# THE LONGEST CRAWL

BY THE SAME AUTHOR

In Southern Waters
The Battle for Dole Acre
Crypts, Caves and Tunnels of London
Parallel Lines
Men and Models

# THE LONGEST CRAWL

Being

An Account of a Journey Through an Intoxicated Landscape

Or

A Child's Treasury of Booze

Ian Marchant

BLOOMSBURY

First published 2006
This paperback edition published 2007

Copyright © 2006 by Ian Marchant

Photographs copyright © 2006 Paul Williams
'Hen Night' copyright © 2006 Catherine Smith
'Finest Half Hour' copyright © 2006 Peter Sansom

The moral right of the author
has been asserted

No part of this book may be used or reproduced in any manner whatsoever
without written permission from the Publisher except in the case of brief
quotations embodied in critical articles or reviews

Bloomsbury Publishing Plc
36 Soho Square
London W1D 3QY

A CIP catalogue record for this book
is available from the British Library

ISBN 9780747585572

10 9 8 7 6 5 4 3 2 1

Typeset by Palimpsest Book Production Ltd, Grangemouth, Stirlingshire
Printed in Great Britain by Clays Ltd, St Ives plc

Bloomsbury Publishing, London, New York and Berlin

The paper this book is printed on is 100% post-consumer waste recycled

www.thelongestcrawl.com

For Alan Raymond Marchant,
Licensed no longer to sell alcohol and tobacco

# ACKNOWLEDGEMENTS

Thanks to everyone we had a drink with, but most especially Bob Cooper, Pete Bright, Deborah Dooley, Julia and Noel Wheadon, Fay Riddell, Rachel Hazell, Chris Garrand, Tony and Dominic Marchant, Tony Green, Tony Allan, Lucy Ramsey, Ruth James, Craig Pope, Saleel Nurbhai, Madeleine Weymouth, George Green, Judy Brown, Catherine Fox, Emmy Manby, Caroline Davy, Jean and Ralph Foxwell, Trapper, Jillian Stuteley, EJMM, ECWM, Adam Gregory, Peter Mustil, Gilly Johnstone, Bob Rowberry, Matthew Bowes, Hag Harris, Dave Bardsley, Isobel Marchant, Revd Heather Parbury, Richard Jarman, Basil Ransome-Davis, Peter Sansom, Catherine Smith, James Long, Paul Farley, Richard Salmon, Sheela Ghosh, Shevaughn Williams, Kit Fraser, Dr Seiriol Morgan, Robert Edric, John Sellars, Chris Brook, Kenny Davidson, Matt Barnard, Gareth Jones and above all to Monique Roffey, the olive in my martini, the lemon in my G&T . . . chin chin!

# St Mark's Eve

I grew restless this evening, and walked through the lanes by starlight for a drink in the next village with my friend Bob. I wanted to buy him a drink, as he has had a heart attack recently. He is my age and a smoker, similar socio-economic group, almost the same postcode, and his heart attack lowered the statistical likelihood of my having a heart attack all of my own in the near future by a sizeable percentage. An actuary told me this, and I believe it. I felt I owed Bob one.

I like walking in the dark, on clear moonless nights, but it's difficult to see by starlight, until your eyes adjust. As I came to the first bend in the road after the last houses in the village, I managed to walk straight ahead, and up a field track, until I felt the surface change under my feet, and I knew that I had gone wrong. When I found my way back to the road, it was hard to tell which side I was on, and I blundered along, occasionally scraping the hedge. A little further, under the trees, over the haunted bridge, it was darker yet, and only the flap of the flooding river to my left helped me stay on course. But as the road rises over a treeless down from the valley bottom, I came out into the stars, and I could see the way ahead.

In town, on a clear night, you are lucky if you can pick out Orion, or the Plough, because of the light from the streets. But out here, they're difficult to pick out because of the light from the other stars. So many stars, and the constellations lose what little definition they had. It's almost vulgar, the night sky, like a child's home-made Christmas card, glitter glued to a piece of black card, the Milky Way a smear of PVA, Venus an acid bead, too big, too bright, looking as if it might come unstuck.

And then, the brow of the hill, and the next village bright in the combe.

This is no man's land; this is deer and fox and otter land, these rolling hills that billow between the Torridge and the Taw. This is Ted Hughes country, the Devon of the *Moortown Diary*. By day, it's the kind of idealised English landscape that men died for in wars, even if they were only familiar with it from chocolate boxes. By night, nothing is familiar, and the only humans on foot are poachers and drunks. A badger skittered past, and made my heart pick up a beat. I walked faster down the hill, back into the safety of real artificial light, past the church, past the shop, and into the pub.

Three pints later, there was no question of walking the couple of miles home. Are you mad? If I'd wobbled about so much sober, what would I be like trying to find my way through the darkened lanes having taken strong drink? So I got a lift, from one of Bob's pals who had drunk almost as much as me. Drinking and driving is endemic in the countryside. You're not going to get stopped. Devon and Cornwall police only have two cars, one for Devon and one for Cornwall, and ours is usually parked up outside Nero's in Okehampton.

In my youth, I cheerfully hiked the six miles there and back to the nearest pub, most nights of the week, through much wilder countryside than this, in the foothills of the Cambrians. It's shameful that these days I don't feel up to it in the same way; a sign that I am getting older, and that the self-abuse is starting to take its toll. If all the exercise you get is walking to the pub and nipping over to the shop for some fags, I suppose something has to give, actuarial calculations notwithstanding. The drink driving is shameful, too, but we all do it out here from time to time, seduced by the ease of the car. If there had been no lift, and if I had more moral fibre, and had drunk less, I like to think I would have walked home from the pub. If it wasn't so far. Or dark.

People always walk home from the pub in towns. We follow soon-to-be lovers, arm in arm, sliding along on icy pavements; groups of laughing friends happy to be together, strolling home as the nights get shorter; stumbling pissheads in rancid August, pancakes of puke showing us their trail – all following well worn paths, private shortcuts, rat runs through snickets and back alleys, on their way home from the pub. Before the car, everyone did it in the countryside too. You can still see the footpaths through the meadow, given over now to ramblers.

I lived in a cottage in the Radnorshire hills for several years in the late 1980s. Every evening, at seven, the eighty-something farmer from the last smallholding in the valley would walk past our house, on his way to the Eagle in New Radnor, five miles away. I would often be chopping wood or working in the garden when he came by, and I would wish him a good evening.

'Aika tayor yife uppa lorngraaass,' he would reply, and I would smile and nod. He had what can only be described as a broad accent; not Welsh that close to the border, but more like Herefordshire with a dash of Xhosa. I didn't understand a thing he said.

Sometime after midnight, he would come singing and shouting up the hill. At first, soon after we moved in, he would wake the baby. But that old man never missed a night in the pub, come rain, hail or snow, and eventually the baby became used to him, and would sleep through his ululations. We could never make out what he was shouting, or gargling, and he wasn't great at carrying a tune. But he was expressing himself, and that's supposed to be a good thing.

Over a few months, though, I became attuned to what he was saying to me on the way *to* the pub.

'I loiker tayor yife upp a lorngrass.'

'I'd loikta take yer woife upp a lorngrass.'

'I'd like to take your wife up into the long grass.'

I still smiled, but I stopped nodding my agreement. In the country, you'd do almost anything to get in with the locals, but here I drew the line.

According to G.K. Chesterton, in 'The Rolling English Road', this act of getting to and from the pub is central to an understanding of English topography, as well as English life:

Before the Roman came to Rye or out to Severn strode,
The rolling English drunkard made the rolling English road.
A reeling road, a rolling road, that rambles round the shire,
And after him the parson ran, the sexton and the squire;

A merry road, a mazy road, and such as we did tread
The night we went to Birmingham by way of Beachy Head.

I knew no harm of Bonaparte and plenty of the Squire,
And for to fight the Frenchman I did not much desire;
But I did bash their baggonets because they came arrayed
To straighten out the crooked road an English drunkard made,
Where you and I went down the lane with ale-mugs in our hands,
The night we went to Glastonbury by way of Goodwin Sands.

His sins they were forgiven him; or why do flowers run
Behind him; and the hedges all strengthening in the sun?
The wild thing went from left to right and knew not which was which,
But the wild rose was above him when they found him in the ditch.
God pardon us, nor harden us; we did not see so clear
The night we went to Bannockburn by way of Brighton Pier.

My friends, we will not go again or ape an ancient rage,
Or stretch the folly of our youth to be the shame of age,
But walk with clearer eyes and ears this path that wandereth,
And see undrugged in evening light the decent inn of death;
For there is good news yet to hear and fine things to be seen,
Before we go to Paradise by way of Kensal Green.

Of course, your French, now in the shape of the 'Common Market',
as it is known in pubs, are still trying to get over here and straighten
our roads (not to mention cucumbers); at least according to the
*Daily Mail* and the UK Independence Party, who stand together
at the saloon bar of public life, shitting off while their beer goes
stale and the world moves on.

It must be true that the old lush in Chesterton's poem, having
slipped and fallen into the ditch on one trip home by starlight too
many, had his sins forgiven. God, after all, invented organisms which
if you give them sugar to eat will piss out alcohol, just like he left
his dope lying around for us to share. Cars leave flowers by the
wayside, too, tied to lampposts by grieving relatives.

Maybe Chesterton was right, and the road was plotted by drunks, and maybe the flowers in the ancient hedgerows do follow in their path. I said earlier that I live in Ted Hughes country. There's more Ted Hughes country, in West Yorkshire, right next to Brontë country. In fact, our Ted Hughes country is locked in bitter dispute with their Ted Hughes country, as to whose country was really Ted's. A short drive away from here is Betjeman's Cornwall. On this side of the Bristol Channel we have Lorna Doone's Exmoor, and on the opposite shore Dylan-Thomas's Wales. An hour's drive east, and we're in Hardy's Wessex. Once again, and with all due respect to my publishers, I would like to advocate the designation of the valley of the River Sussex Ouse as Bloomsbury Country. We like our landscape mediated by fiction and poetry. We like stories, and making our own maps of where stories come from.

The history of roads and the history of pubs are inseparably bound together. I'd like to think of this road/pub continuum as Chesterton Country. It's a conservative territory, resistant to change, natural meeting place of Chesterton's 'Secret People', who suspect that, after all, beer is best. It is not only unfashionable ideas which still have a foothold in Chesterton Country; certain unfashionable emotions have their last strongholds in the pubs of Britain, and these emotions are the ones which are exaggerated by drinking. Pubs are sentimental. Pubs are hearty, pumped up with hail-fellow-well-met back-slapping self-congratulation; they are also hotbeds of nostalgia, and a theatre for expressions of maudlin regret. The authors who write well about pubs are often those who we now regard as over-sentimental, or bumptious and hearty; like Chesterton.

I'd like to map the British landscape in drink, formed as it is by drunken roads running along field and parish boundaries, drawn between village pubs and inns by travellers. There are barley fields and hop gardens, vineyards and cider orchards. The red-brick chimneys of breweries rise on the horizon; distilleries bubble beside peaty lochs; oast-houses, now made over into commuter homes, peep shyly over yew hedges. In cities and towns, we can navigate by pubs, left at the Star, right at the Sun. Dray horses stamp up the South

Circular; the Black Country sizzles with pork scratchings; Islay has whisky on its breath, Plymouth gin, Burton light ale.

If, as Paul Shepheard in *The Cultivated Wilderness* and Simon Schama in *Landscape and Memory* argue, it is impossible to separate landscape and human perception, then I wish to argue that altering our perception alters the landscape. By taking Chesterton's rolling road, maybe we can see that the British landscape is as intoxicated as the people who made it. Drunkenness is built in.

Looked at mathematically, each part of a landscape resembles the whole. This is called 'self-similarity'. A leaf resembles a tree. Rivulets running down a sandy beach form similar patterns to those formed by rivers meeting their estuary. Many phenomena exhibit self-similarity. If you map the fluctuations of stock markets or the distribution of earthquakes over time, the patterns formed over the space of a year are similar to those which occur over hours, or minutes. Things which are self-similar all operate according to the same simple mathematical laws. Mathematicians at the University of Stuttgart have shown that networks of paths across the campus form according to the same laws of self-similarity, as people take shortcuts from the lecture hall to the laboratory to the *Bierkeller*. The Rolling English Drunkard may not have known it as he stumbled into the ditch, but there is an underlying mathematical order in his reeling, a similar order to that found in the shapes of branches. No matter how far back, or how close in, you pull the camera focus, the patterns remain, if the lens is clear.

Life is self-similar, too; broken down into its constituent years, days, hours, minutes, plotted on a graph, the rhythms resemble one another from moment to moment, and year to year; we have good days and bad days, minor ups and downs as a rule, punctuated by wild, inexplicable turns of fortune; peaks and troughs where your life crashes, or springs into a period of uncontrollable growth and change. And if you're British, to help you climb the slopes, and help smooth the slide into the valleys, there's booze. Per capita, the British drink more alcohol than anywhere else on earth, except in the Republic of Ireland, God bless them. We drink champagne at a wedding breakfast, we wet the baby's head at a christening, and when you are called off to the bar of the 'decent inn of death', your loved ones will be drowning their sorrows in your old local. I'm only here at all because my dad got my mum tiddly on Babycham at Margate one Whitsun bank-holiday Monday.

Two years ago today, I went to St Agnes, in the Scilly Isles, which is the most south-westerly inhabited island in the UK. There are neolithic graves and ancient mazes tangled in the island gorse, empty beaches Dysoned white by the wind. At low tide, you can walk over the causeway to the island of Gugh, and climb its hill, and look north and east, and imagine that you are looking back at the whole of Britain, island after island, strung like beads almost to the Arctic Circle. And if you look down, you can see the fishing boat which brought you over to the island moored alone by the jetty. And up from the jetty, there's the Turk's Head. The first pub in Britain. Good pub, too.

I started thinking about drink and landscape while sitting drinking a pint of beer and eating a packet of pork scratchings in the Turk's Head, on St Agnes. It was the pork scratchings that started it. They were just right; tooth-shatteringly crisp skin on one side, a heart-stopping melt of fat on to the tongue on the other. A dusting of MSG made them deliciously moreish.

I idly turned the packet over, and read the ingredients and the manufacturer's name and address. The pork scratchings were made by a small firm in Tipton, in the Black Country, I noticed.

It was as though I had dipped a scratching in my beer. Memories came back to me of all the packets of peanuts, crisps and pork scratchings I had ever read. Sitting in the car outside country pubs in the sixties, waiting for my parents, with nothing to read except the customer-satisfaction guarantee on a packet of Smith's Salt 'n' Shake; trying to pass the time, waiting for my date to return from the lavatory, by answering quiz questions printed on a packet of Nik Naks. That day on St Agnes, I did a *Gestalt*; all the subliminally remembered addresses of pork-scratching manufacturers came together to make a mental map. I realised that ALL pork scratchings are made by small firms in the Black Country. Wherever you go, you get different brands of pork scratchings, made by different small firms. But all of these firms are in Tipton, or Dudley or Walsall. All of them.

Why?

When I got home, I thought about the trip to St Agnes, about the tiny high-walled fields, ideal for growing spring flowers and autumn skunk; about the twitchers lurking behind every gorse bush with insanely expensive and fantastically bulky surveillance equipment slung round their necks, happy to get a hernia in return for a glimpse of a red-throated gobblerbird.

And I thought about that first pub. By vocation, I'm a pub quizzer. I have a pub-quiz mind. I ask pub-quiz questions.

'If the Turk's Head is the first pub, then where,' I wondered, 'is the last pub?'

The last place in Britain is the island of Unst, the most northerly of the Shetlands, home to the only working talc mine in Britain. I needed to know how many pubs the last place has, and which is the most north-easterly. It must have a few, I thought, as talc-mining is probably quite thirsty work. I turned to the interweb for guidance. Unst has just one pub. The most north-easterly, the furthest you can go for a drink if you're going on from the Turk's Head on St Agnes is the public bar of the Baltasound Hotel, in Baltasound, on Unst.

What if, of a Friday night, you didn't find a place you liked after leaving the Turk's Head, and just kept going until you got to the Baltasound Hotel? I've had nights that felt like that.

Now, that's interesting, I thought. That could come up as a question one time. The longest possible pub crawl in the British Isles. I put it away. But this little scrap of trivia nagged away at me, and I kept itching at the scratchings, and their origins, and the more I thought about it, and what beer and wine and gin and whisky and pork scratchings and pickled eggs and crisps have meant both to the British people and to the British landscape, the more I knew that I would have to do the trip. That I would follow in the footsteps of Chesterton, and stagger across the intoxicated landscape, and take the drunken English road between the two most distant pubs. A road trip, after sitting on trains for so long. And a kind of lexicon of drink, from AA to zymurgy.

And I would go with my good friend, photographer and counsellor for people with alcohol problems, Perry Venus. We would set out from St Agnes on the first of April 2004, and hopefully arrive a month later on Unst. April seemed like a good month for pilgrimages. Stephen Earnshaw points out in *The Pub in Literature* that English literature starts in a pub, the Tabard, in Southwark, as Chaucer's pilgrims set off on the road to Canterbury, one April morning.

It's a well-trodden path, the one that runs from inn to inn. A fortnight before the trip, Venus phoned me. During the course of our conversation he asked me what books I was taking. Not many, I answered. Won't be much time for reading. I'm taking a corker I found on eBay, W.T. Marchant's *In Praise of Ale*, written in 1887, because . . . well, I had to, didn't I? And some guidebooks, the AA illustrated *Road Book of England and Wales*, and the companion volume on Scotland. Published in the late 1950s and early 1960s, they are full of line drawings, an excellent historical gazetteer, and fifty-year-old maps for us to get lost by. And I'm taking bundles of proper Ordnance Survey maps too, so we can get unlost.

'What about you, Perry? What books are you packing?'

'Oh . . . *McCarthy's Bar* . . . *Raw Spirit* by Iain Banks . . . *Man Walks into a Pub* by Peter Brown.'

'Yeah, great, thanks . . . I'm sure they're very interesting.'

'They are! And funny.'

'So I'm assured. Anything else?'

'Yes. *Notes from a Small Island*. And *Round Ireland with a Fridge*.'

'How about *Cunt* by Stewart Home? You should bring that.'

'No. But I have got some other psycho-geographers. I've got Iain Sinclair's *London Orbital* and W.G. Sebald's *Rings of Saturn*. Think that'll be enough?'

If you set out to travel in Britain, you become acutely aware that it is not possible to go boldly where no one has gone before. Britain is like an engraved map, cross-hatched by lines etched over the landscape by writers. You can only hope that your lines add something to the picture, even if they are not always straight.

So this is a rambling tale, a rolling story of a reeling trip. We went from Scilly to Shetland, but we went by way of Glastonbury, and Birmingham and Skegness Pier and Kensal Green, where Paradise is now a pub.

# Thursday 1st April, 2004

'Hello,' said Perry Venus.

'What?' I said.

'Day-trippers.'

It was 9.15 a.m. It was raining. Me and Perry, having caught the first helicopter for the Scillies out of Penzance that morning, were now standing in the passenger well of the *Kingfisher of St Mary*, which was due to take us across to St Agnes, most south-westerly of the British Isles, home to the Turk's Head, our first pub, and the place where I'd had my road-to-Damascus moment with the pork scratchings, almost a year before. The *Kingfisher of St Mary* is an open boat, maybe forty-five foot, with benches around the gunwales and a steerer's cabin forward. She was moored up against a similar boat, which was in turn moored to the bottom of a slippery flight of steps leading up to the quay at Hugh Town, capital of St Mary's, the largest of the islands. Perry was mincing about the boat, taking photos, and I wasn't moving from the excellent spot I had copped, leaning with my back against the bulwark of the cabin, facing the stern.

As a seasoned traveller, I have come to understand that my personal safety and comfort are hugely important to me. If you are travelling in an open boat over lumpy open seas, and if you are concerned, above all things, with your personal safety and comfort, you should always go in the cabin. Failing this, if the cabin is too small to take passengers, or the captain too proprietorial, like today, then you should lean with your back to the cabin, and stay out of the wind and the wet. Today was already windy and wet, and cold too, even in the harbour. St Agnes is the most exposed of the inhabited islands. The half-hour crossing takes you from the relative shelter of St Mary's out into the Atlantic, and this one promised to be rough. So I wasn't moving.

There was room for one person standing either side of the cabin door. I was on the starboard side, and an old gentleman with the cheerily mad face of a retired vicar was on the port side.

'Ah, this is the place to stand,' he said, as he found the exact spot against the bulwark and under the shelter of the overhang of the cabin roof where comfort, if not necessarily safety, was best to be had.

'Yes indeed,' I said, from the other side of the cabin door.

'We won't get wet,' he said.

'Not like them,' I said, nodding at our fellow passengers.

The half-dozen or so mostly elderly people who were sharing the boat with us were huddled on the benches; a huge mistake on their part, as they would soon learn to their cost.

Then:

'Hello,' said Perry Venus.

'What?' I said, turning my head.

'Day-trippers.'

Thirty or so people had appeared on the quayside, and were being led, two at a time, down the steps, over the boat we were moored against, and on to the *Kingfisher*. They were all dressed in rain capes, and they all looked a bit fed up. You couldn't blame them, really. No one except looneys would be getting on this boat this morning if they had any choice. As they came on board the boat, it became clear from their sweatshirts that they were excursionists forced out on a jolly with the Bristol Blind Club, and from their specs that most of them were in fact blind. That was why extreme caution was being taken in getting them on board. It was raining, and slippery, and as each of the anxious merry-makers came on to the boat, they were guided to and seated on a wet bench.

'I certainly don't envy them,' said the retired vicar.

'No,' I said.

'They're going to be soaked by the time they get to St Agnes.'

'I'm very much afraid they are,' I said, rolling a cigarette in the lee of the cabin.

The last of the crew came aboard from helping the passengers on to the now-crowded boat. He was carrying a large cardboard box, which he set down on the engine housing. Then he bustled about casting off the lines, and the captain gunned the throttle and spun the wheel, and took the *Kingfisher* away from the quayside and out into St Mary's harbour.

'Smells good,' said the retired vicar to our captain, nodding at the box.

'Them's the pasties,' said the captain. 'There'd be trouble if we forgot those.'

Perry Venus, of course, does not like boats at all, except canal boats. He came lurching towards me, and held my sleeve.

'Oh God, it's rough,' he said. 'Is it always going to be this rough?'

'No,' I said. 'It's going to be much rougher . . . as we come out from behind the island . . . like now.'

Huge rollers loomed above us. Well, not huge. Loomed is over-egging it too. But they seemed big enough. The boat started to pitch and roll. As *Kingfisher* turned to face the wind and St Agnes, waves broke over her bow, soaking all but two of the passengers. A woman with skin the colour of porridge sitting just in front of me started to moan, and leaned over the side, and got a wave in her ear. The captain made a reassuring announcement over the Tannoy:

'If you don't like my driving, you can get out and walk! Har! Har! Har!'

How the retired vicar and I laughed! How safe we felt in the care of this insouciant sailor, who scorned that harsh mistress, the sea.

When we arrived in St Agnes' harbour, anxious hands reached down into the *Kingfisher*, and the crewman passed them the box of pasties. Other, perhaps less anxious hands reached down and helped the dripping passengers from the boat on to the slippery rocks of St Agnes' pier. They were led by their guides in gloomy English people having a nice day out despite the weather fashion up the hill on the concrete track that leads past the Turk's Head. At first sight, it appears as though the Turk's Head is the only building on St Agnes, painted white and built lengthways into the high ground which rises away behind it, staring across St Agnes' harbour to Gugh.

Then you notice the old lighthouse, too, like the giant Cyclops trying to hide behind a hill.

The Turk's Head is five minutes' walk from the pier on St Agnes, and you might think that Perry and I, given that we were about to start the longest possible pub crawl in the British Isles, would get leaning against our first bar. But it was ten in the morning. And (with a very few exceptions) you can't get a drink at ten in the morning in England. The first pub in the British Isles was, of course, closed.

The licensing laws in this country have evolved over centuries. Many histories of pubs end up being fairly dry lists of when and how such and such a law came into operation. In a book of this nature, you can't really avoid the topic. Opening hours were imposed by the State during the First World War because it felt that English people weren't working hard enough at trying to kill other people who the State wanted killed. The laws were greeted with open arms by the Temperance Movement, which had its genesis in the Gin Fever of the eighteenth century, had grown in strength throughout the nineteenth century with the rise of Methodism, and scored its greatest success with the adoption of the Eighteenth Amendment to the American Constitution, which introduced Prohibition. Our opening times, whilst not as insane as Prohibition, had support from similar groups to those that had brought it about, working in concert with the wartime government. These laws are just about to be relaxed, more than ninety years after they were introduced; a relaxation which we could have done with this morning.

But no matter how much it rains, or how cold it is, the law is still rigid, and pubs are not yet open in the mornings, so we took the path that leads away from the Turk's Head to the other side of the island. I wanted to find the Troy Town maze. I hadn't seen it the last time I was on St Agnes; and the centre of a maze seemed like a good place to start. It seemed like a useful model of our journey, or it did when I was sitting at home, planning the trip. A merry road, a mazy road, I thought. I hadn't pictured the wind and rain.

Unlike most mazes, a Troy Town maze, like the one on St Agnes, is not there to get lost in. No one knows what they were for, who made them, when they made them, or why. One story is that Brutus brought them. Brutus was the first Briton, who escaped to Albion with a few followers following the sack of Troy. Britain is named after him, and it's good to imagine that he brought this ancient shape with him on his mythical voyage. Troy Town mazes are unicursal – no decisions have to be made about which way to go. You follow the spiral to the centre, where the path doubles back on itself. Then you walk back out again. That sounds like fun to me, these days.

'Besides,' I said to Perry, 'we don't want to be bumping into the trippers all day.'

'Or, more to the point, to have them bumping into us,' said Perry.

Twenty minutes' walking in the rain took us to Periglis, the first inhabited place in Britain. There is a beach of white sand, a few cottages, and a corrugated-iron boat shed at the top of a slipway. Piles of old fishing paraphernalia – nets, floats, oars – tumble around the shed. The sea is stuffed with more islands, Jackson Pollock islands, splattered across the water; Annet, and the Western Rocks, all uninhabited; and on the horizon, a skyscraper, the Bishop Rock lighthouse. If you come across the Atlantic to Britain by ship, the Bishop Rock is the first thing you see. A light to welcome travellers, and a wonder of Victorian engineering – it is a fine thing to stand at the very start of the archipelago, our Statue of Liberty.

The rain spat in from the sea. An old gentleman working at the boat shed showed us the path to the Troy Town maze. It is hidden in the tiny daffodil fields, and stands on a low cliff top, ten minutes' walk from Periglis beach, among misshapen formations of grey rocks, which offer little shelter from the south-westerlies. It's not spectacular, I guess; not Stonehenge. Just a spiral of white-painted stones, the largest no more than a foot high. It is perhaps twelve feet across. We trod the well worn path, turning in on ourselves, looping into the centre, and then back to where we started. This was a journey that has been made for hundreds, maybe thousands of years. The archaeology has been knocked about, so it is not possible to tell how old this particular maze is. One story is that it was made by a bored lighthouse keeper in the eighteenth century. I prefer the idea that Brutus put it here. Whatever the truth, emerging from the little step dance that the maze made our feet follow, I felt that our journey had begun. It was ten to eleven, and the pub was about to open.

The fields in the Scillies are tiny and have high hedges, to protect them from the wind, and this can make it hard to find your way about; can make it feel like you are stuck in a maze.

'We're lost, aren't we?' said Perry.

'Of course we're not lost. I've got the map, look.'

'According to you, the journey was to start in the middle of the Troy Town maze. Why, I can't work out . . .'

'Oh, it's like a journey through Britain. An ancient and profound symbol, linked with the myths of our origins, now turned into a tourist attraction, following a route that has been followed countless times before for no better purpose than to follow it . . .'

'Yes, all right. Whatever the point, we exit the maze, and then go to our first pub, for our first drink, yes?'

'Yes.'

'And now, ten minutes after starting our journey, we're lost.'

'No . . . I've got the map.'

Perry was right. The hedges were six feet tall, and a track ran around each of them. St Agnes is the size of a postage stamp, and we had managed to lose ourselves. After twenty minutes' seemingly aimless wandering, we finally found the track that leads round the island. You pass the island shop, and then come to a fork in the track. One branch leads towards the Turk's Head and the pier, the other leads to the causeway over to Gugh, St Agnes' conjoined twin. There are two houses on Gugh, strange-looking things with barrel roofs, which can only be reached on foot at low tide. We watched a crocodile of blind excursionists crest the brow of the hill on Gugh, their rain capes billowing in the wind.

'It's bloody cold to be wandering about on a windswept island,' said Perry.

'You're not wrong, friend,' I said. 'Fancy a pint?'

We hurried on to the Turk's Head, overlooking the jetty where the *Kingfisher* had landed us, thus completing a circumnavigation of the first inhabited island. Inside, it is dark with wood, like an old ship's cabin. There is a nautical theme, as you might imagine, with telescopes and oars and models of pilot gigs, fast rowing boats which compete each summer in the World Pilot Gig Championships. Gig-racing is the Scillies' main sport. Charts and photos showing the wrecks around the island cover the walls. There are RNLI testimonials, too, celebrating the part that the islanders have played in saving lives from the countless island wrecks.

Two good-looking lads were serving behind the bar, students who had come to work their holidays in the Turk's Head. By now it was half-eleven, and the pub was starting to fill; trippers all, as it was clearly a bit early for the fifty or so souls who live on St Agnes. We ordered pasties, which had travelled over on the boat with us from St Mary's, and two pints of Turk's Ale, which is brewed for the pub at St Austell Brewery.

Now, here's a thing which we're all going to have to come to terms with, sooner rather than later; Perry and I drink 'real ale' by preference. And, yes, we quite like folk music, too. Late sixties English folk rock, anyway.

By 'real ale' I mean the stuff we drink in the south, stuff which fills northerners, Americans, Continentals, Antipodeans, etc. with horror. It is flat. It should not have any discernible head. It is room-temperature warm; not quite urine-warm, but certainly not cold. It is pulled from the cellar with a hand pump, or, most frequently here in the south-west, tapped directly from the barrel, which is kept behind the bar. It has a bit of an image problem, and I can see why. Some real-ale drinkers really like folk music a lot, and a lot more than me and Perry do. Some like trad jazz. Trad-jazz bands are not unknown at beer festivals. Some real-ale drinkers doubtless have beards. Fair Isle sweaters are not unknown. You might argue that their taste in knitwear renders their taste in drink invalid. I disagree. Not everybody is entitled to their own opinion, but they must be allowed their tastes.

Taste is one of the things in life which cannot be legislated for, or argued with. Some people like the Beach Boys, or Patti Smith; others prefer Iron Maiden, or Dido. Some people like bacon sandwiches; others prefer tofu. And there are those who like drinking real ale, and those who like lager. There is very little point in sitting down with a Dido fan and explaining that the woman has a voice like damp lavatory tissue; that's just how they like her. Perry and I like our native drink, flat and warm though it is, and we both get sulky if it can't be had.

Landlords are not always to be blamed for its absence. This is because it is 'cask conditioned'; which is to say it is still fermenting in the barrel when it arrives at the pub. It is alive, like proper yoghurt, and it takes care and skill on the landlord's part to see that it is served properly. Once the barrel is opened, it goes off quite quickly; a barrel which has been tapped will last about a week, tops. If there is no demand for it, it is not worth while having it for sale. This is not true of all alcoholic drinks. Lager is dead, and will keep for ever. Those dusty bottles of Kahlua or Advocaat behind the bar can quite happily sit there for all eternity, waiting for the occasional curious toper who fancies something new and horrible.

I told the lads behind the bar what we were up to; that we were going on the longest pub crawl in the British Isles, between the two most distant pubs. The landlady brought out our pasties, and the lads behind the bar told her what we were doing. This gave her the opportunity to recommend places that we should visit. We were not to know at the time that everyone, in every pub the whole length of the British Isles, is a living breathing authority on drink, and that, wherever we went, people would tell us where to go, what to see, and what to do. Above all, they would tell us to go to Eli's, in Huish Episcopi. The landlady of the Turk's Head had the distinction of being first.

'I tell you where you should go. You should go to Eli's, in Huish Episcopi.'

I made a note; it's not often you get told to go to Huish Episcopi, or so I naïvely thought. We finished our pasties, and ordered another couple of pints. The Bristol Blind Club came staggering in, their rain capes dripping over the stone-flagged floor, and were shown through into a back room, where lunch had been prepared for them. Me and Perry finished our second pint, and headed down to the quay to wait in a small shelter for the *Kingfisher*'s return. We had ticked off the first pub, and we had a long way to go; it was time to be moving. A few of the other trippers had clearly had enough of the driving rain, and we stood together in the shelter, watching anxiously as several boats pulled up to the quay, none of them the *Kingfisher*. Many of the men who lived on the island were standing by the pier, helping to unload the boats, which were carrying parcels, mail-bags and supplies for the pub and the shop. There was an old tractor and trailer at the end of the quay, and we watched as the locals formed a human chain, taking boxes from the crews of the boats, keen to get them out of the rain, passing them from hand to hand, and stacking them up in the trailer. Next to the trailer, there was a large pile of barrels, waiting for the boat to take them back to St Austell. At least in the season, the Turk's Head was getting through enough beer to make it worth their while keeping real ale.

At last, half an hour or so later than advertised, the *Kingfisher* pulled up to the quay, and we scrambled aboard in streaming rain. Decency prevailed, and I offered my plum spot by the cabin to the woman who had been sick on the way over, which she foolishly declined. So it was me and the vicar again.

'You can't tell some people, can you?' he said.

'No.'

Back on St Mary's, with a couple of hours to kill before our helicopter back to the mainland, Perry and I went for a beer in the Atlantic Bar, which seemed to be the main choice of the locals, and which was packed. The bar was three deep with people waiting to be served. At first I thought that the Scillies were in the grip of a Goth revival, as everybody, young and old, was wearing black clothes. Then I realised that we had stumbled into a funeral party, a very large one. Several hundred people were in the pub, steadily drinking. And like at every funeral I've ever been to, everyone was having a right old laugh.

I remember watching scenes of the Ayatollah Khomeini's funeral on TV, the keening misery of the crowds, and envying that openness, the knowing that it was safe to publicly express grief. Because northern Europeans can't do that, can't let go. We need a drink to unlock, which tends to make us behave inappropriately.

Weddings, christenings, funerals. The three great occasions when we come together in some religious or ceremonial context. Christenings are dull, let's face it. You dress up, the baby howls, but no one really enjoys themselves. You might have a few glasses of bubbly, but lots of the people there will have kids themselves, and will be needing to strap the weans into the people carrier, and drive home. Very few people get pished at a christening. Weddings are much more fun, but tinged with anxiety, especially if it's your own. The closer you are to the bride and groom, the more you are expected to preserve a veneer of sobriety. If you're the best man, or one of the bridesmaids, you can't really begin to hammer it until the happy couple have set out on their honeymoon and the disco is playing 'New York, New York', by which time the thing is almost over. No, as an excuse for a first-class communal drunk, you simply can't beat the funeral.

The best funeral I've ever been to was my old father-in-law's, which was held in Kensal Green. I got a lift to the cemetery with my sister-in-law, Emmy, and my two nephews. Emmy and I had chatted on the drive from East to West London, while the boys had sat quietly in the back, but as we pulled into the cemetery, and started down the long drive to the crematorium, my youngest nephew leaned forward and pushed a tape into the stereo. Black Sabbath's 'Iron Man' filled the car. Good call.

Robert, my father-in-law, was an old-fashioned Soho drinking man whose idea of perfect happiness was making the circuit from the Coach and Horses to the French House, on to Muriel's, and back again. Catch him at the right level of intoxication, and he would tell you funny stories of drinking with Soho legends, like writer Julian MacLaren-Ross, or the artist Robert Colquhoun, back in the fifties. Most of the more colourful characters had pre-deceased Robert by some years, but there was still a decent turn-out in the crematorium; a good collection of Robert's somewhat dog-eared pals and decrepit cronies; a few looking like disappointed creditors, rather than mourners. After the funeral, we all went on to a nearby hotel, where the best thing seemed to be to get stuck into the drink. It's what Robert would have wanted.

Ever since his death, the close family members had been drinking long and steadily. People do; it's what whisky is for. Consequently, there had been a lot of laughter in the days leading up to the funeral. After an hour or so of more drinking, and swapping funny Robert stories at the bar, I felt that I had best sit down, and I found myself next to an ancient crone, who introduced herself as Sylvia. I gained the impression, though I had not met her before, that long and steady drinking was the normal state of things for Sylvia. Gin seemed to be her tipple, at least at funerals.

'I was Robert's first girlfriend,' she said.

This was a bold claim, and one guaranteed to get me interested.

'I lost my virginity to him, you know.'

'I didn't know, Sylvia.'

'Oh yes, dear. In Earls Court. We drank Chianti. I made a fondue.'

'It sounds very romantic.'

'It was. There was nothing sordid about Robert.' She tugged at her wig. I thought of Robert's dead tongue in Sylvia's toothless mouth. I thought too, of the worst funeral that I had ever been to, that of Robert's daughter, my first wife, mother of my eldest child. She had been my first real girlfriend. I fetched Sylvia another gin, me another whisky, and told her of my connection to the family.

'That was a terrible time,' said Sylvia. 'Robert took it very hard.'

'So did I. So did we all.'

And so we had. From the moment of her death from a brain haemorrhage, aged thirty, right up to the funeral, friends and family had gathered round in her flat, where we worked our way through bottles of whisky, which helped to numb the shock and postpone the grief. It also unleashed our hysteria, and there were occasions in that week when we became helpless with laughter. This still seems appropriate to me; the whisky helping to release emotion, emotion expressing itself as laughter as often as tears. There comes a time when laughter stops, and when the whisky hinders rather than helps; this time is after the funeral, when friends inevitably return to life, the shock wears off, and grieving truly begins. Until that time, drink really is your friend.

Today, in the Atlantic Bar, there was more laughter than tears. The dead guy was called George, so much we gathered; he had been much loved, but was quite elderly; had enjoyed what we call in England 'a good innings'. This always puts a different slant on funerals; the drinking becomes celebratory, rather than pain-numbing, the laughter consequently more subdued. We raised our glasses to George. By the time we had finished our pints, the mourners were starting to drift away from the pub; three girls clacked in black stilettos on the slate-grey pavements, clinging to the arms of their boyfriends' suits, all glad to be alive on this wet cold spring afternoon.

I warned you. Spend too much time in the pub, and you lose your immunity to vulgar sentimentality. Be careful, or one day you too will clutch the arm of a stranger and say, 'I love you. You're my best friend, you are.'

Perry and I caught the bus up to the small airport on St Mary's, got ourselves some coffee, and chatted drowsily about the day. From the banquette behind us came a broad Birmingham accent.

'I know that voice . . . Ian!'

It was my pal Professor Sue and her husband Tony, who I hadn't seen for a while. We had first met in Lancaster, where I lived for thirteen years, and where Sue had been head of the French department at the university. She'd just retired and had been down to the West Country to visit Tony's father, who had been unwell. They'd popped across to the Scillies for a few nights, and were now waiting for the fixed-wing aircraft to take them back to Land's End, while we waited for the helicopter to Penzance. I was reminded of the fact that we are all locals in the British Isles; that wherever you go, and whatever you do, someone you know has been there, or is going there, or will be sitting behind you at a tiny provincial airport, waiting for a flight.

And as our helicopter took us away from the islands, and flew over Land's End, I was reminded too that some lightweights walk from the end of the peninsula to John o'Groat's, and assume that they have gone from end to end of Britain. I sneered involuntarily. You can go much further than that; you can go from St Agnes to Unst, where we hoped to be in a month's time, drinking in the Baltasound Hotel. Mind you, we were driving; if we were walking, perhaps we might have been tempted to skip the islands too.

We picked up Perry's car, which we had left that morning in the heliport car-park in Penzance, and drove the ten miles or so to Helston. Astute readers will have spotted that we had already had three pints each, and will be worrying that we were getting near the limit. Wiser counsel perhaps should have urged us to stay in Penzance that evening, but I wanted to see a remarkable pub in Helston, the Blue Anchor. I'd wanted to go to the Blue Anchor because it has been brewing its own beer for more than 300 years. By 1973, there were just four pubs left in Britain that brewed their own beer: the All Nations Inn, at Madeley in Shropshire; the Old Swan, in Dudley; the Three Tuns at Bishop's Castle, also in Shropshire; and the Blue Anchor, by far the oldest of the four. Now there are hundreds of pubs with micro-breweries, but the Blue Anchor is the daddy of them all. After a long day, we didn't need a guided tour (especially since I'd arranged to visit the Three Tuns for just such a tour, later in the trip); all we wanted was some fish and chips, a couple of pints of 'Spingo', the Blue Anchor's legendary brew, and a bed for the night. Well, two beds, in a twin room.

There was a case recently of a Scottish B & B owner who refused a double bed to a gay couple, saying that he did not want their 'perversion' in his home. Fifty years ago, this wouldn't have occurred to B & B owners; they would simply have thought that the chaps were good pals who wanted to stay warm, like Morecambe and Wise. For reasons of economy, Perry and I would be sharing a room for a month, but only up to a point. After nearly thirty years of friendship, we can just about ask one another how our girlfriends are.

In a largely eighteenth-century town, the Blue Anchor is the last thatched building. Inside, it is dark; several small snugs lead off from the corridor. It was difficult at first to see which door led into the actual bars, and when we found one, we discovered that we had entered the public bar, which is always a mistake in Cornwall, where the natives feel about visitors the way I feel about sand under my foreskin. In Devon, visitors are known as 'grockles', a good-humoured word used by the good-humoured locals. In Cornwall, they call us 'emmets', which means ants. Emmets Go Home is a very popular graffito in Cornwall. Cornwall is not really English, and is consequently ignored by the government in London. (Scillonians, incidentally, insist that they are not Cornish.) It's one of the poorest parts of Britain; if the Cornish get the measure of autonomy they crave, maybe they'll become more relaxed about tourists, upon whom the whole county is resentfully reliant. In the mean time, if you want my advice, stay out of the public bar in a Cornish pub.

The little room was packed with coarse-voiced yokels, who were cheered by mine and Perry's appearance; cheered to the point of mocking laughter and talk of 'faggots'. I approached the barman, an ancient, corpulent old lush with a recent black eye, a once-colour-ful snooker player's waistcoat stained to the edge of filthy, and a tricolour handlebar moustache – white with age, yellow with nico-tine, and marbled red with lunch. He was on his own, trying to cope with the demands of a half-six crowd in the public, some all-day drinkers in the saloon, and a party of visitors who took up one of the snugs, who he served through a small hatch.

'Hello,' I said. This was a source of great hilarity to the regulars.

'Oh,' he said, glancing at the smirking clientele.

'Hello,' I continued. 'My name is Marchant, and I've booked a twin room for tonight.' I emphasised the 'twin', not that anything would divert the locals from their instant assessment of me and Perry as London chutney ferreters.

'Oh dear,' he said. 'I'll get the . . .' He wandered off.

The regulars started grumbling. Two of them came up to the bar, and demanded service. The old man came back with the book.

'Oh . . . ah . . . there's no . . . no . . . she's not here, she'll be back in a minute . . .'

He picked up the phone, while the grumbling from the people waiting to be served grew more vocal, their hostility towards me and Perry hardening.

'Hello! There's two gennelmen here . . . booked a twin room . . . but there's no . . . no . . . yes . . . I see . . . yes.'

He put down the phone, and said, 'You see, there's no . . . she'll be up in a minute. I'll get the key, show you the . . . it's a much nicer . . .' He found the keys, and said, 'Follow me.'

One of the locals leaned over the bar and pulled himself a drink. We followed the old man out of the pub, leaving the angry locals shouting at the bar, and walked to an eighteenth-century house two doors down.

'You see . . . this is the key . . . there's no . . . She thought . . . you were . . . oh, it's not the key . . . it's a much nicer room . . . ah, this one.'

The Blue Anchor owns this house, we discovered, and uses it as accommodation. It was an airy and elegant stone-built town house, well decorated.

As the old man led us up the stairs, he continued his mysterious peroration: 'She be here in a minute . . . This is a nicer room . . . thing is, it's got no . . . no . . . this is a nicer . . . but it's got no . . . but she can do it . . . she be here in a minute . . . this one.' He fumbled again with keys, not pausing for breath: '. . . got no . . . Oh, I can't . . . she'll be here in a minute . . . only it's got no . . . hang on . . . this one.'

He showed us into a beautiful room, large, spacious, light, over-looking the high street, *en suite*, tea-making facilities, Corby trouser press, the lot, and in the middle of the room a comfortable-looking double bed. Perry and I looked at one another, and blanched.

'I asked for twin beds,' I said.

'Yes . . . but she can split this into twins . . . she be here in a minute to sort it out for you . . . she'll split it.' It was as if the achievement of this modest goal, that of getting us to our room, meant that he could also finally finish his sentences. It didn't last.

'I'd better . . . there's no one in the . . .'

We waited ten minutes, till a nice lady and her husband came and cheerfully sorted out the beds. We'd been booked into another double room; realising the mistake, she'd arranged for us to be moved to this room, where the double could be split into two singles. They showed us the room we had originally been booked into; ours was much nicer, with that vital two-foot gap between us. They told us where to find a good chippy; and after cod and chips, we went for a walk round the town.

Helston is a town where something has gone wrong. There was money here once, and there are plenty of big stone-built town houses, mostly Georgian, to prove it. We walked around the monumental neo-classical eighteenth-century church; clearly hugely expensive to build, and now locked. Behind the church were several grand houses with scantle roofs, that peculiarly Cornish construction method. Helston had been an old stannary town, and had grown rich on tin. But the tide of money has withdrawn, and the grand old centre of the town looked washed up. Washed up in every sense; the wide gutters run with water from the springs that perforate the town. As the landlady of the Blue Anchor said to us later, these streams (kennels, they call them) keep Helston much cleaner than any street sweeper.

RAF Culdrose is the main employer, and it is thanks to them that the town survives. Also thanks to them for the ugly married quarters that rims Helston. Tonight was payday, and the pubs were full of aircraftmen in their late teens. We didn't fancy joining them, and headed back to the Blue Anchor, which is too eclectic and char-acterful for young people. The decrepit old barman had been replaced by two friendly (for Cornwall) ladies. The public bar was empty now, but the snugs were still full. We sat in the saloon, drinking Spingo with the landlady and her husband. He'd been in the RAF; she'd lived in Helston her whole life; they'd met when he was stationed here in the sixties.

She showed us where the brewhouse was, at the back of the yard. Something very like Spingo has been brewed for 300 years. Her father had been the brewer here, many years before. She can still remember the taste of the brewer's yeast which her father added to all her drinks; and she told us how she'd never had spots, which she attributed to the yeast.

'It's those good bacteria, you see,' she said, entirely wrongly.

Yeast in your drink may be good for spots, but later that night, in the room, in my half of the twin beds, I found out that it is no good for snoring. Perry snored like a donkey with emphysema. His wife had warned me. Only a month to go. I fell into a troubled sleep.

# Friday 2nd April

At breakfast, Perry looked more resentful even than usual.

'Did you not sleep well, friend?' I asked.

'Unlikely, since you snore like a dinosaur gargling wallpaper paste.'

'*I* snore?'

'Yes. Remind me to buy some earplugs later.' He took his camera out of its bag, and snapped his breakfast.

'Did you just take a photo of your breakfast?'

'Yes. I thought I'd take photos of all my breakfasts.'

Few things are designed to make a landlady more suspicious than people taking photographs of their breakfast. Especially if you've made her get you an early breakfast, like we had done. It was 7 a.m., the sun was shining, and we were all up much too early. I don't think she was sorry to see us go.

We left Helston by eight, and drove on back roads in brilliant sunshine to Plymouth, where we were due to visit the Plymouth gin distillery. We have Hitler to thank for modern Plymouth. Bombs knocked the heart out of the old city, and the much-maligned sixties planners did nothing to put it back. But it's a funky town, and that funkiness is most evident down by the Barbican, the one part of Plymouth which the bombers and the planners left untouched, and which is now being redeveloped with vision and verve; the National Marine Aquarium is a fabulous building, for example. If you park up there, and cross the quay by the new lift bridge, you find yourself in the Barbican proper. There are the Mayflower Steps, where the Pilgrim Fathers set sail for America. There is the Dolphin, a raddled old whore of a pub, where Beryl Cook sets many of her paintings. Round the corner you find yourself in a long crescent, a narrow street of high brick buildings, lined with lively shops. At the end of it is the Plymouth gin distillery, whose hexagonal chimney dominates the scene. This is what we had come to see, and it was closed.

'First tour, 12.30,' read Perry. 'Why are we here so early?'

'Because when I phoned they said it was 10.30.'

Perry sighed.

'Let's go and have a coffee,' I said.

'Great. We could have had a lie-in; breakfast at nine. But no. We get up at the crack of dawn, and drive two hours so that we can have a coffee.'

'They did tell me 10.30.'

'Yeah, yeah.'

So we went for a coffee. We had two hours to kill, so it promised to be a long one. The only place we liked the look of was Prete's Ice Cream Bar, a proper old-fashioned caff, one of the many Italian ice-cream places that opened throughout Britain during the early twentieth century. We got our coffee . . . but something was odd . . . we found a table . . . but something was wrong . . . something was very much unlike any caff we've ever been in . . .

'Oh my God,' I said, staring at the end wall of the caff.

'Fucking hell,' said Perry.

We were sitting under a mural done in oils: a painting of the Last Supper, with the guy who had just made us coffee, twenty-five years younger, fatter, and with darker hair, depicted as Judas Iscariot. And in the centre of the huge picture, as Christ holding a Mars Bar, sat the artist, well known for putting himself at the centre of his pictures.

'It's a Robert Lenkiewicz,' said Perry.

We stood up, unable just to sit and drink coffee in the face of this amazing picture. Perry got out his camera.

'No pictures,' said the café owner, a note of weariness in his voice.

'Really?' I said. 'But it's so beautiful. Please.'

'We don't let anyone take pictures of it.'

'But do you have a postcard of it, or something, that we could buy?'

'No. Robert's estate is very complicated. Until it's all sorted out, we can't sell a postcard.'

'You knew him?'

'Of course. Robert came in every day. His studio's round the corner. One day, he asked if he could paint on the wall, and I said yes. Been here twenty-seven years.'

The café owner sounded as though he regretted his decision, and I could see his point. If you own a café, it must be a bit galling to have a major work of art, painted by one of this country's most important figurative artists, up there on the wall. What happens when you want to sell up? If Lenkiewicz had painted it on canvas, or even wood panels, you could flog the thing, at present prices for, say, a hundred grand, probably much more, and think about giving up the day job. But painted on the wall? It had probably brought a great deal of trouble over the years, one way or another. Like the artist himself, a real-life Gulley Jimson, straight from *The Horse's Mouth*, everything that an artist should be.

Still with time to kill, Perry Venus wandered around, trying to take a picture of the Lenkiewicz mural through the window of the café without being spotted by the owner, while I took myself off to visit another of the treasures of the Barbican, the Gypsy Acora. Acora has a consulting room in the same street as the gin distillery and Prete's. I'd passed it before, and had often seen his caravan at Glastonbury Festival, but this was the first time I'd had both the leisure and the inclination to go inside. It was lined with photos of Acora with various celebs: Acora with Lulu, Acora with Tarby. His lugubrious receptionist, who for some reason I suspected of being Acora's mother, sat talking with a young man, moaning about the Gypsy.

'He doesn't put in the time. He's too soft. Look at him now. He's not here. He's in a café round the corner with an asylum seeker, drinking latte. Yes?' She looked up at me.

'I was hoping for a consultation.'

'He's not here. He should be here soon. You can sit and wait if you want.'

I sat and looked at the photos: Acora with Hank Marvin ('You'll never have another hit, but you'll drag round holiday resorts for the rest of your life, arthritically stepping your way through

"Apache'"); Acora with Honor Blackman ('You'll occasionally appear on television and radio chat shows, where the young male presenters will pretend that they fancy you'); Acora with Ross Kemp ('After you leave *EastEnders*, you'll play bald violent men who shout a lot in ITV shows that nobody watches. You'll marry the most evil woman in Britain'). The receptionist continued to moan about her employer slash question-mark son, and I was beginning to think that I might give up on my desire to know the future when Acora bustled in, clearly livened up by his latte. A young fifty, maybe, slight and energetic, he took me through into his consulting room, where he asked me if I wanted a palm-reading character analysis for ten pounds, or a glimpse into my future, via crystal ball, for twenty. Character analysis I leave to my ex-girlfriends and my excellent daughters, so I went for the crystal.

He gazed into the ball, and told me some pretty spooky things in his rich Devon accent. He told me some things about my love life which, discretion being the better part of valour, I shall keep to myself. He told me that I'll live next to water. He told me that I shouldn't work for anybody, a sentiment which my various ex-employers would vigorously endorse. He told me I have a dodgy left knee (I do), but that I would make old bones. He told me that I shouldn't get married again. He told me that I had been cursed, in 1995. As it goes, I *had* been cursed in 1995 by an ex-girlfriend; I remembered the moment well. Acora stood up, and lifted my curse, in Romani. That's what he told me he was doing, anyway, and I trust him, though my Romani is a bit rusty.

I emerged after half an hour, feeling happy and relaxed. Twenty quid is well worth spending for half an hour of someone telling you that you're a good guy who'll live for years. The not getting married again bit was worth the fee on its own. I recommend Acora highly, if ever you have time to kill on Plymouth's Barbican. Perry Venus was waiting for me on the other side of the road; he'd been taking photos of the bottoms of girls looking in Acora's window. It was 12.15, and the Plymouth gin distillery was open for tourists.

Not many tourists. Just us, at that stage. And because we had arrived a little bit early, Fleur, the retail manager, showed us into the still room, and after getting permission from the distillery manager let Perry take some flash photos. You need permission because of 'the angel's share'. This is the case in all distilleries, because 'the angel's share' is the 100%-proof alcohol that hangs in the air; and if you're not very careful, the whole thing will go up in flames. They hastened us through to where we would shortly be going on the tour, and we stood beneath the great copper stills, which looked like overgrown alchemist's retorts. Which was apt, since mainstream European distilling is a direct consequence of alchemical experimentation.

Like everything else, the Chinese seem to have invented distilling, in about 800 BCE. There is evidence that the Romans drank distilled liquor of some kind, too, but it was the alchemists who refined it into a useful art in Europe. These days, alchemy is taken one of two ways. It is seen either as holistic magic, with the alchemists as initiates in a mysterious cult, whose wisdom has been largely lost, due to the rise of phallocentric science; or it is seen as metaphor for self-refinement – in this version, the alchemists are proto-Jungians. Either way, in a secular society, the alchemists are viewed as wise men, adepts, who were on to something. After all, didn't Newton study alchemy? And Newton was a brainiac, so there must be something in it, mustn't there? Well, in fact, the alchemists really were trying to turn lead into gold, by discovering the philosopher's stone, and really were trying to find the secret of immortality, by distilling the water of life, and in both these aims they failed. They weren't trying to do this because they were mad; they were trying to do it because they lived in a world before science, so they thought you could. Their world view was radically different from ours. Alchemy started to die out as the scientific world view took hold. The scientific world view has been successful because it works, and alchemy didn't. Newton didn't study alchemy because he was secretly a magician; he studied alchemy because he was openly a scientist, and alchemy was the best tool he had to understand matter; that is to say, what things are made of.

The results didn't happen, but the techniques the alchemists had developed turned out to be very useful, in a number of ways.

Distilling was at the heart of alchemical practice, and it is perhaps worth noting that it first began to appear in Europe on any significant scale in the early seventeenth century, roughly synchronous with the rise of science. It's as if the alchemists, in the face of Baconian method, decided to stop trying to find the secret of eternal youth, and to just go and get pished instead. The etymology stacks up; whisky comes from the Gaelic, *uisge beathe*, the water of life. The Swedes drink aquavit. The French still make a wonderful drink called eau-de-vie. So does my friend Ash, up in the hills of Ceredigion.

One of the secrets that the alchemists had let slip was that anything could be distilled into spirits. The French distilled wine into brandy. The Russians distilled anything they could get their hands on. But it was the Dutch who started distilling grain on a commercial scale; the Bols distillery near Amsterdam was opened in 1575. The process is very simple. You make a weak alcoholic 'wash' (such as beer), and then put it through a still. You boil it up, collect the vapour, condense it back into liquid, run it through the still again, and *voilà*, you have grain alcohol. Gin is derived from the Dutch for juniper, *genever*, juniper berries being far and away the most important of the flavourings. The spirits that were being drunk in England were mostly French brandy; brandy, incidentally, also comes from the Dutch: *brandewijn*, or 'burned wine'. The evidence would suggest that people in England were not drinking a great deal of spirits throughout the seventeenth century. Charles I granted a monopoly to the Company of Distillers in 1638, but it was mostly employed by apothecaries. Pepys drank it as a cure for constipation: 'Whether that did it, I cannot tell, but I had a couple of stools forced after it, and did break a fart or two.' The restoration of the monarchy in 1660 saw the drinking of spirits become more popular; Defoe said of the population of England in the years immediately following the Restoration, 'very merry, and very mad, and very drunken, the people were, and grew more so every day'. And they were about to get much more so again.

In the Glorious Revolution of 1688, James II was driven from the throne and replaced by his nephew and son-in-law William of Orange. William straightaway declared war on the French and banned all trade with France. This meant no more brandy; hardly a move which would make a new king popular. But William's tipple was Dutch gin, and in 1690 he enacted a bill 'for encouraging the distilling of brandy and spirits from corn'. Not only did this Act allow for the unlicensed and duty-free production of gin, where the ale-houses, taverns and inns had been paying duty for over 200 years on wine and beer, it also supported 'the Landed Interests', who were thus guaranteed a market for their grain. It may also have had military benefits; William encouraged his men to take a wee nip before going into battle, and the greatest of his generals, the Duke of Marlborough, supported this view. It gave the soldiers courage; gave them, in fact, 'Dutch courage'. It is estimated that some half a million gallons of spirit per year were consumed in England in the late 1690s; by 1733 this figure had risen to 11 million gallons, and reached 20 million gallons per year by 1743. As Patrick Dillon puts it in his excellent book on the gin craze, *Gin: The Much Lamented Death of Madam Geneva*. 'Government had declared free trade in a powerful new drug.'

Gin was different from beer and wine; it was exactly 'a new drug'. And, as Jessica Warner put it in her equally excellent book on the same subject, *Craze: Gin and Debauchery in an Age of Reason*, 'Drugs affect the minds of their critics just as much as they affect the minds of their users.' William III had solved the problem of importing brandy from France, had bolstered corn production in England, and had filled his soldiers' bellies with fire. He had also unleashed what came to be seen as the greatest social evil of the next sixty years.

The early part of the eighteenth century was a hard-drinking age, across all the social classes. Gentlemen would have considered it impolite to rise from table in a state of sobriety. Gin, free from excise duty, became the favoured inebriant of the poor, for whom it became a comfort and a consolation. Estimates vary as to how many places sold it; conservatively, 1 in 6 premises in London sold gin; of the population of 600,000 in 1720, 100,000 were regular drinkers of gin. As well as in the 'dram shops', hawkers sold gin in the streets.

London was expanding wildly in the new spirit of freedom after the Glorious Revolution, in what Pope called 'the age of hope and golden mountains'. It was the trendiest, most open and free city in Europe, while English governance and society became the model for Montesquieu's ideal state. It was wild, exciting, violent, and pissed off its face. Slums grew outside the walls of the old City of London, in places like Holborn and St Giles in the Field. This was an ideal environment for 'the dram shops', whose signs advertised the fact that you could get 'Drunk for a penny. Dead drunk for twopence. Straw for nothing' (this last a reference to the practice of providing places where you could collapse after a few glasses). And since the new slums were outside the jurisdiction of the City, it fell to the Middlesex magistrates to attempt some control. They reported in 1721 that 'gin never fails to produce an invincible Aversion to Work and Labour'. I suffer terribly from an aversion to work and labour; I wonder if they used to slip gin in my bottle as a child? It would explain a lot.

Led by the Middlesex magistrates, political pressure grew over the 1720s to deal with the problem of gin. In 1728 the first of the Gin Acts was passed, imposing a duty of five shillings per gallon, but protests from the producers and 'the Landed Interests', meant that the Act failed. It also proved a boost to bootleg production, as most attempts at controlling drugs always do. In 1733, the Act was effectively amended out of existence. The Middlesex magistrates were not happy. By 1736, there were over 7,000 gin sellers in the county. The magistrates pressed for total prohibition, and they got something close to it. The 1736 Act imposed a duty of £20 per gallon, and also forced gin sellers for the first time to apply for a licence, which cost £50. Where a dram of gin had previously cost a penny, it now cost the equivalent of a week's lodgings. There were riots; a bomb was let off in Westminster Hall; the guard was doubled at Kensington Palace. Gin production also doubled. The Act was an utter failure, and was repealed in 1743. It was the closest that England has ever come to Prohibition.

The repeal of the Act did not mean that the problem of gin went away. It clung to its foreign image; gin was alien, beer was British.

Hogarth's famous print of 1751, *Gin Lane*, showing death and disease clustering around the central figure of 'Madam Geneva', has a lesser-known counterpart, *Beer Street*, showing prosperous and happy people enjoying a quiet pint or two.

An Act of 1751 was seen to get it about right. Duty was imposed at £5 per gallon. Distillers were banned from retailing their wares. And gin was only allowed to be sold on licensed premises, taking it into the long-established ale-houses, taverns and inns, which were already under the jurisdiction of magistrates. But, according to Jessica Warner, 'the wave was already on a downward slope'. After sixty years, the English had learned to handle their spirits, and the gin problem was seen to fade away.

But the image of 'Madam Geneva' was slow to die, and transmuted over the early part of the nineteenth century into 'Mother's Ruin'. It was still seen as an abortificant until very recently; fallen women climb into a bath of hot water, down a bottle of gin, and terminate their unwanted pregnancy. It's interesting to note how its socially undermining effects were always given female characteristics, and were seen as particularly devastating to women. This is surely because women did not much go into the ale-houses, whilst gin was freely available on the streets, thus affording to women for the first time the chance of getting off their tits. In *Those That Will Not Work*, the fourth volume of Henry Mayhew's *London Labour and the London Poor*, published in 1861, Mayhew devotes a section to 'Stealing From Drunken Persons'. Not only have the drunken victims largely been drinking gin in 'gin palaces', but those who are doing the crime, often women, are doing it to fuel their pernicious gin habit.

There is one more twist in the extraordinary tale of gin. British colonists in Africa, and, in particular, India, used to take quinine in water to prevent the onset of malaria. Quinine is very bitter, so they mixed it with other more palatable drinks. After some experimentation, it was found that the best way to get quinine water down was to mix it with gin and lemon. The Raj acquired a taste for gin mixed with this quinine tonic water, and brought it back to England with them. Most of these people came from a very different social order from those who had discovered gin-drinking with such enthusiasm in the early eighteenth century. So gin became, first respectable, and then, if taken with tonic water, posh. It is still the great drink of Sloaney girls; their paramours call gin 'panty remover'. After 300 years, 'Madam Geneva' has become a lady.

Perry finished mapping the stills, and we were dumped in a darkened viewing room, where we were joined by two other visitors. Our guide told us that she would shortly take us round the distillery, but not before we had been forced to sit through a PowerPoint presentation. She turned off the lights, pressed Enter on the laptop which controlled the show, and within seconds I had fallen into a blissful sleep. Not once have I ever managed to stay awake through a PowerPoint presentation. Overhead projectors send me off, too. I recommend them as a cure for insomnia; if you have difficulty sleeping, why not try projecting pie charts on to your bedroom wall?

As the show ended, Perry gave me a nudge, and I came to with a start. Now we had a proper guide, and we went back into the still room. We talked with the other two visitors, an engineer and his son from Bristol. The lad was doing a degree in marketing (whatever that is) at the University of Plymouth, and like most undergraduates, spent a reasonable portion of his time screaming 'Gemma! I love yoooooo!' in inner-city centres, while being restrained by his friend Darren, who is telling him to 'Leave it!' because Gemma is being sick in the gutter.

Dad is just showing an interest in the lad's hobbies, by taking him round a gin distillery.

Gin is still the same as ever it was; grain alcohol, to which are added juniper berries and then various other flavouring ingredients. These are known as 'the botanicals'. We were taken into a room and shown the botanicals that Plymouth Gin use. Apart from juniper, there is orris, angelica root, cardamom, orange and lemon peel. The secret is not what the botanicals are; the secret is in the proportions that they use them. We tasted the dry ingredients. Then they brought out the gins. Gin is not like whisky; it doesn't need ageing before you can drink it. It goes straight from the still into the bottle.

We tried the gins. Plymouth Gin is the cocktail barman's favourite, smoother and rounder than the London gins. The guide told us that the distillery manager recommends that you mix his gin with plain water. In fact, all distillery managers recommend that you drink their spirit mixed with water, as it releases the oils. This came as a bit of a shock.

'What about tonic water?'

Our guide made a face.

'Oh no. Just plain water. If you really must use tonic water, then the only one we recommend is Waitrose own brand.'

'Good god.' That's a century or more of tradition brushed aside.

Our guide dropped her voice.

'To be honest, I drink it with lemonade. Don't tell the boss.' We promised.

After the straight gin, we tried the damson, and then the sloe gin. Sloe-gin production takes twenty tons of sloes per annum, which is a lot of sloes. They mostly come from Poland. Are there sloe farms in Poland? Or do kids earn extra pocket money wandering along hedgerows, picking the berries from blackthorn bushes? In the war, my mother used to earn a few pennies collecting rose hips, which were sold to make rose-hip syrup, so I guess that it's at least possible.

Sloe gin has always seemed to me a great triumph of the human spirit. Somewhere in the far-distant past, people must have picked sloes, and eaten them. Horrible! Ugh! But, you didn't die. So someone else must have thought, 'I know, we'll cook 'em up, see what that's like.' No, still utterly disgusting. Then someone else must have thought, 'Well, how about if you cook them up with honey to make them sweeter?' Still completely inedible. I would have given up at that point, and said, 'No, there is nothing to be done with the fruit of the blackthorn tree.' So who thought, 'I know. We'll collect loads of these inedible berries, pierce the skins with needles, pop them into a bottle of gin, add some sugar, shake it up every couple of weeks, and see what it's like after a year?' Genius.

If you've never tried it, you haven't lived. It's one of the great treats of Christmas, and if you can't be bothered to wander about the hedgerows looking for sloes (or if you are unfortunate enough to live in a city), then Plymouth Sloe Gin is available in all fine liquor stores.

After the tastings, we were guided back into the retail outlet at the front of the distillery, and while Perry bought a few bottles, I got talking to Fleur, the Scottish retail manager.

'Which one do like you best, Fleur?'

'I never drink it masel. I'm a recovering alcoholic.'

'God, really?'

'Aye. I'm fifteen years dry.'

'It must be difficult working here.'

'No, not really. Only when we have staff do's. My boss will keep on at me to try a wee drop, but I always tell him no.'

'Do you go to AA, or anything like that?' asked Perry, who, astute readers will remember, is a counsellor for people with alcohol problems by way of a day job.

'No, I've no need. There was a day . . . I've got three children. I was on my own with them. All I did was drink. I was crazy for drink. All our money went on drink. There was never any food in the house. One day, my lovely neighbour went to the corner shop, and bought a load of messages, so that the weans would have something to eat. I took those messages back to the shop, got the money, and bought drink with it. That was my lowest point. The next morning I realised it had to stop, right there and then. So I've never touched a drop since.'

Perry and I glowed at Fleur. She's a brave lady, and later on we raised a cup of tea to her. Distilling and brewing are very open industries, which see visitor centres and on-site retail outlets as important to marketing. Since our visit, Plymouth Gin have opened a new visitor centre, which friends in Plymouth tell me is very good. You can get a coffee there, if you don't want to sit and marvel at Lenkiewicz's mural in Prete's, and you could toast Fleur in latte. Look out for Acora, who might well be in there too, drinking the stuff with asylum seekers.

Scottish alcoholics were very much on our mind as we headed out of Plymouth for our next destination, Buckfast Abbey. The abbey is just outside the village of Buckfastleigh, about fifteen miles east of Plymouth. I'd wanted to go to a monastery because of my thesis that the history of pubs and that of roads and the travellers who use them are intimately linked. The hospitality of the monasteries was a vital part of trade in the Middle Ages. Their guest-houses slowly morphed into inns, over a couple of hundred years. Buckfast Abbey is a Benedictine house, and for the Benedictines in particular, hospitality is central to their philosophy.

Chapter 53 of the Rule of St Benedict deals with the treatment of guests, who are to be received 'as Christ Himself'. I thought that it would be interesting and instructive to stay for a night at a monastery, and that this would give me a perfect opportunity to write about medieval hospitality. I emailed Buckfast, to ask if it would be possible to stay. I phoned. I wrote. I left messages. Nothing. Doubtless there was some perfectly innocent explanation. I told them that I was writing a history of pubs. Surely they couldn't have taken fright because of the reason I wanted to visit Buckfast Abbey in particular, which was, of course, to find out about the production of Buckfast Tonic Wine?

Ah, Buckie. Fuckfast. The favoured drink of Scottish tramps. Scottish tramps are not great readers traditionally, and the chances of anyone else drinking the stuff are vanishingly small, so it is unlikely, dear reader, that you have ever tried Buckfast Tonic Wine, as it is entirely foul. It's quite difficult to get in England, but if you go into any Scottish off-licence, and hang around for half an hour or so, you are bound to see a few bottles sold. The wealth of Buckfast Abbey (Fastbuck, as the locals call it) is founded on the sale of Buckfast Tonic Wine. Is founded, to be frank, on human misery.

Buckfast Abbey church is fairly new. It was built over thirty years in the early part of the twentieth century by the monks, and it is grimly impressive. Fascist architecture, Perry called it, and I could see his point. Neo-Gothic in style, it has neither the soaring grace of the great medieval cathedrals, nor the homely familiarity of Victorian Gothic. It is straightforwardly ugly. Perry and I wandered around it, feeling more and more depressed. There were no monks to be seen; locals who have got in there tell me that there is a monks' bar, so perhaps they were all getting pished on Buckie somewhere. It's difficult to say for sure. The gentleman that we met at the information desk in the gift shop was most unforthcoming about Buckfast Tonic Wine. As I've said, the brewing and distilling industries are very open about what they do, and are universally happy to let people into their plants, and to talk about their craft. It was only at Buckfast Abbey, in fact, that we were stonewalled. This is especially odd, since the Buckfast Abbey leaflet for visitors makes a great fuss about the fact that it is 'the home of the World Famous Buckfast Tonic Wine', and features a picture of a cheery monk holding a bottle.

'Excuse me. I was wondering who is in charge of Buckie production?' I asked.

'Why do you ask?' asked the gentleman on the information desk (Fastbuck is staffed largely by volunteers).

'Well, I'm writing a book on the history of drink, and I was wondering if we might talk to someone about Buckfast Tonic Wine?'

'Father Richard is unavailable,' said the gentleman, without picking up a phone and trying to track Father Richard down.

'Is there any chance we could have a look at the production process?'

'None at all. There's nothing to see.'

'Could you tell us anything about how it is made?'

The gentleman narrowed his eyes, and sighed. 'Well . . . the wine comes in tankers from France or Spain' (from the wine lake, my local source told me later; it's not the very best vintage, you understand, as this would be wasted on tramps). 'The monks add the various flavourings' (which used to include coca leaves until relatively recently). 'Then it goes in another tanker to Andover, where it's bottled.'

'Are the monks concerned that its high alcohol content and low price make it attractive for alcoholics, especially in Scotland?'

'I couldn't comment on that, I'm afraid.'

And that was what we found out about Buckfast Tonic Wine. In the abbey bookshop, however, we did find a number of books about twelve-step programmes (the Minnesota Model, Perry calls it; this is the programme followed by Alcoholics Anonymous); and about Christian approaches to dealing with alcohol problems. This filled us both with loathing. The gift shop, as well as Buckie and sanctimonious literature about the evil of drink, also sells mead, and, in a special shop devoted to monastic produce from around Europe, Chimay beer. We were glad to leave.

We headed down into Buckfastleigh village, where the Valiant Soldier pub has been restored by a local conservation trust. The pub closed in the sixties, and was locked and left completely untouched. Even the money from the last night's takings was left in the till. Now it is open as an attraction, and seemed well worth a visit since we were in the area. Except that it was closed.

'Is it right that you've fixed up visits to several breweries later in the trip?' asked Perry.

'Yes,' I replied.

'And have you organised a piss-up in these breweries?'

'It's a funny time of day, that's all.'

It was four o'clock. Most pubs are closed at four o'clock. Looking at the opening times for the Valiant Soldier, we discovered that we had turned up a day early. Could have happened to anyone. We drove down to Totnes.

In the valley of the Dart, we passed derelict cider orchards, and in Dartington we saw the Cider Press Arts Centre. Defoe came through here in 1722, in his *Tour Through the Whole Island of Great Britain*. He wrote that in Devon 'they have so vast a quantity of fruit, and so much cyder made that sometimes they have sent ten or twenty thousand hogsheads of it to London, and at a very reasonable rate, too'. Now the cider industry is largely gone from Devon, moved north to Somerset and, especially, Herefordshire, but the old orchards are still to be seen, here and there, dreaming of the days when Devon was synonymous with cider.

I like Totnes. It's a hippy town, to be sure, but it still feels real to me. It's stiff with re-birthing therapists and colonic-irrigation workshops, I admit, but it doesn't take itself too seriously, some-how. According to legend, Totnes is where Brutus landed on his arrival from Troy, and if you look carefully, you can find the Brutus Stone in the High Street, where he first set foot in Albion. Legend does not recall the date and time of his arrival; Perry and I arrived at half past four, and we were due to spend the evening at a beer festival, and we had to drive there, so we had an attack of the sensibles, and went for more coffee, in a café pub, called the Barrelhouse.

Café pubs have sprung up all over the place, these days. They are particularly suited to New Labour times; superficially democratic, with glossy but bland food and drink. I like pubs. I like cafés. Café pubs often manage to combine the worst of both worlds. If this book was just about a search for grungy old boozers, with sawdust on the floor and miserable old gets supping in the four-ale bar, then we would eschew such places. But actually, it is about trying to see all kinds of drinking cultures, and, although as a rule I avoid café pubs, we plunged in. And liked it very much. The Barrelhouse is in an old chapel, and they have managed to keep it in a state of relative disrepair, with huge cracked mirrors, and paint peeling from the walls. It is, in fact, quite grungy.

No one seemed to be drinking anything other than coffee. Lots of the customers were students from Dartington College, mostly attractive girls, and one of them, a cutie in a denim miniskirt, tottered over and took a photo of us. So Perry took one back. The rest of the customers were Totnes Beautiful People, and many of them were accompanied by small dogs, who rorted about the place, chasing one another between the legs of the tables, begging for scraps of cake. Really, you shouldn't feed dogs in cafés, especially cakes, but I can't resist small dogs, so I was torn. In the end, I managed to slip a bit of danish pastry to a Jack Russell without its owner noticing, so everyone was happy. The Barrelhouse was good, because it had a good 'atmosphere'.

Very sick middle-aged readers might remember Russ Abbot's only hit record, which was called 'Atmosphere'. Russ sang about how he liked a party with an 'atmosphere'. Well, OK. But atmosphere can be bad just as much as it can be good. Perry lives in the

Welsh-speaking part of Wales, and if you don't choose your pub wisely, you can feel the atmosphere of hostility when you walk in. We've all been to places where 'you could cut the atmosphere with a knife'. Presumably, this was not the kind of atmosphere that Russ was singing about. Atmosphere, like so much in life, is relative. If you are a City banker, then more likely than not you like shouting at people about bill-broking in Corney & Barrow wine bars for an hour and a half after work before heading back to Putney. Lots of people who are interested in nothing but money all gathered under one roof to drink Pinot Grigio will create your idea of a good atmosphere. If you belong to Mebyon Glendower, then your idea of great atmosphere will be exactly the kind that English-speakers find a bit intimidating if they are foolish enough to stop in Blaenau Ffestiniog for a quick pint. I am a West Country hippy, and I liked the atmosphere in the Barrelhouse. Hideous café bars with kooky kewl names clog up the nice narrow back streets of all our provincial towns and cities, but if they were like this, funky, and relaxed, and full of dogs and girls, then people would use them happily. I would, anyway.

We left Totnes, and drove on to the 12th Maltings Beer Festival, at Tucker's Maltings in Newton Abbot. Tucker's Maltings is the only working malthouse which is open to the public. It is not the only one which is open to the public because the others have something to hide. It is the only one which is open to the public because, with the best will in the world, there is nothing of any conceivable interest to see in a malthouse. Malt is one of four indispensable ingredients in beer production. The others are hops, water and yeast, and all four have a particular mythology attached to them. Malt is basically barley grain, which has been steeped in water, and then dried in a warm environment, so that it is almost at the point of germination. This process produces starches in the barley, which are converted into sugars at the first stage of the brewing process, sugars which the yeast needs to produce alcohol. There are different kinds of malt; you can roast it, so that it becomes dark. Light malts are used to make light beer. Dark malt is used to make dark beer. After steeping, the malt is laid out on a drying floor, and it is turned, so that oxygen gets at the grain, which aids germination. All well and good. But watching grain dry does not make a day out for the family, even taking into account the British talent for turning almost anything into a visitor attraction.

Tucker's Maltings is an impressive building. Built in 1900, it is very long, and three storeys high. It needs to be long, so that the huge floor space in what is essentially the attic can be used for drying the grain. Ventilation windows punctuate the roof, to aid the drying process. Inside, the ground floor is dark, the colour of mild ale. It smells of malt, like Ovaltine. For the Maltings Beer Festival, it was lined with hundreds of barrels of beer from the fifty or so small breweries who had brought their wares to Newton Abbot for sampling by the aficionados. The five-pound entry fee gets you a half-pint glass, especially produced for the occasion, a programme listing the various kinds of beer which are available, and a couple of beer tokens, which you exchange for a half from one of the barrels. After that, you can buy as many beer tokens as you like. The people who run it seemed to be, almost entirely, fat guys with beards. T-shirts stretched to bursting point seemed to be *de rigueur*, which is a shame, since in view of the prevalence of beer guts at the festival, something baggier might have been more flattering.

In fact, given the number of beards on view, and the almost total absence of women, I was reminded of pictures of Kabul, or Baghdad, except that at least the lads in Newton Abbot get to have a drink. As a heterosexual male, I entirely fail to understand the attraction of events (or indeed cultures) which effectively exclude women. I like going to the match, but that only lasts ninety minutes, and you get more and more girls these days anyway. It's not that they're barred from beer festivals or anything, it's just that most lasses don't fancy it. And if women don't fancy it, well, neither do I.

The few women who were there were the kind of girls who join in with their boyfriend's activities (beer festivals, steam railways, restoring antique cement mixers, etc.) at all costs, no matter how superficially unattractive they might be. I think this is because some men become so wrapped up in their hobbies, that if the kind of girls who like this kind of men want to keep seeing their boyfriends, then they have to get involved too. Hence biker chicks, female metallists and so on. No girl worth her salt really likes heavy metal, or motorbikes, or beer festivals. They like quite different things, if they are honest. Their heterosexuality lures them into these horrible activities, because certain kinds of men like them; as an old pal of mine once said, 'women like men, and men like hobbies'. When the girls split up with these kinds of men, they suddenly, unaccountably, lose interest in bikes, beer, or whatever. Then these men find new, equally gullible girlfriends.

One of the things that strikes the first-time visitor to a beer festival are the cringe-making names of real ale. I've already owned up to drinking the stuff, but now at the Maltings I was confronted with the cold hard reality of how naff it can all be. Piston Bitter; Rucking Mole; Naughty Ferret; Old Slug. All very depressing, but a symptom of the heartiness with which I'm going to have to come to terms, if I'm to survive a month-long orgy of pub-going. The programme for the festival lists all the beers available, and as well as the names, there are short descriptions of what the beers taste like, so that Burrington's 'Azza Newt', for example, is described as 'hoppy and dry', while Sutton's 'Knickadroppa Glory' (in your dreams, fat guys!) the programme assures us is 'a moreish strong beer'. My favourite blurb is for Hobden's 'Russian Stoat', which is described as a 'dark post-imperial stout'. I imagine Edward Said downing a couple of pints, er, if it wasn't for the Muslim thing.

I got myself a half of Smiles 'Bristol IPA', because I like Smiles beer, and I could ask for it without cringing. Perry, operating on the same principle, chose Butcombe's 'Bitter', and we staggered outside to where a large tent had been erected on the open ground opposite Tucker's Maltings. Here, lots of men were sitting at long tables, earnestly drinking beer, and wiping foam from their beards. It was quieter than a pub, somehow. In a pub, people come to socialise. Here, the punters sat in hushed reverence in the face of such beery abundance. We sat down next to a couple of guys in their twenties, who turned out to be called Ken and Roger.

'All right?' I said.

'Yeah,' said Ken and Roger, who were quite clearly several sheets to the wind.

'Been here long?'

'All day. We're pissed.' They raised their glasses, and smiled benevolently. Pissed young men, statistically, are the most likely to attack you, and the least likely to smile benevolently at strangers. After a few minutes' conversation, it became clear that their benevolence was due to the copious amounts of dope which they were smoking. Dope might make you dull, fat and giggly, but it does not make you violent. One of the reasons that football violence dropped so sharply in the late eighties was the arrival of dope and E's on the terraces. Ken and Roger still preferred dope to beer, but the advent of the beer festival in Newton Abbot, and its concomitant opportunity for all-day drinking had been too much to resist.

Ken was on the sick, off work with stress. He found this odd, since he had a quarter-a-week dope habit, and felt that it ought to help him relax more. I pointed out that dope is a mood elevator, and that if you are feeling stressed, it will heighten these feelings. Perry pointed out that alcohol is a depressant, and that stress is a symptom of depression, so unlikely to help much either. Ken and Roger pointed out that we were self-righteous old bores. We went back into the Maltings for another go. I had a half of Keltek's 10% 'Beheaded', while Perry stuck to the Butcombe. This neatly guaranteed that Perry would be driving for the rest of the night.

Back in the tent, we sat down with John, long hair, beard, sallow skin, fifty-ish, biker type, sci-fi T-shirt, who was marking off beers in his programme.

'What's been your favourite?' I asked.

John jerked his head nervously to the left. 'Eh . . .'

'I said, what's been your favourite?'

He jerked his head again, twice. 'Eh . . . Eh . . . Exe Valley.'

'Oh.'

John had a disastrous tic, and a bad stammer. He had come down from Reading, especially for the beer festival.

'I . . . got the the the tr tr train. Got into Eh Eh Eh Exeter, and h h had three p p pints of Eh Eh Exe Valley. Th th th then I g g got the b b bus to O to O to O to O to Okehampton and h h h had two m m more pints, waiting f f for my f f friends to c come and p p pick me up. I've b been here an ow an ow an ow an hour. Tried f f four different b b beers.'

No wonder he was in such a state. His idea of heaven was going on beer holidays; he'd been all round Scotland a few years before, in search of the perfect Scottish pint, a hilariously pointless task, since Scottish beer is god-awful. I have a pal with drug-induced epilepsy; you couldn't help wondering if John's tic and stammer were caused by devotion to beer. He did give us a useful tip, though, once I'd told him what we were up to.

'You sh sh should go go go to Ee to Ee to Eli's. In Huw in Huw in . . .'

'Huish Episcopi?'

He nodded gratefully.

With this, Perry and I bade farewell to the beardy men of Tucker's Maltings, and headed north on the thirty-mile drive back to my house, where we were due to spend the night. Not many travel writers, I suspect, get to go home after only two days of journeying. But, if we are to look long and honestly at pubs, then we have to spend time in the local. All day Saturday, ideally.

All we have to do now is get into the house without waking anyone up.

# Saturday 3rd April

There are many ways of slipping into the house, and, subsequently, bed, without drawing too much attention to yourself. I fancy myself something of an expert in the dark arts of coming home unnoticed. Always stop for a moment, and check the lights in the bedroom before you open the front door. Are they on? If they are, it is best to move quietly upstairs straightaway, nip into the bathroom and clean your teeth, and then slowly prise open the bedroom door. Is your partner awake? If yes, then just say 'Hi' or something equally noncommittal, sit down on the edge of the bed, and ask how their day/evening has gone. Look them in the eye, and give the impression that you are listening. Try to avoid the topic of where you have been; if asked, it is best to tell the truth, if you possibly can, though you may wish to gloss over some of the details. If pressed further, always try to paint a gloomy picture of how the evening went.

If they are asleep with the lights on, or if the lights are off, then you are clear to enjoy a nightcap before retiring. If you are on your own, this presents little difficulty. If you have your pal Perry Venus with you, however, I have learned from long experience that it is best to move into a room which is not underneath your bedroom. Also, stick to drink; if you have a couple of spliffs as well, it is likely that one or the other of you will start laughing, and nothing infuriates a sleeping partner more than being woken by hysterical hooting from downstairs. Do not be tempted to play your *Ramones Greatest Hits* CD. When you have unwound a little, and reflected on the evening's events, you are ready for bed. Once again, move quietly upstairs (do not tiptoe, as this creates more noise than you might imagine; besides, you are likely to be a bit unsteady on the pins), clean your teeth (never be tempted to skip this), and undress in the bathroom. Turn off any bathroom or landing lights, open and close the bedroom door with love and care, and slide silently under the duvet.

'Hello.'

'Oh! Hello, dear. You awake?'

'I'm hardly likely to be asleep, given the noise that you and Perry made coming in.'

'Sorry, dear.'

'What were you laughing about? You sounded like fucking hyenas on crack.'

'Sorry, dear. Perry does have rather an invasive laugh.'

'Mmph. And must you play the Ramones all the time? You are forty-six. Go and buy yourself a Norah Jones CD, like a proper middle-aged man.'

'Yes, I'm sorry, dear.'

'Mmph. What was the beer festival like?'

'Awful. You'd have hated it.'

'And I suppose you'll be wanting to spend all day in the pub tomorrow?'

'Well, I am supposed to be on the longest pub crawl in the British Isles, darling. Going to the pub is the whole point of the thing.'

'Mmph.'

'Goodnight, dear.'

'Mmph.'

I don't know why I felt guilty. All we'd had was a few nips of gin, some coffee, and a couple of halves, after all. And a drop of Scotch and a couple of spliffs after we'd got in. And there had been no danger of meeting lasses at the beer festival. Perhaps it's just the case that you always feel guilty coming in late from the pub. Perhaps the guilt is part of the fun.

The morning dawned grey and wet; an ideal day for drifting around a few local pubs, and thinking about what makes a great local. I had a pretty good idea, because I used to have a wonderful local. It's called the Yorkshire House, and it's in Lancaster. The landlords were Mike and Sue Edwards. They didn't do food, except crisps and pickled eggs, which sat unloved and ignored by all-comers in a large jar at the end of the bar. There was also a small selection of sweeties, provided for the large stoner community who used their premises. Downstairs, there was just one room, with a tiled floor, and a fire burning in the grate. There was a CD juke-box with Northern Soul compilations, albums by the Clash, the Stone Roses. There were odd pencil drawings of Elvis, Hendrix and Jim Morrison in frames on the walls. There was table football. They sold real ale, and although the Yorkshire House is in the North, and so they felt it imperative to sell their beer with half an inch of foam on top, they were quite happy to take the sparkler off the tap for the occasional southerner like me. They sold rolling tobacco behind the bar, and both green and blue skins. At one end of the bar, there were always a few truck drivers, who had parked up for the night in the truck stop in the next street along. At the other end of the bar, handy for the pickled eggs, sat a group of middle-aged gentlemen known to all as the 'Lancaster Bus Club'. This is because they really did constitute the Lancaster Bus Club, and once a month they would hire the upstairs room, and show slides of buses. The body of the pub was taken up by Lancaster's rock aris-tocracy, poets, punks, hippies, dreamers. Upstairs, there is a perform-ance space, busy most nights of the week, when the bus club weren't using it. Local bands played there, strutting their stuff on the small stage, longing for the day when a London A&R man will wander into the Yorkshire House and snap them up. The poets put on read-ings, the dreamers hold political meetings.

I played up there countless nights; reading stories, singing songs, bickering with members of the SWP. I was on the pub quiz team, more of which when we actually get up there. Most nights, I would get in the 'Yorkie Bar' for last orders. I always knew, with unerr-ing certainty, that some, if not all, of my friends would be there. If they weren't, that just meant that I'd got there slightly earlier than usual, and just as Mike's hand reached out for the bell, in would crash Dicken, or Gary Holland, or Chas, or Neil, or Ron and Sarah, or Simon Norfolk, or Japanese John, or Steven Grew or Tom Crippen or or or. So one of the definitions of a local is this: it's a place where you can go and meet your pals without having to phone anybody up. They are just there, like the fixtures. Another would be this: the bar staff know your name, and know what you are drinking. One more: it is an extension of your living room; you should feel at home there, safe and welcome.

So much was it an extension of home that my eldest daughter and her pals drink there these days, which they used to do in our house when they were underage. Since I've moved away, Mike and Sue have given it up, but it was taken over by a local punk couple, who felt that it was important to preserve the character of the place. I live 300 miles away now, but I know that I could get in my car, and drive up there, and still find the usual suspects, propping up the bar, talking about buses; could still sit around the fire arguing about late-period Electric Prunes albums with musos, still plot Blair's downfall with the dreamers. It's not like that in the Devon village where I live now.

We have a lovely old pub in the village, called the Hunter's Moon. It owns the fishing rights on the river, and fishermen come from all over to stay at the pub, and to fish for trout and salmon during the day. It is less than a minute's walk away, and when we moved here, my girlfriend had visions of tottering over there in her mules of a Sunday lunchtime, for a quick G&T. I saw myself at the bar, chewing the cud with local farmers about this year's lamb crop. But it was not to be. Your local isn't always your nearest pub.

Until six years ago, the Hunter's was packed night after night, a real village pub, the centre of village life. It was run by two brothers, who had taken it over from their father, who had run it since the 1950s. Although, according to the people who used to go there, the brothers could be grumpy on occasion, the place throbbed with life. There was music most weekends. The village took it for granted that the brothers would run the place for ever. But the brothers were getting on in years, and they sold up to a family from the Midlands; a father, his wife, their son, and his wife. Prior to running a pub, father and son had run a firm of debt collectors; good start. One of their first acts on arriving was to take a local (who, admittedly, may have been being a bit of a nuisance), and beat him to a pulp in the car-park. The old man boasts unceasingly about having been in the SAS; about how, in his words, he's 'killed three Paddies'.

When they were debt collectors, he also claims, they used to put dynamite through people's doors. The old man calls his barman 'Lucky Lips', because he's never hit him. The landlord's son is a charmer, too. He was in a fight in another local pub, where he punched a woman in the face, and broke her jaw. Their wives look permanently terrified; on one of the handful of occasions I've been in there, the old man's wife came into the bar, to be greeted by her husband saying, 'Get back into the kitchen, you.' She scuttled away.

Once, a friend of mine was coming to stay with us for the weekend. He arrived earlier than advertised, and finding us not at home, went into the pub for a drink.

'Where are you from?' said the old man, in one of his rare attempts at hospitality.

'London,' said my friend.

'I don't like London. It's full of niggers.'

'I'm sorry?' said my friend, thinking he had misheard.

'It's full of niggers. That's why we came here, 'cos there's no niggers.'

'Why do you think it's all right to say that to me?' said my friend, who refused his pint, and went to sit in his car to wait for us to come home, rather than buy a drink from the vile old man. He was still really upset when we got back; and I could only apologise.

A great local has a great landlord; few things are more important than the landlord's attitude to his customers. You can go in pubs that have great beer, good food, and all the rest of it, but if the landlord is wrong, then so is the pub. The Hunter's Moon is ruined by its landlord. So now we have to cast our nets a little wider to find somewhere decent to go.

I like the Laurels in Petrockstowe, a four-mile drive away. My pal Pete the Thatch goes there, and if there are events on, he lets us know. Mouse-racing is very popular, believe it or not. One day, he called to say that morris dancers were coming to the village, and would we like to go and watch? My girlfriend is new to the country, and so she thought she might like to see some morris dancers, who were performing outside the pub on the evening of the First of May. I demurred. She insisted, saying that it was May Day, and that it was traditional. I groaned, but I hadn't been to the Laurels before, and I like Pete, so I went along with it.

It was a chilly spring evening, the sky clear with a nip in the air and a sharp breeze from the north-west. The Laurels is a plain, square, brick-built building painted white, separated from the road by a small lawn with three weather-weary picnic tables.

We went in for a drink, to strengthen ourselves before the fun started. Inside, the decor of the Laurels called to mind a large version of my mum's front room, *circa* 1973. Same carpet, same wallpaper. The landlord and his wife were serving. To get to the bar, we had to negotiate a throng of loud large lads in their thirties and forties, all wearing rugby shirts, who were propped against it. At tables, their wives and sweethearts, their mums and dads, their granddads and nans sat drinking cider and snowballs, while toddlers staggered around the chairs, clutching bags of crisps. Dogs hid under the tables, out of range of malicious tiny feet. At the other end of the bar, the local teenagers played pool and supped Bacardi Breezers, troubled neither by their parents nor the licensing laws. We bought a pint of mild, a G&T, and a bag of pork scratchings. There was nowhere to sit inside if you weren't a local; not that we were unwelcome, just that the place was rammed. A real old proper country boozer, just for villagers; not a drive-out-from-Exeter-for-Sunday-lunch pub. We went outside, and sat at one of the picnic benches. We pulled our coats around us.

The morris dancing started, and a look of horror crossed my girlfriend's face. Ten minutes later, back in the car, I reminded her of Sir Arnold Bax, once Master of the King's Music, now famous only for the oft-quoted 'You should try everything once, except incest and country dancing.' But I forgave the Laurels the morris dancing; it's a great little pub, and it was mine and Perry's first stop in our search for a decent local.

At the bar of the Laurels, we got talking to Cap'n Ted, a retired navy captain. He looked like a retired navy captain should; solidly foursquare to the wind, aquamarine-blue eyes, Birdseye beard and a Donovan cap. I told him about the pub-crawl project.

'Ah. The last pub must be on Unst. I've had a drink further north than that.'

'Iceland or the Faeroes don't count, because they're not part of the British Isles.'

'Wasn't on the Faeroes. I drunk a gin and tonic in the wardroom of my ship, coming round Muckle Flugga. Not a pub, I admit, but still in British territorial waters.'

'I suppose there's always been a great tradition of drinking in the navy. The rum ration and all that.'

'Most certainly, old boy. Every day at eight bells, the rum bosun piped "Up Spirits", and all the sailors who wanted it got their tot of rum. Nelson's Blood, they called it, after they brought Nelson's body home from Trafalgar pickled in a barrel of the stuff.'

'Every evening?'

'No. At the end of the morning watch. Eight bells is just before midday. Jack Tar was useless for anything in the afternoon.'

'Good God. I didn't know that.'

'Oh yes. The only time we ever had it in the evening was when we were on minesweepers. We all felt that with so many explosives and wires and so on about the place, it was best to wait for the evening.'

We agreed that this sounded wise.

'And do you know how much a tot is?' asked Cap'n Ted.

'No.'

'Three pub measures, old boy. And it was strong stuff; 130%-proof Trinidad rum.'

'What if you didn't like rum?'

'Then you got extra pay; a shilling a day, if I remember. And you didn't get it if you were under twenty. But even those who didn't drink the stuff usually used to take it. It was like snout in prison; it became a form of currency. You had 'sippers', 'gulpers', 'three fingers' and a 'tot'. Jack Tar would cover for someone else at a muster of hands in return for a gulper if he liked his rum a bit too much. Or they would save it up for a special occasion, and get sloshed.'

'I didn't know any of this. What did you do with yours?'

'Officers didn't get it; good Lord, no. It was only for the men. The ratings got it watered down. Petty officers got it neat. Officers only got it when the Queen gave the order to "splice the main-brace".'

'I always wondered what that meant.'

'There were circumstances under which the captain could order extra rum rations to be dished out. I only ever did it once; they'd spent all day pulling decomposing corpses out of the water in Penang harbour. Thought they deserved it. Mind you, the supply officer wasn't very happy; it didn't matter too much if you lost your ship, but if you lost a pint of rum, there was hell to pay.'

'When did it stop?'

'Nineteen seventy-one, I think. The sailors all had their own glasses; after the last ration, the glasses were buried ceremonially at sea. Made sense really; you can't operate an aircraft carrier when the crew are all pissed.'

I looked it up when we got home. Cap'n Ted was a year out. On 28 January 1970 the 'Great Rum Debate' took place in the House of Commons, and 30 July of that year became 'Black Tot Day', when the last pipe sounded for 'Up Spirits' in the Royal Navy.

Cap'n Ted was the only customer in the Laurels that Saturday lunchtime. We were early, so it might have picked up later. I like the Laurels, but I have to disqualify it as a local. At four miles, it's too far away. Your local may not be your nearest pub, but you should be able to walk there. Perry and I finished our pints, said goodbye to Cap'n Ted and the landlord, and headed off for our next candidate, the Torridge Inn, in Black Torrington.

People from our village are wary of Black Torrington.

'Oh, it's a funny place,' they say. It's all of two miles away. Still, more and more people from our village are using the Torridge. I can walk there; I walked there by starlight in the first chapter of this book. The lads I'm pally with use it quite a bit, and you often meet interesting characters at the bar. The beer is beautifully kept; they always have Adnams from Southwold, and Shepheard Neame's Spitfire, as well as Doom Bar from my favourite of the local breweries, Sharp's, in Rock, down Padstow way. The landlord and landlady, Richard and Anne, are friendly and welcoming. They have two excellent and well-behaved dogs, wolfhound/pointer crosses. The bar staff are gorgeous. There is a fire in the grate. A strong candidate for local status, you might imagine. The problem, though, is the food. It's just too damn good.

By the time Perry and I bowled up, it was lunchtime. There were several couples in there eating already. We were hungry, so we thought we might peck at something. Perry went for the ling, cooked in butter, served with organic vegetables and rosemary potatoes. I thought I would go for the medley of game: pheasant, partridge, and rabbit, cooked in a rowanberry sauce, and served over a thick slice of toast. After this, as we still had a few corners to fill, I nibbled at a slice of Richard's frankly world-class lemon tart, while Perry tried the crystallised summer fruits. And unless you are a *Guardian* journalist, nipping up the Farringdon Road for a quick one in the Eagle, your local simply does not serve buttered ling. The Torridge is becoming a gastro-pub, a very good one at that. And with gastro-pub status come associated dangers.

There is a pub between here and Tavistock called the Dartmoor Inn. Here is a selection of their menu, culled from a restaurant review: *'baked eggs with garlic leaves and pan-fried ceps; duck leg with aubergine, sherry vinegar and mint; braised oxtail with a sweet sherry sauce and pureed cauliflower, and cod, fresh from Looe in Cornwall, fried in a light batter with distinctly superior chips.'* Contrast this with the menu at the Yorkshire House: crisps, pickled eggs, Mars Bars for dope heads. The restaurant at the Dartmoor is wonderful; but the bar is now practically non-existent. It serves only as a small reception area to sit and have a drink while you look over the menu. The pint glasses have 'Guardian Gastro-Pub of the Year' on them. You can't smoke. There are no pickled eggs in sight. It's no longer a pub, not really. Or imagine if you lived in Titley, in Herefordshire. Then your local would be the Stagg Inn, the first pub in Britain to earn a Michelin star. The food may be 'Stagg-er-Inn' (note to editor: please take this out; I'm not strong enough), but you've got to book months in advance, and the carpark is stuffed with Beamers and Mercs. What's more, it's closed on Sunday evenings, and all day Monday. You're hardly going to drop in for a few halves of mild and a game of shove ha'penny, are you?

Richard and Anne are working hard to keep the character of the Torridge Inn, to make sure that the locals still feel they have a stake in the place. But Richard's cooking is such that his reputation is spreading. The Beamers and Mercs are starting to appear. I eat there a lot, and drink there too. But I still don't think it qualifies as a local; not mine, anyhow.

After another pint, and our lunch, Perry and I lost our enthusiasm for staying in the pub all day. In fact, we went back to my house, and fell asleep all afternoon.

We are going to need to build up our stamina for this trip, quite clearly.

One more pub to try locally, before we head off back on the road; the Duke of York's, in Iddesleigh, which is about eight miles away, and therefore not a candidate for my local, either. But I wish I lived nearer, and then it would be. I wish you lived nearer, then it would be yours, and you could stand me a pint for recommending it. Any Americans reading this, who are wanting to find the perfect English country pub, should look no further. Here we are, only day three of the trip, and I know I'm going to be hard pressed to find a pub I like more. Me and Perry took my girlfriend and an artist pal called Rachel Hazell out to dinner there that Saturday evening. Rachel was in the area setting up an exhibition of her work; she's a bookbinder, and a book artist, and a good egg.

The Duke of York's is up a back lane next to the church, like country pubs should be. A huge pile of firewood stands outside the front door, which looks good, and stops cars parking there. The sign is battered and unobtrusive; the Duke still looks like a house. Inside, it is dark by the bar, which is good and brown, with curling newspaper stories about the village, dating back to the thirties, pinned to the wall. There are notices about cricket practice, jumble sales, church events. There is a large inglenook fireplace, with blazing logs and a rocking chair either side of it. Locals sit at the bar, chatting to the friendly bar staff. If you don't like dogs, don't bother going; there are always three or four sitting under tables and drinking beer from bowls. There are a couple of cheerful Airedales who hang out there quite a bit; their owners always buy them a bag of crisps each, which they throw, unopened on to the floor. Before the dogs can eat the crisps, they have to open the bags, at which they are rubbish. I'm afraid I find this endlessly funny.

Behind the bar, the beer is kept in barrels, from which your pint is tapped directly; the Duke of York's is one of those pubs that appear year after year in the *Good Beer Guide*. You may meet a short scruffy-looking grey-haired gentleman, sitting at the bar, a pint in his hand, a twinkle in his eye, mud on his wellies, dispensing good cheer and wisdom. This is Jamie Stewart, the landlord. When he's not landlording, he's also a farmer, and much of the produce used in the kitchen comes from his farm. He's been keeping pubs for most of his life, and he has it down to a fine art. He trains all his bar staff in how to be naturally friendly, which sounds impossible, but he pulls it off. They always seem pleased to see you. The kitchen is open all day, and yet the Duke does not stand in danger of becoming a gastro-pub. I had hogs pudding, a local speciality, which is the Devon version of haggis. Perry had a Barnsley chop, my girlfriend had devils on horseback, and Rachel had sea bass. That's just the bar menu. There is a restaurant, but it's tucked out of the way behind the loos, and does not affect the atmosphere of the place, which remains that of a lively friendly local Devon pub. People go there to drink, and to eat, without each affecting the other. It's a superb piece of sleight of hand on Jamie's part, who should be Minister for Pubs.

We talked about the trip, and about where we were going next. Rachel dropped a bombshell. As part of her work as a bookbinder, she spends quite a bit of time running bookbinding workshops in out-of-the-way places, including the Scillies and Shetland. Nobody else I'd ever talked to about the trip knew what the two most distant pubs were; they would always mention Land's End and John o'Groat's. But Rachel knew.

'The Turk's Head on St Agnes, and the Baltasound Hotel on Unst. Know 'em well. I run workshops in Scilly, and one of my friends lives in one of the two houses on Gugh. I always stay with her when I'm there. I like the Turk's Head. But the Baltasound . . . hmm, we'll have to see what you think.'

'How come you've been to Unst?'

'Same as ever. Running workshops. Islands are great; everyone is looking for something new to do. In fact, I'm up there at the end of the month.'

'That's when we'll be there.'

'Give me a ring; we'll meet up. I'll leave you a message at the Wind Dog Café, on Yell, next to where you catch the ferry for Unst.'

At first, this annoyed me a bit. It's a bit galling when on day three of your trip, not only are you sitting in what you already know to be the best pub in England, just twenty minutes' drive from where you live, but you're sitting with someone who's already been lots of times to the utterly obscure places where you are going. But then I realised that this simply reinforces my point, one which I'd thought about sitting in the airport at St Mary's with Professor Sue and her husband: that in these islands, we are all locals.

Jamie gave me a tip, too.

'Where are you going next?' he said.

'Back on the road tomorrow. We're going to a cider-tasting, in Somerset.'

'Somerset, hey? Well, if you get the chance, you should go to Eli's.'

'That's in Huish Episcopi, isn't it?' said Rachel. 'I know it well.'

## Sunday 4th April

Until just a few days before we'd set out for the Scillies, I'd been hanging on a phone call, from a pal of mine called Craig Pope. Craig is a writer, who lives in a little village in Somerset called Churchingford, high in the Blackdown Hills above Taunton. When I first met him, Craig told me about cider-making in the village. It's a community thing, he told me. Everyone in the village gets together to do it. He told me that I should definitely come to Churchingford and meet the cider makers, that it was unmissable. But that he would have to ask Big Al, to see if the cider makers would be willing to talk. I had my own agenda: to weave across the country, from one end to the other, in a month. I kept playing with ideas about where I might go, always trying to leave open a few days when I could go and meet the cider makers of Churchingford, if they would talk. If they *would* talk (and as Craig and I discussed it, it always seemed less and less likely), I needed it to be in a slim time frame; the few days when I could be in Somerset, before we needed to be heading on for the next place. It hardly seemed possible that it was all going to come together.

Then, four days before the trip was due to start, Craig called. 'Big Al has heard the first cuckoo.'

'Has he? Good.' I wasn't sure if this was the right response. I felt a bit like one of Smiley's people, sitting on a bench in East Berlin next to one of my contacts, listening to some gnomic code words, trying to remember what I was supposed to say in reply in order to unlock some vital information.

'When you hear the first cuckoo, that means the cider is ready.'

'God, really?'

'They're having the tasting on Sunday, and they're happy for you to come. Does that fit your plans?'

'It's perfect . . . thanks Craig.'

Sometimes, things fall so beautifully into place, you could just weep. On Sunday morning, Perry and I said goodbye to my girl-friend and Rachel, and headed off towards Churchingford. We took the back road through Crediton and Tiverton, through the so-called 'red' country, where the rich soil is stained vermilion by iron.

'What's that stuff?' asked Perry from the passenger seat.

Large fields were covered in netting or mesh of some kind.

'It keeps pests out. Stops them having to use pesticides. People don't think it looks pretty, but rather that than have organophos-phates all over your swedes.'

'Swedes? All these fields are for swedes?'

'Yeah.'

'That's a lot of swedes. Whoever eats swedes? When did you last eat swede?'

'Couple of days ago, in the pub on St Agnes. They're for the Cornish-pasty industry.'

'You've lived in the West Country too long,' said Perry.

We joined the motorway just outside Tiverton and headed north for a couple of junctions, then turned off at the sign for Wellington, and headed up into the Blackdowns. Most traffic coming off at this point headed into Taunton, but we were straightaway into wind-ing tangled lanes, climbing the Hills. This is hunting country; Craig's instructions said that we should pass the Merry Harriers pub, which gifted Perry a superb knock in the game of pub cricket we had been playing since day one. With five hounds and the hare (who looked much less merry than they) on the sign, this gave Venus twenty-four runs.*

---

* If you've never played pub cricket, you get a run for each leg in a pub's name; so the Red Lion would be four runs, the Duke of York's two, and so on. For the Cricketers, the Fox and Hounds, the Coach and Horses, or in this instance the Merry Harriers, you get as many runs as there are figures on the sign. If you pass a pub that has no legs, such as the Blue Anchor, then you are out, and the other side is put in to bat. To save arguments, we had decided that the King's Head and the Queen's Head should count as one run. Very simple game, keeps the kids amused for hours, unlike real cricket.

I was beginning to worry. The people we were going to see might all be hunting types, big hearty Zummerset farmers, who would find us laughably effete. The closer we got, the scarier Big Al seemed. The lanes became increasingly Chestertonian, winding around to no good purpose. This is a lost little corner of the world, and pretty soon me and Perry were lost. By the time we found Churchingford, we were an hour later than advertised, and we turned up at Craig's to find a note waiting for us, Blu-Tacked to the door.

'Baby due. Have rushed Trina to hospital. Ask at the pub for Big Al.'

We found the pub. We went in. It was FA Cup semi-final day, and it was packed. We'd arrived twenty minutes from time, and Millwall were one-up against Sunderland. Everyone was cheering on Millwall, which was discouraging. We waited till the game was over before we asked for Big Al at the bar.

'I'm Al,' said the gangly smiling man standing next to me. In his mid thirties, and wearing one of the padded checked shirts that all working men wear in the West Country, he made us feel instantly welcome. In fact, he bought us each a pint, which was beyond the call of duty. He told us a bit about the day.

'We'll go back to mine in a minute, and you can meet Steve. All the stuff is kept at my place, but it's Steve's cider press. He's in charge, really. He'll let you try the cider and all the people who helped make it will turn up, and there'll be music, and food. That suit you?'

It suited us just fine, and we walked a few doors down to Big Al's place.

'I'm the only person who ever bought a house and is converting it into a barn,' said Al, but it looked good to me. Al is a joiner, and he has a good-sized house with a workshop and a yard. Steve was waiting in the yard where the cider-making gear was kept, together with ten barrels of cider, all revved up and ready to go. Steve was in his mid fifties, with wild hippy hair and specs, and also wearing the regulation padded checked shirt. He was the spitting image of Jerry Garcia, though he sounded unnervingly like Clement Freud. Finally it dawned on me that, like so many community events in the countryside, this was essentially a hippy do. I decided to relax, and while Steve thrust glasses of cider straight from the barrel into our hands, he explained how Churchingford makes cider.

Not only was Steve happy to talk, he revelled in it; he was the driving force behind seeing that old-fashioned rough cider is still made in Churchingford, and he took pride in what he and his friends achieved every year. As he talked, more and more of the cider team turned up. We were introduced to Dave, yet another fifty-something hippy, who was wearing a Yes baseball cap, if you can believe such a thing still exists. Dave had taken loads of photos throughout the whole process.

'It starts back in the autumn, collecting the apples,' said Steve. 'Everyone in the village who's got a cider-apple tree in their garden brings 'em round to us. Most of the farms in Somerset and Dorset had cider orchards. It was very important; a good farmer always made good cider for his workers at harvest time. There was nothing to choose in terms of wages on the farms, so the guy who got a reputation for making good cider could attract the best workers. So, if we're driving around and we see an old cider orchard, we stop and ask the farmer if he's using his apples, and if he's not, can we have them, in return for a drop of cider come the spring. There's a dedicated team of about ten of us. The crack is, we collect apples on a Sunday morning, aiming to be finished by opening time, so we can have a few pints. Then we come to Al's on a Tuesday and a Friday night for the pressing. When we've got the apples, the first thing we do is wash 'em.' Dave showed us a photo of a couple of guys scrubbing an enamel bath full of apples. They looked very cheerful, fuelled as they were by last year's cider.

'Next, we pulp them.' Steve showed us the pulping machine; Dave showed us photos of cheerful men feeding apples into the pulping machine. I was beginning to feel increasingly cheerful myself.

'Do help yourself to more cider,' said Steve. He pointed to where the ten wooden barrels were stacked in an alcove at the back of Big Al's yard.

'The top row is sweet cider, and the bottom row is dry. You could try mixing them. I wouldn't have just sweet. It can do serious damage. A couple of pints of that and your legs go, and you just can't stand up.' He grinned.

'What's the difference in making sweet and dry?' I asked, pouring myself a pint of half and half.

'Well, there are many varieties of cider apples. The big commercial concerns discriminate between sweet and sharp apples. But we don't get enough for that. We make a *mélange* of all the apple varieties we get, and press them together. So with us, the secret's in the barrels. This year, we had four new rum barrels. Rum barrels are very popular for making cider. The wood is saturated with rum, and it's this that gives the cider its sweetness and strength. We use old bourbon barrels for the dry. Anyway, when the apples are pulped, you need a pressing medium, to hold the apple pulp together. In the old days, they used straw, but we use hessian. Much easier to handle. And the straw made the cider cloudy. Here are the mats . . .' Steve showed us the hessian, stored now in the flat bed of the great cider press that dominated the yard. It looked very much like an old printing press, with a heavy platen that was screwed down on to the apples which were wrapped in hessian, waiting to be crushed.

'How old is the press?'

'I've had it about twenty years. I bought it off an old farmer, who said it came from one of the big estates. Got to be a hundred years old, I'd have thought.'

'So you've got your pulped apples. What then?'

'You build it up, with layer on layer of apple pulp wrapped in hessian, until it's about a metre high.' Dave showed us some photos of cheerful men piling up apples and sackcloth.

'That's called a "cheese". And even before you start to lower the frame, it's amazing how much apple juice starts pouring out of this thing.' Steve sighed. 'It's just so beautiful . . .' I could only agree; my second pint of Churchingford cider was slipping down very nicely.

'Then we lower the frame, and all this beautiful juice comes pouring out. And we sieve it through muslin into buckets, and then we pour it through a funnel into the barrels. And that's it really. There's no clever thing about it. You don't add anything.'

'What about yeast?'

'There's no yeast. Apples have their own natural yeasts on their skins. It's quite hard to make apple juice, actually, because it wants to turn into cider. All you have to do then is to keep an eye on the barrels, to make sure they're topped up. We use juice to top it up while we're pressing, and water after that. You have to do this religiously every day.'

'Religious is a good word . . . this stuff is holy.'

Steve smiled again.

'It is, isn't it? It's nectar. So, there comes a point when you have to decide that it's ready. Some people say it's when you hear the first cuckoo. One of the guys lost a nail a few years ago, and an old boy told me that cider takes as long as it takes to grow a nail back.'

'That's what Craig told me; that Big Al had heard the first cuckoo.'

'Did he? Load of bollocks, really. Anyway, you have to decide somehow. Then you need to rack it off; you pump out one of the barrels into a clean one, and you've got loads of shit left, called the lees, which you clean out; then you've got another clean barrel, which you use to rack the next lot off into. And then you collect all the lees from all the barrels, top it off with water, and leave it, and you'll get some half-decent cider out of that, too.'

'So now you've got ten barrels of cider. How many gallons to a barrel?'

'Forty.'

'So you've got about four hundred gallons of cider. What happens to it now?'

'Well, there used to be a tradition of doing this.' Steve waved his hand around at Al's yard. 'People would come to a cider shed on a Sunday, and sit around drinking cider, and telling stories, and playing music, like today. There's still a bit of that which goes on, but it's few and far between now. And we need a lot of people to help us make the stuff, so really they just come and help themselves. We've got some containers, and some labels, and we sell a

65

bit at Glastonbury, too, just to cover our costs. It's called Tricky Cider. Do help yourself.'

Now Big Al's yard was full of the cider makers and their families, as well as several hangers-on like me and Perry. Craig had arrived with his wife Trina, who looked about eleven months pregnant. Everyone was asking how the dash to the maternity unit had gone; clearly she hadn't just given birth. They sat her down, and gave her a drop of cider, to steady the nerves.

'False alarm,' said Craig. 'Couple more days yet, they reckon.'

Food was brought out; I had local pork, cooked in this year's Tricky Cider. Steve's partner is a fiddler, and she was striking up some music in the corner of the yard with a four-string-banjo player, with whom I fell instantly in love. They played mountain music, just right for the occasion. We helped ourselves to some more cider to wash down the food, and as I drunk my third pint, I realised that, for the first time on the trip, I was pissed.

'I love Churchingford,' I said to Craig.

'It's a great place. A magical place. We have a beer festival every year, and we use the money from that to fund peripatetic music-teaching in the Hills. It's a real community.'

I wondered how some villages had managed to maintain their sense of community, where others had lost it years ago. My theory is that the hippies who started moving out to the countryside in the sixties and seventies re-invented rural living. Those towns and villages that still have a lively community life, like Totnes, or Presteigne in Radnorshire, or Alston in Cumbria, owe it at least in part to the right kind of incomers: people who have come to make a life, not to retire, or to buy second homes. Certainly, most of the people in Big Al's yard that day were hippies, or the children of hippies, or hippy fellow-travellers. Most, but not all. I was introduced to Ernie. He's the oldest member of the cider-making crew; Dave showed me some photos of Ernie helping to pulp apples back in the autumn.

'I'm eighty-four,' he said, a pint of cider in his hand.

'Have you been making cider for long?'

'Seventy year.'

'Wow. And what do you think of this stuff?'

He wrinkled his nose, and sipped the new cider.

'Yas, it's all right. Not like it used to be.'

'Why's that, do you think?'

'Wall, they use those cloths for pressing. We always used to use straw. Oat straw was best. Makes it sweeter.'

'But it's good that people still make cider in Churchingford?'

He smiled, and showed me his dentures. 'Oh yas. Cheers!'

Now it was early evening, and Perry said that we needed to be heading off. Big Al gave us a gallon container of cider to help us on our way, and directions to our next destination, which was odd, since I'm sure we hadn't mentioned where we were going.

'How did you know where we were going?'

'Well, since you're writing a book about pubs and that, I was sure that you'd want to go to Eli's. Now, Huish Episcopi is just the other side of Langport. Go down into Taunton, follow the signs across the levels to Langport, and Huish is the next village you come to.'

Although for days now, people had been telling us to go to Eli's, it hurt to leave the cider-tasting. The bluegrass was getting louder, people were starting to dance, the banjo player rocked my world, the cider was superb, and the cider makers of Churchingford had been so lovely, that I didn't want to go.

'I don' wanna go,' I said to Perry, as he forced me into the car.

'Well, we're going.' Perry, as the day's designated driver, had only had one pint of cider. He had not formed the same deep sentimental attachment to Churchingford as I had.

We followed our instructions, and drove out across the Somerset Levels towards Langport, which struck me as a case in point. Although Glastonbury is only twelve or so miles away, the incomers have clearly not arrived in Langport, and many of the shops were boarded up. It's a beautiful little town, if somewhat spoiled by the road that runs through it, but it's waiting for a makeover. Huish Episcopi is right next door, and we drove through the village several times without spotting Eli's. We asked a goth girl at the bus stop, and she put us on the right road.

'It's not really called Eli's,' she said. 'Really, it's called the Rose and Crown. Go down there, and you can't miss it.'

We pulled up in the informal car-park next to a plain-looking early nineteenth-century brick-built pub. Sure enough, the sign said 'The Rose and Crown'. It was difficult to see why we had been told to come here by so many people. Until we went inside.

We walked down a corridor, and glanced into the room on our right, which was empty of customers. There were a few plain tables and chairs, an old cast-iron range and a couple of photographs of long-dead soldiers framed on the wall (the landlady's great-uncles, we learned later, both killed in the Great War). We turned the corner into the bar.

Except there was no bar. We were standing in a room with barrels and bottles and boxes of crisps and a few optics of spirits ranged round the walls. In one corner was an elderly till; in a second corner, a door opened into a further room. Another door led into the kitchen, from which the landlady appeared, wiping her hands on her apron. She smiled, and asked us what we'd like; we both ordered a pint, and while she was tapping them from the barrels, we told her that we were on the longest pub crawl, and that everyone in the West of England had told us we had to visit Eli's.

'Hang on a minute,' she said. 'I'll just finish getting these for you, and I'll call Mother down. She generally comes down still. She'd love to talk to you.'

'I've never been in a pub without a bar before,' I said.

The landlady smiled. 'There's not many left, I don't think. We've just got a cellar.'

'Where?'

'You're in it. We call this the cellar.'

As she finished getting our drinks, one of the regulars came into the cellar, tapped himself a pint, walked over to the till, rang it through, and put his money into the drawer.

'Thank you, Liam,' said the landlady.

'Cheers, Eileen.'

'I'm Ian and this is Perry.'

'Nice to meet you both. If you'd like to sit down next door, I'll get Mother and we'll come and have a chat,' said Eileen. We went through into the sitting room; I'm not sure what else you'd call it. There were a few tables lined with benches in the whitewashed room, with one guy in his thirties sitting alone, nursing a pint. At the other end of the room was the one concession to modernity, a small conservatory, where a group of eight young people, including Liam, sat laughing and talking. Eileen and her mother Maureen, a lady in her eighties, came through and joined us round the table.

'Why do they keep telling us to go to Eli's, when the sign says "The Rose and Crown"?'

'Eli was my father,' said Maureen. 'He had it for many years, and ran a little shop here too, so it became known as Eli's. Do you remember, Eileen, a few years back, when those tourists were looking for this place? And they asked old George Hascombe up in the village for "The Rose and Crown". Old George said, "I've lived here all my life, and I can assure you there's no such pub as the Rose and Crown in Huish Episcopi." And when they insisted, he said, "I tell you what, you ask 'em at Eli's. If anyone'll know, they'll know at Eli's." So he gave 'em directions here, and I told him when he came in next, and he said, "Well, I've been coming here fifty years and I never knew it was called the Rose and Crown." It's always been Eli's as long as anyone can remember.'

'So Eli was your grandfather, Eileen? Did you take over the pub from him, or from your father, or . . .'

'Oh no. It wasn't really Eli's pub. He married my grandmother. It was hers really. It comes down the distaff; has done for the best part of 150 years. Eli was an important man in the village; he was churchwarden, and a farmer and a stonemason as well. But it's handed down from mother to daughter.'

This might seem radical, or modern, but it is, in fact, medieval. Brewing, like baking, was always women's work. Wallingford, in Oxfordshire, in the early thirteenth century had between fifty and sixty brewers, and only four of them were men. The women who kept ale-houses were known as 'ale-wives'; a female brewer is known as a 'brewster', which is where the surname comes from. Incidentally, a female baker was called a 'baxter'. Ale-house-keeping remained a relatively respectable trade for women well into modern times, and the myth of 'the widow with a pub' still lives on. My father wanted nothing more from life than to find such a paragon, but unlike Eli, he never got lucky. The ale-houses may have been run by women, and until the emergence of large brewing firms in the late seventeenth century, brewing may have been largely conducted by women too, but the ale-house customers were always overwhelmingly male, as, it is probably fair to say, they still are.

'Has it changed much since Eli's day?'

'Oh no,' said Maureen. 'I was born here, and I've lived here all my life, and it's still just as it was.'

'We had the conservatory put on a few years ago,' said Eileen.

'Did you see the men's kitchen as you came in?' said Maureen.

'I don't think so . . .'

'Come and have a look.'

Maureen took us to the small whitewashed room we had passed on our way in.

'We still call this the men's kitchen,' said Maureen. 'The farm workers used to come in here, and bring a bit of bread to toast up, or a potato to bake up in the oven. And they didn't like women coming in here. It was years before I got up the nerve to come in. And see the floor?' We looked at the worn flagstones.

'Worn down with hobnail boots, they are, because the men would come in here and do their step dancing. Have you heard of Cecil Sharp?'

We had. Sir Arnold Bax might not have approved of Sharp's interest in folk dance, as it was Sharp who was largely responsible for the modern revival of morris dancing, but as a collector of folk song he was the most important figure of the early twentieth century. His five-volume collection of the folk songs of Somerset, although subsequently criticised for their perceived bowdlerisation of some of the racier lyrics, was the greatest work of folklore scholarship in the period before the First World War. The revival of interest in English folk music which so influenced composers like Vaughan Williams and Elgar (and Bax) had its roots in Sharp's work. He was

the first serious collector of American folk songs, too, and he gathered together over a thousand songs in the Appalachian Mountains,
so it was possible that some of the mountain music we'd heard in
Churchingford that afternoon was also collected by Sharp.

'Well, you know he used to stay at Hambridge Rectory, just
down the road?'

We didn't.

'Oh yes. Well, I was told that this was the first place he ever
heard a folk song, here in the men's kitchen.'

I'm not sure if this is strictly true, but it is certainly the case
that he came to Eli's and collected some songs early on in his great
enterprise. Standing in the men's kitchen, looking at the flagstones,
worn to an ice rink by generations of step dancers, it was easy to
picture Sharp, sitting in the corner with a notebook, writing down
'The Queen of the May' or 'Lord Lovel' sung by the men in hobnail
boots, while potatoes baked in the old range. Sharp felt that the
folk songs were a survival of the 'peasantry'. Marxist scholars have
questioned this idea, but I think we can safely say that Marxist
analysis lost all its moral power in Tiananmen Square. I come of
'peasant stock', from a long line of landless farm labourers and
servant girls, and standing in the men's kitchen at Eli's I felt proud.
The Rose and Crown is a survival, not a revival, not brown-sign
English Heritage 'ye olde worlde' nonsense, but a true echo of pre-
industrial England. Back in the car, heading for our hotel in
Glastonbury, we put Fairport Convention's *Liege & Lief* on the CD
player, and it had never sounded better.

We were booked into the George and Pilgrims, one of the oldest
inns in England. It was once the guest-house of Glastonbury Abbey.
Before the dissolution of the monasteries, Glastonbury, as well as
being our most holy site, was also home to the most important
library in these islands, and the guest-house would have thronged
with pilgrims and scholars. By the time we bowled up, the great
days were clearly long gone.

The place seemed to be run by children; the receptionist was
fifteen, if she was a day; too young to be on licensed premises, never
mind running them. Behind the reception desk, where even the

most humble of B 'n' Bs might put up a certificate from the tourist board, showing their star or rosette rating, there was only a certificate of authenticity from 'UK Ghost Investigators', 'who undertook an inspection and believed to have found evidence of paranormal activity'. Glastonbury is Glastonbury, after all, and the George and Pilgrims displayed several posters for forthcoming events. We had just missed a workshop dealing with 'The Healing Shaman in the Native British Tradition'. We were sorry to have missed it, as it was advertised as 'a valuable primer for all those who wish to contact the shaman within', which, after all, who doesn't? Later in the month, the George and Pilgrims would play host to 'The Glastonbury Psychic and Holistic Event', where the delights on offer were to include aura photography, psychometry, psychic art, reflexology, Indian head massage and a 'Rune Magick' workshop. Sadly, we couldn't wait around for the Event; besides, the whole place smelled of drains, and there was no loo paper in our room, and we were hungry, so we went out into the night for a curry.

Sitting in the curry house on Glastonbury High Street, Perry pointed out that nothing had changed; that the place would have smelled of drains and been a magnet for hucksters a thousand years ago. But there would have been no Indian food in Glastonbury, so we counted ourselves lucky. While we were waiting for our curries, a tall wasted blonde, a ruined beauty like the Parthenon, came and sat at the next table, nursing a large glass of wine.

'Scuse me,' she said, 'I'm sorry to bother you, but can I have a roll-up?'

'Of course,' I said, handing her my rolling gear.

'Can you do it for me?'

'Sure,' I said. 'Do you like a roach?'

'No, 's'OK. Here comes your curry.'

The waiter brought our lamb rogan josh and chicken dansak, and I handed our new friend her cigarette.

'Cheers,' she said, and ordered another glass of wine. The waiter was unsure.

'I'm jus' waitin' with my frens here, till my take-out is ready. So please can I have another large glass of white wine?'

The waiter looked at us.

'Is this lady bothering you, sir?'

'Not at all,' I said. The waiter fetched her wine.

'You're a Christian,' said our new friend. 'My name is Sam. Wos yours?'

We told her.

'You're Christians. Have you seen *The Passion of Christ*, Ian?'

'No. Can't say I fancy it.'

'I saw it in Yeovil yesterday. S'a new film, by Mel Gibson, about Christ's crucifixion. Fuck. I'm an agnostic, but I'm not any more. They fuckin' flay him. He's like a piece of fuckin' meat.'

'Is he?' I said, a forkful of lamb halfway to my lips.

'Ian, honestly, he's like fuckin' hamburger meat. They fuckin' whip him an' torture him, and the skin comes off him in sheets, till he's like a fuckin' bloody piece of hamburger meat. You should see it.' I could tell that Sam was arousing Perry's professional interest. She gave us a blow-by-blow account of *The Passion* while we finished our curries, without much enjoyment. I rolled a couple of fags, one for me, one for Sam, while she elected to tell us her life story.

'I fell off my fuckin' bike las' week, an' my arm was like meat, I tell you.'

'You'd never get me on one of those, Sam.'

'Thing is, it's the drink. I could ride it fine, if it wasn't for the drink. S'ruined my life, drink.'

'Have you ever tried giving up?'

'I'm givin' up next week, Perry. I've promised myself. I go'doo. S'ruined my life, all my relationships. My little girl hates me. I los' my job. I'm 'n actor an' a director when I'm not pissed an' I was head of the drama department at a posh public school, but I lost it 'cos of the drink.'

'What about cutting back a bit?'

'I can't control it, Perry. I only have to have one an' it goes off like a fuckin' bomb in my head. Thas why I'm givin' up nex week. An' then I'm going to write a book. It's all written in my head. Do you know what it's going to be called?'

73

'No.'

'Life Through the Bottom of a Glass. S'all in my head. I've jus' got to write it out.'

The waiter brought Sam her food in two white carrier bags, and she stood up.

'Good luck, Sam,' I said.

'Cheers. Was nice to meet you both.' She picked up the bags, and took them to where her pushbike was propped against a lamp-post outside the restaurant. We watched as she hooked her carrier bags full of curry over her handlebars, and cycled uncertainly from our view.

I thought Perry looked really sad. 'What's the matter, mate?'

'She won't eat any of that,' said Perry.

# Monday 5th April

Hung-over. Full English, with extra black pudding, cooked and served by children. The black pudding glistened at me. Perry was taking photographs of his breakfast. Not an auspicious start to the day. The smell of drains was worse in the morning than it had been the night before. This might have been an impression caused by heightened awareness; all your senses running on hangovertime, working hard to detect all that is most horrible; the drains stink, the light glares, Perry scrapes his knife and fork across the surface of his greasy plate.

Perhaps not a great moment for definitions. But this was, at least in part, one of the reasons that I'd wanted to stay at the George and Pilgrims; to offer it as a living example of 'the good old English wayside inn', and to talk about how such inns had their roots in monastic hospitality. I really really wished I'd laid off the sweet cider in Churchingford.

Broadly speaking, there were in the Middle Ages three historically well defined kinds of drinking places – ale-houses, taverns, and inns – the function of each enshrined in law. This structure can still be unearthed. Eli's was an ale-house, a house that served ale. Ale-drinking was central to Anglo-Saxon culture, and so was regarded as inferior by the Normans, who had learned to drink wine. Since the English class system has its origins in the Norman Conquest, pubs are still seen as lower class. Taverns, licensed to sell wine and to serve meals, were almost exclusively urban and middle class. Wine bars are the nearest thing to taverns that have survived, though café bars like the Barrelhouse in Totnes might fall into this category too. Top of the tree were the inns. The George and Pilgrims was an inn, a place that offered food and accommodation to travellers and their horses, just as now they offer sea bass, and parking for your Merc.

It was built in 1475 for the Glastonbury pilgrims that the abbot and his guest master were unable to accommodate within the wall of the abbey. It is outwardly unchanged since that time; the parapets and turrets, the wide archway, the ecclesiastical windows have all survived pretty much unscathed. And, as I mentioned at Buckfast Abbey, these abbey guest-houses were of central importance both to the medieval traveller, and to the souls of the monks who maintained them.

The Romans had inns, or *tabernae*, along their system of roads in order to provide rest and shelter for travellers. These taverns were signified either by a bush or a chequerboard hanging outside. Thus, 'The Bush' and 'The Chequers' are the oldest surviving pub names. The hanging bush had another function, other than as a sign. Yeast multiplies during the brewing of beer, and it needs to be skimmed off the brew, and preserved until the next time a batch is made. Brewers used a bush for the purpose, and hung it outside their establishment, so that the yeast would be well kept, a practice that survived into early modern times.

Although Romano-British culture did not disappear with the departure of the last of the Roman soldiers, the system of military roads began to fall into disrepair. There was to be no coherent programme of road-building, or indeed maintenance, until the late seventeenth century, so for well over a thousand years, travellers in England clung to the routes of the old Roman roads. The *tabernae*, like the roads, fell into ruin. The Saxons brought ale-houses into the villages, but they were early versions of the local, not proto-Travelodges. Travelling was seen as perilous, not just in physical terms, but as potentially inimical to the soul. Travellers needed somewhere to eat, a place to rest, and a place to pray for their safe-keeping from the dangers of the road. The monasteries and abbeys which sprang into life in the early medieval period were ideal for these purposes; indeed they were obliged to offer hospitality by their own rules, chiefly St Benedict's rule that guests be received 'as Christ Himself'.

In early medieval times, the travellers would have been looked after by the *hospitarius*, or guest master, one of the most important offices in a medieval monastery. Rich and poor, kings and beggars, all who were travelling could be assured of a meal and a place to stay within the monastery walls. Some travellers would have been on pilgrimage; others would have been travelling for political reasons (such as the progress of the royal court around the kingdom); merchants would need to travel for commercial reasons; labourers would be tramping the country looking for work; and all were to be treated equally by the guest master. It was his job to present the house in a good light; the reputation of the monastery and the monastic life were in his hands. The guest master was to welcome the guest, and to put him at his ease. According to one monastic rule book, 'By showing this cheerful hospitality to guests, the good name of the monastery is enhanced, friendships are multiplied, enmities are lessened, God is honoured, charity is increased, and a plenteous reward in heaven is secured.'

It was the guest master's task to see that the guest-house was in good order; that there was plenty of straw for beds; that the fire was lit; that lights were prepared; that writing materials were provided for those guests who needed them. It was also his function to see that horses were fed and watered, and shod if need be. This last could be a considerable drain on monastic resources, and small bequests were often left to the monasteries to help provide for pilgrims' horses.

Guests were first taken to the church, where the guest master would sprinkle them with holy water, before they knelt down to say a prayer together. After this, the guest would be conducted to the guest-house, where he would be fed and watered too. Important guests would be taken by the guest master to introduce them to the abbot. Strangers would be entertained for two days and nights without question; and at their departure, the guest master would be on hand again, to wish them Godspeed for their journey.

By the late medieval period, such personal attention had become untenable, certainly in the large centres of pilgrimage, like Glastonbury. Glasto is still a centre of pilgrimage; imagine all the people who camp in Farmer Eavis's field knocking at his door and asking if he has any milk and eggs for sale. The establishment of

guest-houses outside the monastery gates was an inevitable step
once the number of travellers grew too large for the guest master
to deal with personally, as was their survival after the dissolution
of the monasteries. They were sold off, or gifted by the king, but
the monastic inns were too vital a part of English life to be allowed
to disappear, and too profitable for anyone to want them to. The
George and Pilgrims is one of the best-preserved of the old guest-
houses, at least externally, and the children who were running it
were obviously doing their best (the breakfast was especially good,
despite the hangover). But the old guest masters would be turning
in their graves to know that there had been no loo paper in our
room, and will rise to haunt the owners unless they sort out the
smell of the drains.

One of the principal reasons that pilgrims came to Glastonbury
was, and still is, the Chalice Well. Perry suggested that I might
deal with my hangover by taking the waters. After all, according
to the Chalice Well brochure thingy, 'The healing power of the
waters is not in its mineral content but in subtle forces carried in
the water that are released when it leaves its subterranean home
and interacts with the forces of light and air above ground.'

'If this stuff can't clear your head, you whining bastard, then
nothing can.'

Chalice Well Garden is at the top of the town, hard under the
tor, and there is nowhere to park. I grumbled at the walk. I had a
bad left foot, and had had it for well over a year. I had 'policeman's
heel', which is the butchest member of the tennis-elbow and house-
maid's-knee family. I also had an open sore on my left heel; that
had been there for six months, and it was painful to walk on. Since
our circumnavigation of St Agnes, I had been walking with a bad
limp; according to Perry, this was how the Gypsy Acora had been
able to diagnose that I had a dodgy knee. It was also cold and pissing with rain. But the pain in my head overruled the pain in my
foot, and I hobbled up the High Street after Perry.

At the entrance to the Chalice Well, we bought a few plastic
bottles to fill with the healing waters, and walked through the
orderly gardens towards the spring. Twenty-one thousand gallons

bubble up daily. The water is red; red with the blood of Christ, if you believe the legend that Joseph of Arimathea buried the chalice of the Last Supper under Glastonbury Tor. Or red with iron, if you don't. I stopped at the Lion's Head, the place where the spring is channelled for drinking, and gulped down a few cupfuls from the enamelled mug chained to the wellhead. It tasted like spinach. We filled our bottles, for the ghost of hangovers-still-to-come, and walked up to King Arthur's Court, where the water is channelled into a small healing pool, a little bigger than the ones you have to walk through in municipal baths to make sure you haven't got verrucas. There are steps down into it, and steps to walk out by at the other end. The healing pool is overhung by trees, which dripped with rain.

'Take off your shoes, and walk through the pool, so I can take a picture,' said Perry.

'Fuck off. No chance.'

'Yes. Do it.'

'No. It's cold, and wet, and I'm not walking through some hippy dipshit puddle for your amusement.'

'If it's cold and wet, it won't make any difference if you get cold and wet, will it? Just take off your shoes and socks, and get into the pool.'

'And I've got a bad foot.'

'Shut up moaning, and just fucking do it!'

I love it when Perry is stern. I bared my feet, rolled up my trouser legs, and stepped down into the water, which came half-way up my calves. The water comes out of the ground at a constant 11°C, and it felt bastard cold to me. I yelped with misery while Perry took his photos, and then I climbed out. We didn't have a towel with us, and I put my socks on to my soaking wet feet, sitting on a soaking wet bench by the poolside, thus neatly rendering my arse soaking wet too. How Perry roared.

Funny thing is though, and I struggle to write this, my foot felt better straightaway.

'Must be the cold,' I said, as we walked back to the car.

'Shut up about your bad foot.'

'Yes, you're right. It's the cold. Ooh, my foot feels all tingly and warm.'

My policeman's heel had gone, after a year. And I know this is weird, but it has never come back. Weirder still, the six-month-old open sore had completely cleared up within two days of my reluctant walk through the healing pool. There is, of course, a rational explanation, such as it might have healed up two days later anyway, and that policeman's heel goes regularly into remission. Or it could be 'subtle forces' activated because the Chalice Well is at the crossing of England's two longest ley lines, the 'Michael' and the 'Mary', though I doubt it. Whatever the explanation is, it can't be faith. It never for a moment crossed my mind that my walk in the pool would do anything for my foot. My hangover cleared up, too.

We drove out from Glastonbury towards the Avalon Vineyard, in East Pennard, maybe eight miles away. Everyone knows that the Romans drank wine, but until recently it was a matter of dispute as to whether or not they also made it in England. In 1996 archae-ological evidence showed that they did, with the discovery of the first Romano-British vineyard, at Wollaston, in Northamptonshire. At the time of Domesday in 1087, there were 48 vineyards in England; now, there are over 400. Although the tradition of English wine-making goes back a long way, the modern industry is just that, modern; all 400 vineyards have been established since the end of the Second World War.

Driving out to the vineyard, we could see that we were really in Avalon, the Isle of Apples. We drove past cider orchards, with cows grazing under the trees; we passed the Apple Tree Inn, and in West Pennard stopped outside the fifteenth-century Court Barn, tall and proud, surrounded by orchards, waiting for apples. This cider country is also good for growing grapes, and there are several vineyards around Glastonbury. I chose a visit to the Avalon Vineyard, because it is all organic; because they make English Table Wine from grapes and English Country Wine from their own soft fruit; and because the viticulturalist and winemaker is called Dr Hugh Tripp.

Dr Tripp, when we found him, looked like he could be running shamanic workshops on the sly. He had a pointy beard, coal-black eyes and big teeth, and was the living image of Faust. He looked slightly uneasy, as though one of his conjurations had gone awry.

He apologised for his unease. 'My mother is staying, and it's not all been plain sailing.'

Like many small vineyards, his on-site shop is an important part of his marketing strategy, but it was early in the season, and we were the only visitors, so he opened the shop for us, and we tried some of his wines.

'This is the 2002 English Table Wine. We make about a thousand bottles a year.'

We tried it; it was very good, as dry as you like.

'Two thousand and three will be much better,' said Dr Tripp.

'Two thousand and three was a good year?'

'An amazing year. The best-quality grape crop in over twenty years.'

'How often do you get good years?'

'Say, two in ten. Two good years, four average years, four bad years; that's the pattern.'

'What do you think this year will be like?'

'Can't be as good. We are slaves to the weather. It's a constant battle.'

'What's the main problem? Is it the cold?'

'No, not really. The worst is a wet July. The vines flower in July, and if it rains, the vines don't set, and you don't get grapes. Frost you have to try and judge. You try to leave the grapes on the vines as long as possible, and crop just before the first frost. Most years, it's October, but we didn't crop until November last year.'

'Can English wine compete with German?'

'Not in terms of quantity, but for quality, yes. The problem is marketing it; people are reluctant to buy English wine. My stuff is sold in Rick Stein's shop in Padstow, and in his restaurant, and all my bottles have a Rick Stein sticker on them, look.' They did.

'And he's done his best to promote English wine, but people still won't buy it,' said Dr Tripp.

'Ooh, I will,' I said. Dr Tripp smiled at me with his big teeth, and I handed over six quid for a bottle of the 2002.

'Then we do the cider, straw-pressed . . .'

'Doesn't that make it cloudy?' I said, cocky with new knowledge.

Dr Tripp frowned. 'No. Not if you do it properly. We use straw and the cider press for crushing the grapes, too.'

'Do you make fruit wine the same way?'

'No. Grapes, like apples, have their own yeasts on their skins. The soft fruit has to be crushed, and then you add sugar and yeast. Care to try some? We're the only producer of English Country Wine who grow all our own soft fruits.'

We tried the gooseberry and the tayberry wines, and we liked them too, so we bought a couple of bottles. Dr Tripp had cast a spell over us. Perry in particular can only get his wallet out when he has been enchanted.

'Like to take a walk through the vineyard?' said Dr Tripp.

We walked up the hill along rows of wires; the vines were only just springing back into life.

'There's not much to see at this time of year. But, look, the sap is starting to rise.' Dr Tripp showed us where the ends of the branches were becoming sticky, and we touched the tacky vines.

'So how do you get round the English-wine thing? I mean, how can you earn a living from 1,000 bottles?' I asked. We were standing at the top of the vineyard, looking back from Pennard Hill over the flatlands of the Somerset Levels. Light cold rain misted in across the Levels, from the direction of the sea.

Dr Tripp grinned. 'We do much better with the fruit wine. We make 6,000 bottles of that a year. And we mainly sell it on the neighbour's farm . . .' He grinned again, and pointed up the hill. The penny dropped. Pennard Hill. Pilton Festival. Glasto. For a week every summer, the biggest city in England west of Bristol.

'You're next door to Worthy Farm?'

'Yes. Just over the hill, and you come to the sacred space. I hate it when Michael doesn't do the festival. I rely on it really.'

'How have you found it since the new fence went up?'

'Much better. We still sell a lot of wine, but I don't get people traipsing through my vineyard, waiting to hop the fence.'

'Did they before?'

'Hundreds of them. You'd have a steady stream of people walking up through here.'

'Where do you set up?'

'In the Avalon field. Pennard Country Wines. We sell it by the cup.'

'We're both working at Pilton this year,' I said.

'You'll have to drop by and say hello,' said Dr Tripp.

And, come June, we did. Or at least, we visited the Pennard Country Wine Bar when we both had a moment to spare. It was rammed; a marquee full of hippies drinking gooseberry wine is a remarkable thing to see. There were tables and chairs outside too, all full of people drinking Hugh's excellent fruit wine. There were cheerful bar-persons serving the stuff by the cupful. But, of the good doctor himself, there was no sign. Which just goes to show what I've always said: 'You can never find a trip when you want one at Glastonbury Festival.'

We headed from Avalon, and drove towards Bath. Just outside Shepton Mallet, we drove through the Blackthorn Cider factory, which straddles the road. All the cider orchards that we passed earlier made sense; this is where the apples end up. Blackthorn Cider sponsor Bath Rugby Club; this is rugby country. Lads in Bath wander around in Bath Rugby Club Blackthorn Cider shirts, bought from the Bath Rugby Club shop, in the same kind of quantities that in other towns you see Arsenal and Manchester United shirts. We parked the car in Walcot Street, tucked around the back of the Paragon, and went for a pint in the Bell.

'Why are we in Bath?' asked Perry.

'To visit the Bath Postal Museum!'

'Why are we going to the Bath Postal Museum?'

'To see how important Bath was as a centre of postal innovation.'

'I see. What has this to do with pubs, as such?'

'Coaching inns! The mail coach! Coachmen hunched in their high-collared coats, accepting a hot cup of something from the landlady's daughter! The passengers: an unmarried lady peeping coyly from beneath her bonnet at a dashing captain just back from Trafalgar, under the disapproving eye of an elderly clergyman and his talkative wife, all gulping down a cut off the roast and two veg in the common room of the inn! Blazing log fires! The jolly ostlers, bustling about the yard! The snort of horse, the stamp of hoof, the merry jingle of the harness! The scarlet-coated guard, with his blunderbuss! The mail shall get through! Snow and robins. Christmas cards! Nostalgia. England . . .'

'I understand. So why are we sitting in the Bell?'

'Er, because the Bath Postal Museum closed half an hour ago.'

Perry's chin fell forward on to his chest, and he blew air from between his lips, like a horse: 'Pouffffffffffff.'

'It's a good pub, though.'

Perry looked up at me. 'Any link with coaching?'

'None whatever, so far as I know. I've played here a few times. It's a rock 'n' roll pub. That's Don, the landlord.' A black guy with an afro somewhat corroded by male-pattern baldness, wearing his trademark jodhpurs and with a red neckerchief tied at his throat stood chatting to a girl at the bar.

'But the coaches came down Walcot Street. The last turnpike gate on the London Road was at the top, up by the Hat and Feather. The mail coach passed toll gates free, and the gates had to open ready for the mail to pass, or the gatekeeper was liable to a fine. We'd better go and have a quick one there.'

We walked up Walcot Street towards the Hat and Feather, a walk of perhaps five minutes. Perry had never been to Bath before.

'It's a good town, I think,' I said. 'They declare Walcot Street an independent nation for one day of the year, and hold a street festival, called Walcot Nation Day, and the Bell and the Hat and Feather go crazy. They put up barriers at either end of the street, the Natural Theatre Company dress up as border guards, and you have to buy a passport off them to get in. So sometimes, you still have to pay to get through a gate at the top of Walcot Street.'

In the Hat, I told Perry more about Bath and the Post Office. 'In the eighteenth century, the Bath Theatre Royal's manager was a guy called John Palmer. At that time, post was carried by post-boys on horses, kind of like the Pony Express, except they were far from express. They were easy targets for highwaymen, and post-boys were not above putting their hands in the mailbag themselves. If people had to send money by post, it was the custom to cut the notes in half, and send them by separate letters. Like now, the Post Office had a monopoly on letters, and it was illegal to send letters by stage-coach, though people very often did, disguised as parcels. Palmer wrote a book called *A Plan for the Reform and Improvement of the General Post Office*, where he proposed using fast coaches to deliver and guard the mail. He claimed that the trip from Bath to London could be done 'in sixteen to eighteen hours'. The Post Office thought he was bonkers, but Palmer's pal, William Pitt, the 23-year-old Chancellor of the Exchequer, and soon to be Prime Minister, supported him. In 1784 Palmer was given permission for a trial run from Bristol to London. It left the Rummer Tavern in Bristol at 4 p.m., and arrived eighty minutes later at the Three Tuns, in Bath.'

'Let's go there, then.'

'It's not there any more. But the mail coach traditionally started from the White Hart, and that's still there, in a way. It's the Royal Pump Room Hotel now. We could go and have some tea.'

So we did. The Royal Pump Room Hotel is much changed from its coaching heyday. Now it is a tourist trap, and we paid tourist rates for a cream tea, though it was compensated for by being served by 'Nippies'. I do like a girl in uniform.

I sipped my tea, and nibbled a scone, and went on at Perry. 'Thirteen hours later, the coach was at the General Post Office in Leadenhall Street, and Palmer was vindicated. Pitt made him Controller-General of the Post Office in 1786. He was one of the first people to insist that things ran by the clock; the mail coaches were timed to the minute. He used light coaches which carried four passengers inside with the coachman and guard outside. Every six to eight miles, there would have to be a change of horses, which was always done at an inn. While the ostlers changed horses, the barmaid would come out with drinks for the passengers, while the guard picked up and dropped off any mail; the stops were timed at five minutes each, but the ostlers were so efficient that they could change four horses well inside the time allotted them by Palmer. They got a dinner stop of twenty minutes at one of the inns; that's why they had to eat quickly, because the coach wouldn't wait for passengers.'

'So if you were slow, you had to stay in the inn?'

'Yes. Inns were essential to the whole enterprise. Innkeepers owned the horses, and leased them to the Royal Mail. People would wait for both the mails and the slower stage-coaches in an inn, the journey would begin and end at an inn. Inns were like stations, pubs and post offices rolled into one glorious whole. The sixty or so years that the mail coaches ran were the great years of the English inn. This place would have been full of travellers, as opposed to tourists.'

'Sixty years?'

'About that. The roads weren't good enough before the late eighteenth century, and the railway took over delivery of the mail in the 1840s. But by 1830, the mail coaches were the most efficient land-transport system in the world. They were good, and people liked them; and the coaches became the symbol of the days before the coming of the railway; coaching days really were the good old days. Difficult to imagine now an efficient system of transport which stopped at a pub every eight miles. We still buy into images of coaching at Christmas; "God Rest Ye Merry Gentlemen" sung round a fire in the inn. Presumably, the implication is that Mary and Joseph would have found room in these good old inns along the Bath Road. They'd have had a bit of good old English beef, and drunk a nip of gin, taken warm, to help the baby along, and really been much better off altogether.'

We left Bath for Limpley Stoke, a few miles outside the town, just over the border into Wiltshire, where we were to stay the night with an old friend of Perry's called Caroline. We pulled up in front of her tiny stone cottage, and fought our way inside past the three dogs, two cats and a rabbit who wandered cheerfully about the place. One of the dogs was elderly, and he breathed like Darth

Vader, except Darth Vader never stuck his nose in my groin and wagged his tail.

'Mind the rabbit,' Caroline warned. 'It'll chew anything you leave on the floor.'

Caroline cooked, and we presented her with a bottle of Dr Tripp's table wine.

After dinner, talking about the crawl, she said, 'Ooh, what about opposite?' and sent me over to her neighbour's house, 'The Old Maltings', where Jill, the owner, was kind enough to give me a guided tour. It's a family home now, but for a century or more, it had been a malthouse, which operated right up until after the Second World War. It had been owned by George's, a relatively large Bristol brewing concern; it was easy to think of malt from Limpley Stoke being sent by wagon to Bristol, brewed into beer, and served in the old White Hart in Bath for the waiting travellers.

When I got back, Caroline and Perry were giggling together and sampling Dr Tripp's Fruit Wine. The rabbit was stuck up the chimney. I made my excuses, and took myself to bed.

## Tuesday 6th April

The next morning, the sun was shining, and Perry was in one of his good moods. I was pleased, because today was Perry's day in charge. I was driving, he was navigating and talking. The idea was that we'd drift through Wiltshire, cross Salisbury Plain and end up in Hampshire, just outside Winchester. Perry had the bridge because this was the area where he spent his boyhood, had gone to school, and first experimented with drink and drugs. This was Perry's earliest intoxicated landscape.

We started the day in Devizes. When I first met Perry it was 1976, we were both eighteen, fresh from sixth form, and students at St David's University College Lampeter, in the middle of rural Wales. I used to boast about Brighton, where I didn't live and wasn't from, but which was the nearest big town to where I grew up, entitling me, I felt, to claim a degree of ownership. For Perry, it was Devizes which ran through all his stories; much less glamorous, in my mind, than London-on-Sea. These days, I'd happily swap. Chesterton's rolling English drunkard went to Bannockburn by way of Brighton Pier, but I thought we'd give them both a miss. There are other piers, and other battlegrounds.

We parked beside the Kennet and Avon canal, right by the top of Caen Hill locks, a real giant's staircase, sparkling in spring sunshine. There was a school minibus parked by the canal's edge, and a group of sixth-formers, both sexes, unloading canoes from a trailer. Their teachers were talking and laughing with the kids; the kids were good-looking, lively, healthy, well-spoken. They all wore blue polo shirts saying 'Westminster to Devizes Canoe Race, 2004. Dauntseys School team'.

'My old school,' said Perry.

'Were you that good-looking?'

'Yeah,' said Perry.

'Shame you didn't lay off the booze and drugs when you were their age, or you could still pass for good-looking now.'

'Cheers.'

Devizes was the first town we had come to which smelled of brewing, that sweet and strong smell of malt which hangs in the air. This is the home of Wadworth's 6X, one of the great beers of England, and the smell is something to be proud of. The red-brick brewery, built in 1885, dominates the town, its six-storey-high tower leaking pungent steam from louvered ventilators. A 6X flag fluttered proudly from a flagstaff on top of the tower.

Wadworth's is one of the breweries that keeps its dray horses. The horse was replaced by lorries for beer delivery after the First World War. About 200,000 suddenly unemployed dray horses were slaughtered in the 1920s. The breeds descended from the Great Horse indigenous to the plains of Europe – the Shires, Percherons, Clydesdales and Suffolks – all but disappeared in England, except for a few ceremonial teams. Then came the oil crisis of the seventies, and Wadworth's began using the horses again. Eight English breweries still use dray horses to deliver beer; Wadworth's, Young's, Thwaites, Samuel Smith, Vaux, Adnams, Hook Norton and Tetley. Oddly, this is quite a useful list of my favourite brewers. Perhaps the firms that keep the dray horses also know how to keep much else that is slow and quality-led in their processes. These horses do something motor transport can't do; they memorise their routes. It is reportedly very hard to get the teams to pass a pub on their normal route without stopping. The story goes, a Young's dray was rammed by a car, startling the horses, who threw the driver and ran off to the next pub on their route, where they waited for the driver to catch up. Lorries can't do this, or bring on your rhubarb.

I used to have a girlfriend who lived in a flat in Wandsworth on the South Circular, virtually opposite the Young's brewery. Every morning, the South Circular would be glacial with vehicles. Moving at just the right pace for the traffic, I would always see a couple of Young's horse-hauled drays. No one else was going faster than three miles an hour, so the horses made perfect sense. I especially liked the expression of petulant rage on the faces of those commuters in Porsches, driving from Wandsworth or Clapham into the City, who were now stuck behind a horse-drawn beer wagon. In Leeds, the traffic department complained that the Tetley's horses held up traffic in the city centre and tried to ban them. Within four days thousands of letters had poured into the *Yorkshire Post*; all of them telling the Leeds Corporation to forget it. People would rather wait behind the horses than see them disappear.

Devizes was, and clearly still is, an important place. The centrepiece of the town is a fine old market square, burbling with shoppers. Devizes was on the Bath-to-London road, and was a vital stop for the mail coach. Its coaching inns still seem to be thriving. The market square is ringed with them; the Pelican, the Black Swan, and the magnificent Bear, with a carved black bear above the entrance, a chain around his neck to symbolise his captivity. If a pub is called the Bear, it is often a sign that bear-baiting could once be enjoyed in the yard of the inn. I think it's a shame that we did away with those old traditional country sports. It's a way of life! Thousands of jobs would have been lost in the bear-baiting industry. When Erasmus visited England in the reign of Henry VII he noted that there were 'many herds of bears maintained in this country for the purposes of baiting'. Queen Elizabeth was a big fan, and she liked to entertain important guests with a bit of good clean bear-torturing fun. When her sister Queen Mary came to visit the then Princess Elizabeth at Hatfield House, a 'grand exhibition' of bear-baiting was laid on after mass, with which 'their highnesses were right well content'. After bear- and bull-baiting were made illegal in 1835, the bulldog almost died out, just as pro-hunting lobbyists say that foxhounds will after hunting with dogs is banned. But the bulldog didn't die out, though it is shorter in the leg these days than in its bear-baiting heyday; and neither will foxhounds. And as for jobs being lost? Retrain the huntsmen as Environmental Health Officers, I say; much more in tune with the times.

We went in to the Bear for a morning coffee and a Wiltshire pasty. Since you ask: in a Wiltshire pasty, unlike in the better-known Cornish variety, the meat is minced.

'Did you come drinking in here in your youth?' I asked Perry.

'Not really. It's the kind of place my parents would take me if they were down visiting at half-term or something.' And so it was; the up-market nature of the inn reflected in the farmers' wives taking morning coffee.

'Did your folks go to the pub much?'

'Not much, I don't think. Yours?'

'All the time. My dad did, anyway. We're going to some of his old boozers later in the trip. Not so much my mum and stepfather. But I can remember lots of pub gardens from when I was quite small.'

'I can, too,' said Perry.

'The other thing was, if there wasn't a pub garden, or if it was raining, you'd sit in the car while your parents went for a drink. Your mum would bring you out a bottle of Coke, and a bag of Smith's Crisps with a little screw of salt in it, and there you'd sit. You just don't see it any more, kids sitting in cars outside pubs. In our day, it was just unheard of for kids to go in pubs. Mind you, that's one reason why I'm good at British geography.'

'Why's that?'

'There was nothing to do while my parents were in the pub. I used to read the maps in the *RAC Handbook* my dad kept in his glove compartment.'

'Did you drink at home?' asked Perry.

'Yeah. My stepfather worked on Newhaven docks, and he was always bringing wine home. We had wine with most meals, if we wanted it. He kept it in plastic containers. The dockers tapped it out of wine tankers. Probably on its way to Buckfast for conversion into Buckie. The Old Feller used to drink the good stuff at work. If a dozen or so cases of wine were being unloaded, one case would be discovered to be "broken", and all the lads on the docks would drink a few bottles at lunchtime. My Old Feller is the only person I know who's drunk Château d'Yquem from an enamelled mug. Only person I know, now I come to think of it, who's drunk Château d'Yquem at all. And so now he's a bit of a wine expert. I saw him holding his own with a posh wine merchant a few Christmases ago, bickering about *terroir*.'

'What was that story you used to tell about Customs?' asked Perry.

'Yeah. We came home from school one day to find loads of Customs officers, swarming over the house. The Old Feller had been stopped driving out of the docks, and they searched his boot, which was full of booze off one of the boats. Customs men don't need warrants; they've got loads more rights than the polis, so they turned the house upside-down. My mum was really upset, but me and my brother thought it was very funny. He was fined sixty quid, if I remember rightly, but that's because they didn't find his bottles of '62 vintage Warre's port up in the attic. My parents always wanted me to join Customs and Excise after school. You'd think being busted for smuggling would put you off.'

'You'd have done very well,' said Perry, 'with your uncanny ability to sniff out other people's drugs.'

'I've always offered my kids wine with their meals. In fact, when Minnie was about eight months old and teething, I put a drop of brandy in her bottle, to see if it would send her off.'

'You're a very good parent, Ian. I've always said that.'

'No, but I bet they don't have drink problems. Charley doesn't. She's twenty-five, and she's a sensible social drinker.'

'Yes, but she's a raving pothead.'

'You ask your clients. I bet the worst alkies weren't brought up to drink properly.'

'I do think there's some truth in that, actually.'

'OK; where next?'

'Potterne,' said Perry. 'It's a village, five miles south of Devizes.'

A pretty one, too, banked along a High Street that curls down the side of a hill. Nothing is quite even in Potterne. One side of the street is higher than the other, the half-timbered houses lean into one another. The George and Dragon is a large thatched establishment, three storeys high, with a long flight of brick steps leading to the door to the bar on the first floor. The ground floor is for the superb skittle alley. Built as a guest-house by the Bishop of Salisbury sometime between 1450 and 1500, it retains its character, as they say in old guidebooks. When we went in, there was only us and four ladies *d'un certain age*, who were taking their fort-nightly lunch together.

'Ooh, look, young men!' said one of their number as Perry and I came into the bar.

'Good afternoon, ladies,' I said.

'Is he talking to us? Who are you calling ladies?'

'Oh come. If we're young . . .'

'You're about the same age as my son, and that's still young to me.'

'Well, you are still ladies to me.'

One of the ladies had just got back from six weeks in Marbella, and so had missed a few lunches. She was certainly looking very brown.

'Do you like my new handbag?' she said. 'It's Louis Vuitton.'

'What did you have to do to get the money to buy that, dear?' asked her friend.

Although there were only a few of us in, it felt as though there were more, as though we were in the centre of a throng of locals. One of the problems with country pubs is that some of the heartier regulars insist on keeping tankards behind the bar. This was certainly the case in the George and Dragon, where there were at least fifty hanging from the ceiling, but what made it feel friendly, as opposed to gittish, was the fact that each of the tankards was labelled with a pen-and-ink caricature of its owner, which dangled over the bar. If we came back in the evening, we would feel that we had already met the tankard men. George, we could see from his picture, was an amiable soul, with a big beard and a red nose, like Santa on 6X. Michael scowled; he wore a jacket and a cravat, and was a dead ringer for Disgusted of Tunbridge Wells. Gabriel looked refined; he had a long nose; he might be the local antiques dealer, or a horse breeder, perhaps.

'Brilliant, aren't they?' said the landlady.

'Yes. Who did them?'

'Cartoonist bloke who lived in the village. He's moved now, more's the pity.'

With any luck, they'll be kept together and hidden away, and turn up again in 300 years, when they'll be seen as a remarkable document of English village life in the twenty-first century. There'll be an exhibition at the V. & A., 'The Potterne Caricatures'. President-for-Life Blairbrown IV will open it.

'This is a really nice pub, Mr Venus. So was this where you had your first pint?'

'No. It was in Potterne I threw my first bluey. Nineteen seventy-five. Belinda Clarke had booked the church hall for her birthday party. Because it was the church hall, we weren't supposed to "play our music too loud", and we certainly weren't allowed drink.'

'It was such fun when grown-ups said that.'

'Yeah. We went into Devizes, and bought loads of booze. Then we came in here, and I drank three pints of cider. Then we went up to the church hall, and got stuck into the booze we'd bought. It was gin, I think. I made a lunge of some kind at Belinda. Next thing I knew, I was on my back on the floor, staring up at the ceiling, which was spinning round and round. The DJ was playing "Riders on the Storm". I think I lay there most of the night.'

He sipped his pint of 6X. 'There was a stink about it afterwards. The music was too loud, there was sick all over the hall, and a window got broken. Happy days.'

'Yeah. We used to go to people's houses for bottle parties. Most Friday nights, from about age fifteen on, it would be someone's turn to host a party. You'd take a bottle of cider, or a few tins, or a Watney's Party Four . . .'

'The girls would take Dubonnet, or Cinzano.'

'Exactly so. We'd drink till we were merry. We'd always dance to the same records; "Brown Sugar", "Hi Hi Hi", "Virginia Plain", "The Jean Genie", "Suffragette City" . . .

'"Hi Ho Silver Lining". "Voulez-Vouz Coucher Avec Moi" . . . ?'

'. . . "Ce Soir". Only in our dreams. But we did get to snog with the girls. Tit rub on a good night. That was the best bit. And the girls had always fixed it so there were equal numbers of boys and girls. They were snog-fests really, all over someone's front room. And we swapped partners. We were swingers, and we didn't know it.'

'If only we'd known then what we know now, we'd have stuck with the swinging,' said Perry.

'That's about the sum of my underage drinking. Oh, and on Saturday, we'd go to see the Albion, and have a few tinnies on the train. But we didn't used to go down the swings and drink White Lightning after school. I was always keener on smoking and its various permutations. I know I got tiddly on Friday nights, but I was much too concerned with getting my hand on Madeleine Pocock's A-cups to want to get really pished. Enough taken to steady the nerves, to embolden the young lover, but no more.'

'And falling-down drunk? When did you first pass out?'

'Not for years. My mum's got a story about me being brought home by a couple of pals one night, but my first real wipe-out was Bryony's twenty-first.'

'Oh, that was a terrible night,' said Perry. 'You're never going to tell the story of Bryony's twenty-first?'

'Maybe . . .'

'Oh God, no.'

Perry's right; best not. Most of the participants are still alive, after all. I claim that Bryony's father led us on; that he knew what he was doing when he gave us great tumblers full of Scotch on our arrival, and that all the rest of it – Perry's insane heckling during Bryony's father's speech, the food fight, the unconscious bodies all over the lawn, my projectile-vomiting over a rather lovely Wilton shag pile, which opened the gates to a great flood of sick from my fellow party-goers, pretty much totalling a very expensive carpet – all could have been easily avoided if Bryony's father hadn't made the mistake of treating us like adults, just because we were 21 or 22. It did have one consequence for me. When I was throwing up all over the walls of the downstairs loo in the morning, I swore to myself 'Never again'. Everyone says that at one time or another, blinking in the bright glare of a morning after, but I meant it. Between the ages of 22 and 29, I did not drink alcohol at all, and just stuck to the far healthier hallucinogenic family of drugs.

We drove on again, up and over Salisbury Plain, high, treeless and fought-over by innumerable armies. We crossed the Ridgeway near West Lavington. In prehistory, in Albion, the builders of Stonehenge used this road, part of the system of roads that we now call the Icknield Way. For thousands of generations, traders, travellers and pilgrims came along this ancient trackway, which runs from Norfolk to Devon, through the capital of Albion at Avebury. There was freedom of movement in this country, once. We can't go on the Ridgeway any more, however, as it cuts right across that part of Salisbury Plain the State uses to practise killing folk. Even the main road we were driving down was closed at certain seasons; it is bifurcated by tank crossings, and Perry told me that we were close to Imber, the village that the military stole from its inhabitants to be used as a place for playing war.

West Lavington is home to Dauntseys School; I could just picture old Perry at twelve, getting off the bus from Amesbury in his diarrhoea-coloured shorts and blazer; yes, and at seventeen, just before I met him, the rebellious sixth-former in his Afghan coat and Dee Dee Ramone bob with *Trout Mask Replica* tucked under his arm. Perry told me that they used to drink in the Stage Post, the pub that adjoins the school grounds; and that there is reputed to be a secret passage linking pub and school. The teachers would join them on occasion, so drinking at the Stage Post would tend towards the sensible, a staging post both on the difficult road across Salisbury Plain and on the even more difficult road to successful social drinking.

Higher yet on Salisbury Plain, we passed signs to the Bustard Inn, right on the edge of the firing ranges. Perry's father worked as a photographer for the M.o.D. and between rocket launches and explosions, this is where Perry's dad would come for a drink with his mates. It's also where the great bustard is to be reintroduced into this country, and I would like to look, but Perry told me it's a shocking toilet of a place, and we did not stop. So, through Larkhill, where larks still rise singing to the sky. You can see them, but you can't hear them any more; Larkhill is home to the Royal School of Artillery, and the sound of Chinooks cackling overhead drowned out the birdsong. As we came to the scarp of Salisbury Plain, and looked down into the soft country beneath, Perry insisted that we stop and have a look at Woodhenge, quite frankly the crappest prehistoric monument in England. Even in its day clearly outshone by Stonehenge, the site of each of the pillars of wood which made up the site has been replaced by a Ministry of Works concrete post; they should call it Concretehenge. We drove down into Amesbury.

From stone-and-thatch buildings in the morning, we had crossed into the chalk lands; so now, at Amesbury, we saw for the first time pantile and knapped flint; we had left the West Country, I realised, and entered the south.

'I was born here,' said Perry, wiping his mouth.

'What, here in the Friar Tuck café?'

'No. I was a home birth, here in Amesbury.'

We had enjoyed a late fried lunch in the café; it had sabres for door handles, and quite sharp they were, a reminder that Amesbury is a military town. Sitting at the table behind us were two military nurses, talking about make-up.

'I gotta be careful what foundation,' said one, in a Welsh accent. 'I go red with alcohol.'

Opposite us was the Bell, an old pub that relies on squaddies for its living. Fake blackboards stood outside. 'Fish and Chips, £3.50.' 'Happy Hour 5 to 6. All cocktails half price.' 'Sky Sports. Wide screen.'

'I can remember walking through the town with my mum when I was a kid, and the pavements out there slick with vomit.'

'So was that where you had your first pint in a pub?'

'No, it was much too full of squaddies. Too scary. My first pint was in the George, round the corner. Shall we look?'

On the short walk, I thought about the first time I got served in a pub. It was the spring term of our fifth year, Year 11 they call it now. Me and two pals, Andy and Nik, had headed into Newhaven at lunchtime with the intent purpose of getting served. We'd chosen our target, the Prince of Wales, which was covered in green ceramic tiles, not because of how nice it looked, or because it was hip, or because we'd heard reports from other fifth-formers that they could get served at lunchtime, but because it was down a back street so we could be certain that there would be no one in there to catch us. We held our breath, and pulled open the door. As we'd hoped, there was no one in the darkened public but a thin stooped greying man behind the bar. He wore a green tank-top cardigan, I seem to remember. My pals sat down quickly at the nearest table, because they were short.

'Whaddya want?' said the landlord.

'Three halves of bitter, please,' I said, as casually as I could muster.

The landlord looked at Andy and Nik.

'Are they eighteen?' he asked. Andy's nascent sideburns had not taken him in.

'Yeah,' I said, with a little laugh of surprise in my voice.

'Are you sure?'

'Yeah!'

He pulled us three halves, which we drank quickly, because we had to get back for double maths. On the way up to school, I was triumphant, and Nik and Andy were a bit downcast.

'Are THEY eighteen! Not me! He KNEW I was eighteen! Hoo hoo!'

A watershed had been crossed. At almost sixteen, I now knew that I could pass for an adult. It was a huge confidence boost. Thirty years later, I still enjoy the memory. It was crushing for my mates, obviously, but fuck 'em.

'This is the George,' said Perry, in front of an imposing coaching inn. A sign on the wall told us some of its history; it had been built in 900 CE as a guest-house for Amesbury Abbey, which according to the legend is where Guinevere lived as a nun until her death. It had been Fairfax's headquarters in the Civil War, and was the model for the Blue Dragon in Dickens's *Martin Chuzzlewit*, the dragon on the sign 'rearing, in a state of monstrous imbecility, on his hind legs'. Now one half was the Dickens Coffee House, and the other half was a sports bar. We walked into the empty sporty half, and had a shufti round. It was empty, and shut, the chairs were on tables; the bar was being got ready for that night's squaddies. It seemed an unlikely place for a boy's first go at getting served.

'Why here?'

'It wasn't a sports bar in 1974. I'd come to see a gig. My first gig, actually. I ordered cider.'

'Wow. Who was playing?'

'Fungus.'

'No, who was playing really?'

'Fungus. They were a Dutch folk-rock band. They played Dutch folk music on electric instruments. They were quite big in Holland at the time. They were a kind of Dutch Steeleye Span.'

'Oh dear God, no. What were they like?'

'Shit.'

'Ha ha ha ha ha!'

'Yeah, and who was your first band?'

That wiped the smile off my face.

'Er . . . Soft Machine. In the Dome in Brighton.'

'What were they like?'

'Dreary prog bollocks.'

'There you are, then.'

'That was in a concert hall. The first band I saw in a pub was Ducks Deluxe.'

We'd brought a Ducks Deluxe CD on the trip with us, and we were soon back on the road, bowling past Old Sarum, singing along to that first-wave pub-rock classic, 'Don't Mind Rockin' Tonite'.

'I had to sleep there once,' said Perry, as we drove past what is now essentially a hill with a few ruined walls around it.

'Where?'

'There. Old Sarum. Under the shelter of one of the walls. Me and one of my pals had been up to London to see Patti Smith and the Ramones, at the Roundhouse, 1975.'

'A bit better than Fungus, I'd imagine.'

'A bit. We knew that the last train into Salisbury would get us back too late to catch the last bus to Amesbury, so we walked it. Or thought we would. It's about nine miles. But by the time we got off the train, we were pissed, and we only made it as far as Old Sarum. So we tried to kip there, but it was too cold. As soon as it got light, we walked back into Salisbury, and got the first bus to Amesbury. I got home just in time for my gran to wake me up for school.'

We parked in Salisbury, and walked towards the cathedral. Perry had come home. We had come to Salisbury Cathedral to see the Magna Carta. There are only four copies left, where once there were forty, one for each county. We walked through the nave of that great old church. The Dean and Chapter have a policy of commissioning modern art to go in the cathedral, and there is always something new to see. This time, though, it was the Chapter House that held my attention. There, in a glass case in the middle of one of the glories of thirteenth-century Gothic architecture, is one of the glories of thirteenth-century law. The corner stone of the rights of a free-born Englishman.

There is a desk around the glass case, on which were several modern translations of the Norman French in which Magna Carta is written. I sat at the desk, gazed in awe at the Great Charter, and flicked through the transcript.

'Blah blah blah, rights to trial by jury of peers, blah blah blah, no imprisonment without trial, blah blah blah, ah ha! Here we are: "Let there be one measure of wine throughout our whole realm and one measure of ale". So it's enshrined in law.'

'What is?' said Perry.

'The pint. The good old British pint! It's here, in Magna Carta. I'd like to see those Eurocrats come over here and take away the good old British pint, and give us half litres instead! I'd like to see them try and go against Magna Carta.'

'But they don't want to take away the pint.'

'I know, but if they did, they can't.'

'It just says there shall be one measure. It doesn't say what it is.'

'No . . . but I expect they meant the pint. You can't argue with Magna Carta. Why, it's the corner stone of the rights of every free-born Englishman.'

'It doesn't mean shit,' said Perry. 'The government can do what it likes. It locks people up without trial. Magna Carta's not worth the vellum it's enscribed on any more. Give me the European Act of Human Rights any day. And I prefer my cucumbers straight.'

We had one last drive, from Salisbury to the Travelodge on the outskirts of Winchester where we were staying for the night. On the way, we came into Stockbridge, and stopped for dinner. Perry pointed out that we had entered a new economic zone; that Stockbridge was palpably the richest place we had come to. It is a very pretty village, dripping in weatherboards and pantiles, with tributary streams of the Test flowing through the streets, and if I was all right for a bob or two, I'd fancy it myself. We went for dinner at the Three Cups Inn, and ordered from the beautiful French barmaid. We sat with a pint at a table next to the bar, and enjoyed our dinner, which was served to us by a friendly French waiter called Michel. We listened to the chatter of the half-dozen locals gathered at the bar. Listened, but didn't understand, as they were all speaking French. When the waiter came to collect our plates (after an excellent French meal), I asked him how come, here in Stockbridge, everyone seemed to be French.

'Well, the landlady, she likes French food, so she 'ired a French chef, and 'e said, why not get some French waiters and some French bar staff too. So now everyone in 'ampshire who is French comes 'ere to drink.'

'As long as they don't try to straighten the roads,' said Perry.

'Monsieur?'

'In France, when you are children, do you all drink wine at home?' I asked.

'Of course. We are brought up around wine. Drink is part of life. Children are part of life. Only the British don't let children into bars. If you did, you'd have less problems with drunk teenagers terrorising all the city centres. You don't see that in Paris.'

'Thank you, Michel.'

'Thank you, monsieur. Have a nice evening.'

In the Winchester Travelodge, we lay on our (twin) beds in our underpants, and watched telly. I wrote up my notes. Perry snored. So much for Michel's good wishes.

# Wednesday 7th April

Suppose you were visited by aliens. Suppose they had travelled for thousands of light years across the Galaxy to ask you this question: 'What can you show us of England?' Suppose they only had a fortnight before they needed to be getting back.

Where would you take them? You'd take them down the pub, of course, and to a jumble sale or car bootie; they would be like the Bible and Shakespeare on *Desert Island Discs*; you'd get those anyway. Other than that, though? If you get stuck for places to take them here are five English journeys which I suggest would do a lot of work in a short time.

1) Travel by narrowboat from Oxford to Leeds, via the Trent and Mersey, Ashton and Huddersfield Narrow canals. This might take the whole fortnight, and that's with the aliens helping at the locks, but it would be worth it.

2) Take the miniature railway between Ravenglass and Eskdale, and then climb to the summit of Scafell Pike.

3) Walk at night from Farringdon Underground station through the City and Spitalfields to Brick Lane. Have a Balti Chicken Tikka Masala.

4) Cycle from Jaywick Sands, on the Essex coast, through Clacton, Frinton-on-Sea (where there is now a pub), Walton-on-the-Naze, Aldeburgh and Walberswick, ending in Southwold. This is a beautiful trip, and a useful introduction to the English class system at the same time, but it takes for granted that the aliens have the appropriate limb structure.

5) Borrow a dog. Stroll along the banks of the River Itchen from Winchester Cathedral to the Hospital of St Cross, and take the Wayfarer's Dole. If it's in April, just as cricket is getting started, then so much the better.

Perry and I had neither dog nor aliens, but we hardly minded. The sun was shining, the birds were singing, and we were off for a free beer.

Lots of other people had dogs, though; the walk is the perfect length for a morning constitutional. The way is metalled as it first leaves the Cathedral Close, but it soon turns into a well looked-after gravel track, at the point where it squeezes past a whitewashed water-mill. The Itchen gently meanders, and the path runs between the river and the old mill race. To your left, on the other side of the river, cows graze in ancient water meadows; low hills, newly green, bank away to a near horizon. To your right, on the other side of the mill race, the buildings and playing fields of Winchester College.

It must have been one of the first cricket practices of the year. It was sunny, but still cold, and the boys in their whites had their sweaters on, and swung their arms as much to keep warm as to loosen the bowling arm. A teacher brought the boys to order; some were sent into the nets, others to bowl, while the rest practised field-ing. This is one of the first places in England where people played a form of cricket, and they're still doing it now, 500-odd years later. Winchester was important in the early development of football, too; they play their own unique version, Winchester football, as well as soccer. Wykehamists, as the old boys are known, traditionally leave school and go on to become Archbishop of Canterbury or Cabinet Secretary or Master of the Rolls, but I guess (I'm no cricket buff) that several of them have played cricket at the highest level, before going on to run the Empire. It's difficult to imagine, though, that many of them became top footballers; it would look odd on the CV: Winchester, Balliol, West Bromwich Albion.

Anthony Trollope was a Wykehamist. The school wasn't entirely ashamed of him for treading the primrose path of literature since he did also have a respectable Wykehamist day job running the Post Office. (Not *a* post office. *The* Post Office.) When he wasn't inventing the pillar box, he was writing some of the greatest and most popular novels of the nineteenth century; chief among which are the series of novels called *The Barsetshire Chronicles*. The first of the novels, *The Warden*, is set in a fictitious medieval foundation, the almshouse of Hiram's Hospital. Trollope had a ready model for Hiram's Hospital five minutes' walk from his school, a real medieval foundation, the Hospital of St Cross and the Almshouses of Noble Poverty. From the playing fields of Winchester College he could have watched the poor of Winchester walking along this path between the river and the mill race to collect one of the most remarkable charitable survivals in England, the Wayfarer's Dole. No charity could be more worthy in its aims. They give away beer, to anyone who asks.

The Hospital of St Cross and the Almshouses of Noble Poverty rise from the water meadows like a dream of medieval England. There was something about the arrangement of the buildings that reminded me of an Oxbridge college, with domestic buildings ranged around an inner and an outer quadrangle. But actually the buildings at St Cross seem much bigger. The gatehouse linking the two quadrangles would not be out of place in the wall of a castle, and where you might expect a Perpendicular chapel, there is a four-square Norman church dominating the space.

The Hospital of St Cross was founded in 1132 by Henry de Blois, the Bishop of Winchester, to provide retirement homes for 'thirteen poor men, feeble and so reduced in strength that they can scarcely or not at all support themselves without other aid'. The hospital was placed under the care of the Knights of St John, and the thirteen brothers of this foundation still wear black gowns with a red badge of the Cross of Jerusalem. Then, in 1445, there was a second foundation, the Almshouses of Noble Poverty, so that more of Winchester's worthy elderly could be accommodated. These new brethren wore red gowns with black crosses. The distinction between the hospital and the almshouses is now blurred, but the 'brothers', the elderly people who live here, still wear either black or red gowns according to which foundation they belong to.

In addition to the almshouses for the elderly, St Cross administered the feeding of Winchester's poor. The Wayfarer's Dole was originally a daily meal for 100 people, as well as a source of beer and bread for those wayfarers who asked. The meal is long gone, but for almost 900 years, the porter of St Cross has refreshed travellers. William Howitt, a prolific nineteenth-century travel writer, said of the Dole:

> Not a stranger, from the days of King Stephen to the present hour, on presenting himself at that wicket but was, and is, entitled to receive bread and beer. Accordingly, the horn, a genuine vessel of the good old times, no glass or crockery of these artificial days, was produced, and the eleemosynary[*] bread; and we ate and drank, and praised great Henry de Blois, and the porter, that the bread they gave was good bread, and the beer good beer, for, sober itself, it would keep all who drank it sober, so that even a teetotaler, though a kind of creature unknown to de Blois and his times, might taste it with a conscience, and no weary wayfarer need dread its bewildering him on his journey.

The Wayfarer's Dole appears in every single book about customs and folk practice in Britain. According to the books, you have to ask for the Wayfarer's Dole. You turn up at the porter's lodge, the books say, knock at a window, and then demand the Dole. You are not even supposed to say please. This worried me as we walked through the outer quadrangle towards the formidable gatehouse, as I don't like not saying please. I steeled myself to be butch; to thump the counter, if need be, in the face of a recalcitrant porter. We came under the gate, and entered a little gift shop, with a nice smiling lady sitting behind a till.

'Good morning,' she tinkled.

'Oh, good morning. Are you the porter?' I had expected a grumpy jobsworth in a medieval costume of some kind; the nice lady was wearing a twin set and a tweed skirt.

'Yes, I am,' she said, smiling. It was going to be hard for me not to say please to the nice lady. Clearly, it was sometime since the books had come through this way. I took a deep breath.

'We are travellers . . .' I began.

'Ooh, have you come for the Dole?'

---

[*] 'Eleemosynary' means something given as an act of charity.

'Yes please.' It felt good to say. 'I thought we were supposed to demand it?'

'Well, you are really. But I'm not very strict. Sometimes I even offer it to visitors who haven't asked. Here we are.'

She reached under the counter top, and put out a tray, with a plate full of white sliced loaf cut into centimetre squares, and two beautiful ceramic beakers, bearing the Cross of Jerusalem. Into each of the beakers she poured perhaps a third of a pint of beer, and offered the beakers and the plate to me and Perry. We each picked at a morsel of bread, and drank our beer.

'Thank you. Where does the beer come from?'

'It's brewed by Gales Ales, of Horndean, especially for the Hospital.'

'It's very good.'

'So they tell me. I don't drink beer. The Dole nearly had to stop a few years ago, until Gales kindly offered to donate the beer.'

'How much do you get through?'

'It comes in eighteen-pint pins. One of them lasts us a week.'

The eleemosynary bread has been reduced almost to nothing, and the horn – the genuine vessel of the good old times – has been replaced by the beakers, but the beer has kept well, and I suspect that the majority of recipients are glad that the balance is still that way. It really was good beer, 'sober beer', and a third of a pint goes down nicely at ten in the morning.

'What sort of people ask for the Dole?'

'Well, tourists mostly, and then we get long-distance walkers who stop by. There's still a few of the older tramps who know about it.'

We turned into tourists ourselves, the only ones that morning, and paid the entrance fee so that we could wander about the site. Two black-gowned brethren were walking along the path next to the brothers' lodgings. In the church, knocked about a little in the fourteenth century but otherwise pure twelfth-century Norman, another brother, a red-coat, knelt at his morning prayer. A black-cassocked priest hurried through, genuflected in haste at the altar as he passed, and ducked into the vestry. It was like walking in Trollope's fiction, in Hiram's Hospital. I expected to see Septimus

Harding kneeling in the chapel, Obadiah Slope concealing himself behind a column.

One end of the quadrangle contains the medieval kitchens, the only part of St Cross that is a museum piece rather than a living culture. Once, not so long ago, they would have brewed the beer in this kitchen. Now it comes thanks to the charitable heart of one of southern England's finest brewers. Wayfarer, say a prayer for the soul of good Henry de Blois when you come through, and for the health of the independent brewers.

Perry and I drove out of Winchester on the A272 towards Petworth, a typical West Sussex country town in flint and brick and tile about twenty-five miles away. If the Anglophile aliens had chanced on Dutch teacher Pieter Boogaart, and asked him to show them something of England, he would have known where to take them at once. He would take them for a trip along the A272, which runs ninety miles from Stockbridge, through Winchester, and on to Poundford, in East Sussex, about fifteen miles north of Eastbourne. We know that he would do this, because he has written a book about the A272. It's called *A272, An Ode to a Road*. It's one of the best English topographical books of the last twenty years, written with an outsider's eye, like a whimsical Sebald; a work of love and a work of art. It took Boogaart years of cycling and driving to write, design and photograph.

Here's what Boogaart says about the A272: 'The A272 is the most English of English roads. With all its history. With the people along the way. With its hills and valleys, its forests and rivers, its towns and villages. With its diversity, its inconsistencies, its richness and its beauty. The A272 is England.' And you can't argue with that.

We were going for a lunch date, and Perry was feeling a bit anxious, as our guests were to be my ex-wife Lily and my younger daughter, Minnie. Perry and Lily have always been a bit cool with one another. Perry is one of those friends who wives and girlfriends see as essentially naughty, guaranteed to lead your husband/boyfriend into trouble. This is a role I also perform, in my turn. Lily and Min live in Brighton, and Petworth was the nearest that we were coming on the longest crawl. From here, we would start heading north; through Surrey and into London. And Daddy had chosen the Easter holidays to go off round the pubs of Britain, so if I was going to see my daughter at all in these holidays, this lunch was going to be it.

We met in the Star in the middle of Petworth, a nice country-town pub, with a bright newly modernised interior. It's been a bit gastro-ised, but that's not a bad thing when you're looking for lunch, and you have a teenager in tow. Our youthful experience of waiting outside pubs for your parents is a thing of the past. Kids in pubs are a good thing. So is food. Purists might hate it; but back in the eighties, driving from Brighton to Gloucester, there was nowhere much to stop except a Little Chef just south of Basingstoke. Now food is everywhere, and it's getting better all the time. Those places that don't have food usually have widescreen TV instead. President-for-Life Blairbrown has decreed that where there is food, in future there shall be no smoking, as he wishes to live (and rule) for ever, so the only places you'll be able to go for a pint and a tab will have Sky TV assaulting your eyes and ears.

Hurrah.

I gave Minnie a hug and a kiss, and she came with me to the bar to order drinks and food, while Perry and Lily sat at a table, trying to make small talk. Minnie was wearing her Clash t-shirt, as she is a raving punk nut, which is a good thing for a fifteen-year-old to be. While the barmaid fixed our drinks, Minnie told me about going to see 100 Reasons at the Concorde Club, on the seafront at Brighton.

'I've never heard of them,' I said. 'Are they a nu-punk band?'

'Uhh! Nu-punk? No, of course they're not nu-punk. They're EMO.'

'Oh.' I felt like a High Court judge. Not only had I not heard of the band, I didn't really know what nu-punk was, never mind EMO; I don't think you get either on Radio Two. Some of my friends still read Q, Perry, I felt confident, amongst their number. I resolved to ask him. The only thing I read about pop music these days is Marcus Berkmann's column in the Spectator, and he tends to write about ELO, rather than EMO.

'Can you get in the Concorde, then?'

'Nuhh! How else would I get to see bands there?'

'Yes. Silly of me.'

Minnie grinned.

'And I get served at the bar,' she said. Now I felt ancient; an old-timer.

According to a recent survey (in the *Express*, so you may want to nip off and get yourself a pinch of salt), 48 per cent of fifteen-year-olds in this country regularly drink alcohol, the largest figure in Europe, just ahead of the Maltese and the Danes. Minnie was clearly one of their number. At least she hadn't quite reached the stage of drinking in front of her mother and father in the pub. That comes a few years later. Drink, when you are fifteen, is used for getting pished, and not as a social lubricant. She had a Coke; she carried her mother's white-wine spritzer and I carried Perry's beer back to where they were both sitting, desperately in need of a little social lubrication. Lily was trying to smile at Perry's jokes, and Perry was trying to nod his head in agreement at Lily's coruscating feminist critique of men, all men, but in particular men who took photographs and made jokes. They both sucked down their drinks with evident relief. Lil could switch her funny, astute but still coruscating critique over to absentee fathers who went on very long pub crawls, while Perry chatted to Min. I tried to get Lily to talk about her youthful drinking, but she claimed that she didn't do it; that her family had no real tradition of drinking, and the fact that Minnie liked to go out with her mates and have the odd cider came down through my side of the family.

Whether this is entirely true, I'm not sure, but it is certainly the case that both sides of my family liked a drink, and from Petworth on we would be driving through darkest Sussex and Surrey, the landscapes where generations of Marchants and Bulbecks (my mother's maiden name) had, on a regular basis, been more than a little intoxicated; though the two families' approaches to the various problems associated with getting pished could hardly be more radically different.

This awkward lunch was access parenting at its worst. Lily told me that Min had nicked a bottle of Pimm's to take to a Halloween party, and I reflected that Min had probably picked up the habit of Pimm's-drinking while staying at my house during the summer holidays, when my girlfriend had shown her how to make it.

Best not mentioned, I thought.

I tried talking to Min about my days playing in bands, about how we had played often at the Concorde, about how, in particular, a ten-piece Maoist funk/noise collective which I fronted had something of a following in mid-eighties Brighton.

'We were revolutionary,' I said.

'Dad, you are about as revolutionary as an iron-on Che Guevara patch,' said Min.

We walked them to the car-park, both sides, I think, relieved to see the other go.

As we got back in our car, Perry said, 'You're quiet.'

'What's EMO?'

'I don't know.'

'I thought you still read *Q*.'

'No: I read *Mojo*, said Perry. 'Very different.'

If the lunch had not been a great success, then at least I would be compensated by the drive through my family's landscapes, dense with trees, where Perry's had been windswept and bare. If people know Sussex, they mostly know the coast, or the belt that follows the London–Brighton railway line and the M23. If they think of Surrey, they think of Purley, Esher, Virginia Water; they think posh, suburban, moneyed; stockbroker belt. Living up North, as I did for many years, telling people your family come from Surrey is a guarantee of social death. But where my family came from was not like that at all.

The landscape of much of Surrey is still unchanged from the Bronze Age. There are very few entries for Surrey in Domesday; despite its proximity to London, the land was simply too bad for useful agricultural exploitation. The Normans only bothered building two castles in Surrey, as it hardly seemed worth defending. Defoe described the hills and heaths of Surrey as a desert. The Sussex Weald at least had iron; Surrey had nothing. It was the railway that turned Surrey into a dormitory for London. Land values were low, which meant that developers could buy up prime sites around the stations, and start building the suburbs. People wanted to live there because it was very beautiful, as well as close to London, now that the train had come.

We turned off the thrice-blessed A272 at Wisborough Green, and jinked our way northwards, through narrow lanes with hedges coming back into life, the banks spattered with primroses. Perry was navigating us into one of Surrey's Empty Quarters, south of Cranleigh, an area of old woods and occasional small fields, towards Ewhurst, the village where my mother grew up, under the eaves of the slopes of Pitch Hill.

I find it difficult, looking now at the half-a-million-quid pretty pantiled cottages where my mother lived with my Nanny Bulbeck and my Uncle Frank, to imagine them as the theatres of squalor and deprivation which she describes. The family didn't have loos, or bathrooms, or tap water. They didn't have electricity, and although they had a gas lamp in the front room, the kitchen and the bedrooms were lit by candles. They cooked on a small coal range. My mother didn't live in a house with a bathroom until she was thirty, when I would have been just five; I still remember being bathed in the old tin tub in front of the fire. This memory, one of my earliest, is my only memory of how they lived, a last link.

In the 1930s, this was one of the poorest places in the south of England; now it is one of the most prosperous. The south of the county, largely untouched by concrete and roads and motorways, looks much the same, but it has been culturally built over. The old rural poor have been largely modernised; turfed out of the cottages and shipped off to Crawley or Woking. I've heard the stories all my life of my mother's childhood; but I have to look quite hard behind the BMWs and the 4x4s parked outside Godalming Waitrose to see the landscape take shape.

My Nan, Ellen Field, was born in 1886, and had been in service since she was fourteen. When she was sixteen, she was got into trouble, and she gave birth to my Aunty Joyce. Ellen was shipped off to a home for wayward girls and put back into service. Joyce was brought up by her grandparents, calling them Mum and Dad. Ellen came home in her holidays from the big houses where she worked, and Joyce was told that 'Nen' was her older sister. Joyce didn't find out that Nen was really her mother until she was sixteen. They always behaved like sisters; it was difficult to think of them as anything else. Perhaps Nen, with a child/sister in her past, was not a great catch. She worked hard, and must, I think, have had some talent; she was cook/housekeeper at one of the better houses on the outskirts of Ewhurst; perhaps her employers had not wanted her to leave. Whatever the reason, Nen didn't marry until she was in her early forties, when she married Albert Bulbeck, some four years her junior. Albert was known as Cruiser. He had been regimental sergeant-major and a champion boxer in the Queen's Regiment; he was a big man, six foot four – a handsome man, with wavy auburn hair. According to my mother's memory, he was a ganger on the railway; according to her birth certificate he was a bricklayer's labourer. He may have been both, at one time or another. Joyce always hated him, although she was off and in service herself by this time, the late 1920s. He was the worst kind of savage drunk, a brutal bully with a vicious short-fused temper.

My mother has evidence of his brutality from before her birth. My mother was born with a large scar on her upper arm, which was a result of Albert beating Nen when she was pregnant. My mother has no good memories of her father at all. She can only remember him drunk, raging and screaming. He never touched his son, my Uncle Frank. He certainly beat Nen up. But most of his savagery was reserved for my mother. As well as the scar she was born with, she has other scars on her arm, from where Cruiser attacked her with a knife. She has scars on her back, from beatings with belt buckles. When Nen tried to get in the way, she would get punched, and my mother's beatings would continue. But it wasn't all Dave Pelzer, my mother's early childhood, as Cruiser had one redeeming feature. He would disappear on drinking binges, for days, and weeks, and the odd month at a time. Then my mother's state of fear would evaporate, and she could be happy for a while. His going-off had economic consequences. Cruiser would steal any money that could be found, leaving his family destitute. My mother tells a story about how they had been evicted from one of their hovels, and were destined for 'the workhouse', which would not then have existed, I think, but was still clearly a potent source of fear for the poor. In the end, they were taken in by neighbours. My mother didn't mind being evicted, as long as Cruiser wasn't about. But he would return, without warning, and start his brutality over again. This is the sum of my mother's memories of her father. My grandfather.

Just before she was seven, Cruiser went off on one of his drunks. For the first month, everyone still expected him back one day soon. But he didn't appear. He had gone, and no one knew or cared where he had gone. Life was hard for Nen with two kids to look after on her own, but infinitely preferable to life with Cruiser. Joyce sent money home, and somehow they managed; mostly through Nen's hard work cooking and cleaning for the burgeoning Surrey middle class. When she was thirteen, my mother contracted TB, and was sent to a sanatorium in the north of the county, where she stayed for nearly a year. One day, Nen came to visit my mother. She announced that after six years, Cruiser had come back – but before my mother could begin to cry, Nen assured her that she hadn't let him in, and that he had now gone away for good. That was the last time my mother heard any news of her father. For years, she could not even be sure that Cruiser was dead; only now, in her seventies, does she really accept that he is gone, and that she is safe. She still doesn't like being grabbed by men, even playfully.

So that was dear old Grandad Albert. That's all I know. I've never even seen a photo of him. I see his genes when I look at Minnie's auburn hair, or my red beard, if ever I'm forced to grow one. But what is missing is the drunken inheritance, the intoxicated gene. My mum likes a drink; a bottle or two of wine most weekends with friends, with my Old Feller. My Uncle Frank, who lived in Ewhurst his whole life, would nip down the Bull's Head for a couple, or go to the working men's club for a pint or two with Eric Clapton, a Ewhurst resident who Frank was proud of having introduced to the club. Even Nen, my old Nanny Bulbeck, liked a glass of port at Christmas, and she was strict Chapel. No one had drink problems, of any kind. They didn't get lashed night after night, nor were they scared of drink, or dissuaded of its enjoyable side. They didn't blame the drink for Cruiser; they blamed Cruiser, himself, alone.

And genetics? Some people want to establish a genetic model for alcohol abuse, in order to strengthen the argument that alcoholism is a disease. If it's there, if Cruiser had it, my mum and Uncle Frank didn't exhibit it. I'm not saying that this proves that there is no drunkard's gene; it could be recessive. I got a different dominant gene, from my father's side, from generations of cheerful social drinkers, for whom drink is a pleasure, and not an instrument of fear. For whom drinking is associated with people, and conviviality, and thus, above all, with the pub.

I showed Perry around Ewhurst; the cottages where they had lived, the church where my parents were married, the graves of Nen and Joyce and Uncle Frank. I took him up Pitch Hill, and we looked back at the village over the tops of trees. My mother still calls it home, after fifty years away. Whatever damage Cruiser did, this is where she will always be from. I'll bury her there, and the Old Feller, and me too, one day, thank you very much. Where Cruiser might be buried, I don't care.

Maudlin, you see. It's the drink.

We left Ewhurst, and drove along the old bus route into Guildford that my mother took on Saturdays. We passed through Cranleigh, as she had, and Bramley, and we came to Shalford, ten miles further north, where my dad got on one day in the early 1950s, and decided that he had met his future wife on the top deck of a green London Country bus.

According to my birth certificate I was born in Shalford, but I wasn't. I was born in Guildford, four miles up the river, and that's too shameful for me to face up to, so in my blurb (see blurb) I always say I was born in Newhaven. Shalford exemplifies the poverty of the land in Surrey. It's a proper workaday little village, ranged on two corners of a green the size of four football pitches, which in turn gives way to Shalford Common, a large area of shrubby heath. Even the greatest enthusiasts for land enclosure just couldn't be bothered parcelling up such shitty territory, so common land it remains. The common drops down to the River Wey, and on the other side of the river water meadows run up to the base of a low sandy hill.

There is a road that runs through the common, and crosses the river by a stone bridge. In 1760 the engineer Joseph Smeaton, hotfoot from knocking together the third Eddystone lighthouse, was asked to improve the navigation of the River Wey, and as part of this scheme a new wharf was built by the stone bridge. A canal started from here once, the Wey and Arun, which linked the two rivers and thus London to the sea at Littlehampton. You can still see the first few hundred yards of the canal, which now serves as moorings for river boats. Shalford Wharf was an important place. When I was a kid there was a factory looming over the water, a factory for vulcanising rubber. Now it's flats; riverside apartments. Behind the old factory, with its back turned to the river, is the Parrot Inn, looking over the common towards the village.

This was my Grandpop Marchant's local. My other grandfather. He was a master builder, and a funny and dear man, called Charlie. Every night of his life, and every Sunday lunchtime, he walked to the Parrot for two pints. Nothing could stop him. My father tells a story about the old man, with serious flu, off from work for the first time that anybody could remember, dragging himself from his sick bed, painfully getting dressed, and setting off for the Parrot, a walk of at least a mile.

'But you're too ill to move,' said my father. 'Why don't you have a night off from the pub?'

'If you miss one night, boy, they'll remember,' said Charlie, nodding at my grandmother. 'Then they'll always have an excuse for not letting you go again.'

I lived in Shalford from being brought back from the hospital till we moved away, when I was aged five. The Parrot is the first pub I remember. I didn't go there; I stayed at home with my mum and gran while they put crosses in Brussels sprouts. I heard tell of the Parrot. I remember that it was where the men went during food preparation and during the washing of the dishes. It was implied that one day, when I was much older, when food was being prepared and the dishes washed, I too would be able to go to the Parrot with the men. I played in the garden, and looked forward to their return. Good-humoured men, my grandpop, my dad, my Uncle Tony, came home up the side alley for Sunday lunch, smelling of beer, shouting jokes, tickling the kids, carving the joint; they were the sum total of what I wanted to be.

Little could menfolk have foreseen, from the sunlit uplands of 1962, that bloody Betty Friedan was just correcting the proofs of *The Feminine Mystique* and that the 30,000-year-long male domination of the planet was grinding to a halt. Alas for those childhood dreams of Sunday lunch waiting when you get in from the pub! They have turned to ashes. All too often, my typical Sunday was spent pacifying kids with sweets and *Postman Pat* videos, burning chickens and scraping grease from plates, while Lily sat around reading Simone de Beauvoir. Thirty thousand years, my friends, and we missed it by so little . . .

Now, forty and more years later, I was sitting at the bar for the first time, waiting for my Uncle Tony and cousin Dominic to turn up and have a drink. Minnie was going to the Concorde; now I was in the Parrot with the ghosts of the good-humoured men. My moment had come. I was to join their company at last.

Tony walked into the bar, tanned and handsome and good-humoured as ever, looking prosperous in a blue blazer with a silk handkerchief in his top pocket. He still heads the family firm, Marchant and Cheale, Builders, though he leaves the day-to-day running to my cousin Dominic, built like a rugby player and with the family ease in company. I stood, shook hands, introduced Perry, and tried to buy Tony and Dominic a pint, which they weren't having. Tony insisted on buying us pints, and on buying us dinner too. We sat down at a table, and talked family.

'Your dad loved to sing,' said Tony. 'He was fuckin' funny.'

'Was he?'

'Course he was. You know he was. This used to be two bars back then,' said Tony, gesturing around. 'Old Grandpop would be on one side of the bar with his cronies, and your dad would be in the other side, leading the singing. Old Grandpop never used to know whether to be embarrassed or pleased.'

'Was there a piano?'

'No boy. They just used to sing, all together. And old John Girdler's father would sing the Cornish "Floral Dance", and your dad would sing "She Wears Red Feathers and a Hooly-Hooly Skirt". He was never happier than when he was singing, your dad.'

'I stayed with him in the States last year, and he's still singing "She Wears Red Feathers". I've tried to move him on from the Guy Mitchell thing, but he's not having it.'

'He's not still singing it, is he? Well I'm buggered.'

Tony and my dad have not spoken for years.

Dominic said, 'You and Alan played cricket here, didn't you?'

'The Parrot was the centre of the social life of the cricket and football teams, and your dad played for both. Cricket was his favourite. I played cricket, too. I remember one time getting the bus to go and play in Bramley, where there's nowhere to get changed, your dad in his whites, getting everyone on the bus to have a sing-song. Yeah, singing, that was your dad. And the ladies.'

'He was fairly successful?'

'Coh, I should say so. He was a charmer. I tell you one I saw him do in here loads of times. He used to carry a tape measure in his pocket, and he'd tell some girl that she had like a very slim waist, an eighteen-inch waist. And she'd say he was a flatterer, and he'd get out this tape measure, and say that he needed to measure her waist, so that he could see for himself. This was so he could put his arms around 'em, maybe steal a kiss.'

'But did you ever used to get slaughtered?'

'Grandpop didn't. He had two pints, every night, never less, never more.'

'And Dad?'

'Once I remember. It was John Girdler's stag night. Your dad was best man; they'd fixed it up when they were kids. Old Flo Cordery was the landlady; she was very short was Flo. Your dad used to say to her that she was only the landlady 'cos she was the right height to rest her tits on the bar. She liked your dad, 'cos he was cheeky. So on the night of John Girdler's stag do, Flo kept John and your dad back. They'd both had two pints of mild, but she gave 'em a whisky, and then another one. Coh, he was in a state that night, your dad. He was sick all down the Fair Isle jumper your nan had knitted. He was too hung-over to make the wedding.'

'Two pints and a couple of Scotches doesn't sound too bad.'

'We weren't used to whisky. We didn't go out to get blind drunk. We went to the pub for a laugh.'

I understood a crucial difference between pub men and drinking men. My grandpop, Tony, my dad, went to the Parrot to see their mates, to sing songs and to meet girls. It was the pub they liked. Drinking men like Cruiser might start the day in the pub, but at some stage they would be too pished to get served, if the pub was well run. Then they would need to get drink elsewhere, shops, off-licences, and find other places to drink it. A well run pub, there-fore, where good cheer is a shared goal between the customers and the staff, regulates drinking. You can get merry, tiddly, but if you get hammered, then you can't get served.

I managed to buy my uncle a pint, a belated passage of manhood. If my father had stayed in Shalford, then I would have been drink-ing in here from sixteen up. As it was, at forty-six, this was the first time I'd been served here. I was glad to be a pub man, like them, after all.

At the end of the evening, Perry and I said goodbye to Tony and Dominic. Perry drove through Guildford, and across to the M23, from where I knew my way to the friends' house where we were to be staying the next three nights. Up the A23 into Coulsdon; up through Croydon, Brixton, across Blackfriars Bridge, up Farringdon Road, Rosebery Avenue, Upper Street and into Islington. Perry thought that the best thing to do was drive at sixty miles an hour, and screech to a dramatic halt at all the lights and behind any cars which were braking. We had arrived in London, and I had begun to suspect that Perry couldn't drive. I put it to the back of my mind, and fell asleep on my friends' sofa, dreaming of an early start.

## Thursday 8th April

You meet all sorts who tell you they are morning people.

'I'm a morning person, me! Yes, I'm always up with the lark! It's the best time of the day.'

Funny thing is, you never seem to meet these people in the morning. In the morning, especially at 7 a.m. on the Victoria Line Tube from Highbury & Islington to King's Cross, everyone seems as miserable as sin. Where are these rays of early-morning sunshine? Not to be seen. Perry and I should have been cheerful. Everyone else was going to work; we were going to the pub. Yet we were as mired in gloom as the next person. It is not in our nature to be up with the lark. We like to get up at the same time as the three-toed sloth and the slow loris. Let the early birds have their worms. Nothing is worth getting up this early for, certainly not a pint with your cooked breakfast, which I was already dreading. We walked in crowded clattering silence through the booking hall at King's Cross, and hung from straps to Farringdon, where we joined a grudging surge of office workers making their way to the surface.

Perry spoke for the first time in half an hour. 'Have you got the directions?'

I grunted, and summoning all my energy, pointed the way.

It was 07.30. We trudged off looking for the Fox and Anchor, right by Smithfield Market. It opens early, so that the porters at Smithfield can get a drink after work. The market was winding down. Outside, the porters in their high-necked aprons were hosing blood from the pavement, and loading carcasses into refrigerated meat wagons. In the market itself, the stallholders were wiping down and packing away. There didn't seem to be many buyers left; perhaps they were all in the pub with the butchers and porters, sealing their deals over a pint and a full English. From the outside, the Fox and Anchor is a good example of an art-nouveau pub, high and narrow, covered in tiles, a strange mix of decorative styles, with a slight Egyptian feel perhaps predominating. High on its Dutch gable, there is a picture of a fox canoodling with an anchor, and a date, 1898. Tiles seemed to go with Smithfield Market; would make it easier to sluice down.

We stepped inside.

Stale beer, fags, fried food smacked my nose, and I heaved. I shouldn't be awake! Even a pint at lunchtime makes me sleepy and spiky at the same time. At breakfast? I swallowed hard, felt acid at the back of my throat, and looked around. The pub was full, not with men from the meat trade, but rather with City types power-breakfasting in shirt sleeves and braces, jackets over the backs of the chairs. A hum of important conversation filled the long dark bar. A secretary was taking dictation from between her boss's mouthfuls. I should have suspected something when we had to book a table two weeks in advance.

We had arranged to meet a pal for breakfast, Christopher Garrand, architect, historian and writer, bon viveur, gourmand and expert on the pubs of the City of London. This was going to be the first stop on a daylight guided pub crawl. Chris had told me it was possible to drink all day in the City, though not all night, as most pubs in the City close at eight, when the action shifts to the West End. I should leave it to him, Chris said. He'd see us right. He'd come up with an itinerary. It seemed a good idea, until faced with the reality of the Fox and Anchor at 7.30. We asked the wildly attractive forty-something waitress for Mr Garrand, and she showed us to a cubicle, blackened with age and dried blood, where Chris sat grinning, bouncing with cheeriness and energy, flapping the menu with enthusiasm, the foam of his first pint glistening on his upper lip. It looked very much as though we had found our morning sunbeam.

'Ah ha! Mr Marchant! Well met! And you must be Mr Venus!'

Perry twisted his face into an approximation of a smile.

I forced air from my lungs up through my larynx, and I made a sound, which was intended to be, 'Hello Chris.'

'Come on, slide in, sit thee doon. Now, first things first . . .

what's to drink? Perry? Mr Marchant?' The waitress stood by ready to take our order.

'Poufffffffff . . .' said Perry, making his horse noise. 'Erm, well . . . a pint, I suppose. London Pride.'

'Excellent choice,' beamed Chris. 'Mr M?'

'I suppose I can't just have a cup of tea?'

'Of course you can't,' said Chris. 'Don't be ridiculous. What would be the point? Three pints of London Pride, please.' Chris smiled at the waitress, and polished off his beer.

'Now, have a look at the menus. I take it you'll be wanting the full English?'

Perry and I looked at one another soulfully, and nodded.

'Good. Here we are.' The waitress bought our pints.

'Thank, you,' said Chris. 'So, that's three full breakfasts . . . And can I have an extra portion each of bubble-and-squeak and black pudding? Lovely. Now, enjoy your breakfasts. There's no rush. We can stay here till half-nine, if we like, eat our breakfast, have two or three pints, and move on.'

I wasn't sure that I would be able to get just the one down. The waitress brought our breakfasts, glistening eggs, gleaming sausages, black pudding that sucked in light, a pile of crusty bubble. I stared at it, and sipped my beer, trying to pretend it was cold tea with no sugar.

Chris made us tell him where we had been so far.

'Scillies? The Turk's Head is the first pub, isn't it? Friendly place. Good pasties. Did you know that Scillonians call the inhabitants of St Agnes "turks"? All supposed to be descended from Spanish sailors shipwrecked from the Armada. That's where the pub gets its name. Where else? Somerset? Did you go to Eli's, in Huish Episcopi? Did you meet the landlady and her mother? Devizes? 6X! Yum! I tell you where you should have gone; St Cross, Winchester.'

'We did,' I said.

'Did you? And did you take the Dole? I've taken it three times, once when I was walking from Land's End to Fort William. Another pint, Mr Venus?' Any moment now, I felt, Chris was going to ask me how my Uncle Tony was.

'How's Monique?' asked Chris. (My girlfriend and his cousin.)

'She's good. I spoke to her last night. She'll be asleep.'

'Well, lucky us, to be awake and enjoying life. Ah hello!' (To the waitress) 'A pint of London Pride, please, and three rounds of buttered toast for me; Perry? A pint? Come on . . . yes, two pints, please . . . Mr M?'

'Please can I have some tea now, Chris?'

'But you've still got half your pint! Drink it up, and you can have some tea . . .'

By a gargantuan act of will, I got my pint down, and Chris ordered my tea.

A third of a pint at ten in the morning, I had discovered yesterday at St Cross, goes down very well. Even half a pint at eight was too much. A pint made me want to hurl, and then go back to bed all day. My head span, and took my stomach with it. Chris was happy as a sandboy. Perry looked queasy as the waitress brought his second pint, Chris's third, and my lovely pot of tea. I rolled a fag and poured myself a cup with shaking hands.

'This is wild,' said Perry. 'Most of my working life I spend dealing with people who get up in the morning and start drinking at breakfast-time.'

'Good, isn't it?' said Chris, tucking into his toast.

'No, Chris, it's fucking mad,' I said.

'Oh, I wish I was coming with you on the whole trip,' said Chris. 'Up with the lark, hearty breakfast, couple of pints, long walk, nice warming lunch in a pub somewhere . . . Where are you ending up? The Baltasound?'

'You've been there too?'

'Many a time and oft. I lived on Shetland for three months, conducting a survey of redundant housing stock.'

'What's the Baltasound like?'

'Hmm. You'll have to see. Anyway, it's not the most northerly bar.'

'Of course it is . . .' I said, a little uncertainly.

'No. If you go on another three miles, you'll come to RAF Saxa Vord. The bar there is the most northerly in Britain.'

'Not open to the public though, is it?'

'I got in all right.'

I expected that Rachel Hazell, my artist friend who'd also already been to both the Turk's Head and the Baltasound, would be on guard duty at the RAF base when we tried to get in. I decided that Chris and Rachel should get married, though choosing a honeymoon venue might be tricky, as they'd both already been everywhere.

'When you get to Unst,' said Chris, 'you must walk up through the bird sanctuary at Herma Ness to Muckle Flugga. That's the end of Her Majesty's domain. But carry a big stick.'

'Why?'

'Skuas. Have your eye out if you're not careful. Now, let me tell you about Smithfield . . .'

Nothing will now stop old Chris talking until he leaves us at five o'clock.

Perhaps this is a moment to reflect on one of the major problems in writing a book of this nature. It is an obvious problem, an inescapable structural difficulty, but one which hadn't really occurred to me before starting out. It is just this; for reasonable periods of time during the journey, I was going to be pished. How would I remember what had happened? I had my trusty Moleskine notebook, and my Fisher Space Pen, and I made thousands of notes. But sometimes my notes, looking at them now, don't always make sense. It is like reading pages of notes written by a meths drinker, quite frankly. I also had a tape recorder. Have you ever tried taping yourself getting pished with your pals? Don't. Very little point. How journalists cope, most of whom like a goodish lunch, and whose notes must often be incomprehensible when the time comes to write the story, I don't know. They just make it up, I suppose. This early start was one such case in point. I remember going to the pub at 7.30, the breakfast, but after that, there are distinctly hazy periods.

I know I only had a pint, but it was very early. Next thing I can remember clearly is us standing in St Bartholomew's Church, Gabby Garrand chattering away about an unusual piscina, why, I don't know. Then, after that, we went into another pub, and I didn't want to feel like an utter wuss; so I drank another pint. Huge mistake. So far as I can remember, Chris said it was the place where the condemned went for a last drink on their way to the scaffold. I would find it a struggle at the bar to choose what I was going to have. A pint of crème de menthe, maybe, so that you would feel less pain, and so that you would projectile-vomit over the crowd at the key moment. Projectile-vomiting certainly seemed like an option for me right now.

Anyhoo, next we seemed to be in the Barbican. Chris likes the Barbican, I know, as I've heard him enthuse about it before; perhaps that's why we were there; I couldn't say. Not the easiest of places to find your way around at the best of times. Today, in my increasingly fragile state, it was like wandering about in an episode of *The Avengers* set in Cold-War Berlin, after the KGB have dropped ketamine in your morning coffee. I was scared. As we came into the theatre complex from the bit where people live, old Chris seemed to be riffing about pre-stressed concrete and theatre bars. It's a shame I missed this bit. Pre-stressed concrete means nothing to me, but I like theatre bars. I like being crushed up against glamorous ladies in evening wear.

I have a vague recollection of leaving the Barbican via an underground car-park. Next thing I remember is standing in front of an eighteenth-century building that had been turned into a conference centre. Chris said that it was the original Whitbread brewery, and that we must go into the Hogshead pub attached to the building. I had a coffee, and sat with shaking hands, trying to remember all that I knew about the Whitbread brewery, and about its most famous and long-lived brew.

After King Billy's pro-gin legislation, the brewers responded by upping the strength of some of their beer. Higher strength meant higher prices, and the porters of Smithfield and the other London markets got around this by mixing the various strengths of beer, so that they got higher alcohol content at a slightly lower price. As I said at Tucker's Maltings, beer has four essential ingredients – malted barley, yeast, hops and water – and each of the ingredients has a mythology, which varies from place to place. The very hard water of Burton-on-Trent makes it ideal for brewing bright bitter; the softer water of London suits a much darker brew. The eighteenth-century porters liked mixing their beer three ways; one third strong London beer, one third slightly less strong London beer, and one third pale Burton ale. This was called 'three threads', and you can imagine that although it was popular with drinkers, it drove the pot boys who had to draw it from three separate casks to distraction. Step forward Ralph Harwood, of the Bell Brewery in Shoreditch, who in 1722 managed to come up with a brew which combined the qualities of the three threads in one. He called it 'entire', but by the 1740s, it had been named after the market porters who drank it; London porter. It was almost black in colour, and heavily hopped for extra bitterness. It was so popular that it came to be brewed anywhere that soft water was available; most notably in Dublin, where on 31 December 1759 Arthur Guinness set up production of the new style beer.

Due to the process of its fermentation, porter lent itself to mass production, which meant that it was capital-intensive. Its popularity meant that it became highly profitable, which meant that more capital could be invested in its manufacture. This in turn led to the establishment of larger and larger brewing concerns. In 1700 there were 1,914 brewers in London; by 1808 there were just 127 left in business. Samuel Whitbread set up his brewery here in Chiswell Street with the intent purpose of brewing porter, in 1750. In 1775, he installed a Boulton & Watt steam engine for grinding his malt; the six vast cisterns, the largest of which contained 3,600 barrels of porter, were built by Smeaton, the designer of the Eddystone lighthouse (and Shalford wharf). In the year of Whitbread's death, 1796, this brewery was producing more than 200,000 barrels a year. The giant brewing concerns had arrived. Whitbread's did not even have the largest vats in London; that honour went to the Meux Brewery, in Grey's Inn Lane. One of their vats had a capacity of 20,000 barrels; but in 1814 the fashion for huge vats was shown to be somewhat suspect, when one of the Meux vats burst. This was one of Meux's smaller vats, containing around 3,500 barrels, or about a million pints; but it was large enough that eight people were drowned in a flood of porter.

I felt a bit like I was drowning in beer myself, and although we were on the site of one of the most important and historic breweries in London, I couldn't face another pint just yet. A couple of cups of coffee and a nice sit-down revived me slightly. Perry was off the booze, too, but Chris did his fifth pint of the morning, despite disapproving of the pub.

He looked around him, and said, 'It doesn't matter what time of the day you come in here, it always feels like you've come in at the wrong end of an office party.'

This displays great fortitude, in my view. Garrand didn't just know the good pubs, he knew the shit ones, too, and was prepared to take them on. I didn't care; I just wanted to sit and drink coffee until the morning was over. Chris was having none of it. Twenty minutes later, we were out of the door, and on to our next scheduled stop.

This proved to be Bunhill Fields, the Nonconformist cemetery where Blake, Bunyan and Defoe are buried. All cemeteries are oases of calm, but Bunhill Fields, surrounded by the tower blocks of the City, cultivates an especial peace. All these old Ranters and Dissenters now lie in silence, their voices stilled, their fervour dissipated. There is a distrust in England of enthusiasm, and it seemed to me that part of the reason was in Bunhill Fields. The English Civil War was fought because both sides were over-enthusiastic, but most especially the citizens lying here in Bunhill. The eighteenth century saw the rise of pallid Anglicanism in response to religious enthusiasm – cool, rational, slow to raise its temperature. No one must get too enthusiastic about anything, or the religious wars might kick off again. This is one reason for that famous 'British reserve'. It's also why we think anyone who is keen on anything is a nutter. You'd have crossed the road to avoid Blake and Bunyan, if you're honest, like you do with all mad street evangelists. Visions? Prophecy? Oh . . . no thanks, I'm English. Defoe would have been much more comfortable company, I suspect. There is a monument to Defoe in Bunhill Fields, raised in the 1870s. It says: 'This monument is the result of an appeal in the *Christian World* newspaper to the boys and girls of England for funds to place a suitable memorial upon the grave of Daniel De-Foe.' I thrill at the idea of anyone asking Minnie to hand over some of her allowance to build a monument, unless maybe it was for Sid Vicious.

The coffee in the pub and the walk in the cemetery seem to have cleared my head, and memory begins to kick back into life as we approached midday. Chris took us from Bunhill Fields to Liverpool Street Station, and into Hamilton Hall, once part of the Great Eastern Railway Hotel, now a Wetherspoon's. This, according to Chris, has the highest turnover of any pub in the UK, and so was worth a look. It is a great rococo barn of a place, with gilded cherubs and plaster curlicues, and was slowly filling with more City types as lunchtime approached. The beer (for I was drinking again, determined not to be an utter pantywaist) was OK; good even. Which just goes to show that good beer doth not a good pub make. Founder Tim Martin set up his first pub in London in 1979, and the story goes that the chain is named after a teacher at his old school, J.D. Wetherspoon, who told him that he would never amount to anything. Well, you know what, sunshine? I'm behind Mr W 100 per cent. So what if you own 600 pubs? So what if the beer is OK, and the food reasonably priced? And the loos clean? So what if you have designated non-smoking areas and anti-swearing policies? Your pubs are all cheerless temples to corporate Britain, the pub equivalent of Little Chef.

And the Wetherspoon's in Hamilton Hall features one of my pet hates: rubbish shelf furniture. There are hundreds of books about the place with titles like *Corn Law Reform in Maidstone*, *Bulgarian Watercolourists of the Nineteenth Century*, *Bus Stops of Huntingdonshire*, *Pass School Certificate Chemistry*. There are swathes of novels unread in a hundred years: Bulwer Lytton, Mrs Humphrey Ward, George Moore. People like to ask writers where their ideas come from, but they very seldom ask where their ideas end up. This is where they end up, unread on unreachable bookshelves in horrible pubs, somehow mysteriously adding atmosphere, in the mind of Wetherspoon's corporate-design division, at least. In Hay-on-Wye, they'll sell you this stuff by the yard. The price varies according to the quality of the bindings; the books on offer in Wetherspoon's would set you back maybe a fiver a yard.

Good. I've woken up. It was now midday, and I'd managed three pints, to Perry's four and Chris's six. We walked through the City, while old Chris kept up his unceasing commentary; but now I was awake, and lively, and I began to find it enjoyable. If you are inter- ested in the difference betwen minimalism, brutalism, and post- modernism, then there is no better guide to London than a tame architect. Especially one with a big appetite.

'Time we were thinking about lunch,' said Chris. 'How about the best hot beef roll in London?'

'Sounds good. Whereabouts?'

'The Lamb, in Leadenhall Market; follow me.'

Leadenhall Market, a web of Victorian arcades in glass and cast iron, with the Lamb at its centre, is hard by the Lloyd's Building. The proximity of Lloyd's and the excellence of the beef means that the Lamb is packed at lunchtime; Garrand managed to get us there by twelve-thirty, just before lunch hour hit its height. We were lucky enough to find the last table upstairs. The ground floor was packed with Lloyd's types, youngish, over-dressed, shouting shop in public-school accents. They spilled outside into the arcade, with beer and fags and beef rolls. I expected the hoorays, but there were plenty of older gentlemen too, with immense bundles of files tied with ribbons under their arms. One of them even had mutton-chop whiskers; it was a Dickensian scene as much as it was a Thatcherite one. I had imagined that the clerkly class had been swept away by call centres and computerisation; but next to us in the Lamb sat two gentlemen in their early sixties, drinking ale, eating beef, and rummaging quietly together through piles of papers from bundles of files.

How grim their lives must be, both those of the Dickensian clerks and the Thatcherite hoorays.

I suppose that insurance pays well, and I know that money has its attractions, both superficial and otherwise, and that the lack of it is a source of unhappiness. But every study conducted into 'happi- ness' by psychologists shows that beyond about fifteen grand a year, money seems to make no discernible difference to levels of happiness whatsoever. What is it then that drives men to make more and more of it at the cost of their personal liberty? In the words of G.K. Chesterton, 'To be smart enough to get all that money you must be dull enough to want it'. The happiest, freest man I know sits outside his van in a wood in the Cambrian Mountains, tending his still; his name is Ash, and he is a week away in the future. I'm sure that these insurance men know freedom and happiness from time to time, but it is difficult for me to see how.

The beef rolls were very good though; hot pink meat, zinging with horseradish. Ben Rogers in his excellent book *Beef and Liberty* quotes the Swiss traveller M. Muralt, writing in 1726: 'roast beef . . . is the favourite dish as well at the king's table as at a tradesman's; 'tis common to see one of these pieces weigh from twenty to thirty pounds . . . and this may be said to be (as it were) the emblem of the prosperity and plenty of the English.' And it still is; nothing lifts the English heart more than a bit of beef, Yorkshire pud, the lot.

Vegetarianism is not English, but I guess it is an emblem of prosperity and plenty, that people can afford to be fussy these days. It always reminds me of George Bernard Shaw; on the occasions I am forced by social circumstance to eat vegetarian meals, I keep expecting my hosts to urge me to wear natural clothing and to advocate spelling reform. And they never give you a choice, do they? If a veggie comes to your house, you go out of your way to cook them something nice; but when did you ever go to a dinner party at a veggie's house where they said, 'Ooh, and we've done a leg of lamb for you'? So you are forced to chomp your way through a plate of alfalfa sprouts in a rich tofu sauce like a fucking water buffalo, and then pretend it was nice, even though you've left three-quarters on your plate, and your face while you were eating it clearly registered disgust verging on nausea.

Real vegetarians can't drink most beer. This is because real beer is not vegetarian. At the end of the brewing process, the beer is full of gunk, and it needs clearing. This is done by adding 'finings'. The most commonly used substance for fining is called isinglass, which is made from the flotation bladders of fresh-water fish. You might agree with me that, like the manufacture of sloe gin, isinglass represents a triumph of human ingenuity. Your beer is cloudy; you've tried everything to make it clear. What are you going to do? 'Well,' said an enterprising brewer (probably Russian, since isinglass was originally made from sturgeon's swim bladder, and probably in the eighteenth century), 'we could try adding the powdered flotation bladder of a fresh-water fish, see if that works.' Which it does, beautifully. I want to celebrate this remarkable discovery. But not your veggie.

'Poor things,' they say. 'It's cruel to fresh-water fish. Surely there's another way to make beer clear?' And there is; there is such a thing as vegetarian beer, which uses polyvinylpolypyrrolidone instead of isinglass. Veggies are clearly quite happy to let chemicals into the temple of their bodies, so long as no fish have been harmed during the making of this brew. Madness, I call it: I avoid vegetarian beer where possible, and unless you like drinking polyvinylpolypyrrolidone, then I advise you to do the same.

Ah, all-day drinking! Not only have I now woken up, I have become properly grumpy. Wetherspoon's! Shelf furniture! The financial sector! Vegetarianism! A few pints in the day, and divine discontent is pumping through my veins. I whine, therefore I am! Filled with artificially induced self-righteousness, I now felt ready for an afternoon of drinking in the City.

Chris took us staggering off to see one of his favourite pub interiors, the Blackfriars, down by Blackfriars Bridge. It is the shape of the Flatiron Building in New York, occupying a similar corner site. It is on the CAMRA National Inventory, a list of some 250 pubs whose interiors have remained unaltered. And it really is astonishing. The builders ran with the friars theme big-time, and there are carvings and mosaics celebrating the links between monasticism and merriment. No detail was spared; the tables, the stools, everything is in a style which falls in the centre of a triangle with art nouveau, the arts-and-crafts movement and Byzantine revivalism at its three corners.

At the back of the bar is a vaulted area with mosaics in different kinds of marble. Chris knew the names of all these marbles, and listed them for our edification. There are monks all over the ceiling in mosaic, and it is like nothing so much as a chapel in Greece, except that it is crammed with screaming office girls. I guess this adds a note of authenticity, since many of these girls are probably off to Faliraki for their summer hols, and one or two of the more serious-minded of them might visit the odd Byzantine chapel on Rhodes during the day, to get their strength up for a night of drinking ouzo, screaming and showing their arses to the locals. Around the walls, and along the bar, are inscribed words of wisdom: 'A good thing is soon snatched up', 'Silence is golden', 'Finery is foolery', 'Industry is all'. What I needed was one which said, 'Ian, you can't manage five pints in the day'. But it was not there. After that fifth pint, my afternoon was effectively over, and my cheerful grumpiness dissolved into incoherent muttering.

I can remember Chris making us wander up and down Ely Place, off Fleet Street, making us look for a pub which he claimed was there, and then leading us triumphantly down a tiny alleyway to where the Old Mitre Inn lurks, waiting for the aficionados who know where to find it. It was very dark, I remember, and full of the crusty-faced afternoon topers one might normally associate with Soho. I can also remember old Perry ranting about the furniture. He was an antiques dealer before he took up sorting out pissheads for a living, and he was highly impressed by the chairs, which he said were oak, and eighteenth-century, and that you could tell they were right from the colour. All I know is that I was glad to have somewhere to slump, and how good the patina was on the chairs didn't matter to me in the least. Garrand was still drinking; this must have been his eighth pint of the day.

I used to be able to do a gallon reasonably cheerfully of a Friday night, in my youth, but day-time drinking has never been my bag. Some smokers can't face the thought of a fag before six in the evening, whilst I cheerfully smoke morning, noon and night. I like a drink, me, or I wouldn't be doing this trip. In the evening, I like a couple of pints, or a bottle of wine, and I don't mind a pint at lunchtime. But five pints by two o'clock is ridiculous. I admire alcoholics. How they manage it is beyond me. Chris Garrand is not an alcoholic by anybody's standards, just a man with a healthy appetite. He had set himself the task of taking us on an all-day pub crawl, and he was going to enjoy it, and have at least a pint at every stop, and all it was going to do was make him more enthusiastic and garrulous. But I was coming to the end of what I could stand.

He took us to another of the pubs on CAMRA's National Inventory, the Citie of Yorke on High Holborn; a great cavern of a place with a Tudorbethan interior, contemporary with and in the style of Liberty's. But I put my foot down, and refused to stay for a drink.

Back on the street, I said, 'I must have air. Please God, let's walk around for a bit.'

Chris's face fell.

'Well, I had at least another four pubs in mind . . .' he said.

'No,' I said. 'No more pubs. No more beer. Just air.'

'I know. Ever been to the Inns of Court?'

'No more pubs.'

'The Inns of Court are not pubs.'

'No, sorry, of course not. I've never been, no.'

'Through here.'

Chris disappeared through a crack in the wall, and Perry and I followed up a narrow alleyway.

'Here we are,' said Chris. 'Lincoln's Inn.'

Crims reading this may smile with pleasant memories of Lincoln's Inn; it is a huge and beautiful space, a lost world and difficult to find for the casual passer-by, where medieval and Georgian buildings rub shoulders to make a perfect and harmonious whole. Peace hung in the air; it reminded me somewhat of St Cross, except that instead of the deserving poor, the inhabitants are largely the undeserving rich, hidden away from the noise of London. In every doorway there are plaques with the names of barristers, but there was not a soul to be seen. Presumably, they were all in court, or snoozing after a long lunch, like I should have been.

The Inns of Court (Lincoln's Inn, Inner Temple, Middle Temple, and Grey's Inn) are not just the places where barristers have their chambers, they are also where barristers train. In order to become a barrister, you have to come and have a number of dinners in the hall of one of the Inns, which entitles you to membership of these exclusive clubs. After you've had the requisite number of dinners (and after you've served your pupillage in one of the sets of chambers), you are called to the Bar. I was most definitely a bit wobbly on my pins, so we sat on a bench while I tried to sober up.

'Why Inns?' asked Perry.

'Originally, an inn could be a manor house or mansion, just as much as it could be an up-market pub,' I said. 'The plot of Oliver Goldsmith's *She Stoops to Conquer* turns on the fact that it was possible to confuse a private house and an inn. There used to be others; Pip, in *Great Expectations* lives in Barnard's Inn when he moves to London. Doesn't mean he lived in a pub . . . he lived in a place like this, although Barnard's Inn was slummier, and was knocked down sometime in the nineteenth century.'

'This place nearly got knocked down by the Nazis,' said Chris. 'Look, you can still see shrapnel damage on some of the walls.'

We walked about for a while, until I had recovered some of my composure.

Then Chris said, 'Ever been to Sir John Soane's Museum?'

Neither of us had, so Chris guided us out of Lincoln's Inn proper, and into Lincoln's Inn Fields, the largest private square in London. Liveried flunkies sat at the gates of Lincoln's Inn, the only humans we saw in the half-hour or so we had been there.

Sir John Soane's Museum is one of those places that native Londoners enthuse about, but which few out-of-towners ever get to see. Soane was a very rich man, who like many gentlemen of the Enlightenment delighted in putting together cabinets of curiosity. It's just that his was a bit bigger than most. His eponymous museum had been his home, and is crammed with fascinating stuff; most excitingly, the originals of Hogarth's *Rake's Progress*. Ben Rogers in *Beef and Liberty* has a fascinating chapter about Hogarth's food imagery. Hogarth used beef and beer as symbols of health, and thus Englishness; and fish and gin as symbols of poverty and disease, and thus the unfortunate condition of unEnglishness. Standing in front of the third picture of the *Progress*, set in the Rose Tavern, and looking at the debauchery so cheerfully depicted, with its drunks and working girls, I thought about current concerns around drinking; about how drunkenness and debauchery have always been central to the English character, and about how no amount of well-meaning legislation is going to stop people going on the piss and on the pull. It is in the grain of the nation. I particularly liked the picture set in the Fleet prison, with the beer boy hassling Tom Rakewell. If today's prisoners, banged up with nothing to do except smoke heroin, were still visited in their cells by pretty boys with foaming tankards of ale, I suspect they would be a lot happier.

After a walk and a visit to the Sir John Soane, Chris was ready for another pint, and I was at least able to think about going into a pub, our last of the afternoon. He took us to the Seven Stars, a lawyers' pub behind the Royal Courts of Justice, with lovely Harvey's beer from Lewes, and a proper buxom barmaid, who took a bit of a shine to Perry. Chris had his last pint of the day, while me and Perry stuck to coffee. The walls were covered with posters for legal films, most of which seemed to star James Robertson Justice. Like the whole of London's legal enclave, it was deserted, even though it was now five in the afternoon, when presumably people would be knocking off work. Where all the lawyers hid themselves that afternoon, Lord only knows. It was Maundy Thursday; perhaps everyone had gone home early for Easter. At five-thirty, we said goodbye to Chris, with thanks for his exertions around the pubs of London. I'd lost count of the pints he'd drunk in our day-long pub crawl; all I know is he showed no sign of being even slightly tiddly, while I was almost legless, and Perry was grim and pale-faced, despite the attentions of the buxom barmaid.

Frankly, we were in no state to get the Tube back to the Islington squat where we were staying, so we hailed a black cab, and dozed on the twenty-minute journey home.

I used to live in this house, and it was good to see my old house-mates, Richard, Ed, and Sheela. Richard had cooked us dinner, and offered us wine, which neither Perry nor I could face. We had picked up another lady too, Perry's wife Shinaid (really . . . when her mum registered her birth, she didn't know about the Sioned thing), who was in town for a couple of nights, and who was waiting for us back at the house. Chris Garrand might have gone home to sleep off a day's worth of beer, but there was no relief for me and old Perry. As soon as dinner was finished we headed out with Mrs Venus and all my old housemates to the Hope and Anchor on Upper Street. We were off to investigate the state of pub rock.

Pub rock is a pejorative term these days. Noel Gallagher described the fourth Oasis album as 'the usual pub-rock bollocks'. It carries with it notions of lumpen meat-and-potatoes rhythm and blues; sad old feckers belting out 'Mustang Sally' to nobody except their girl-friends. But in our day, 'pub rock' denoted cutting edge, exciting new music, which was a vital precursor of punk. In the mid-seventies, rock 'n' roll music was moribund. Bands like Led Zep, Pink Floyd, ELP, Yes, Genesis, Jethro Tull, Deep Purple, and their countless imitators, the great bloated dinosaurs of punk legend, dominated the British music scene. If you wanted to see them, you had to go and sit politely in concert halls, where the stewards would ask you nicely to sit down if you had the temerity to get up and dance, as if anybody could dance to 'Smoke on the Water', 'Stairway to Heaven', or 'Tales From Topographic Oceans'. It was a horrible time to be young, in many ways. Hip boys like Perry and I trawled the pages of the *NME* and *ZigZag*, looking for something inter-esting to listen to. Hip girls discovered Bowie, Roxy Music, Lou Reed, and turned us on to them too, God bless their cotton socks, while we tried to find albums by the MC5, the Stooges, the New York Dolls, which was not always easy. There was certainly no chance of seeing them. So we went to the concert halls, and sat politely through gigs by Renaissance. Or Curved Air. Nasty, it was. If you had ambitions to play yourself, you could forget it, unless you had Grade Eight music and enough money to buy a mellotron.

So when pub rock started to happen in the mid-seventies, it was a godsend, a revelation. Bands like Ducks Deluxe, Brinsley Schwarz, and Dr Feelgood played a small circuit of London pubs. They played actual three-minute three-chord rock 'n' roll songs, direct and from the heart. Occasionally, they got down to Brighton, and played in the Hungry Years on the seafront, instead of the Dome, where the dreary prog stuff was played out, week after week. You could dance to this music. Nobody told you to sit down; in fact, the bands actually wanted you to dance. And it wasn't all rock 'n' roll or rhythm and blues. The thrice-blessed (and now sadly deleted) Kokomo were a superb vocal/funk band, somewhat after the style of the Voices of East Harlem; Chilli Willi and the Red Hot Peppers were a Western Swing band, a bit like Dan Hicks and His Hot Licks. They all had great names, too; Bees Make Honey, Duke Duke and the Dukes. A few of the bands had hit singles, for example, 'How Long', by Ace and 'Little Does She Know' by the Kursaal Flyers (whose drummer, Will Birch, has written a superb book on pub rock, *No Sleep Till Canvey Island*). There is even one superstar band who emerged from the circuit: not to my taste, but Dire Straits were essentially pub rockers; my musical partner, C.C. Ambler, still talks about booking them into the White Lion in Putney in 1975, when they were paid a whacking seventy quid. Loads of the punk bands benefited from pub rock; Nick Lowe from the Brinsleys became punk's first important producer; Stiff Records, set up by the Brinsleys' managers Dave Robinson and Jake Riviera, became the first half-decent independent label since the rise of Island back in the sixties. And of course, many of the people who went on to invent punk/new wave actually played in pub-rock bands; Strummer in the 101 'ers, Costello in Flip City, Dury in Kilburn and the High Roads. But the most important legacy of pub rock was that it established a circuit of places where you could actually play. And the Mecca of pub rock, its Shea Stadium, was the Hope and Anchor.

One of the things that happened as a consequence of pub rock was that people started bands of their own. I did; my school band was called Ruby Crystal and the Diamonds; the fact that none of us could play didn't seem so daunting any more. All that I wanted from life was to hack up and down the motorway in a battered old Transit van packed with scuffed AC30s and characterful Telecasters. As it happens, this was how I spent most of my twenties, playing first in an outfit that Radio Caroline described as 'Britain's Best Unsigned Band' (why ruin it, we thought, let's stay unsigned); and then in the ten-piece Maoist funk/noise collective that Minnie had dissed so cruelly. Three or four nights of the week we would bowl up at various pubs, and hack it out to a largely indifferent world. I loved it; loved the poverty, the fist fights, the drugs, the sex and even, on occasion, the music. Julie Burchill said, 'Show me a boy who doesn't want to be a rock 'n' roll star, and I'll show you a liar.' What better way of life could you possibly conceive when you are in your teens and early twenties? I couldn't, anyway. I must have played hundreds of gigs in dozens of grotty old pubs in my time; and once, just once, we made it into the hallowed basement of the Hope and Anchor. It is a tiny space, with room for no more than a hundred people, with the bands crammed on to the corner stage. There were ten of us, and nine people in the audience, but I really didn't care; I was playing in the Hope, treading the same boards as Brinsley Schwarz, and that was all that mattered to me.

So as soon as our posse entered the Hope and Anchor, it felt like coming home. The male customers wore unfortunate leather trousers and ill-judged sunglasses, whilst the lasses had dyed their hair blue. Just what I like in a pub. You could tell that everyone in there was in a band, or was in the process of forming one; they sat at tables, hunched together, planning their rise to the top. Even the friends I had come with were not immune: Perry, I had played with in punk days; and Richard and I still play together at parties. It's a thing that boys do, play together. The habitués of the Hope and Anchor might think they are cool; might try very hard to look cool, but all rock 'n' roll musicians are in their hearts just boys who like playing together, and a good thing too. I would much prefer to be in a pub with these playful dreamers than with a miserable bunch of old geezers moaning about asylum seekers and the Common Market, who seem to be the default regulars in most bars.

We went down into the basement. Ed, Sheela and Shinaid had never been down there before; for me and Perry and Richard it was everything a venue should be: packed, sweaty, and loud. We hadn't known beforehand who was going to be on, but we had struck lucky. The band were called The Jukes, and they were proper. A four-piece with great songs, they struck out their chords in the MC5/Stooges style beloved both of a new generation of post-punks and of those of us who remember it all the first time round.

Me and Perry and Richard grinned at one another; Ed and Sheela and Shinaid put their mouths next to our ears and shouted, 'It's very loud.'

We shouted back, 'Yes! It's supposed to be. It's called rock 'n' roll music!'

Five minutes later they put their mouths next to our ears again, and bellowed, 'We're going upstairs.'

'OK,' we shouted, and got back to grinning.

After the set, we went back upstairs too, our ears ringing, to find our friends.

'Cor, that was great,' I said.

'Bit loud for me,' said Ed. 'You couldn't talk over that noise.'

Musicians get used to people talking all through their set. The jazz critic Leonard Feather suggested that someone should make an album of conversation to play solo piano to. There really is little point in explaining to civilians that actually, you like *listening* to music, and could they please shut up. Music, for most people, is just something to set the mood for your dinner party. Playing loud is one of the best ways I know to shut people up (being very good is another sure-fire way, incidentally).

The Jukes came up into the bar, and once they had got themselves drinks and been kissed by their girls, I had to go up and tell them what I thought. Young gunslingers love it when middle-aged men come up and tell them they are great, especially when they say, 'I used to play a bit myself . . .'

This was only their fourth gig, but they all been knocking about the London scene for a year or two. The singer was an Australian, in his mid-twenties; he told me that they had brought about thirty people along that night, and had been paid forty-seven quid. 'Twas ever thus, my friend. At least there were only four of them; we used to have to split forty or fifty quid between ten of us. Young people today, they don't know they're born.

Pub rock, I would like to tell Noel Gallagher, is not bollocks; not all of it, anyway. If your idea of a good night out is going to see Lionel Richie at the Wembley Arena, then clearly you are not going to get off on seeing The Jukes at the Hope and Anchor. But if you want to hear something new, cutting-edge, exciting, then really you are going to have to go round the pubs, and open your ears.

On the way home Ed bought a falafel pitta and some chips, but he couldn't hold it all. So I became Ed's chip bitch. I carried his chips; and ended up eating most of them. By the time we got in, it was half-twelve. Me and Perry had been on the pish since half-seven in the morning, and all we had to sleep on were the sofas in the front room, and then not until we'd shared a spliff with Richard and Ed. By the time we got to bed, it was around three.

This was unfortunate, since in the morning, we were due to get up, and go on another all-day pub crawl round London. It really didn't bear thinking about.

# Good Friday 9th April

Gilbert Keith Chesterton was, in his day, one of England's most popular and prolific writers. As a poet, polemicist, journalist, novelist, biographer, critic, Catholic apologist, crackpot political theorist, magazine editor and broadcaster, his written output was huge by anybody's standards. So was he: six foot four, well over twenty stone; he once said, '. . . just the other day in the Underground, I had the pleasure of giving up my seat to three ladies.' He was a canny PR performer; he carried a sword stick and dressed in his trademark cape and battered hat, because he knew that it would make it easier for editors and readers to remember him. Born in 1874, he died in 1936, overworked, over-fed and over-watered. He liked a drink, did GK.

He's best remembered now for the Father Brown stories, about a Catholic priest who solves crimes, but I must admit that I always found the stories a bit laboured. What I like about Chesterton are the aphorisms. His work crackles with them:

'A dead thing can go with the stream, but only a living thing can go against it.'

'What embitters the world is not excess of criticism, but an absence of self-criticism.'

'To have a right to do a thing is not at all the same as to be right in doing it.'

'The comedy of man survives the tragedy of man.'

I could see why my anarchist and libertarian pals liked him too:

'Men are ruled, at this minute by the clock, by liars who refuse them news, and by fools who cannot govern.'

'A citizen can hardly distinguish between a tax and a fine, except that the fine is generally much lighter.'

Chesterton has the only funny defence of Catholic birth-control policy I've ever seen: 'Let all the babies be born. Then let us drown those we do not like.'

And who can argue with 'You cannot grow a beard in a moment of passion.'

And I like the poems. When I first came across 'The Rolling English Road', I looked about to see what collection it was published in. It wasn't, not at first; it first appeared in a very strange novel, *The Flying Inn*, published in 1914. The novel is set in an England where Prohibition is being introduced. Even a fictional English politician wouldn't have the nerve to actually ban alcohol. So they pass legislation which bans the sale of alcohol from premises which do not have a signboard outside. And then they ban signboards. The ruling classes would still be fine if they wanted a drink, of course:

> . . . by restricting the old sign-posts to a few places so select that they can afford to be eccentric, and forbidding such artistic symbols to all other places, they could sweep fermented liquor to all practical purposes out of the land. The arrangement was exactly that at which all such legislation is consciously or unconsciously aiming. A sign-board could be a favour granted by the govering class to itself . . . if a gentleman wished to claim the liberties of a bohemian, the path would be open. If a bohemian wished to claim the liberties of a gentleman, the path would be shut.

Two anarchist pals, Humphrey Pump, inn-keeper of the Old Ship, and the Fenian adventurer Patrick Dalroy, joined later by aristocratic poet Dorian Wimpole, travel around the country in defiance of the government with a cask of rum, a large cheddar cheese, and the sign from outside Humphrey Pump's inn. They put up the sign and set up impromptu pubs in locations designed to agitate the authorities. To amuse themselves on the road, they make up drinking songs, and 'The Rolling English Road' is one of these.

The best-known example of a popular novel which used poems and drinking songs in this way is *The Lord of the Rings*, and no one reads those bits, do they? If any of Tolkien's poems do stick in the mind, it is only 'The Road Goes Ever On and On'. *The Flying Inn* is a much inferior book to *LOTR*, but its poems are much better. In reading Chesterton, you can see the debt that Tolkien and his circle owe him. C.S. Lewis was converted to Christianity after reading GKC. The same hearty muscularity which informs Chesterton's drinking songs runs through the hobbits' revels. It is the welcoming glow from the windows of the Green Dragon in Bywater that is the light at the end of Frodo's tunnel. Chesterton's England and Tolkien's Middle-earth have a lot in common.

I wanted to inhabit the last couplet of the Chesterton poem,

> For there is good news yet to hear and fine things to be seen,
> Before we go to Paradise by way of Kensal Green.

I wanted to visit the Paradise Bar, and go to Kensal Green Cemetery.

And I thought I'd found two perfect guides to help me on this quest: comedian Tony Green and another architect friend, Rudja Matthews. Yes, that's what I thought.

Perry and I had arranged to meet them in the Paradise Bar at midday. Kensal Green is a long way from where we were staying, so we were reluctantly off the sofas and heading for West London by half-ten. We left the car behind, and decided to get about by public transport because we are very environmentally conscious and nobody needs a car in London, and also so that we could both get pished. My old housemate Sheela, finding herself at a loose end, had asked if she might come too, which was cool with us. Sheela is also an architect, and since I maintain that architects are the best guides to any city, I reasoned that you could never have too many when you are out exploring.

As we walked towards Highbury & Islington Tube, two hi-tech coaches passed us on St Paul's Road. One had a sign saying Arsenal, the other Liverpool. They were the team coaches, on their way to Highbury for the midday game. We peered expectantly as they passed, hoping for a glimpse of Steven Gerrard or Thierry Henry, but the windows were blacked out, and there was no way to see into the coaches. As we got nearer the Tube station, coming towards us on the street with an Arsenal scarf round his neck was no less a figure than the poet laureate of the bespectacled, Luton's own John Hegley.

'Hello John.' I said. 'Off to see the match?'

'Oh, hello Ian. Yeah, I am. I'm a bit late.' said John. 'What brings you to London?'

'Well, I'm doing the pub crawl I was telling you about.'

'Oh yeah. I remember. Where are you going today?'

'Ah. Oh. We're . . . well, we're going to meet Tony Green for a drink, actually.'

Hegley always looks a bit suspicious of the world around him, but the mention of Tony Green was guaranteed to add to his paranoia.

'Oh.' He frowned. 'Well, say "Hi" from me. Better get a move on.'

'Good to see you, John.'

'Yeah. And you.' Mr Hegley hurried on his way to Highbury. Sheela was impressed.

'That was John Hegley,' she said.

'Yes.'

Thing is, I felt a bit awkward. Once, long ago, Tony Green and John Hegley were comedy partners and best friends. They were like brothers. They started out together on the long and bumpy road to showbiz success, but their paths divided, not without some acrimony. John became popular, probably the most successful performance poet in Britain today. And Tony? Well, I think it fair to say that he took the road less travelled. He performs as Sir Gideon Vein. His refusal to compromise his anarchist principles, his addiction to improvisation at all costs and his tendency to call Jesus a word which, used in this sense, is said by feminists to hate women, make it difficult for the average comedy club to accommodate him. But on his night, he is the funniest man on earth. He's a political comedian, a genuinely threatening one, who makes Mark Steel look like a Tory. I've sat and watched him perform for two hours, where I've been barely able to draw breath between my screams of laughter. And I've seen him come on, abuse the audience for not being anarchists and then storm off after three minutes. Sheela had seen Sir Gideon perform a couple of times, and was genuinely scared at the prospect of meeting him. I can see why he would be difficult to work with, and why Hegley felt that he wanted to branch out on his own. Yet he haunts Hegley's work. If ever you see Hegley perform (and you should, because he's very good), notice how often he refers to his mythical friend Tony.

Tony's also a legendary drinking man, one of those people like Harris in *Three Men in a Boat* who always know a place just round the corner where you can get a half-decent drop of something. I've bumped into him in various towns on the alternative cabaret circuit, and he always has a pub up his sleeve.

'Just down here, Ian,' he says, and you find that all the time you have been five minutes away from one of the best pubs in Bath/Edinburgh/London without knowing it. And, to top it all, he's a big fan of Chesterton, and had promised to take us to some of the pubs that had been important in the great man's life.

The hero of *The Flying Inn* is Patrick Dalroy, an Irishman. In the final section of the book, Dalroy and his companions Humphrey Pump and Dorian Wimpole are being hunted by the authorities, and they drive for days across the country to escape their pursuers. To speed the journey along, Dalroy challenges his English companions to explain why the English roads can never run straight. He tells them that they must each produce a poem on the subject, and that he'll write one too. He also decrees that each poem have the same title; not 'The Rolling English Road', but 'An Inquiry into the causes geological, historical, agricultural, psychological, psychical, moral, spiritual and theological of the alleged cases of double, treble, quadruple and other curvature in the English Road'. He also tells them they should strike a lyric note. So actually, there are three poems, of which 'The Rolling English Road' is both the best and the best known. Strictly speaking, it's not even by Chesterton, but by his fictional creation, the effete poet Dorian Wimpole. (You can see the other two poems on my website, www.ianmarchant.com.)

The Paradise was not actually one of Chesterton's haunts, so far as I'm aware. There is a doorway on the side of the building, in what looks like moulded earthenware, above which is a date, 1892, and the sign of the Plough. Sometime in the eighties, when the skips started arriving in Kensal Green, a sure barometer of upward mobility for any area, an enterprising landlord bought the place up, and renamed it the Paradise, in honour of the poem.

The whole text of Wimpole's ballad is painted on to the front of the bar at the Paradise. If there were separate bars and snugs in the Plough, they have been swept aside in Paradise. Big comfortable sofas are arranged around the tables in the large open bar; it is a gastro-pub, decorated in shabby chic, and at night it is packed. We waited for our experts to arrive. Which they did almost at the same moment; Rudja on foot, and Tony by the unlikely medium of the bus, when I had always previously associated him with taxis.

Have you ever held a dinner party where you thought beforehand that the guests you had invited would be ideally suited to one another; would get on like houses on fire; would in fact probably become best friends, and blow you out altogether; only to realise, at the very moment of their arrival, that you had made an appalling mistake, and that it should have been obvious from the first that they would hate one another instantly? So it was with Tony and Rudja.

I'd met Rudja in the early eighties, through my sister-in-law, with whom she had been to school. An Amazonian blonde, six foot in her stockinged feet, she had a reputation for naughtiness, back then, and had been rumoured to have had a highly inappropriate walk-out with my father-in-law, Robert. I hadn't seen her for years until Robert's funeral, when it became evident that the naughtiness had grown into an overdeveloped taste for winding people up. She would fearlessly expose the weaknesses and foibles of anyone she came into contact with, and think nothing of their reaction. I thought she was great, but I knew that not everybody agreed.

After that, we stayed in touch, from time to time. Since she had spoken to me before about her love for Kensal Green Cemetery, and lived just round the corner from the Paradise, she seemed an ideal person to take us around. Why I thought that this street-fighting woman and Britain's most abrasive comedian would get on with one another, I still don't know. They were scrapping within seconds of their arrival, and would continue to fight for most of the rest of the day, except when Rudja was scrapping with someone else.

Tony is garrulous, like Mr Garrand, and he has the disarming habit of talking to people he's never met as though he has known them for years. When I first bumped into him, at a festival in Cornwall at which we were both appearing, he did this trick on me, and I've loved him ever since. He started talking as soon as he came into the bar.

'Ian, I've bought you a copy of *The Club of Queer Trades*, and I've brought my copy of *The Napoleon of Notting Hill* to show you the cover, because there's a good pub up there, and it's right where Chesterton was born and I thought we might go after the cemetery.'

Rudja said, 'Aren't you going to give him that too?'

'Well, no. It's mine.'

'That's a bit selfish, isn't it? You give him a book, and then take it away.'

'But, I'm not giving him this. I'm giving him *The Club of Queer Trades*. This one's mine.'

'Don't you like sharing?' said Rudja.

'But it's mine . . .'

'Mine mine mine. Is that any way to live?'

This before they had been introduced. Perry and Sheela looked anxiously at one another. Rudja wanted wine, and I thought I might join her, after my experience of getting beered up the day before. Tony, Perry and Sheela had a pint each.

With a beer in front of him, Tony turned into Sir Gideon as though a switch had been thrown, and started to tell a long story about queer tradesmen he had been involved with. We started to laugh; not Rudja though. She stared boggle-eyed at Tony, and after a minute or so, she stopped him in mid-flow.

'Why are you dressed like that?' she asked.

'My dear,' he said, turning towards Rudja like a Gila monster rounding on a hamster, 'I'm one hundred and forty-four years old. I've dressed like this for as long as I can remember.'

Tony is a dandy. He habitually wears a Homburg hat, an ancient suit with a cravat, and a black overcoat that comes from before the dawn of time.

Rudja rolled her eyes. 'How old are you really?' she said.

'I told you my child. I'm a hundred and forty-four years old. And how old are you?'

'A gentleman wouldn't ask.'

'And what leads you to believe that I am a gentleman?'

'Nothing, actually.'

'Shall we order lunch?' I said. 'My treat.'

'Not for me,' said Tony. 'I can't keep solids down. This fermented vegetable drink is all the sustenance I need,' he said, tapping his glass.

'You'll die then,' said Rudja.

'Ready to order?' I said brightly.

While we waited for lunch, Sir Gideon, for some reason best known to himself, began to caricature Chesterton's idly held anti-Semitic views.

'The Jew,' said Sir Gideon, paraphrasing GK, 'has much neglected virtues, as well as his well known faults . . .'

'Don't you like Jews?' said Rudja.

This stopped Sir Gideon in his tracks.

'I am Jewish,' said Tony.

'No you're not. I'm Jewish, but you're not.'

Colour came into Tony's face, something I for one had never seen before. He is normally the colour of a piece of A4 paper.

'Er, yes, I am.'

'No you're not.'

'My father was Jewish,' said Tony.

'There you are, then,' said Rudja. 'Judaism is matrilineal. My mother *and* my father are Jewish. I'm a Jew, you're not.'

'Everybody's mother's a bit Jewish,' said Perry. 'Mine is.'

'Mine was, too,' said Sheela.

'You're all goyim,' said Rudja.

'How dare you call me a goy, young woman,' said Sir Gideon.

'Funnily enough,' said Perry, 'you get very few Jewish alcoholics. Or Chinese.'

'Or Hindus,' said Sheela, born in Birmingham of Indian parents.

'I know why you don't really get Asian drinkers,' I said. 'It's to do with different approaches to unclean water. In Asia, people boiled it; in Northern Europe we fermented it. Alcohol was always used lightly in the East, where in Europe it was part of everyday life. I wonder why you don't get Jewish drinkers, though. After all, you use wine in the Friday-night rituals, don't you?'

'Don't ask him,' said Rudja. 'How would he know?'

'Because I'm a fucking Jew!' said Tony.

'I'm asking you, Rudja,' I said.

'Yes, we do. But no, Jewish people don't drink a lot. I've been to weddings where there's been a free bar, and at the end of the night there's still loads of drink left. It's not really in the culture, I suppose.'

'What about Noah?' I said.

'What about him?'

'It's the earliest drunk story there is. First thing that Noah plants after the Flood subsides is a vineyard. And the first thing he does after his grapes are ready is to get slaughtered. Absolutely pished, and he falls into a drunken stupor. In the morning, his son Ham goes into his father's tent, and sees his dad's todger. He backs out, and tells his brothers Shem and Japheth that their dad is lying there naked and hung-over. Shem and Japheth back into the tent, so they can't see Noah's cock, and cover him up. Noah wakes, mysteriously realises that Ham has seen him *in flagrante delicto*, and curses Ham's son Canaan. Says that all his descendants must be servants, and servants of servants for ever. It's a very odd story, actually.'

'Bit harsh, too, I'd say,' said Perry.

'I've always thought so,' I said.

'Where do you get all this crap from?' asked Rudja, the note of menace in her voice directed at me for the first time.

'First Book of Moses, Chapter Nine, verses twenty to twenty-seven.'

'Bullshit,' said Rudja.

'Not at all. I'm a proddy dog. We read the Bible.'

Like the Bible, *The Flying Inn* deserves to be read not for its plot and characterisation, but for the ideas and the rolling aphorisms. In 1914, just before the First War, Chesterton predicted PC, and the kind of problems that it might produce. The Prime Minister of Great Britain, Lord Ivywood, is slowly converted to Islam through the course of the book not by divine revelation but political expediency, in order to secure an alliance with the Ottomans. Prohibition is one of his concessions to his new allies. Chesterton has lots of fun at the expense of Mohammedism, in a way that we can't. Sir Gideon can say that terrible word about Our Lord Jesus Christ, and get laughs, but you try saying it about the Prophet, peace be upon him. Chesterton's prose is therefore quite daring and exciting to read in the present climate. One of Chesterton's themes is that English people prefer English Common to Sharia law, and that one day, it might come to a fight.

Like we were having over lunch in the Paradise. Our own little religious war. I decreed that a nice walk in the cemetery would be just the thing to cheer everyone up. I like to think that I'm unfit, but compared to Tony, I'm a cross between Mr Motivator and Sebastian Coe. So I walked ahead with Rudja, leaving Perry and Sheela to look after Tone. Best too, to let things cool off a little.

The cemetery was closed. I could hardly believe it. Apparently, nobody wants to visit graves on Good Friday, or hold a funeral. I would have thought that it was the ideal day, what with one thing and another. Perry, Sheela and Tony caught up with us.

'What are we going to do?' said Sheela.

'Break in,' said Rudja. 'I know another entrance.'

We walked around the walls of the cemetery, slowly so that we stayed together, but Rudja clung to my arm, and refused to speak to the others. Sure enough, when we tried Rudja's gate, it opened just sufficiently for us all to slip through.

The huge necropolis was utterly deserted. Rudja kept control of my arm and hurried me away from my other friends, because, she said, she wanted to show me Brunel's grave. It was small and plain; Isambard Kingdom Brunel, it said, Engineer. I felt sure that Isambard had gone to Paradise, by way of Kensal Green and God's Wonderful Railway. I thought again about funerals. The Irish have ritualised the drinking in the form of the wake, where everyone who knew the deceased comes round for a glass or two, by way of farewell. In Wales, up until the nineteenth century, sin-eaters were paid to come to the funeral, and eat a meal using the coffin as a table, thus consuming the sins of the departed. At my wife's funeral, we had gala pie and seafood vol-au-vent in the upstairs room of a pub on the Level in Brighton. Very stylish, no expense spared.

Chesterton would say that this is where the rolling road ends, and the straight road begins. I hope he was right.

We rejoined our companions by the catacombs, where Sheela was laughing as Perry took photos of Sir Gideon enacting his show-stopping impersonation of Boris Karloff. Usually, Tony's Boris Karloff impersonation is a good sign that an evening in his company should draw discreetly to a close. I always knew that it was time to throw him out of my house when he kicked into it, usually round about four in the morning.

'You are throwing me, Sir Gideon Vein, out of your house and into the night?' he would cry.

Enough graves for one day. The time had come to get Tony back into a pub.

'So, Tony; you're the boss,' I said. 'Where are you taking us next?'

'The Windsor Castle, I thought. It's by the place on the cover of *Napoleon of Notting Hill*, a couple of streets up from where Chesterton was born. Used to be his local. Shall we get a taxi?'

Since it was me picking up the bills, I looked at the A–Z, and decided that it was perfectly walkable. So it was arranged, and we set out on what I thought was the modest walk from Kensal Green Cemetery to Campden Hill Road. As on our way to the cemetery, Rudja took my arm, and sped me away from my other compan-ions, who walked at Tony's pace, which is that of a fifty-year-old man who refuses to eat. Once again, I had been deceived by the A–Z into believing that London is a small place and that it is easy to walk everywhere. Half an hour later, we arrived at the Windsor Castle.

It's called the Windsor Castle because you can see Windsor Castle from an upstairs room on a clear day. It's divided into three areas, each area divided from the other by the lowest doors I've ever had to try and get through. They came up to my chest. How Chesterton managed is a mystery. I bent double to get to the loo. Half an hour later, Perry, Tony and Sheela turned up, Tony almost on the verge of tears. Even little Sheela had to bend her head to get through the doors into the area where I stood with Rudja at the bar, supping Pinot Grigio. We tried to get Tony to eat something, which he refused. We sat around a big table, with bottles of wine and pints of beer. Tony, Sheela and Perry were deep in conversation with the couple on the next table, an Irish lass and her boyfriend. Perry told me about this later. He said the Irish lass had taken a shine to Sheela, and that her boyfriend was uncomfortable with this.

'There had clearly been some friction between them. I got the impression that she had been involved in a bit of bi-action at some point in the recent past, which was still causing upset.'

'What a strange thing to get upset about,' I said. 'To be encouraged, I'd say.'

Rudja was drunk, and becoming maudlin. She wanted to talk about Robert, my old father-in-law, who was buried in Kensal Green.

'He was a lovely man,' she said.

'Well . . .'

'No, he was. I know he drank and womanised, and was horrible to his children . . .'

'Yes?'

'But he was always lovely to me. He encouraged me to study architecture.'

'We always wondered if you'd ever . . .'

'Ever?'

'Shagged him.'

'Ian, don't be so horrible. Buy another bottle, and I'll tell you.'

And she did.

Tony had one last pub to show us, one of the great journalists' pubs, the Cheshire Cheese, on Fleet Street. The day before, Perry and I had come past here in the daytime, when the City had been full of life. Now it was bleak and deserted, a Lonely Financial Zone, in the words of the old Jonathan Richman song. I understood what Chris Garrand had meant when he'd told us it was very difficult to get a drink in the City after eight. Once it would have been full of journos, but now they've all been hived off to Canary Wharf, and Fleet Street is dead at night. The Cheshire Cheese was the only pub open. Chesterton used to drink here, laughing with his fellow journalists, writing his copy and arguing with his friends. I wondered how he would have got on with Rudja.

I paid off the cab, and while Perry insisted on trying to take a few night photographs of me and Tony, Rudja went into the pub. Five minutes later, the rest of us followed her in. She was shouting indignantly at three men at the bar. They'd told her a racist joke, she said.

'Why do you think I'd find that funny? How fucking dare you talk to me like that?'

The three men looked sheepish as we came in, and took their leave. That only left our party and a middle-aged man with his two daughters in the bar. We got talking. He was a Manchester barrister, in London for Easter, and had brought his student daughters down to show them something of London. They'd borrowed a friend's flat in the Barbican, and the Cheshire Cheese was the nearest pub that was open, at ten o' clock on a Friday evening.

Sir Gideon said, 'I very rarely meet lawyers out of court.'

'How can you be Jewish,' said Rudja, 'and not know a few lawyers?'

We drunk a lot more wine. Tony talked to me in one ear, Rudja in the other. They were telling me how much they hated one another. They were both very drunk. I was, too. Sheela was sitting on Perry's lap.

They slung us out at closing time. I managed to find one cab for Tony, heading to Kennington, and another for Rudja, to take her back to Kensal Green. She kissed me, and said, 'Thank you, darling Ian, for a really lovely day.' She turned and waved as her cab pulled away.

'How can you put up with that dreadful woman?' said Sheela in our own cab back to Islington.

'Sheela, that is the kind of woman you throw everything away for: job, career, happy home, the lot.'

'And six weeks later, she'd spit you out like a dried husk,' said Perry.

'Yes. But it would be worth it,' I said.

The cab dropped us outside the house. Perry's car was parked there, and it had been clamped. There was a £115 fine to pay before the car could be released.

'But there aren't any parking restrictions on this street, are there, Sheela?' I asked as very drunk and very angry Perry negotiated on his mobile with the all-night division of Islington Council's parking fascists.

'Oh, yes. I forgot to tell you. You need a resident's permit on match days. There's a tiny sign, look, halfway up the tree.'

'What, when Arsenal are playing at home?'

'Yes.'

'So you have to memorise the Arsenal fixture list before you can be sure your car isn't going to get clamped?'

'We've got it pinned up in the kitchen.'

'But today's Friday. They don't play on Friday . . .'

I remembered the team coaches on St Paul's Road as we set out that morning, and the Arsenal scarf around Hegley's neck. I remembered it was Good Friday. I remembered that I hadn't mentioned meeting John Hegley to Tony Green. Probably just as well.

# Easter Saturday 10th April

It's always good to be heading west out of London. Go north, up to the M1 from Marble Arch, and although you have the thrill of being at the start of Watling Street, it is not enough to compensate for crawling along Kilburn High Road, inching over the hilariously named Shoot Up Hill and getting stuck behind a bus in Cricklewood. South to Brighton is an interminable trip through a brutal labyrinth of poverty and apathy, whose characteristic buildings are godless carpet warehouses, and which only feels like it's over once you get the other side of Crawley. Heading east is unlovelier still. Yore 'avin a larf, entjya? Leave it aht!

But the route west goes past King's Cross, St Pancras, Euston, Madame Tussaud's, Regent's Park, before soaring up on to the Westway. You can imagine the Clash rehearsing somewhere down there; Portobello Market is under your wheels; in August, the Notting Hill Carnival rattles beneath the road. The Westway is funky. Who has not wondered what it would be like to live in the Trellick Tower? And then you drop down on to the Western Avenue, the only really modern arterial road that leaves London, a fascinating legacy of 1920s city planning, one which went badly wrong.

For years I was intrigued by the Western Avenue, and what it must be like to live in the houses that squash up against the roaring road for mile after mile. Built in the 1920s and 30s, the rows of once-respectable semis have been largely boarded up and abandoned to squatters. Here and there, vast thirties roadhouses, a new breed of inn for a new breed of traveller stand unloved at intersections. But when it was built, this road was a ribbon of hope; a realisation that the idea of a city had been changed by the internal combustion engine. Edward Platt has written a plangent and moving account of the Western Avenue in *Leadville*, a book about roads and broken dreams. And Elvis Costello has written a song, 'Hoover Factory' ('Five miles out of London on the Western Avenue, must have been a wonder when it was brand new, talking 'bout the splendour of the Hoover factory, I know that you'd agree if you had seen it too'), a hymn to the extraordinary art-deco palace that Hoover built next to the road in the early thirties. Hoover have gone, but the building, or at least its façade, is intact; it is a branch of Tesco's now, who have handled the preservation of this great industrial building with some sensitivity. So if you have to drive in and out of London, the A40 is by far the most interesting route to be stuck in jams. On Easter Saturday, the traffic heading west wasn't too bad, and it only took an hour from Islington to the start of the M40.

I expect you think you are a good driver, but you are not. No one is, except me. I think about my friends who drive me about from time to time. My girlfriend drives like an ancient dowager on crack. Lily, as soon as she turns the key, ignites into permanent seething road rage. Her dream vehicle is an armoured Humvee, so that she could shoot other road users. C.C. Ambler, my musical sidekick, is blind and mean. His spectacles are worse than useless; he can't see a thing when he's driving, but they give him a misplaced feeling of confidence. He refuses to get new specs, because they are much cheaper in the Czech Republic than they are over here, and next time he's in Prague, he'll get some new ones. He hasn't been to Prague for ten years, and, so far as I am aware, has no plans to go in the near future. My friend Saleel is blind and generous to a fault. His good-natured loving generosity makes him unable to make a decision. I've sat next to him as we've bowled up towards red lights, and overheard his thought processes. Hello. A red light. That means stop. But will the accelerator be offended if I apply the brakes? And what if the brakes are busy; I hate to bother them. Still, a red light's a red light, so I suppose there's no choice. Sorry to trouble you, brakes, but do you think you might help us stop? Oh, I've gone over the line a bit. Hope it doesn't think I was ignoring it. Why is Ian crying?

If I seem ungrateful to everyone who's ever given me a lift, then

I wish to say that it is not so, that I am grateful. Grateful to be alive. No, after a great deal of thought and self-examination, it seems to me that the world is a much safer and better place when I'm driving. But today Perry was at the wheel, and we were all in peril of our lives. The fear that had struck me as we drove into London, that Perry can't drive, had hardened into certainty. And he has a very bad habit; he endlessly taps his right foot along with the bass guitar on whatever is playing on the stereo; the right foot, which is traditionally used for regulating speed, via the accelerator pedal. This . . . Means . . . That . . . You . . . Jerk . . . And . . . Stutter . . . Up . . . The . . . Fecking . . . Road. Which made me want to boak.

Perry needed to drive so that I could navigate. We were looking for a place called Wheeler End, which is tacked on to the village of Lane End, about thirty miles west of London, just outside High Wycombe. We found Wheeler End, nothing much more than a hamlet clustered around a green, and tucked back from the road, the pub we were looking for, the Chequers. It's a Fuller's pub in brick and tile, smartly painted in black and white, with climbing plants up the wall and an attractive front garden with half a dozen tables and seats, just the kind of place that you might stop at for lunch if you were passing.

I had been here once before. For two years, back in the eighties, the landlord was my father. I can remember seeing his name above the door: 'Alan Raymond Marchant, Licensed to sell alcohol and tobacco'. I came here only once in the two years he had it because I became somewhat estranged from my father in the 1980s. I don't think he approved of my choice of career; batting around England playing in bands at night, and writing up the results of horse-races in bookmakers' shops by day. In my turn, I don't think I approved of his third wife.

He'd split up with my lovely stepmother Isobel a few years before, and run off with a lady called Pat, who he'd met on holiday in Torremolinos. Although I did my best to be nice to her, they always seemed incongruous to me, given that my Dad is six foot two and Pat was four foot eleven. Aesthetically, it just didn't work for me.

I was very pro-Isobel, too. And something had happened between my father and I, which I found unforgivable (it wasn't, given the passage of time; nothing is really). When my wife died, who I thought my father adored, he refused to come to her funeral, as he and Pat had booked to go on holiday, and were due to fly out from Gatwick that morning. To have delayed the flight by twenty-four hours would have meant paying a supplement, which my father could not face. I regarded this as just the teensiest bit insensitive. With hindsight, I think he was scared of running into my mum. So, for whatever reason, in the two years that he owned and ran the Chequers, I only made it up there once for a visit.

It was a huge mistake for him to buy a pub, one that lots of men make when they take early retirement. It must seem so attractive, after the hurly-burly of cost accountancy or whatever. You picture yourself sashaying into the bar for an hour or two in the evening, patting the behind of your buxom barmaid, quaffing a few pints of ale with some cheery locals, then cashing up at the end of the night, and counting your loot. Where this picture comes from, I have no idea. Five minutes' conversation with any pub landlord will very quickly show you that they get up at the crack of dawn to set up the bar, work all through everyone else's lunch hour, then maybe get a couple of hours off in the afternoon, not to have a nap, but to go to the cash-'n'-carry, before spending all evening kowtowing to beered-up bores, who feel that England should leave the Common Market and that asylum seekers should be shot, then sent back to wherever they came from, and then shot again. The luxurious mansions that the council give the asylum seekers to live in should be sold, and the money used to fund hospitals. The hospital is very important from the pub bore's political standpoint. It's a measure of value.

'See that arts centre? Could have built a hospital with that money.'

'That new swimming pool? A maternity unit.'

'New library books? An intensive-care bed.'

All public money should be used to build more hospitals, except, of course, the defence budget, which should be quadrupled as asylum seekers are also insane suicide bombers, who need to be taught a lesson. As a pub landlord, you're going to hear this stuff every night of your life, up until closing time, when, after you've managed to get the punters out of the door, you tidy up and clean the bar, before falling gratefully into bed at about two o'clock. Then you get up at seven, and the whole thing starts over again. Holidays and days off become all but impossible. This is why all pubs are for sale, if the money's right. The landlord's lot is not a happy one. But year after year, gullible men in their fifties sink their golden handshakes into the Shitkicker's Arms, and are then surprised that their lives have become even more miserable than previously. So it was with my father.

Talking to him now, he says that the main mistake he made was in buying a pub that was not surrounded by chimney pots. Standing outside the Chequers, I could see his point. Wheeler End is very pretty; but it is not big. Clearly, the larger part of your clientele is not going to come from Wheeler End; there are not enough chimney pots. But we had already been to pubs in villages that were both smaller and more isolated – the Duke of York's in Iddesleigh, for example – that were thronged morning, noon and night. The main ingredient for a successful country pub these days is food. If you don't have enough locals to make it pay, you have to attract the drive out from Beaconsfield and High Wycombe for dinner market. The Chequers has gone down this route.

Inside, it is now a light and attractive place. The bar staff were efficient and friendly and the beer was good, as you'd expect from Fuller's. A new restaurant area had been built on to the pub at the back, and a few couples and families were out there, eating their lunch. We ate in the bar; good pub grub, from a smart and efficient kitchen. The racing was on the telly, and a dozen or so locals were watching it with the landlord, clearly a big racing fan. It was a lively village pub, one to which people were making a special trip for food. But to do all this takes a great deal of work, and your fifty-something ex-businessman who has bought a pub upon taking early retirement does not want to do a great deal of work.

My father certainly didn't want to do food, which meant that he had a very low turnover, which meant that he could never afford

bar staff, so he had to sit there himself, night after night, and entertain the handful of locals. Pat popped down from time to time to
show off the thing that had lured my father into her clutches, viz.
her remarkable bosom; no bad thing in a landlady. Even that didn't
pull in the Hillmans. He tried putting on a few special nights to
attract people from Lane End; he told me about a forties night,
where they played tapes of Vera Lynn, air-raid warning sirens and
Churchill's speeches. Since it was a special night, he did do food;
Woolton Pie, and jellied snoek with dried eggs. Oddly, the evening
was not a roaring success. My visit was just after forties night, and
things looked bad.

The business was haemorrhaging money, and as my father had
demonstrated by his reluctance to pay a small supplement to an
airline so that he could attend his daughter-in-law's funeral, money
was a thing that mattered a great deal to him. So he hit on a plan.
He would serve underage drinkers. It started in a small enough
way; a few likely lads came in, thinking that the pub was a step
out of Lane End proper, and the landlord was new, so he wouldn't
know how old they were. My father wasn't taken in, but he took
their cash. When they got served, they told their mates.

Soon, the Chequers was busy with 16- and 17-year-old chavs on
mopeds. And their 14-year-old girlfriends. They were coming, not
just from Lane End, but from as far afield as Piddington and Ibstone.
Yamaha 50s were parked all up the lane, and when the little fuck-
wits weren't drinking in my father's pub, they were sitting out on
the green, revving up their bikes. The fact that the pub was now
full of illegal drinkers who my father hated did not encourage him
to get bar staff, as that would have meant handing over cash to
someone. He still served behind the bar, and he had to try and
engage with his new customers, who had no conversation. So he
decided to get a jukebox, to encourage his teeny clientele to keep
coming, and to stop him having to try talking to them.

Music has always been a struggle for my father. Although he
loves to sing, and has a beautiful voice, like most people born before
1940 his idea of what pop music should be doesn't engage with a
post-Presley world. So a jukebox that played endless '45s from the

Hit Parade' was my father's idea of hell. After two years, he could stand no more; he sold the pub, split up with Pat, despite the bosom, and buggered off to Thailand, another popular fifty-something destination.

The landlord pointed me towards Dusty, one of the locals. 'He's been coming here for years. He'll remember your dad.'

Dusty screwed up his face. 'Alan? Alan and Pat? It's been through a lot of hands . . . it was quite rough for a bit. Just full of kids; I went into Lane End to drink. It's difficult to remember them all. Alan?'

I blushed. 'Tall bloke. Liked singing Guy Mitchell songs. Ran forties nights.'

'And Pat, you say?'

'Tiny woman. Yorkshire. Regal bosom.'

'Wait a minute . . . Pat?'

'Yes.'

'And Alan?'

'That's right.'

'No . . . it's gone, I'm afraid. Sorry, mate.'

Dusty told us that the following night was charity auction night at the Chequers, the proceeds going to search-and-rescue helicopters. It was a shame we were going to miss it, he said. I promised that when this book was published, I'd send him a copy for next year's auction. It seemed the least I could do to make up for the Yamaha 50s and jukebox.

We drove on. I'd never been this way before, through the deepest Chilterns, not that I could remember. I always thought the Chilterns were suburban, but I was wrong. They are very beautiful, and seem remote.

'Look,' said Perry. 'A red kite.'

I'd never seen one before, even though in Radnorshire I lived on the edge of the Cascob valley, one of the last places that kites could be found. Now the kites are coming back, creeping nearer to the cities where they belong, and where, up until the nineteenth century, they could be found hopping about on rubbish heaps, the most lordly of the carrion birds. We drove on another half mile, and saw another two kites high above the trees. I promised myself that one day I'd come back to this lost corner of rural England, thirty miles outside London.

We stopped to stretch our legs in Ewelme, surely one of the most picture-perfect villages in chocolate-box England. Watercress beds run alongside the road up to the wonderful church, with its cloister of medieval almshouses. Jerome K. Jerome is buried in the churchyard. Rooks fluttered around high trees; daffodils pushed through the earth over the graves.

Back into the car; I managed to get a *Round the Horne* CD on the stereo, so that Perry would stop pumping his foot along to the music. It made for a smoother ride, except when Rambling Sid Rumpo came on to do his bit. We crossed the Thames at Shillingford Bridge, and made for the village of Harwell, where my father and Isobel lived for ten years. We were going to the Kicking Donkey, the first pub I ever went in. It was 1971, and I was thirteen. It was my father's local.

It was built from brick, left unpainted, the dark red brick of the Oxfordshire/Berkshire borders. It was a two-minute walk away from his house, which was a good thing. My father could not rest easy unless he was in a pub, any pub, for last orders, and so it was necessary that his house should be an easy and quick walk away from a boozer. My stepmother suggested that he have an alarm fitted and linked to the pub, like MPs do in their flats to alert them when the division bell is ringing and they must attend the House to obey their orders, but my father pointed out that his own internal pub clock functioned perfectly, and that having an alarm fitted represented an unnecessary expense.

When I was staying with him, he would take me too. At five minutes to eleven we would leave his house, and at three minutes to we would walk in through the door of the Donkey, and turn left into the public bar. Maybe 20 by 25 foot, the thirty or so locals in there were enough to make it seem packed. There were no tables, just benches around the walls, where the old men and women of the village sat. The young people all stood around the upright piano, where an old guy called Frank would sit and play 'Two Lovely Black

Eyes', or 'Daisy Daisy'. Everyone would sing along. The floor was covered in sawdust, and there was a coal fire burning in the grate. It was 1971, but it felt like something out of *Lark Rise to Candleford*.

My dad would buy two pints of bitter for himself, and a half of shandy for me, and then Harry the landlord would ring the bell for time. Like his father before him, two pints was what my dad liked. One of my father's heroes when he was a boy before the war was a middle-distance runner called Sidney Wooderson, who at the time held the world record for the mile. Wooderson wrote a training manual, which my sporty father read, hoping to emulate Sidney's achievement. Wooderson said that every day he drank 'two pints of ale drawn from the wood'. My father liked this, especially the detail about 'drawn from the wood', and stuck rigidly to this useful advice until the day he moved to America. I like it too; fantastic to imagine today's sports stars recommending anything so healthy and sane.

The thing my father liked most about the Donkey was the singing. He'd join in with the general sing-song, and then yield to requests for a solo. His specialities were 'Nelly Dean' and his legendary rendition of Guy Mitchell's 1953 hit 'She Wears Red Feathers (and a Hooly-Hooly Skirt)'. By midnight, people started to leave, still singing as they walked up the lane.

After I'd been going there for several years, I noticed that there was another bar, an old-fashioned parlour. I looked in once. It was dark, like chocolate. Heavy old armchairs huddled around dingy tables. No one ever went in, except, my father told me, when there was a funeral. Then Harry would lay on refreshments in there. Outside, there was a large beer garden, where on summer evenings the local men played Aunt Sally. Aunt Sally is peculiar to that part of the country. The sally is shaped like a champagne cork, though much larger; as large, perhaps, as an orange. It is balanced on top of a spring, which is mounted on top of a short stake, maybe three feet high. The locals stand fifteen feet or so away, and throw sticks at it. If they knock the sally cleanly from the spring, then they score a point. If they hit the stake or the spring and the sally drops off, that doesn't count. There were several other pubs in the area that played, and there was a local league. The biggest rivals were the team from a pub called the Leathern Bottle, which was about five miles away. The rivalry was hardly deadly – once a year all the locals would go on the Harwell Village Walk, which started at the Donkey, and culminated at the Bottle.

All subsequent pubs were ruined for me. The first pub I drank in was one of a tiny handful of real village pubs which still stood at the heart of their community. I thought that this was what all pubs were like. Nothing else has ever quite measured up. Years later, I read Orwell's essay 'The Moon Under Water', about his search for the perfect pub, and I realised that the Kicking Donkey had come pretty close. I couldn't wait to see it again. I was prepared to be disappointed; to see it turned into a Harvester or something. I wasn't prepared for it to be gone.

The building is still there, in a way. It's been turned into a private house. But the Donkey has gone. The brick has been scrubbed, so that it looks almost new. UPVC windows and doors have been installed, which I'm sure are easy to maintain. They've put coach lamps up on the wall. They probably come on if a stranger approaches the door. A conservatory, also in shiny UPVC, has been added at the back. The old pub now looks almost new; it could pass for a neo-Georgian house on one of the windswept estates for salarymen that are spreading across the countryside. In the old beer garden where we played Aunt Sally, a new house has been built, a hideous mockery of the vernacular. On the gatepost there is a small sign, a last reminder of what it was: 'The Kicking Donkey'. I walked up to the front door and rang the bell; no one was home. Perry took some photos.

'Bad one,' he said.

'Bloody Margaret Thatcher,' I said, a bit choked.

'You can't keep blaming her for everything,' said Perry.

'Why not? She's been in power since 1979, her and her evil clones, and look what they have done to this country.'

'Lots of pubs get turned into private houses,' said Perry.

'I know, I know. It's the coach lamps that get me.'

'Why?'

'Because once, in my lifetime, this place was authentically part of rural England. It was proper. It certainly didn't have coach lamps outside. And these bastards have scrubbed it up to make it look nice and new and tidy, and then have stuck up fucking fake fucking coach lamps, because they think it makes it look old and quaint.'

'It was never going to still be a spit-and-sawdust village alehouse any more, you knew that. How many of them are left?'

'Thirteen.'

Perry laughed.

'No, really, thirteen. I found a list, in Lucy's in Hay.'

This is true; true, at least, at the time of our journey. In the middle of Hay-on-Wye there is a pub called the Three Tuns, run by an old lady called Lucy. Nothing has changed since the 1920s, when her father took it over. I was in there a few months before the trip, and Lucy showed me a list, compiled by a madman, of the thirteen completely unspoiled pubs in England; a list that grows smaller by the year, as the old landlords and landladies die off. So mad is this list, it excludes places like Eli's, because they've put a small conservatory on at the side of the building. Lucy was proud that she was one of the thirteen. Sadly, no longer; during the writing of this book, the Three Tuns was gutted by fire. Friends in Hay tell me that Lucy was unhurt, and that she is hoping to refurbish and reopen. But she is in her eighties; if the Three Tuns does manage to reopen, it will never be the same again. (You can see the full list on my website, www.ianmarchant.com.)

'We're going to one of the thirteen tomorrow night, in Worcestershire,' I told Perry. 'Unless some wanker has PUT COACH LAMPS ON THE WALL!!!'

'Ian, stop ranting. Get in the car.'

So I did. Railing at fakery does not roll back the crimes of developers. Nothing does. We are powerless, really, like we always have been, unless our much-vaunted power as consumers counts for anything, which I doubt. Even if it does, our tastes are so debased that people scrub good old brick, buy coach lamps from B&Q, and mortgage their existence away so they can lead their lives of quiet desperation in fake Georgian houses.

'I blame the Prince of Wales, big-eared wanker.'

'Do leave it out. You were blaming Thatcher a moment ago.'

'And the Prince of Wales. Have you been to Poundbury?'

That wiped the smile off Perry's face. Poundbury is the fake village that Charles has flung up on the outskirts of Dorchester. It is one of the most vile places in England, a Hollywood set, a façade, a bad joke.

'And did you see the house they'd put up in the garden? Fake! A bad fake, too. Why can't we build houses that look like they were built in the twenty-first century?'

To shut me up, Perry put a rare groove compilation on the in-car stereo and . . . we . . . stuttered . . . off . . . to . . . our . . . final . . . destination . . . of . . . the . . . day.

Thame is an attractive market town six miles or so to the east of Oxford. According to local legend, it has the second-widest High Street in England. Standing in the middle of that street is the Spread Eagle. In 1922, the Spread Eagle was taken over by John Fothergill, poet, art dealer, archaeologist, and friend of Robert Ross and Oscar Wilde, who now had a wife and a young son to support. Fothergill decided to buy an inn, and run it his way. This meant that he would serve good food, well cooked, which was as revolutionary then as it is now. The Spread Eagle has good claims to being the first gastro-pub in Britain, and I wanted to stay there, as Chesterton, H.G. Wells, Augustus and Dorelia John, Lytton Strachey and Dora Carrington had in Fothergill's day.

One of the best-written exposition scenes in English literature is set in the Spread Eagle. Fothergill hated the hearties, especially huntsmen. He liked the rackety aesthete undergraduates who drove out from Oxford to dine at the Spread Eagle, especially Harold Acton and his crowd, who included the cheerful bugger Tom Driberg, MI5 spy, MP, and later chairman of the Labour Party; and Evelyn Waugh. Waugh and Fothergill became friends. It's well known that Waugh liked writing in hotels, and the Spread Eagle was one of the first places he used; Fothergill used to let him have a room at a cheap rate on week nights. Waugh repays the favour in *Brideshead Revisited*, when the aesthete Anthony Blanche takes Charles Ryder out to dinner, both to warn Ryder against the charms of Sebastian Flyte, and to tell him that he has genuine artistic talent.

> He [Blanche] asked me to dinner, and I was a little disconcerted to find that we were to dine alone.
>
> 'We are going to Thame,' he said. 'There is a delightful hotel there, which luckily doesn't appeal to the Bullingdon.* We will drink Rhine wine and imagine ourselves . . . where? Not on a j-j-jaunt with J-J-Jorrocks, anyway . . .'

Waugh moves the action from the pub where they meet, into a taxi, on to the Spread Eagle, through the meal and back to Oxford, all by means of the torrent of Blanche's talk, which also manages to tell Sebastian's 'back-story' (the bit that shows what happens to a character in the past, which the reader needs to know, but which doesn't necessarily move the plot forward; very difficult stuff to handle for a writer). It's a superb piece of writing. In a way, the fact that Anthony Blanche with his over-refined tastes happily dines at the Spread Eagle is a ringing endorsement of how good it must have been, even though Blanche is fictional, and the kitchen was real. Thomas Burke, in his *Book of the Inn*, published in 1927, certainly thought so; he picks out the Spread Eagle as the best inn in England.

If Fothergill was welcoming to some of the wilder elements of Oxford undergraduate life, he could be very rude to customers he didn't like; once famously adding sixpence to the bill of a party he considered ugly. Fothergill wrote a very funny book, called *An Innkeeper's Diary*, published in 1931, a copy of which is in all the rooms of the Spread Eagle. While Perry had his shower, I lay on my bed and read from it. Fothergill's main bugbear was people who came in to use his loos; lots of entries in the *Diary* concern Fothergill's confrontations with people who had used his convenience without saying 'please' or 'thank you' (as Chesterton says in *The Flying Inn*, courtesy is the one saving grace of the upper classes). I found an entry for 1929, about Waugh visiting Fothergill with a

---

* A dining club for hearty undergraduates.

copy of his first novel: 'Evelyn Waugh, wasting his time at Oxford on himself rather than others, with his shy propriety rapidly came through with *Decline and Fall*, the wittiest book of all time, a copy of which I keep chained to a shelf in the lavatory marked "Private Sitting Room".'

There is also a list of the seven requirements for a good inn-keeper:

(1) 14–16 hours a day and few even half days off, (2) some capital with which to have good food ready and to waste, (3) a mind for the tiniest details, (4) an all-round outlook, (5) an ability to formulate a policy and courage to carry it out, (6) to have had first a good time in life oneself, and (7) a natural, not enforced, love of the job.

My father's failure as a landlord was writ large. I'm not sure he had any of these qualities. My own occasional desire to take over a pub, measured against this list, makes it clear that I too would be disastrous, since I have only two of the qualities: an all-round outlook, and having had a good time. And I worry about the all-round outlook.

When Perry emerged from the shower, we headed down to the restaurant, which is called Fothergill's. I really liked the idea of dining in the same restaurant as Charles Ryder and Anthony Blanche. But the interior is much altered from Fothergill's day; it is light, a riot in beige and stripped pine. And the menu was a bit over-fussy for our taste (Supreme of Gressingham Duck with Kumquat and Orange Sauce, Confit of Lamb wrapped in Parma Ham with a Port and Redcurrant Jus). After three nights in London, we were looking for something plainer. Luckily, Fothergill offered a solution. In another of his books, *My Three Inns*, he gives a list of things to look for when you're buying an inn. One of these is 'Is there a fried-fish shop near?' I'm not sure if this was a good thing in Fothergill's view, but there was such a place just up the road, and after a couple of pints at the bar, we went off to the chipper for haddock, chips and mushy peas, washed down with a pot of tea. It was run by a bunch of Portuguese guys from Madeira, and they clearly thought we were very funny; they kept coming to look at us while we were eating, alternating between goggling and giggling. Clearly, the exertions of the trip were starting to show.

It was obvious from the shape of the building that the chip shop had once been a pub; good that it had been saved from conversion to a private house, at least. I'd seen enough of that. A walk round Thame after our dinner showed us that there had once been twenty or more pubs in the town, a fair few of them now converted into shops. And all of the old pubs still kept their signs, so that Thame High Street is one of the best places to see the old signscape of England. And the best of all is the sign of the Spread Eagle, a real signpost, freestanding in the middle of the pavement, rather than a signboard swinging from the building: wings extended, talons at their sharpest, a glint in its green eye, it was painted by Carrington.

London had exhausted us, and all we wanted was an early night; we went back into the Spread Eagle for a nightcap, and then hit the (twin) sacks. Easter Sunday tomorrow. We had to be up early, to take communion in a church up in the Cotswolds. Perry was very nervous, not really approving of churches other than as places to take photos. Some people are uncomfortable with their sinner status, I know; not me. Perry refused to come to the Easter service. It looked like I would be taking communion on my own.

## Easter Sunday 11th April

Everyone at the Spread Eagle was sorry to see us go. Not that we had especially distinguished ourselves as guests, but because we needed to be away very early, and so the ancient night porter had been forced to prepare us a 'continental breakfast' and to haul it up to our room at six-thirty in the morning. He looked as delighted to see us as we were to see him. Perry and I sat gloomily in bed, chomping on leathery croissants.

An hour later, we were on the road again, heading for the village of Great Wolford, about thirty-five miles north of Thame, on the north-eastern edge of the Cotswolds, hoping to be in time for the Easter communion service, which was due to start at nine. I wanted to take communion, because it was Easter Sunday, and I usually do, but also because I'm endlessly puzzled by religion and its relationship with intoxicating drink, and I wanted to muse. I chose Great Wolford, because in W. T. Marchant's *In Praise of Ale* there was a transcript of an inscription from one of the graves in the churchyard:

> Here old John Randal lies
> Who counting from his tale,
> Lived threescore years and ten,
> Such virtue was in ale.
> Ale was his meat,
> Ale was his drink,
> Ale did his heart revive,
> And if he could have drunk his ale,
> He still had been alive,
> He died January 5, 1699.

Old John Randal's grave seemed well worth a pilgrimage.

Church and pub, pub and church; these have been the two main-stays of English life for a thousand years. In a village, they are invariably next to one another, the parson and the landlord the most important inhabitants. English pubs were the secular arm of the Church of England. Until well after the Reformation, churches sold beer themselves on occasion, at 'church ales'. The churchwarden would buy some malt, and give it to those of his parishioners who brewed. They gave back the beer when it was ready, and the church would turn into a pub for a few days, over Christmas or Whitsun, selling the beer . . . 'to repaire their churches and chappels with, to buy bookes for service, cuppes for the celebration of the sacra-ment, surplesses for Sir John,* and other such necessaries . . .' (Phillip Stubbs, *Anatomie of abuses*, 1585). Stubbs was being puritanical; the money didn't just go on gaudy raiments for Popish priests. John Aubrey, the seventeenth-century antiquary, remembered that 'in his father's day', before the Poor Law of 1601, all money for the poor and needy was raised by church ales and church feasts.

The use of church premises for drinking had long been an issue. Village ale-houses were private homes, with little or no room for people to sit and drink. The church was the obvious place to go, and up until the Reformation, the church had little problem with this. The problem for the church was when the priests started join-ing in; Dunstan, Archbishop of Canterbury in the reign of the Saxon King Edgar, wrote as canon law that 'No priest should be an ale-scop nor in anywise act the gleeman'.

Christianity insists that believers take a drink, every time they approach the altar rail. Drinking alcohol is not a sin, according to Christian belief, but a duty. This is my blood, said Christ; do this, as oft as ye shall drink it, in remembrance of me. If drinking is a sin what are we to make of the wedding at Cana, where Christ performed his first miracle? Six waterpots, 'containing two or three firkins apiece' were turned to wine by Christ's agency. A firkin is nine gallons; so Christ produced somewhere between 108 and 162

---

* The priest.

gallons. A vicar pal estimates that that's about an extra three bottles per guest, on top of what they'd drunk over the previous two days (weddings in those days lasting three days; now it just feels like it). This is a serious piss-up; the Jewish weddings that Rudja had been to, where free bars are left largely untroubled, are clearly a recent phenomenon.

Readers of *The Da Vinci Code* and the book that 'inspired' Dan Brown, *The Holy Blood and the Holy Grail*, will tell you that this wedding was Christ's own, where he got hitched to the Magdalene. You can forget all the guff about Templar conspiracy theories, but there are certainly some clues that this was a family wedding. Mother Mary insists that Christ perform the miracle, despite him telling her that 'his hour is not yet come'. She ignores this, and pretty much tells him to get on with it. It was the responsibility of the bridegroom's family to provide the wine, and it would have been shameful for anyone else to do so. For Mary to be so upset about running out of booze, it must have been a wedding that the family were very closely involved with.

After the wine appeared, the governor of the feast called over the bridegroom, and said to him, 'Every man at the beginning doth set forth good wine; and when men have well drunk, then that which is worse: but thou hast kept the good wine till now' (John 2: 10).

People still do this at parties; fill their guests with a drop of the good stuff, and then, when they are beyond caring about quality, get out the cheap shit. I picture drunk old uncles at the wedding at Cana, finding that all the wine had gone, desperately hunting about for anything to drink, triumphantly finding a bottle of Advocaat in a cupboard somewhere, or unearthing a bottle of Dubonnet that no one could face until they were pished. They must have been very pleased with Jesus.

Think about how odd it is that the Temperance movement was largely led by Christians. Nonconformists, who do not take the communion very seriously, drink a sickly sweet kind of alcohol-free grape squash during the service, rather than wine. But since Christ quite clearly enjoyed a drink, and old Noah liked a drop, there is no biblical precedent for abstinence; and I thought the whole point of evangelical Christianity was that it is based on the text of the Bible. Evangelicals are especially fond of the Psalms; well, why don't they read Psalm 104, which thanks God for 'wine that maketh glad the heart of man'?

There only seems to be one place that drink is banned, and then only for priests, and that's in the Temple: 'Do not drink wine nor strong drink, thou, nor thy sons with thee, when ye go into the tabernacle of the congregation, lest ye die: it shall be a statute forever throughout your generations' (Leviticus 10: 9).

And that would seem to imply that the vicar shouldn't drink communion wine in church; except Christians will tell you that Christ rewrote the Covenant, so Leviticus doesn't exactly count anyway, and that's why it's all right to eat lobsters, too. And what happens if you're a Catholic member of Alcoholics Anonymous? On the one hand, you are obliged to take communion; on the other you are told that if a drop of drink passes your lips, you are off the wagon and back to square one, and you might just as well go down the offy and buy yourself a four-pack of Special Brew.

It's all very confusing.

All I know is that I would rather the cure of my soul was in the hands of a whisky priest, or a cheerful ruddy-faced parson who enjoys a drop or two of port after dinner, than a pinch-faced parsimonious abstainer. I would have liked Bishop Earle, who was Charles II's tutor, and subsequently his chaplain during his exile in France.

The good bishop wrote that 'A tavern is the busy man's recreation, the idle man's business, the melancholy man's sanctuary, the stranger's welcome, the inns-of-courts man's entertainment, the scholar's kindness, and the citizen's courtesy' (*Microcosmographie*, 1628). He might also have added that they make monarchs merry.

St Michael and All Angels Church in Great Wolford was rebuilt in the nineteenth century, but there has been a church on the site since the twelfth. So old John Randal could not have worshipped in this church; but he would certainly have drunk in the Fox and Hounds, the village pub, where I intended to take Perry after the service. It's been there since the sixteenth century.

'You're sure you don't mind if I don't come in?' Perry said miserably at the gate to the churchyard.

'Of course not, godless heathen. You go off and enjoy yourself. While you can.'

Great Wolford is close to the Rollright Stones, the most impressive stone circle in the Cotswolds. While I sat and listened to the ringing phrases of the Prayer Book, sung the great Easter hymns and took part in the mysteries of the sacrament, old Perry was taking himself off to stand on a windswept hillside in a stone circle, to smoke a spliff and read his Julian Cope book.

'I'll pray for you, hippy,' I said.

'Whatever.'

I was nervous as soon as I entered the church. The churchwarden handed me a printed service sheet, which promised me a nice family service. I was worried that there would be guitars and hugging. I sat in a pew near enough the back that I would appear inconspicuous; a hopeless ambition. The only time in my life I've ever appeared inconspicuous was when I was working for a time as an ugly model, and would get sent to auditions with other similarly fat bald speccy men. Today in church, everyone had a good old stare. I stared back. There were a couple of extended families, each filling a pew on opposite sides of the aisle. There were several well-kept elderly couples, clearly retired to the Cotswolds, all nicely tanned after a couple of months in Gozo or wherever. There was a sprinkling of the sixty- and seventy-something spinsters and widows without whom the church could not survive. And there was me. The spinster in the pew in front turned round and whispered to me in conspiratorial tones.

'There's not many in,' she said.

'No,' I replied.

'I'm going to have a word with the vicar, see if she'll do a Prayer Book service instead of this modern rubbish,' she said, shaking her service sheet with contempt.

'Good idea,' I whispered back.

The spinster stood, and accosted the vicar, who was bustling around preparing the service. The vicar was not terribly pleased that the battle between traditionalists (like me and the agitated spinster) and the modernisers who want to make the service relevant to a modern audience (who were absent) had once again broken out into the open. The vicar spoke to the churchwarden, who smiled and started handing round the Book of Common Prayer. The spinster sat back down in front of me.

'Much nicer,' she said. And I agreed. Tradition is the democracy of the dead, wrote Chesterton.

So Cranmer filled the church, the same words that old Jack Randal would have listened and responded to; death hath no dominion. And we sang 'Alleluia! Alleluia! Hearts to Heav'n and voices raise'. And once again I found myself kneeling at an altar rail, being offered the unleavened bread of sincerity and truth; and then the vicar stood in front of me, and tipped the communion cup towards my mouth, saying, 'The blood of our Lord Jesus Christ, which soul was shed for thee, preserve thy body and soul unto everlasting life: Drink this in remembrance that Christ's Blood was shed for thee, and be thankful.'

A trickle of viscous liquid, like sweet cough medicine touched my tongue.

'Amen,' I said.

She wiped the edge of the cup, and moved to the next communicant; 'The blood of our Lord Jesus Christ . . .'

It's actually QC British sherry. If you're a Catholic, then you believe that QC British sherry is transmuted by the mystery of the Mass into the blood of Christ. If you are a Baptist, then you're . . . well, you're not reading this book, are you? But if you were, then you'd see it a papist foolery to imagine that it really was anything other than a symbol, and typical Anglican prevarication to allow the demon drink in church. Since the ritual is symbolic, then Nonconformists see no difficulty in using symbolic wine. A friend of mine whose father was a Baptist minister told me that on one occasion her dad used orange squash with a bit of red food colouring. But I'm a Zen Anglican, a sect of one; to me, the communion is a symbolic mystery, a dream of miracles. As a Zen Anglican, I feel free to believe whatever weird shit I choose. I do know that few alcoholic drinks lift the heart more than this consecrated wetting of the whistle.

The vicar stood at the church door, shaking hands with the small congregation. Her name was the Reverend Heather Parbury, a tall attractive woman in her late thirties, with a well conditioned bob. I told her about my quest to find Randal's grave.

'Oh. I've no idea at all. I've certainly never seen it. I'll ask Marjorie . . . Marjorie! Marjorie, this gentleman is looking for a grave . . .'

Several of the parishioners gathered round, and I showed them the book where I had found out about Randal's grave. None of them had either seen it or heard of it.

'It could have been moved when the church was rebuilt,' said the vicar. That seemed plausible; the post-Restoration/Glorious Revolution zest for life being swept aside by grim Victorian modernisers.

'I tell you who might know, and that's Stephen . . .' said Marjorie to the vicar.

'Yes, Stephen would be the man to ask. He's the expert on the tombstones.'

'Is he here?' I asked.

'No, he's not due back from Capri for another fortnight.'

So that was that. I wandered around the churchyard, but of John Randal's grave there was no sign. Ale was his meat, ale was his drink, ale did his heart revive, but now he is remembered only by antiquarians. I looked forward to a pint in his local, the Fox and Hounds. I'd arranged to meet Perry there at twelve.

I was a little bit early, and the pub was still not open when I walked into the old bar, which was empty.

I called out, and the landlord came through, and served me a pint. Perry turned up minutes later, clearly shaken. I bought him a pint, too.

'What's up?'

'The Rollright Stones . . . you've got to come and see them.'

'I was hoping we might get lunch here . . .'

'Fully booked, I'm afraid gentlemen,' said the landlord. Mercs and Beamers were starting to pull up in the car-park.

'Come on then,' I said, 'drink up.' Perry drove me the three or four miles up to the stone circle.

The Cotswolds are funny hills. If you come at them from the

east, you hardly notice that you are climbing at all, until you come to the scarp, and find yourself high over the valley of the Severn, looking across the river at the Malverns, the Forest of Dean, and, on a clear day, into Shropshire and Wales, as Hay Bluff, the Black Mixen, and the Stretton Hills stand out on the horizon. The Rollrights are a long way from the drama of the western edge of the hills, but it was obvious that we were quite high up, on top of a down, looking east into the farmland between Oxford and Stratford. The circle is looked after by the Rollright Trust, rather than by English Heritage, and there is a small hut at the entrance, where you are asked to pay 50p. The volunteer on the gate looked as upset as Perry.

'What?'

'Look.'

Someone had been round the circle, and poured yellow paint over all the stones. According to legend, the stones are uncountable; if you count as you walk round one way, and then change direction and count again, you will always reach a different total. We walked round both ways, and so we could see that every stone, however many there were, had been spattered with the paint; a horrific act of deliberate pre-meditated vandalism, which would take months and a lot of money to put right. We spoke to the volunteer on the gate.

'It happened a couple of weeks ago. I don't know what's wrong with people,' she said.

'Who do you think might have done it?' I asked.

'Religious nutters, we think. We let druids and witches hold ceremonies here. Looks like someone doesn't approve.'

'How was church?' asked Perry with some bitterness.

'Good. Very good. Prayer Book.'

'I don't know how you can do it,' said Perry. 'Look at what religion does. Never mind religious wars; look at what the fanatics did to the stones.'

'I can't imagine anyone being fanatically C. of E.,' I said. And I can't. But the idea that the stones were attacked by someone who felt that pagan rituals were satanic seemed entirely plausible. I couldn't help thinking that whoever did it came from Christianity's non-drinking arm. Zen Anglicans enjoy a bit of pagan ritual; Perry and I shared a spliff in the vandalised circle, and headed back to the car to find somewhere for lunch.

After a few miles, we passed the Four Shire Stone. If Middle England were a place, instead of a nonsensical politician's fiction, then it would have to be around here somewhere. The stone marks the meeting place of four of the historic counties, before the boundaries were changed in 1974. Each side of the stone has a name of one of the counties on its side, thus:

Warwickshire

Oxfordshire                                       Worcestershire

Gloucestershire

We drove into Gloucestershire, towards Moreton-in-Marsh. The Fosse Way comes through the town; we had last crossed it outside Glastonbury. Moreton was full of antique shops and crowds of antique shoppers, bussed in by tour companies. We wanted a proper English Sunday lunch, so we went into the imposing Redesdale Arms, where Perry had lamb and I had a wonderful steak-and-kidney pudding, which I hadn't had for years. Batsford Park, once home to Lord Redesdale and his family, is just on the outskirts of the town. Lord Redesdale was a famously eccentric man (who had once owned the village of Great Wolford, selling it in 1924), best remembered now for his daughters, the legendary Mitford sisters: Jessica, the communist and writer; Unity, the fascist and personal friend of Hitler; Diana, also a fascist, who married Oswald Mosley; Deborah, the Dowager Duchess of Devonshire; and Nancy, the novelist and intimate friend of Evelyn Waugh. So this was another pub where Waugh had strong associations, and, as we drove on into the Cotswolds that afternoon, we passed yet another, the Lygon Arms in Chipping Campden. There is another, better-known Lygon Arms, also in the Cotswolds, at Broadway. Waugh had been great friends with the Lygons, and his experience of visiting the family home, Madresfield, fed into the imagining of Brideshead.

We came down from the Cotswolds, and into the Vale of Evesham. Wherever we looked, we were surrounded by apple trees. We were headed for one of the thirteen completely unspoilt pubs, at least according to the mad list that Lucy had shown me in Hay. This one was called the Cider House, and it sits on the outskirts of a village called Defford, in Worcestershire. I'd phoned ahead to check they were open that evening, since we didn't have such a great record of just rocking up. They opened at seven, so we drove around Bredon Hill, which I'd never done before, and which is very beautiful, and found a place to stay in Ashton under Hill. After our early start, we were both knackered, and we slept off our lunches for a couple of hours.

By seven we had arrived at the Cider House. It's not easy to find. It has no sign, other than the licence over the door, and is set right back from the Pershore to Upton-on-Severn road. There is a yard to park the car, and a gate, and a path to a half-timbered cottage whose thatch looks as though it is losing the battle with gravity. I'd never seen thatch that looked shaggy before, like a bear's coat. It drooped towards the earth, almost reaching the ground-floor windows. It was black with age, and was held on with chicken wire. There were benches in front of the cottage and, off to the left, a small shed, maybe twelve foot by ten. This was once the bakehouse; through the windows we could see pews round the walls and a few scrubbed pine tables. There is no bar. The landlord stands in a lean-to on the side of the cottage, selling his cider through a stable door. If the weather is good, you sit or stand in the garden; if it's bad, you go into the old bakehouse, where there is a stove. That's it. There is nowhere like it left in Britain; a unique survival of a rural cider house. Its survival cannot be accounted for by isolation; the M5 passes within three miles of its door, as does the Birmingham-to-Bristol railway line. Strensham Services is just up the road.

'What can I get you, gents?' said the landlord.

'Two pints of cider, please.'

The landlord was wearing overalls and a flat cap, and looked to be about sixty. He poured us two pints. I told him how we'd found his pub; he said that he'd never seen the list of thirteen.

'This is good cider,' I said.

'Brewed for me special, by Bulmer's.'

'It's good strong stuff.'

'Ar.' Not the most garrulous of men. We took our cider into the garden. It was a beautiful spring evening, and we were the first in. The lawn had been recently mown, and that most characteristic of English scents, new-cut grass, filled the air.

'Here we are, Perry, in the green heart of England.'

'Ar.' (It was catching.)

'Peace and tranquillity surround us.'

'If you'd shut up for five minutes.'

'God is in his heaven, and all is right with the world.'

'Poufffffffffffffffffffff.'

'You know, people pay lots of money to go to India, searching for inner peace and spiritual enlightenment. But all they have to do is go to church, have steak-and-kidney pudding for lunch, and then sit drinking cider in a pub garden, to know what peace really is.'

A large minibus pulled into the yard, and a dozen or so very drunk men clambered out, with a sad-looking eleven-year-old girl in tow. They marched through the garden, screaming obscenities. Perry and I pursed our lips in disapproval. Peace and tranquillity are probably false idols, anyway. They ordered their cider at the top of their voices, and milled around us in the garden.

They were members of a rugby team, and they'd been out all day, getting aggressively drunk. The little girl was on an access visit to her father, and this was how her day had been spent. She sat on her own on one of the benches, sipping a bottle of Coke.

'I bet you anything her dad belongs to Fathers 4 Justice,' said Perry.

We picked up our pints, and went over to talk to the landlord, leaving the boorish rugger buggers to shout in the garden. We told him about the longest crawl, and he told us something of the history of the place. Like Eli's, it had been passed down through the female line, and had been in the family at least since the census of 1851, when his wife's great-grandmother had been the owner. But the landlord and his wife had no daughter; their son was in the Navy, and he had no interest in taking it on. They only really kept it going themselves because they felt it was their duty; they owed staying open to their regulars. Last year, the landlord had asked the magistrates for a change in his licensing arrangements. A few of the regulars' wives didn't drink cider, so he'd asked that he might sell wine as well. The magistrate granted the landlord's wish, while admitting that he was sad to see the last cider-only licence go.

'But you've got to keep up with the times,' said the landlord, whose name was Graham.

Above the stable door from where Graham dispensed the cider and the occasional glass of wine, there was a handwritten notice on a piece of cardboard: 'This establishment does not accept euros'. It was amazing that the establishment accepted decimal currency, quite frankly, despite Graham's avowed commitment to staying abreast of the *Zeitgeist*.

As the light faded from the sky, the regulars started to turn up, and the rugby players headed off for their next destination, the sad little girl dragged along in their wake. Peace returned to the Cider House. I noticed that the regulars were being served their cider in half-pint china mugs; crocks, they called them.

It used to be the case that anything that could hold liquid would be used as a drinking vessel. Thomas Heywood in his *Philocothonistra or the Drunkard Opened, Dissected and Anatomized* of 1635 lists a few:

> Of drinking cups, divers and sundry sorts we have, some of them elme, some of box, some of maple, some of holly etc; Mazers, broad-mouthed Dishes, Noggins, Whiskins, Piggins, Crinzes, Ale-bowls, Wassal Bowls, Court dishes, Tankards, Kannes from a bottle to a pint, from a pint to a gill . . . small jacks we have in many ale-houses of the Citie and suburbs, tip'd with silver, besides the great Black Jacks and Bombards . . . we have besides cups made out of horns of beasts, of cockernuts, of goords, of the eggs of ostriches; others made of the shells of divers fishes.

But by the eighteenth century, the glass had achieved the prominence which it still holds. The beauty of glass is that it is see-through; you can get a good look at what you are drinking. The discovery of isinglass meant that beer could be clear, and so would look good in the glass. Cider could be cloudy, whether straw-pressed or not, and so landlords preferred their customers not to look at their brews too closely. This is why, on occasion, you will still find cider being drunk from a crock; not that most modern ciders are not good-looking, but just that the tradition has survived.

The regulars invited us into the parlour. They loved old Perry taking photos, loved our interest. It was an honour to be invited into 'parliament', as they called the tiny room.

'What brings you to the Monkey House, lads?' asked one of the ladies.

I told them about our journey, and asked why they called it the Monkey House.

'That's what all the reg'lars call it. It's because there is a long hill to it from Pershore, and after getting drunk on cider, people would fall off their bikes, get cut, then tell their wives they had been fighting with monkeys,' she said.

'Do you all come from the village?' I asked.

'Ooh, no. They're a bit like that in the village,' she said, pushing up the end of her nose. 'We come from all over; Pershore, Evesham, Tewkesbury, 'round about Bredon Hill.'

'Is it the cider you come for?'

'No,' said an old gentleman sitting next to me. 'It's the company. We like getting in here for a natter. We're family.'

'You should come by on a Thursday,' said another of the ladies, who turned out to be Graham's wife. 'We all bring a bit of grub to share; bread and cheese and that. We've had some smashing times in 'ere.'

The parlour is so small that private conversations are hardly possible. This is a true talking room, where they like to put the world to rights. (Which mostly involves leaving our old friend the Common Market.) And to tell music-hall jokes about their wives.

'How's the wife?' asked one of the regulars of a new arrival.

'Better 'n nothin',' he replied.

The old gentleman sitting next to me said, 'I bought a dishwasher; cost me seven and six for the marriage licence, and it's worked for fifty-three years.' I'm afraid I laughed.

After three pints of Graham's excellent cider, I was more than ready for a slash. The gents is a breeze-block cube, open to the air, with a gutter running around it to take away the piss. They call it the Observatory.

'It was a bloody good place to watch Halley's comet,' said my neighbour.

One of the ladies said, 'Ooh, we're posh. We get a door; and a roof.'

Perry asked if it would be OK to take some photos of the loo, but the landlady said that she'd rather we didn't. The gents loo will not pass Health and Safety's strictures. It is Health and Safety that will close the Monkey House. The parlour is another of the reasons why the Cider House is doomed; Graham can't see into it from his place at the stable door. Health and Safety can't be doing with this. The half a dozen or so men and women, mostly elderly or late-middle-aged who get into the parliament hardly constitute a threat to themselves, one would have thought, and they've been quite happy sprinkling their boots and looking up at the stars for a hundred and fifty years or more; but there you are, the State knows best. It's not the EU that wants to close the Monkey House, despite the beliefs of the regulars; these are not regulations that are coming from Brussels. But the government is quite happy for people to believe that they are. Nor should anyone believe that Health-and-Safety regulations exist to improve the health or the safety of customers. Health-and-Safety legislation exists to make sure that insurance companies have to pay out less often. Fight the power.

'You're ranting again,' said Perry, who was just barely this side of legal, and so driving us back to our B 'n' B. after closing time.

'I know. It's the booze.'

'It's the cider. There's a cider mentality; all cider drinkers are headbangers. That's why they drink it in halves. No one else was drinking it in pints.'

'Oh, I'll be sorry tomorrow. Glastonbury all over again, and no magical water to cure me.'

'Drink some ordinary water before you go to bed,' said Perry.

'I will. But I'll be up and down all night like a bride's nightie.'

'Thank God I've bought those earplugs,' said Perry.

# Easter Monday 12th April

In the hideous glare of a bright spring morning, we crossed the liverish river at Upton-on-Severn, and dragged ourselves by sheer force of will (and a car) up into Great Malvern. We were looking for more water with magical properties. Once again, I had been the victim of cider. Never ever again. Only now we had crossed the Severn we were in the West, and that's cider country, as everyone knows. Bulmer's of Hereford . . . Weston's of Much Marcle . . . Dunkerton's of Pembridge, all lay in wait on the other side of the Malverns, with their sweet sweet liquor and their nauseous headaches. Chesterton wrote a poem about the country we would pass into on the other side of the Malvern Hills;

> The wine they drink in Paradise
> They make in Haute Lorraine;
> God brought it burning from the sod
> To be a sign and signal rod
> That they that drink the blood of God
> Shall never thirst again.
> The wine they praise in Paradise
> They make in Ponterey,
> The purple wine of Paradise,
> But we have better at the price;
> It's wine they praise in Paradise,
> It's cider that they pray.
> The wine they want in Paradise
> They find in Plodder's End,
> The apple wine of Herford,
> Of Hafod Hill and Herford,
> Where woods went down to Herford,

And there I had a friend.
The soft feet of the blessed go
In the soft western vales,
The road of the silent saints accord,
The road from heaven to Herford,
Where the apple wood of Herford
Goes all the way to Wales.

Well, fair enough, since I guess you don't get hangovers in Paradise. But no more cider for me, not in this life. Just coffee. And aspirin. And cool clear water.

We parked the car and went for morning coffee and a handful each of aspirin at the Foley Arms Hotel in the middle of Great Malvern. The Malvern Hills are a sponge made from volcanic rocks, some of the oldest in Europe. They bubble with water; the towns and villages of the hills – Great Malvern, Little Malvern, Malvern Wells, Malvern Link and so on – are blessed with the purest water in Britain. The Queen always takes a few bottles with her when she goes abroad, because you can't trust the water there, can you? Malvern water was drunk in the Middle Ages as an aid to fertility; the first well in the town was dedicated to St Ann, mother of Mary, mother of mothers. In the eighteenth century the drinking of Malvern water was popularised by Dr John Wall, founder of Worcester Porcelain, who subjected it to analysis and declared it free from minerals and salts. The water's purity meant Malvern's popularity as a spa slowly grew during the latter half of the eighteenth century and the first half of the nineteenth. The Foley Arms Hotel, where Perry and I sat ogling waitresses in black Nippies uniforms, was built in 1810, and is a good example of a largely unmucked-about Regency hotel. Malvern was quite smart when the hotel was built, a mini-Bath. In 1810 a little over 800 people lived in the town. By 1921, the population had risen to 20,000, with an additional 25,000 visitors a year.

This population boom was due to a renewed interest in taking the waters, coupled with the arrival of the railway. In the 1840s Doctors Wilson and Gully persuaded the public of the efficacy of

The Turk's Head, St Agnes, Isles of Scilly.

Steve the cidermaker, Churchingford, Somerset.

Eli's in Huish Episcopi.

Gravestone in Ewhurst, Surrey.

Tony Green, aka Sir Gideon Vein.

The Kicking Donkey, Harwell, Oxfordshire.

The Cider House, Defford, Worcestershire.

Liquid gold from Ash's still.

The Ivy Bush, Lampeter, Ceredigion.

Marston's Brewery, Burton-on-Trent, Staffordshire.

Whisky enthusiast at the Bruichladdich Distillery, Islay.

Barman at the Isle of Jura Hotel.

Brooky on Jura.

Hauf and hauf, West Highland Hotel, Mallaig.

Sign in Lerwick, Shetland Isles.

The author in the public bar, Baltasound Hotel, Unst, Shetland Isles.

hydropathic cures. Dr Wilson's book *Water Cure in Chronic Disease* was published in 1846, and ran into twelve editions. The great and good flocked to the doctors' clinics in Malvern, most notably Charles Darwin, who swore by the water cure as the only thing which helped his chronic hypochondria. A strenuous regime of abstemious diet, long walks in the hills and lots of cold water taken internally and externally was the order of the day. Doctors Wilson and Gully would wrap their patients in soaking linen for hours at a stretch, douse them under powerful jets of cold water, and encourage them to drink up to thirty tumblers of water a session. Since exercise, careful diet and drinking lots of pure water are pretty much good for everybody, many people felt a great deal better after a visit to Malvern. The most likely cause of Darwin's illness was what we would now call an 'anxiety disorder', the kind of malady that the water cure was ideally suited to treat. His daughter Anne, his favourite child, was, however, very ill, and the water treatment proved less useful. Some modern commentators have said that the cure probably made her worse. To Darwin's lifelong distress, she died at Malvern in 1851, aged ten.

Darwin wrote: 'Poor dear little Annie, when going on very well at Malvern, was taken with a vomiting attack, which was at first thought of the smallest importance; but it rapidly assumed the form of a low and dreadful fever, which carried her off in ten days.'

Anne Darwin is buried in the churchyard of Malvern Priory, and we went to pay our respects. Hers was the only grave that had flowers growing on it; nice to imagine they were planted by the great naturalist.

Hangovers seemed to fall well within the compass of ailments that the water cure could help. We walked up a steep winding path to St Ann's Well, the nearest of the six wells to the town centre. Old Perry is not as fit as once he was, and we had to make frequent stops. As we climbed the hill, more of England opened up beneath us like a relief map; on a clear day you can see one sixth of the landmass of England and Wales from the top of the Malvern Hills. This is where William Langland had his vision of Piers Plowman, looking down into the 'fair fields full of folk'. We were climbing the Worcestershire Beacon; over the brow of the hill lay the hop gardens and orchards of Herefordshire, the hills and forests of Wales. At the start of the climb, we thought we might make it on past the well, and up to the summit of the Beacon. But, no, let's face it; by the time we were halfway up, it was quite clear that the cider was beginning to take its toll. We were both pleased to wheeze up to the cottage that houses the wellhead, and to drink a few glasses of the most pure water in Britain. Even better than the water was the fact that there was a café in the old well cottage; we sat outside, drinking tea and eating cake, feeling the fog lift from our poor old heads, looking back over England, its fair fields full of housing developments and investment opportunity. The summit we decided to save for another day. Beneath us in Great Malvern, the bells in the priory were ringing. We drank some more water, and bounced down the path back to the car. A stiff walk on a spring morning, with four glasses of water at the end, is the best hangover cure I know.

We were due that evening in Bishop's Castle in Shropshire, where we were going to have two piss-ups in two breweries. I had organised them by the simple expedient of asking my friend Pete Mustil to organise them for me. Pete lives in Presteigne, just over the Welsh border, and we were picking him up at six to drive over to the Castle. We dropped down from the Malverns and headed west into the fertile plains of Herefordshire. There were apple orchards and pear orchards and cherry orchards along the way, some starting to come into bloom. But above all, this part of north Herefordshire and western Worcestershire is known for hops; Charles Faram, one of the largest independent hop merchants, have their headquarters in Malvern. We were too early in the year to see much activity in the fields, I thought, but I had planned to go to the Hop Museum in Bromyard, so that we could find out something about England's second-most-important hop-growing area. (Astute readers will have noticed that we didn't go to Kent, and so you are saved all that stuff about chirpy cockneys going hop-picking for their holidays, interesting though it is.)

As we came over the brow of a small hill, we passed a bow-top caravan parked in a lay-by, in the charge of a young couple. Their horse, still hitched to the van, was munching grass. We stuttered past (Perry was driving), but I asked that we turn round, and go back for a chat.

In Lancaster, during April and May, it is a common sight to see bow-tops coming through the city, as travellers head for the Appleby Horse Fair. These are mostly Romani families, looking forward to their annual knees-up. Almost everywhere else, horse-drawn bow-top caravans are lived in by what the *Daily Mail* used to call 'new-age travellers'. This young and glamourous couple, to my surprise, were Romanis, the first I'd met south of the River Ribble, and they were happy to talk. In winter, they live in a house in Worcester, but come the first sign of spring, they spend as much time as they can in the caravan, looking for work and a place to park up for a week or two. This was only their second day out of the year. They had stopped in the lay-by to give the horse a chance to rest before he had to pull the van up the hill.

'Do you get work in the hop fields?' I asked.

'Used to,' he said. 'This time of year, I'd be stringing. Then tying.'

'Sorry to show my ignorance . . .'

'Stringing is the first job of the year in the hop gardens,' he said. 'That's going on now. Hops grow very tall, and they're supported on wires stretched between the hop poles. Wiring 'em up, that's stringing.'

'My dad worked all his life in hops,' said the girl. 'All winter, we used to sit at home as kids, tying ribbons on the wires, to show where the plants should go. To space 'em out.'

'Then, when you've strung the hop ground, you plant out the hops, and when the bines start growin', you tie 'em on to the wires as they get bigger to train 'em. That's tying.'

'Tying was always women's work, in the past,' said the girl. 'My mother always helped with the tying.'

'So, are you off to do that now?'

He smiled. 'No. It's not worth it now. Farmers keep cutting the wages. The only people who can afford to do it are illegals.'

'Asylum seekers and that,' she said.

'Really?'

'Yes. Give it a couple of years, there'll be no more gypsies working on the hops at all.'

'I don't think it's right,' said the girl. 'My dad worked all his life in hops, and now he can't barely walk.'

'Why? Did he have a fall, or something?'

'No. They all get it, all the old stringers and riggers. It's from spending your life standing on tiptoes on ladders. Your calves go.'

I asked them how they got on with the 'new-age travellers'. I have friends in that community, who travelled in that area, or at least, a little further west. I thought we might have pals in common. They didn't recognise any of the names I mentioned.

'They're drop-outs, most of the travellers,' he said.

'We try to stay out of their way,' said the girl.

I'd forgotten how conservative Romanis can be. They are, in their eyes, the aristocrats of the travelling community, and drop-outs and illegal workers are well beneath them in the social order.

'Is there anywhere we might find gypsies working in the hop gardens now?'

'There's a place out by Suckley, round that way. You could try down there.'

We thanked them for their time, and headed back on the road.

A quick note about hops; hops are the difference between ale and beer. Beer is made with hops; ale isn't; or wasn't. You can't actually buy 'real ale' at all, and if you could, you wouldn't like it. The first beer was imported into England from the Low Countries in 1400; before that date, ale was made of just malt, water and yeast. The ale that the Saxons introduced into Britain, and which was the staple drink in this country for almost a thousand years, would taste very sweet to modern palates. Hops grow wild in the hedgerows in bines of up to twenty feet in length. It is a close relative of cannabis. But nobody in England seems to have thought of adding the aromatic 'petals' to ale. It's not easy to cultivate; it's only really Kent and Herefordshire where the soil and climate are right. Hops were first grown commercially in Kent, to any useful degree, by Flemish immigrants, in 1524. Hops added flavour, and bitterness, and, most importantly from a brewer's perspective, they acted as a preservative; beer flavoured with hops lasted longer than the unhopped ale. Throughout the fifteenth century, more and more beer was brewed, although not without opposition from those who felt that ale was best drunk unadulterated. It was not until the end of the seventeenth century that unhopped ale disappeared completely. Now, although some lightly hopped beers are still described as 'ales', beer has become our national drink. It's worth noting that two of the drinks which have played a central part in British life, beer and gin, were both introduced from the Netherlands. Now I come to think of it, skunk is Dutch, too. Is it some evil master plan to render the British insensible?

We turned south off the A44 (a road to rival the A272 in beauty and interest) and wound our way over Bringsty Common towards Suckley through the lanes, looking for places where we might find illegals working. We couldn't find any hop gardens, but we did find some beautiful orchards, with sheep grazing under the boughs.

'Look at these, Perry. Aren't they something? Let's take a photo.'

'I thought you were through with cider? Anyway, they don't look like apple trees to me.'

'Of course they're apple trees. Hundreds of years old by the looks of them.'

'Pouffffffffffff.'

These trees were so ancient, and they so perfectly symbolised the ageless nature of the cider maker's art, that I just had to make Perry take some shots. There was a cottage on the other side of the road, with an old gentleman working in his garden. This being a friendly part of the world, he strolled across to say hi to the two hippies taking photos of the old apple trees.

'These are wonderful trees. The oldest apple trees we've seen,' I said.

'Bless you, they're not apple tress. They're cherries.'

Perry snorted.

'And they're younger'n you, boy. Thirty-nine years, they are.'

Perry snorted louder.

'Still, it must be lovely for you, living next to such beautiful trees.'

'Ar, well, it's all right, I suppose. Problem is, the blossom smells so intense. When they're in blossom, you can't sleep with your window open. Fills the house, the smell does. Specially after rain.'

'We were looking for hop gardens, really. To see if we could meet some people who work with hops.'

'Well, it's Easter Monday, boy. No one works on Easter Monday, do they? Nearest you're going to get to a hop worker today is me.'

'You worked in the hop gardens?'

'Course I did. Forty year 'n' more.'

'What did you do?'

'I did it all, boy. First you did the stringing; tied knots in the strings, big knots like bees. Then you pegged 'em out, and passed the strings up to the joker on the jockey. That's the stiltman. Then you had to come back ten days later, and peg 'em out again, 'cos the hares dug 'em all up. They get all excited in the spring, dig 'em up for fun.'

'Did they use stilts?'

'What, the hares?'

'No, I mean, the guys at the top of the hop poles.'

'Ar, in the old days. Ladders were no good for stringing. I was a stiltman too.'

'You walked on stilts?'

'I told you, boy. You had to be able to walk on stilts if you worked in hops, 'fore they mechanised it . . . it's all cherry pickers now.'

His name was Harry Davies. He must have been in his late sixties. His hands were as big as my head, and looked as though they were covered in soft brown leather. Talking to Harry made me feel like a Bangkok lady-boy. I would rather set fire to my eyebrows than walk on stilts. I told Harry this.

'Oh, I was good on stilts, I was. Born to it, everyone round 'ere was. There was even one old family used to make all the sieves for hop-collecting. You got paid by the sieve load, you see. Yes, there was even an old family up in the village made the sieves from willow. And they did all the shopping baskets for the local ladies. They taught me how to do it. I could do the sides all right, but I never could master the bottoms. That was the hardest part, the bottoms. They've all died off now.'

'Did the farmers use the gypsies to pick the hops?'

'Did they? Cor, I can remember fifty or sixty caravans parked up just over in the next field at picking time.' Harry pointed beyond the cherry orchards. 'Used to come from as far afield as Cornwall. And all the horses, and their fires . . . marvellous, it was.'

'Not so much now?'

'No, boy. Not any more they don't come. I miss them most of all. I loved having the old gypsies about.'

'Do the farmers use illegal immigrants instead?'

Harry looked at me what my mum calls 'old-fashioned'. 'Well, they find it all but impossible to find anyone at all. I wouldn't be surprised if they had to.' No more would he say.

'Thanks, Harry. Is there a pub near by we can get lunch?'

'Ar. Now, thereby hangs a tale . . .'

Harry is a commoner. This means he has certain rights over what happens to Bringsty Common. Harry's cottage is right on its edge. The nearest pub is a couple of miles away, on the other side of the common. It's called the Royal Oak. Although it's right on the A44, business has been slow, and the owners put it up for sale as a private dwelling house. The commoners objected, exercised their rights, and were able to stop their pub being turned into another Kicking Donkey.

'And all the commoners have chipped in a few bob to save it, 'n' all. It's not open yet, but if you come back later in the year . . .'

'Not everything has been lost, then,' I said.

'No, boy. Not quite.'

In the mean time, Harry sent us to the Talbot Inn at Knightwick.

'A good pint. And there's a big hop-yard behind it, though you'll not find anyone working. It's Easter Monday.'

We stopped at the Talbot for a late lunch. Harry was right, it was a good pint. And was there, perhaps, a hint of head on the beer? At some point, we were going to cross from the South, where there is no head (because we don't like fizzy drinks, and because we want a whole pint), and into the North, where beer served without a head is regarded as an insult. Would the change come abruptly, or would there be, as I suspected, a transitional zone? The beer at the Talbot seemed to confirm this theory; there was, for the first time on the trip, a ghost of foam on the sides of our glasses as the beer went down.

After lunch, we walked through the hop-yard behind the pub. Harry was right again; there was no one working. It was difficult to see that there was much left to do, anyway. The hop gardens look like a hundred thousand string vests hung up to dry. Rows of poles stretched into the distance. Wires ran between all the poles, both lengthways and across the rows. Every couple of feet along each of the rows, there was something like a tent peg stuck in the soil. From each peg, three lines of twine fanned out to meet the wires. There were countless thousands of lengths of twine, a mad cat's cradle, ready to support the hops as they grew. The whole effect was like a Cartesian graph in string, and as we moved through the hop grounds the straight lines joining the co-ordinates seemed to converge to form insubstantial curves.

By each of the pegs, there was a hop plant, six inches high. They looked more like brambles than they did like the other members of the order cannabinaceae. By late September to mid October, the bines will have grown up to twenty feet in length. Then the scaly petals will be picked, and dried, and be ready for the brewers. Some of the bines will be sold intact, for pubs to hang over the bar, and for *Country Living* readers to zhoosh up their kitchens.

A hop garden is one of the seven wonders of British agriculture. The level of skill and manual dexterity which goes into stringing the gardens boggles my mind. Growing hops is one of the most labour-intensive parts of the brewing process, and all the workers, at every step of the way, are grossly underpaid. It's good that we have the chance these days to buy Fair Trade bananas and coffee. Why not extend the scheme to British produce, too? Why not pay more for beer, and pay the highly skilled men and women who work in the gardens the minimum wage?

We drove on into Bromyard, to find the Hop Museum, newly

located in the Tourist Information Office. It was closed. We peered through the windows at mannequins on stilts, mannequins carrying sieves full of hops.

Perry said, 'I am looking forward to the piss-up in the brewery this evening.'

I said, 'Fuck off.'

We headed west once more on the A44, through Leominster, and towards the Empty Quarter that is Radnorshire and South Shropshire. This is my favourite part of Planet Earth, and friends and family get sick of me going on about how it's God's Own Country. But it is. A little bit ahead of schedule, due to the Hop Museum being closed, our first stop in Presteigne was at our friend Gilly's house. Gilly is a photographer and a gardener. We go back a long way; she was one of the witnesses at my wedding to Lily. Perry first met Gilly at our post-wedding party. Ever since, Perry and Gilly have had just the tiniest perceptible twinkle in their eyes for one another; perhaps it's the photography. So when Perry suggested that she accompany us on our piss-up in two breweries, Gilly agreed at once. The three of us went and picked up Pete Mustil.

It is difficult to believe now, but there was a time, not so very long ago, when fitting in with your neighbours, agreeing with the government and working like a dog to pay a 110% mortgage was seen as a bad thing. This time was called 'the sixties'. In those days, young people saw themselves as what was known as 'free'. They had watched their parents flog their guts out for a pittance and the silent approval of their neighbours, and, although they were grateful, they didn't fancy it for themselves, and they went off and did things with their lives. Pete remembers this time, and so has dedicated his life to doing interesting, valuable and rewarding things. He sets things up; festivals, community music projects, a craze for the tango. He is currently the founder and editor of the best monthly events magazine in Britain, which is called *Broad Sheep*. Although Presteigne is a lively town by Radnorshire standards, there are not really enough events to sustain a monthly events magazine, not even if you count the knitting circle and the Presteigne Model Railway

Society, so Pete's catchment area extends from Shrewsbury in the north to Ross-on-Wye in the south, from Leominster in the east to Llanwrtyd Wells in the west. No one knows what's happening in this patch better than Pete Mustil.

The two breweries were both in Bishop's Castle, twenty miles to the north of Presteigne across the Clun Forest. The first was called the Three Tuns, at the top of the town. It was one of the four extant pub breweries which CAMRA identified in 1974; the Blue Anchor in Helston was another. The second pub/brewery was at the bottom of the town, and was called the Six Bells, and was set up ten years or so ago by the pub's landlord, Big Nev. Pete told me about Big Nev as I drove, while Perry and Gilly giggled like schoolchildren in the back seat.

'He's a good bass-player, is Nev. Runs a nice little R 'n' B band. He looks after the brewery, and his brother Colin does the pub. He actually makes a brew called "Big Nev". I bet you haven't met many people who've got a brew named after them.'

'And the Three Tuns?'

'Run by a guy called Bill Bainbridge. A real-ale buff. Very keen. We're meeting him at seven, and Nev at nine.'

We parked the car by the Six Bells (a useful tip this; always park your car at the bottom of the hill, by your last pub, and then walk up the hill to where you mean to start). Perry and Gilly walked behind me and Pete, tittering inanely. These days, the Castle is a hippy town, like a mini-Totnes. Twenty years ago when I first came there with Lily, tumbleweed rolled up the High Street. Nothing else moved, except for a skanky dog we saw disappearing down an alley. Then the hippies discovered the Castle and brought it back to life. One of the breweries had survived because Bishop's Castle was a forgotten backwater in the unending flood of time. The other brewery had started because the town began to fill up with lively creative people attracted by low property prices. Hippies add value.

Bill, in his mid- to late fifties, was waiting for us in the bar of the Three Tuns. He had a beard, and an anorak, and was wild-eyed with enthusiasm. He was already talking to a couple also in their fifties, who he introduced as John and Carol.

'You see, the thing is, I only own the brewery. It's actually quite separate from the pub. Try the 3X. They keep it well. Mind you, not so well as they do at the White Horse in Clun. Exhibition standard, that is. Hello. Yes. Got your beer? Good. Now, I only bought the brewery this year. So we're not in full production. We aim to do seventy barrels a week, but at the moment we're doing about ten . . . hello? More friends of yours?'

It was more friends. It was Matthew and Kate. Matthew used to go out with my girlfriend. Kate is a yoga instructor. They live in London, and have a place in Presteigne.

'Ian! Perry! Pete! Gilly! Hi!'

'Hello! What are you doing here?' I said.

'We've been up for Easter . . . been walking on the Stiperstones. Came in here for a quiet drink on the way back to Presteigne,' said Matthew. 'What about you?'

'Well, we're here for a trip round the brewery.'

'God, how fantastic,' said Kate. 'Can we come?'

'Of course you can,' said Bill. 'Refresh your glasses, and I'll take you round. Why don't you come too, John and Carol?'

We all had another pint of 3X, and then the eight of us followed Bill outside into the yard.

'Now, the earliest part of the brewery dates back to 1642, but the really interesting part of the building is the tower, built by John Roberts in 1890. Now, this is the only surviving miniature tower brewery. Big breweries still have them; a good example is St Austell. They operate by gravity. The Victorians worked out that if you could get your water pumped to the top, either by steam pump, or town pressure, as in our case, and if you could winch your malt to the top too, then all the other processes can operate by gravity. This prevents the need to pump or ladle the beer. So I think the best place to start would be at the top . . .'

'Hello, Will,' said Pete to his friend Will, who was just about to go into the pub.

'Oh, hello, Pete. What are you up to? Oh, hello, Ian.'

'Hello, Will. We're going on a guided tour of the brewery.'

'That sounds interesting. Can I come?'

'Of course you can,' said Bill.

'Hold on a minute,' said Will. 'I'll just get a pint.'

'That seems like a good idea,' said Matthew. 'Anyone else?'

'Yes, please.'

When Will and Matthew came back with the beers, Bill took us into the brewery building.

'Now,' said Bill. 'Because this is a tower brewery . . .'

'What's a tower brewery?' asked Will.

'I'll explain later,' said Pete.

'. . . we should start at the top . . . this way . . . mind your heads . . . stairs are a bit narrow . . . that's it . . . one more floor . . . come on . . . keep up . . . here we go . . . this is it. Now, this is the malt loft. Three storeys up. Look, this is the original winch for the malt, but we use this electric one of course. And this is the hot liquor tank. That's what we call water. After the water has been burtonised . . .'

'What's burtonised?' asked Matthew. I knew this one.

'Brewers add mineral salts to their water, so that it mimics the water in Burton-on-Trent,' I said.

'What, all breweries?' said Kate.

'Well, not the ones in Burton-on-Trent, obviously,' I said.

'Yes, that's right,' said Bill. 'If you are making a pale ale, then the water in Burton is the best. If you are making a darker ale, of course, then you'd want your water more like London water, which is more suitable to a darker ale, such as porter.'

'That's because all the water in London has been pissed through people seven times,' said Matthew.

'Why would that make it dark?' Will asked. 'Wouldn't that make it piss-coloured?'

'Well, now, of course, you also use darker malts, roasted malts for darker ales. So, well, after the malt has been hauled up, you put it into the pre-masher with the hot liquor. We use a high mashing temperature, as the beta enzymes leave more non-fermentable sugars, which gives a thicker beer . . . hello? Where are John and Carol?'

'Who are John and Carol?' said Matthew.

'They were there in the pub, and outside,' I said, 'but I'm not sure they came up here with us.'

'Really,' said Bill. 'I thought they were right behind us. Are you sure?'

'Fairly sure,' I said.

'That's odd,' said Bill.

'Where's Perry and Gilly?' said Pete.

'We're down here,' shouted Perry from the floor below. 'Just taking a few photos.'

'We'll come up,' shouted Gilly.

'Are John and Carol down there with you . . . ?' said Bill.

'Who are John and Carol?' said Gilly, as her head popped through the hatch to the malt loft.

'I don't think they came into the brewery,' said Perry, following her.

'Really? Are you sure? Well, never mind,' said Bill. 'Lets go down and visit the mash tun on the next floor. That's where the starch in the malt is converted to sugar . . . careful on these steep stairs . . . that's it . . . here we are. The mash tun. Now, the mash tun is the heart of the brewery. This one was installed by John Roberts when he built the tower . . .'

'Who's John Roberts?' said Will.

'He's the man who built the brewery,' I said.

'Yes, that's right,' said Bill. 'And John Roberts the second wrote the recipes for the beer we make today. Some of the older locals have been kind enough to say that it's as good now as it's ever been. It was John Roberts the first, of course, who installed the mash tun, but we've just lined it with stainless steel. Traditionally, they used gunmetal.'

'Does it make a difference to the flavour of the beer?' I asked.

'It doesn't seem to. Now, some breweries use stainless steel for the coppers, but as you can see, mine is copper. That doesn't really seem to make a difference either. After the mash has worked for a couple of hours, it gets fed through to the coppers, where the malt liquor is boiled, and you pitch in the hops, and get it in a good rolling boil. Now, we don't put all the hops in at once. You put it in in three stages, a couple of stages of hops for bittering, and then, just before the end of the boil, some further hops for aroma.'

'Ooh, what's all this foamy stuff in tanks?' said Kate from the next room. We all went through to have a look.

'Well, now, that's the beer,' said Bill, following us, resigned by now, no doubt, to indifference from less technically inclined visitors towards his mash tun.

'You keep it in open vats?' said Pete, peering at the beer, which was working so vigorously that spume spilled down from the tanks and on to the floor.

'Yes,' said Bill. 'We might have to change that. We had a couple of brews go wrong in the autumn, and couldn't work out why. Then we realised that it was because of yeast from the apple tree in the garden next door.'

'Really? It's that sensitive a process?' I said.

'Yes,' said Bill, smiling. 'Just yeast from the skins of apples outside the tower is enough to make it go wrong . . .'

'When does the yeast go in?' I asked.

'Well, that's after the boil. In the fermentation tanks. You pitch in the yeast as the wort cools. Fermentation won't start until the wort reaches eighteen degrees.'

'Where are you off to, Will?' said Pete.

'Just going for a slash.'

Matthew and Kate followed Will down the steep stairs to the ground floor, so we did too.

'And finally, it comes down here for barrelling,' said Bill. We all gathered hungrily around one of the barrels.

Bill tried to soldier on, but his cause was lost, and he knew it.

'Now, barrelling takes place . . . by . . . you . . . er . . . would you like some beer?'

'Yes please, Bill.'

'Don't mind if I do.'

'You're too kind.'

So we ventured on to our fourth pint. Will came back, and he had one too. Bill's enthusiasm for his craft had been swept aside by his visitors' enthusiasm for his product. It really is very very good.

You should go to the White Horse in Clun, and try it for yourself.

'We've got to go now, Bill,' said Pete, as he finished his beer. 'We've got to go to Big Nev's. He's expecting us.'

A small moue of disappointment mingled with disapproval crossed Bill's face.

'Yes, of course. Well, I hope it was of some use.'

'It was, Bill. Thank you so much for showing us round,' I said.

Now we headed down the High Street towards the Six Bells, a lively, friendly place with some folk musicians holding a session in the public bar. John and Carol were in the corner; we waved hello. While we waited for Big Nev, we all had a pint of 'Big Nev', and it was very very good too. When Nev turned up, he was wearing a T-shirt which bore the legend 'Everybody Loves A Big Fat Bastard'. He took us out the back, to the old barn where he brews 'Big Nev'. But really, he was much more interested in talking to Will and Pete about motorbikes than he was in showing us where he worked. I pressed him.

He sighed. 'Well, there's not much to it really. You mix malt and hot water, add yeast and hops, then barrel it up after a few days. Will, did you see that Kawasaki parked up outside?'

'Yes, but I bet there's an interesting story behind your mash tun. The mash tun is the heart of the brewery,' I said.

Big Nev looked at me like I was mad. 'Well, it's an old milk tank. I got an old milk tank and cut it in half. Pete, did you see Cradley Heathens might be getting a new track? I haven't been to speedway for donkey's years.'

We all agreed that we would be more comfortable back in the pub, where I bought everyone a pint. John and Carol had gone home, but the musicians were still in session. Matthew and Kate headed back to their car. Will went home, too. Me and Pete and Perry and Gilly went for a curry, because you have to be in a very small town before you can't get a curry.

'You see,' I said to Perry, as he drove us back to Pete's, where we were crashing for the night, 'I *can* organise a piss-up in a brewery.'

'Your friends can, anyway,' said Perry.

# Tuesday 13th April

In the morning, we said goodbye to our Presteigne friends, and worked our way on hill roads back to the A44. It really is a superb road; it starts in Moreton-in-Marsh, and ends up in Aberystwyth, and if a latter-day Pieter Boogaart wanted to write another book about a British road, he could do a lot worse. The road climbs high over the Radnor Forest towards Llandrindod Wells, known to the locals as Landod. Radnorshire is the size of Surrey, but it has a population of just over 20,000, and much of the county is taken up with thrilling mountain scenery. I learned to drive on the stretch of the A44 between New Radnor and Landod; it took me ages to pass my test because I kept staring open-mouthed out of the window at the view. The road bypasses Landod, goes right through the middle of Rhayader, and on to Llangurig, under the shadow of Plynlimon. Then it starts to really climb. Plynlimon is not a spectacular mountain, but it is the third-highest in Wales, and we were soon up in the clouds. The road winds along the headwaters of the Wye, crosses the watershed, and starts its slow descent into the Welsh-speaking bit of Wales. Just as you see the first road sign for Devil's Bridge, there is the George Borrow Hotel.

Borrow was a nineteenth-century writer, whose best-known work is still *Wild Wales*, in which he travelled all over Wales with his wife and children. The hotel where once he stayed and which now bears his name stands alone on the westerly side of Plynlimon, relying on the A44 for pretty much all its trade. We stopped for lunch. In the gents, there was a picture of Jane Fonda as Barbarella, which I found a bit troublesome after a fortnight of sharing a room with Perry Venus.

And here, dear reader, I need to blindfold you, spin you round, and lead you by the hand through the woods. If you take the

Ordnance Survey Landranger map, put the point of a compass on the George Borrow Hotel, and set it to measure out a circle with a radius of fifteen miles, where we are going next will fall within its circumference. I could write about scoring twenty quid's worth of spliff and Customs & Excise or the police would not bat an eyelid. But this trip will drive them crazy. We were off to meet a pal of mine who does something very very illegal indeed.

Call him Ash.

I phoned him up a few days before Perry and I set off for the Scillies to make sure we were OK to come and visit him.

'Yeah, of course. Look forward to seeing you. I'll brew some ale.'

Brewing unhopped ale is not illegal of course, but putting it through a still is. That's what Ash does to keep himself in spirits. We were off to make hooch. Moonshine, as they call it in the Ozarks.

In the eighteenth century, home distilling was part of everyday existence. Big houses would have a still room, looked after by the still-room maid, and the mistress of the house would take great pride in producing perfumes from the garden, and in making her own essences. Good cooks didn't buy vanilla essence; they distilled it. But since the Excise Act of 1823, you need a licence for a still, and you can't get one. In Scotland, the illicit whisky trade went straight, with the consequence that you can go to the pub later and buy a dram of Glenlivet, though 70 per cent of the purchase price is excise. In the States, making moonshine is still illegal, but lots of people are at it; you can buy a still quite openly, though you have to go up into the woods to use it; it is almost a constitutional right in the mountain states of the South. Spend a couple of hours in a pub in the west of Ireland, and someone is going to offer you a bottle of poteen. But in England and Wales, the tradition of home distilling has largely died out. Old Ash is merely keeping alive the guttering flame of the art.

Ash is a traveller and the happiest man I know. He always wears a filthy pair of dungarees and a tea cosy for a hat. It's quite hard to pin down his age, but to judge from his stories, he must be sixty-two or sixty-three. He's been travelling, one way or another, since 1959, when he read *On the Road*.

'Day I finished reading it, I packed a bag, put on my duffel coat, went down the road, stuck out my thumb and never went home again.'

Home was in Liverpool, but all trace of Scouse accent has long gone. Now he sounds like Danny from *Withnail & I*. In fact, since he claims to know Bruce Robinson quite well, he has to be a contender for Danny's original. He looks a bit like David Essex, with Robert Redford skin, gold earrings and a smile of dazzling beauty. He is a legendary ladies' man. I was talking to a girl in her thirties in a pub in Lampeter a few years ago, and for some reason, I asked her if she knew Ash.

A dreamy far-away look crossed her face.

'Oh, I did love him, Ian. I know it was wrong. I was only fifteen, and he was forty. My brother threatened to kill him. But I did love him.'

These days, Ash rents a few acres of woodland for a shilling a year. That's 5p to our younger readers. He parks his big old Iveco van up there for much of the time, and goes round the festivals all summer, where he makes and sells mobile sculptures from scrap metal. The van is both his living space, and his workshop; he opens an awning on its side, gets out his work bench and tools, and it becomes a travelling forge. He keeps his previous van in the wood, too. It doesn't run any more, but it acts as a bedroom for his daughter Rowena and her boyfriend when they come to stay. And he's even gone permanent these days; he's built an open-sided shed from some poles he has cut in the woods and some corrugated-iron sheeting he skipped in Tregaron. So far as is possible, he likes to be self-sufficient. He has permission from the landowners to take wood for his fire. He's made a veg patch in the woods. He has a few spliff patches too, hidden around the hills. And he runs a still.

We bumped along the bit of abandoned railway track that leads to his homestead. After perhaps a mile driving through pine woods, we saw smoke from his fire. We parked up by the van. Rowena and her loppy boyfriend Max were hammering away on the work bench. Ash has trained Rowena how to make beautiful things from scrap metal, and she in turn has trained Max to do some of the less delicate work. She and Max were making necklaces to sell at Glastonbury.

I had brought the gallon of rough cider the team had given us in Churchingford.

'Hello, Ian,' said Rowena, with a heart-breaking smile, inherited from her father.

'Hello, Rowena. Where's the old feller?'

'He's just gone into the woods for a shit. What's that you've got there?'

'Rough cider.'

'Well done. I'll get some glasses.' She climbed into the van, and came back with five half-pint tankards. Ash came down the track, with a water jug in one hand, a spade in the other, and a towel over his arm. He has no time for people who moan about the loos at Glastonbury. He put down his requisites and we hugged. I introduced Perry.

'Nice to meet you. Come and sit by the fire.' Two folding camp chairs and an old wheelchair made up an impromptu three-piece suite. Ash settled in the wheelchair, while me and Perry took the flimsy camping chairs, with a degree of caution. Rowena brought us each a glass of cider. I told Ash where it had come from.

'That's good. It drives me mad when you meet pissheads who don't know how to make booze. You see these fucking brew-crew lads at the festivals; always buying beer off me they are. I say to 'em, it costs fucking nothing to make. Nothing! And it couldn't be easier. What do you fucking do? Stick some sugar and yeast in some water, with some malt and hops. Make your own! But they don't.'

'What about distilling? Is that easy?'

'Distilling is easy; the difficult bit is making the still.'

'So where is it?'

'Next to you.'

We were sitting by the shed. A couple of old oilcans, one advertising 'Shell Grease', were linked together by bits of old hosepipe to half a copper immersion heater chopped about to look like an overblown kettle with a whistle instead of a spout.

The old immersion heater was on a small Calor gas ring, which was up on a bench Ash had built from some pallets. Next to me on the ground was a flagon, almost full of a clear liquid, with a hosepipe leading into it from the last of the oilcans.

'What, that's it?'

'What do you fuckin' think?'

'I don't know really. Some huge contraption up in the woods.'

'No need. This works a treat. The bottom can is what they used to call a worm tub. The condenser. Here's an old one,' he said, scrabbling about in a pile of scrap metal to show me better. Copper piping was tight wound in a spiral inside a rusty old can.

Ash talked me through the stages of his still.

'You put the ale in here,' he said, pointing to the old immersion heater, 'and you heat it up so it boils. The still is like a giant sealed kettle. The steam from the beer is forced into the tube of the condenser; cold water comes in at the bottom here, from the top tank. The water gets heated by the steam in the tube. As it warms, it rises, and comes out the top here. This draws more cold water in from the top tank. The steam condenses as it loses heat coming down the worm tube, and it turns into liquid gold, which you can see dripping into the flagon. Shall I do a spliff?'

'What about having a drop of the good stuff?' I asked.

'Fuck, no,' said Ash. 'That's the first time through . . . what's called "firsts". Here, taste it . . .' Ash pulled the hose from the flagon, let a few drops of the clear liquid fall into a spoon, and put the hose back. He held out the spoon for me to try. I sipped a drop.

'That hurt,' I said.

'I wouldn't have swallowed it,' said Ash.

'Will I go blind?'

'You already are blind, you wanker,' said Ash.

'Am I going to go more blind?'

'When did you start, Ash?' said Perry.

'Early eighties. There was an oil crisis. I thought I might learn how to make fuel, so at least I could run the bike into the village.' Ash keeps a little Yamaha 50, big enough for local errands, small enough to stick in the back of the van when the summer comes and he's travelling.

'How did you learn?' Perry asked.

'Read a few books.'

'Fuel?' I croaked.

'Yeah. That stuff you just drank. Once I tasted it, I thought it was much too good to burn. By the time it's been through three times, it's 100% proof.'

'Three times?'

'Yeah. Firsts is nearly through . . . hang on. You roll that spliff.'

Ash passed me his home-grown, took the flagon, which was now full, poured the contents into the still, adjusted the flame on the gas ring, and sat down again in his wheelchair.

'Don't you put the hose back into the flagon?'

'No. The first lot through is called the feints, and it's no good. Full of nasty stuff. So, as they say, you let the feints fall to the floor. You got to keep an eye on it, make sure you don't let too much run away. The bit you want is called the middle cut. We'll have to sit here by the fire and drink your cider while it goes second time through. That's called "doubles". Where's that spliff?'

So we sat by the fire, drinking cider as the afternoon wore on. The sun was shining through the trees. Rowena and Max were making jewellery at the work bench. A light breeze caught smoke from the fire. The gas ring hissed, and the still bubbled. We smoked Ash's home-grown. Clear liquid leaked out from the end of the hose. Ash let it run for a minute or two, and then put the hose back into the flagon, which slowly began to fill.

I got Ash to tell Perry some of his stories.

In the early sixties, Ash shared a flat with the blues singer Long John Baldry. They used to go busking together up Ladbroke Grove, Baldry singing and playing guitar, and Ash handing round the hat. Often, they were accompanied by a young ukulele player known as 'Long-Haired Eric'.

'Clapton,' Ash told us. 'Baldry was giving him guitar lessons. But he always used to play the ukulele when we went busking. This would have been '61, '62. Didn't see him again till about '68.

I never really followed music, and I'd been in Afghanistan for a couple of years. I was the first person to import Afghan coats into this country . . . did you know that? Met him up the King's Road. Ash! he said. Long-Haired Eric, I said. What are you up to these days? Still playing the ukulele? Cunt never spoke to me again.'

He met the Beatles with Baldry, in the 2i's coffee bar, in late 1962.

'What did you think?' I asked.

'Not much,' said Ash. 'I was into jazz. What would you think if you met Busted?'

'Did you prefer the Stones?'

'Oh yeah. I still think of Jagger as a mate.'

So we sat around the fire some more, until the afternoon began to shade into evening. The flagon was three-quarters full, and the cider was more than half gone. Rowena and her boyfriend were packing away their work, and tidying the bench.

Ash stood up, and stretched. 'Nearly ready to go through one more time . . . Are you hungry?'

We agreed that we were.

'What about you?' said Ash to the workers. They joined us by the fire, and accepted some more of the cider. Ash poured the flagon into the still, threw in a couple of handfuls of orange peel, and turned up the heat on the gas ring a little.

'Is that all you use as your botanicals?' I asked.

'Yep. Lemon peel if I've got it, as well.'

'Where do you get your water from up here?' asked Perry.

'Rainwater. I collect it in butts.'

'So the hooch is made from rainwater?'

'Yes, my friend. Pure rainwater.'

Then he made us chilli beans and rice on the fire. The hose went back into the flagon for the last time. We ate our beans, washed down with the last of the cider. After dinner, Rowena and Max went off to the van that served them as a bedroom, while Ash passed his pipe, and told some more of the stories.

'I had this cat, called Procol Harem,' Ash told us. 'A Burmese, a sweetie she was. At this time, '66, '67, I was dealing acid to the beautiful people. Sold it to Hendrix a few times. Gary Brooker was one of my regulars. He played in a group called the Paramounts. He was always round mine. What's your cat called Ash? he asked me. Procol Harem, I said. So they changed the name of the band.'

'But Ash, that's one of the great unsolved mysteries of rock 'n' roll!' said Perry.

'What is?'

'Who owned the cat that Procol Harem were named after.'

'Is it? Well, it was me.'

As evening turned to night, Ash fetched some more wood, and we drew a little closer to the fire, pulled our jackets around us. The moon was rising behind the hill. The flagon was almost half full.

'Is it ready now?'

Ash stretched. 'You're always in a fucking hurry. That's your problem.'

'You're the only person who ever said that to me.'

'He's the slowest driver on God's earth,' said Perry.

'I'm like the Cadbury's Caramel bunny behind the wheel,' I said.

'If you think you can drive slow,' said Ash, 'you should try driving my van from here to Glastonbury.'

'How long does it take?'

'A week. Ten days.'

He stood to attend to the still. The trebles had run through. After a slow day of love, Ash had made half a gallon of hooch. He held it up to the light of the moon.

'Lovely. Now to test it.' He tipped the flagon, put his finger inside, wetted it, and held a lighter to his fingertip. It burned with a blue flame.

'See? Hundred per cent proof. Burns too quick to feel anything. We need to get it down to about 40 per cent. You know it's right when you can feel it. A little sting. It's too weak if your finger hurts. Want a go?' Ash asked me.

'Fuck off. You do action, I do reflection.'

Ash had a gallon of water he had already run through the still. He added it to the flagon, until it was three-quarters full. He dipped his finger; once again, he set light to it.

'Bit more. First time I did it, I had a glass of this stuff in one hand and a fag in the other. When I looked, I saw my glass was on fire. Just the spark of my fag set it off.'

He tipped another slug of the water into the flagon, dipped his finger, lit it.

'Nearly,' he said.

'Do you sell it?' said Perry.

'No, it's for friends and family only. I sell the stills.'

'No?'

'Not no. Yes. This is the eighth still I've built. Sold all the others, and showed the people who bought 'em how to do it. I'm the Godfather of distilling in these hills . . . I am no longer alone.'

Ash added a couple more jiggers of water. Dipped his finger. Lit it.

He shook his finger, and blew on it.

'Perfect. Warm hooch, anybody?'

'Yes please, Ash,' we said.

We took the glasses that had held our cider, and Ash poured us each a half inch.

It was warm, like mother's milk.

'You're a lucky man, Ash,' said Perry.

'Well, yeah. I am. It's like I always say; the past is a comfortable void . . . the future is a less comfortable void, waiting to be filled . . . but the present is lovely. Cheers.'

# Wednesday 14th April

In the morning, I was woken by bright sunlight behind white blinds. When I opened my eyes, I could see that I was in a white room, with an old schoolroom map of Africa hanging on the wall. I was lying on a futon mattress under a white duvet. Despite my over-enthusiasm for Ash's brew, I could still see. My head hurt less than I deserved. I reached for my specs, walked over to the window, and pulled up the blind. I looked over small fields to the Irish Sea, calm in the morning sun. On the other side of a blue bay was a white Welsh seaside town, climbing away from its fishing harbour up two narrow valleys. We had crossed the country to the wild Welsh coast, and I was in one of my most favourite places in the world: the house of Perry Venus. I pulled on my jeans, and tottered downstairs. Perry was cooking breakfast.

'Were you OK to drive?' I asked.

'Yeah. I only sipped the hooch. Slipped most of it back into the flagon when Ash wasn't looking.'

'Did I snore on the way back?'

'You always snore. I enjoyed sleeping with my wife for a change. Have some breakfast.'

'Thanks, mate. Where *is* Shinaid?'

'At work.'

'Oh yeah.'

'It's a thing people do.'

'I remember.'

Perry put up a very creditable plate of bacon and eggs, which he photographed, and I ate. Then we looked forward to a day of inaction, of doing some laundry, of baths. In the evening we were going for a pub crawl with an old friend. But for a few hours, we luxuriated in not going anywhere, and not doing anything. We were two weeks in, and this was the first moment we had really stopped. A day of lolling about in the bath and hanging out clothes to dry was just what the doctor ordered. But by five o' clock we were primped and pampered and rested, and were back in the car, heading fifteen miles inland to the small market town of Lampeter, Llanbedr Pont Steffan yn y Gymraeg.

Lampeter has something that no other small market town in Wales can lay claim to: a university. When it was founded in 1822, it was the first university establishment in England and Wales outside Oxford and Cambridge, older than University College London by five years. It was established by Thomas Burgess, the Bishop of St David's, as a training college for clergy who were unable to afford to go to Oxbridge. As St David's University College, it became part of the University of Wales in 1971. A well-known writer once described Lampeter in my hearing as 'the Cannabis University'. In 1972, a young bright-eyed undergraduate called Hag Harris started a degree in geography. He soon discovered that the main social activity for Lampeter students was smoking dope. Hag also discovered that one of the most horrible side effects of spliff is weight gain. This previously fit young man found himself unable to say 'No' to cake and sweeties. By 1976, he had ballooned into a fully fledged fat guy.

When I started to apply to go to university, also in 1976, Lampeter was one of four places on my shortlist. The others were Bradford, Leeds and Bangor. I wanted to study philosophy; I needed a place where you didn't have to have a foreign language at 'O' level, and which was at least 250 miles from home. Leeds was my favourite, because Bob Marley and the Wailers were playing at the Freshers' Ball. Lampeter was bottom of my list, because no bands of any interest seemed to play there, and I did not yet realise its international reputation as a centre for drugs. But a trip to Lampeter for a prospective students' open day was two days off school, so I was happy to make the trip. It was a comfortingly long and obscure journey, three changes of train and an hour-and-a-half bus journey through the largely empty hills of Carmarthenshire. There was a formal interview with the head of the philosophy department to be got through, where my having read and not understood *Zen and the Art of Motorcycle Maintenance* was enough to secure me a place. Then there was a trip round campus, hosted by a third-year undergraduate. Our little group was assigned to a very fat hippy, with long straggling red hair, who introduced himself as Hag. He was standing for election as Union President, he told us.

The first thing I noticed as we wandered about was that I was the only lad in a group of four or five devastatingly beautiful lasses, all wearing name tags on their bosoms. And you can't argue with that. Then I came to see that devastating beauty was the order of the day. A stream flows through the middle of the campus. Light twisted in the water. We stood on the footbridge which links the two halves of the campus, and I managed to raise my eyes from Elizabeth Braithwaite's breasts. Lampeter sits in the Teifi valley, and is surrounded by hills. In mid-March, the hills were tipped with snow. Half-way up the furthest of the hills, three or four miles away, was an isolated whitewashed cottage. The space, the loneliness, the white under the sun, the absence of males, and the fact that I'd been offered a place if I got three 'C's were starting to have their effect.

I had three good reasons for wanting to go to university. These were, to lose my virginity, to experiment with drugs, and to sing in a fuck-off rock 'n' roll band. Hag, I suspected, would be unable to help me with the first, and was quite clearly a living endorsement for the benefits and otherwise of the second, so I asked him about rock 'n' roll.

'Does anybody play here much?'

'The Velvet Underground were here in my first year.'

'I didn't know they ever played in this country.'

'Post-Reed. The Doug Yule version.'

That was it. I was coming here, I decided. This was a place where candidates for election could discriminate with ease between Velvet's line-up changes. I loved the lasses with name tags on their wobbly jumpers. I loved the obscurity of Lampeter, its distance. I loved its beauty and inaccessibility, the woods, the whitewashed cottage on the hill. And I rightly took Hag as representative of the promise of lots of druggy boys who understood the rock media for me to form bands with. I started in September 1976. Hag had lost the election by then, and had left college, but he stayed on to live in the town.

By January 1977 I was a confirmed weed head, singing in a punk band without a name, still a virgin, but making headway. Perry played bass. Me and Perry, as first-years, lived in college. People who lived miles away in the hills needed somewhere on campus to hang during the day, to listen to records and smoke spliff when they came in to town for a lecture. This place was Perry's bedroom, which became an impromptu green room for Lampeter's rock aristocracy. Our friend Wee Boab played guitar in our band. Wee Boab was a second-year, and he lived with four of his mates in the whitewashed cottage on the hill that I had so admired on the open day. It was called Coed Mor Fach. As the spring approached, the lads with cars drove us out to Coed Mor in the evening, so that we could all sit on what they called 'the verandah', listen to records, smoke, talk, look down on the town and the campus. It came to be the routine that Wee Boab and his mates would hang at Perry's most days, while we went up to theirs most evenings to get stoned, before coming back into town to drink in the Union Bar. Lots of people would walk or drive out from the town to Coed Mor for a chat and a brew and a smoke. I met my first wife there.

There was a long concrete roadway to Coed Mor, which zigged and zagged up the side of the steep hill. It really was quite high. You could see Lampeter at your feet, the sunset over the hills on the other side of the Teifi. On occasion, we watched practising RAF jets fly below us along the valley. The highlight of an evening at Coed Mor was watching Hag jog out from town. He was one of the first joggers most of us had encountered, and by far the fattest. We would sit out in front of the house, skinning up and taking bets on how long it would take him to run up the long hill. The first time, it was an hour between his arrival at the bottom of the track, and his reaching us up at the house. Every few steps he would stop, and hold his knees, and pant for breath, before staggering onwards and upwards for a few more yards, every step of the agonising climb clearly visible from the verandah where his pals sat smoking spliff and drinking tea. When at last he made it to the top, we would cheer, and make him a cup of tea, which he would gratefully gulp down before beginning the somewhat easier downhill leg of his self-elected hell.

I think I first realised that he was changing shape as the celebration of his nightly arrival grew more and more muted. By the end of the summer term, when we were all leaving for home, he had become merely plump. When we came back for our second year, he was like a gazelle. He now worked as Lampeter's window cleaner. His gimmick was wearing shorts, no matter what the weather. He was lean, and fit, and muscly, girls loved him suddenly and it was horrible. By the time we left Lampeter, Hag was on the Welsh Orienteering team, dating Jan, one of my third-year housemates, and was still cleaning windows. Sadly, his hair had gone along with the fat.

Next I heard of Hag, he had opened a record shop, called Rip-Off Records. They advertised every week in the *NME*, and bought and sold thousands of records a month. Dealers from all over Britain made their way to Hag's. When we moved to Radnorshire, I started dealing second-hand records on the markets of the Welsh borders, and I would drive over to Hag's to make sure I was stocked up on my *Dark Side*s and *Thriller*s, which you always need to have. Hag could get Jim Reeves eight-tracks too, which, take it from me, sell at a premium in Llandrindod Wells to this day. Hag looked better and better as time went on. He started to look prosperous and respectable. Rip-Off Records was going well, and I was always pleased to see the first person I ever met at Lampeter, still living and working in the town he had always believed in. He and Jan married and had three kids. He was elected town councillor, then county councillor. In the 1997 General Election, he was the Labour candidate for the Aberystwyth constituency. Luckily, he was beaten by Plaid Cymru. He's still on both the town and county councils, though. In fact, he's the Mayor.

So now the overweight hippy who had helped me make up my mind to come to Lampeter is a lean mean fighting political machine, one with an intimate knowledge of the back catalogue of the Stooges, the Velvets, and the MC5, whose first, live album opens with a call to arms: 'THE TIME HAS COME, BROTHERS AND SISTERS, THE TIME HAS COME . . . FOR YOU TO DECIDE . . . IF YOU ARE GONNA BE PART OF THE PROBLEM, OR IF YOU ARE GONNA BE PART OF THE SOLUTION!'

That's politics in the second-hand record game. Hag decided that he wanted to be part of the solution. I wanted to talk about the political regulation of alcohol with the Mayor. Perry, whose office is next door to Hag's shop, had fixed for us to meet him at six, in the King's Head.

Alcohol in the United Kingdom is a political problem in a way that it just isn't anywhere else, and histories of pubs and drinking always end up as histories of legislative attempts to control excess, curb drunkenness, and to raise tax revenue. It's an old problem, one which faced the Saxon kings just as much as it does President-for-Life Blairbrown's New Party. Lots of commentators who have studied the history of drinking feel that this fifteen-hundred-year-old attempt at control has exacerbated the problem; that restricting opening times and regulating the amount that people can drink, or for how long they can stay in the pub, has had exactly the opposite effect, and has served only to encourage people to drink, to get it down their necks while they can. Exacerbated the problem, but not caused it; St Boniface got to the heart of the matter, in about 750 CE, when he wrote to Cuthbert, who was then the Archbishop of Canterbury: 'It is reported in your dioceses the vice of drunkenness is too frequent. This is an evil peculiar to pagans and to our race.'

St Boniface could say much the same thing today, except that he evangelised lots of the pagans, which just leaves Johnny Saxon on his own. Lots of cultures have stories about individual drunks; but ours seems to be the only one where getting drunk together is the norm, and is accepted as a fun thing to do. The French and Italians get together for dinner parties, and drink a little wine, but they don't get falling-down drunk, whereas I've shoved people out of my door, perfectly respectable middle-class people, lawyers, journalists, doctors, who then trip over and fall in the gutter, and who phone you up the next day, not to apologise, but to proudly tell you how rotten they feel, and how much they had to spend on dry cleaning.

As I finished that sentence, my girlfriend called down to me, to say that I needed to go over to the village shop to pick up the Sunday papers. The lady who works in the shop on Sundays is in her early sixties, a widder woman, a pillar of church and community. I picked up the papers, and asked her how she was.

'Oh,' she said. 'I feel dreadful this morning, Ian. I had much too much to drink last night, so it's my own fault.' And we laughed, as we always have, and probably always will, when people tell us about their hangovers. In England, drinking to excess is socially acceptable. It is also a matter of personal responsibility; we feel dreadful, but we know that it's our own silly fault.

Early attempts at the social control of drinking came mostly from the church. After his correspondence with St Boniface, Cuthbert made it canon law that 'monastics and ecclesiastics do not help themselves to drink before the ninth hour be fully come', which is probably still quite good advice. The first real legislation came in the reign of King Edgar, on the throne between 959 and 975 CE, who ordained that there should be no more than one ale-house in a village; who insisted that there should be one system of measurement throughout the realm (later enshrined in Magna Carta), and who seems to have started the practice of restrictive legislation which only served to make things worse. In those days, people used to go out and get pished together by passing round a four-pint loving cup, called a pottle. Edgar decreed that there should be pegs inside the pottles, dividing them into sixths, and that no one should drink more than a peg at a sitting. What Edgar had done was launch a new opportunity for drinking games, and topers started 'taking one another down a peg or two'. People challenged one another to show their prowess as drinkers, which led to people fighting. Aethelred II, in 997, passed legislation which laid down fines for scrapping in the pub: 'In the case of breach of peace in an alehouse, six marks shall be paid in compensation if a man is slain, and twelve ores if no one is slain.'

And we think we have problems with drunken disorder.

Cut forward a thousand years or more, and our masters are still grappling with the problem. Only, after all this time, they seem to have learned a lesson. If you are running a country where drunken bad behaviour is enculturated, then to try and place restrictions on how and where Her Majesty's subjects can drink serves only to make the problem worse. Most fights happen because the pubs and clubs all chuck out at the same time; in the words of the government's Alcohol Harm Reduction Strategy, 'fights and disputes occur over scarce infrastructure' (and over whether or not Wayne has been looking at Sharon's tits, but even the New Party see legislating for that as beyond their purview). 'Scarce infrastructure' means things like fast-food outlets, and bus and taxi queues. So the 2003 Licensing Act aims to liberalise opening times, in order to stagger chucking-out times, in the hope that pressure will be taken off the scarce infrastructure, so that there will be less trouble. Licensing will be taken away from magistrates, and given over to local councillors. The thing is, it could really help. If draconian licensing laws have only pushed the English further into the arms of drink, then some degree of liberalisation has to be worth a try. The Act also demands that the licensee is licensed, as well as her/his premises, and in order to get such a personal licence, she/he will have to undergo training. It also increases the penalties for selling alcohol to minors. I hate to admit it, but it does seem like a well-thought-out piece of legislation.

Oh, and you should be able to get a drink at midnight in most towns and cities, which will be a good thing too.

Hag powered into the King's Head, looking better than ever, a fuck sight better than he did thirty years ago, sleek, shaved head, tanned, carefully dressed in a sports jacket and slacks. The King's Head is opposite the house I shared in my third year with Hag's wife. We shook hands.

'Good to see you, Mr Mayor. How's the Mayoress?'

'She's good. She sends her love.'

Hag went up to the bar and shook hands with the landlord, and with a couple of old boys at the bar. We introduced ourselves, too.

'We're on the longest pub crawl in the British Isles,' I said.

'Ooh,' said the landlord, 'You'll have been to the Turk's Head, on St Agnes. I got a postcard from there last week from one of my reg'lars. 'Ave a look.' He showed us the postcard, and we showed it to the Mayor, so he could see where we had started. On the back, the King's Head regular had written to the landlord, 'They have a strange habit here. They have a bell in the pub which they ring at 11 o'clock; then people stop drinking.'

'Is there a problem with student drinking in Lampeter, Hag?' I asked.

'No, not really. They mostly drink in the Union Bar.'

'Like us, really,' said Perry.

'Yeah,' agreed Hag.

'Is Lampeter still dry?' Back in the day, the pubs always shut at 10.30 on a Saturday night, and they stayed shut till Monday lunchtime. There was no drinking on Sundays in Cardigan District Council. The other side of the River Teifi, a mile from the town centre, was Carmarthenshire, which was wet; and the Cwmann Tavern on the right bank only stayed open because of people walking there for a drink on Sunday. The Union Bar was a members' club, so drinking was permitted on Sundays.

'No, it's been wet for ten years.'

'What do you both think about the new Act, then?' I asked Hag and the landlord. The landlord, to judge from his postcard, was not a man overly concerned with the regulation of opening hours, and he hadn't really heard about the new laws. Hag explained the two key points: that opening hours were to be liberalised, and that licensing was being taken away from magistrates and given to councillors, like him.

'I think it's a good thing,' said Hag. 'It will make life much simpler. Instead of having to apply for extensions, and special licences, you'll just need two bits of paper: a licence for the premises, and a personal licence for the landlord.'

'I think it's a good idea, too,' said Perry, who is, after all, Lampeter's pisshead tsar.

'What, having the pubs open all hours?' I said.

'It won't happen, not here,' said Perry. 'No, what's good is that licensing becomes the responsibility of local councillors, who are answerable to their constituents. Communities will have a say in what opens when, that they don't have now. In Newcastle, which goes fucking ape every weekend, the council have already said that they won't allow any new applications for drinks licences within the city centre, unless it's something that offers a reason for drinking, like a comedy club. If a pub is causing a nuisance to its neighbours, then people will be able to lobby their councillors to take away or amend the licence. And the police will have closure orders, so they can shut down a place which is being a nuisance.'

'Oh. I didn't know any of this,' said the landlord, anxiously.

'Don't worry,' said Hag. 'I'll pop by in the week with some information.'

'Thank you, Hag.' We shook hands all round, and were off in Hag's wake.

Our next pub was the Ivy Bush, in our day a legendary hippy haunt. Not any more; now it is a Welsh-speaking pub, but a very polite one. As we came through the door, the landlord was by the bar with a couple of his pals, speaking Welsh, but when they saw the Mayor come in, they switched to English.

''ello, 'ag! What brings you 'ere?' they said. Hag shook hands all round, and I bought some drinks. The head on our beer was now definitely there, not so big as they like it oop north, but there.

Bev, the landlord, was well up on the 2003 Act, and was uncertain. 'Thing is, 'ag, magistrates were supposed to be impartial, weren't they? What happens now, look, if you're being granted your licence by a councillor who owns a couple of pubs himself up the road? He might not fancy the competition, might he?'

'Well, he wouldn't be on the licensing committee, would he?' said Hag. 'He'd have to declare an interest, wouldn't he?'

'Yes, but what if 'is mate 'as a pub? I'm sorry, 'ag, but politicians do look after their own int'rest, don't they?'

'Have you seen all the information about the new Act? Did you go to the meeting about it in Swansea?'

'I've got a pub to run, 'aven't I? I can't go runnin' off to Swansea all the bloody time, can I?'

'Shall I pop some information in later in the week?'

'Nobody in 'ere can read, 'ag,' said a cheerful fat man in a Wales rugby shirt.

'What does it say on your shirt?' I asked.

He looked down. 'I've always wondered,' he said.

'Oh, I've read all about it, 'ag, haven't I?' said Bev. 'I suppose we'll just 'ave to wait and see 'ow it goes, won't we?'

Hag shook hands all round, and we moved on to the third pub, the Castle. It was much busier than the others. One of Hag's sons was working behind the bar. Hag shook hands with everybody, and said a few words in Welsh to some of the locals.

'Ian, come and meet John.'

John was the landlord. He had worked in the South Wales coalfields until 1986, when he was made redundant as the pits were closed after the miners' strike. 'So I became a pub landlord. What else can an ex-miner do?'

John had been treasurer of the local branch of the Licensed Victuallers' Association, and he was enthusiastic about the change in the laws.

'But won't it see you working longer hours? If the opening times are liberalised?' I asked.

'No, and I'll tell you why. Imagine now you run an 'otel or a pub, and you do lots of weddings, and you 'ave to keep applying for an extension every Sat'day night. Under the new reg'lations, you apply, once and for all, to stay open till two, say. But that doesn't mean you 'ave to stay open till two, just that you can when you need to. So it'll cut back on the paperwork, and you won't 'ave to keep going to the magistrate's court all the time. If people don't like the way a pub is run, if there's trouble an' that, they can talk to their councillor about it. It's bringing the licensed trade under democratic control. An' it's two licences you need, now, one for the premises and one for the person. And you 'ave to demonstrate experience or training to get your personal licence, so 'opefully standards will improve, see? If someone plays silly buggers, they could lose their personal licence, without 'ooever takes over next 'aving to relicense their premises.'

'And do you think it'll stop people getting tanked up before closing time? The idea is that people will drink as much, but spread it out over a longer time, so they won't be so leery at chucking-out.'

'Not in this country, it won't. You know what people are like.'

'It's not going to turn Britain into a nation of laid-back *boulevardiers* overnight,' said Perry, 'no, but over time we might get more relaxed about getting those last few down, if you lose the urgency.'

'And there's nothing more embarrassing than having visitors from Spain or France over, and not being able to get a drink after eleven,' I said, 'even in the centre of London.'

Hag told me to tell a gentleman in his early sixties who was sitting at the bar about the longest crawl. This gentleman would clearly benefit from any liberalisation of the laws. His huge red nose looked like a road map of Portugal.

'Well, we're travelling between the two most distant pubs in Britain, the Turk's Head on St Agnes in the Scillies and the Baltasound Hotel on Unst in the Shetlands, only we're taking the long way round, and we're going to pubs and breweries and distilleries and quiz nights and karaoke nights, and . . . yeah. That's what we're doing.'

The old gentleman roared with laughter, and called over his friend. ''Ere, you listen to what these lads are up to . . . best thing I've ever 'eard. Tell him. Go on.'

'Er . . . Well, we're travelling between the two most distant pubs in Britain, the Turk's Head on St Agnes in the Scillies and the Baltasound Hotel on Unst in the Shetlands, only we're taking the long way round, and we're going to pubs and breweries and distilleries and quiz nights and karaoke nights, and . . . yeah. That's what we're doing.'

Now both men laughed.

'You doin' it for charity, like?'

'No. I'm writing a book about pubs.'

'That's brilliant, that is. Well, I never. Dai! Dai, come and hear what these lads are doin' . . . go on, tell 'im.'

So I told Dai, and then the old gentleman called over two more pals, and I told them too. I thought that I was going to have to tell everyone in the pub, one after the other; I was relieved that Hag had business to deal with, while we were off for a bite in the only pub in Britain with an elephant buried in the garden. Hag shook hands with everybody in the pub, said encouraging things to them, sometimes in English, sometimes in Welsh, and then he walked us back to the car, where he shook hands with us, too.

'Good to see you guys,' said the Mayor.

'Good to see you. I like it when you take me on guided tours.'

'Any time,' said Hag. 'It's good for me to be out round the pubs talking with people about this stuff. It's an election year.'

'When I first met you, you were standing for Union President. It's always an election year, it seems to me.'

'Remember the MC5,' said Hag.

'What have you learned from listening to too many records?' Perry asked me, as we drove off.

'It's a mighty long way down rock 'n' roll,' I said.

We took the back road from Lampeter to Tregaron, nine miles or so to the north.

The Talbot in Tregaron is a drovers' pub, dating from the thirteenth century. The old drove road across the Cambrian Mountains to Abergwesyn started here. The Talbot would be an ideal stop in Chesterton Country, a pub whose history is intimately linked with the history of a road. Up until the late nineteenth century, Tregaron market would be packed with sheep and geese and black cattle, which were shod in the yard behind the Talbot before the long walk to the English markets. Tregaron was an important place; the busy pubs and markets meant that it was home to one of Wales's oldest banks, 'The Black Sheep'. I'm not sure if the drovers used talbots to help them in their work, but it seems a good bet that that's where the pub gets its name from. A talbot was a large kind of hound, and it's a pub name that goes back at least to the reign of James I. Old Perry didn't know this, so he disputed my claim for four runs in our endless game of pub cricket. But four runs it is. If local legend is to be believed, there is an elephant buried in the back garden. The circus came over the hill, in 1848, and while it was in Tregaron, its elephant died, and was duly interred. All the locals believe this, but no one has actually investigated if it is true; just in case it isn't, presumably. You can still see shows there; it's one of the best venues for roots music in Mid Wales.

Perry comes to the Talbot once a fortnight, after his badminton nights in Tregaron Leisure Centre, and he was unsurprised to find two or three of his badminton buddies in there. We ate sausage, egg and chips in the dark old pub, washed down with beer, and after we finished, we were joined by one of the badminton crowd, who Perry introduced as Rod. Rod is a cartographer, and an expert in the sacred landscape of Wales. I learned later that because of his interest in standing stones and their putative channelling of earth energy, his pals call him 'Divining Rod'.

I told him about my idea that much of the landscape is given over to intoxicating the population, and that the intoxicated portion of the population must see landscape differently from their straight brethren.

'Of course,' said Rod. 'Altering your consciousness peels back layers in the land. I do it all the time. There are places I've been going for years round here, up in the hills, and I just sit and look and look and try to understand what's happening in the landscape. I'm off for a walk at the weekend, and I've bought some Mexican mushrooms to take with me. It renders the landscape sacred, gives you new ways of looking.'

I wonder how many cartographers take this view of their work? Are road maps drawn up by shroom heads? I think we should know.

Driving home to the coast on the back road from Tregaron to Aberaeron, Perry told me a tale. Back in the 1970s, according to the legend, there was a pub on that back road called 'The Last Visible Dog'.

'It was Divining Rod who told me the story,' said Perry. 'Some hippies thought it would be a good idea to buy up an old pub in West Wales, and run it along the lines of a commune. Soon, their traveller friends from all over were turning up to use it. You could get a bath there, which is a luxury if you are a traveller, and they did macrobiotic pub grub. The communal landlords allowed travellers to park up in the car-park, so it was hugely popular as a meeting place for the tribes. Above all, the hippies liked it because the landlords allowed their regulars to smoke spliff in the bar. Which they did, lots and lots of it. It was far enough out in the backwoods that they never got busted by the polis.'

'Like an Amsterdam coffee shop?'

'Kind of. But it was still a pub. A coffee shop makes money from selling spliff. A pub makes money from selling beer.'

'Oh.'

'You see the problem. If you're smoking spliff all night, you don't want gallons of beer as well, do you?'

'Not really, no. You'd never stop pissing.'

'What *do* you want?'

'A nice cup of tea and some cake.'

'Exactly. The hippies would come in, order a half at most, and then sit about getting out of it all night.'

'They probably got through quite a few crisps and snacks, though. So what happened?'

'"The Last Visible Dog" closed after two years. You can't make a profit on a pub that doesn't sell enough alcohol. It was busted by the market.'

I don't know if there is any truth in this at all. Where does the name come from, for example? It seems to be a quote from Russell Hoban's *The Mouse and his Child*. At least one writer of my acquaintance has told me that it is a fairly well known pub name, and is a hunting term, referring to the slowest hound in the pack – I have found no evidence for this at all. Not only are there no pubs currently called 'The Last Visible Dog', I can find no records of any pubs ever having been called that. I'd really love to know if there is any truth in Perry's story (ian@ianmarchant.com).

Later, lying in Perry's guest room, trying to get to sleep, I thought about how lots of ex-Lampeter students of our generation still drink quite a bit less than their contemporaries from other universities. When we were lads, drunken behaviour was almost frowned upon, something that only rugger buggers were interested in, whilst drinking mushroom tea and snarfing up lines of amphetamine sulphate were completely socially acceptable. In order to understand how drinking lager, throwing up in the gutter and shouting 'Chloe, I love you, Chloe!!' at your ex-girlfriend has become more attractive to today's youth than prising open the doors of consciousness, it was becoming increasingly clear that Perry and I were going to have to spend an evening with some young people, within the next fortnight. It was not an attractive prospect.

# Thursday 15th April

Some people don't like pork scratchings, which is fair enough, given the inviolability of taste. Others won't eat them because they've got hair on them, or because they don't know what they are made of. Pork scratchings are made of pig skin. It's crackling, that's all. Just try to ignore the hair thing. In this age of over-abundance in the West, we are free to be picky about what we eat, and are increasingly prone to 'food intolerance'. People can't eat sugar, or wheat, or yeast, or whatever. I met somebody recently who couldn't, or wouldn't, eat anything red, such as tomatoes, kidney beans, or red peppers. I find this all but incomprehensible, especially 'wheat intolerance'. The whole of human civilisation was predicated on the cultivation of grain. The first cities appeared because the cultivation of grain meant that food surpluses became available for the first time, freeing some people to do something other than collect food. It's difficult to imagine people in Ur or Nineveh saying, 'Ooh, no bread for me, thanks. Makes me feel a bit bloated. Got any gluten-free wild berries?' Intolerance is a consequence of over-abundance.

Others are forbidden by their gods from eating pork scratchings. Gods are down on pork generally, rather than the actual scratchings, claiming that our humble friend the pig is unclean. Since the gods claim to have made the pigs, this seems a bit dim-witted on their part. Why, we might ask the gods, when you were making the pig, did you not make sure that it was clean? Gods often set restrictions which make a lot of sense, such as 'Don't kill', and 'Don't shag around', but it is difficult to see how 'Don't eat pork' is commensurate with the more sensible prohibitions. The gods get bees in their bonnets about the oddest things. For example, Hindus can eat pork, but they can't eat beef. Muslims, Jews, and some fundamentalist Christians can't eat pork, but can cheerily chow down on a steak. My friend Saleel is the product of a mixed marriage; his father is Muslim, and his mother is Hindu. When his mum went out shopping, his dad gave him corned-beef sandwiches. When his dad was at work, his mum gave him bacon sandwiches. Saleel is one of the nicest and goodest men in the world. When he gets to heaven, as surely he must, is he going to be condemned from all sides for all eternity because of this meaty miscegenation? Not by any God worth worshipping, surely. Go on, try a pork scratching. They're lovely. If there's any trouble on the other side, blame me.

From the first moment that I realised that all pork scratchings hanging from cards behind pub bars come from Walsall and the Black Country, I'd been determined to visit a pork-scratchings factory, and research demonstrated that if I wanted to see the best, then I would need to visit G. Simmons & Sons in Walsall. Simmons are the champagne of pork scratchings. The fat is soft and buttery like babies' bums, the crackling crisp like frost in February. When I phoned to ask if we might visit, they were more than happy, because they take great pride in the food they produce. All kinds of factories are happy to show visitors round. If you are worried about the food you eat, try ringing the manufacturer, and gauging their willingness to let you come and have a look round their premises. If they are happy, then go and judge for yourself if something is good to eat. If they won't show you their processes, then maybe you are right to be worried. On this index, Simmons come out at the top. They weren't merely happy for us to come and look round, they were positively enthusiastic.

Walsall makes sense when you come to it from the west down the old road from Wales, the A5, Watling Street, that ancient artery of British trade and politics. This is the first important industrial centre that the various cattle driven from places like Tregaron to England would have reached. Its industry was leather. There is a Leather Museum, and there are still ninety or so firms in Walsall producing leather goods today, most famously, saddles. Walsall FC are nicknamed the Saddlers; Bloxwich, the neighbouring town, Hove to Walsall's Brighton, was famous for making bits and stirrups. Walsall's fortune has been made from processing animal skins. No wonder it's the home of pork scratchings.

Simmons make their pork scratchings from a unit on a utilitarian industrial estate in the heart of Walsall. Industrial estates are becoming increasingly alien to British people, because most of us don't make things any more. We got lost easily, and had to be talked down the anonymous, identical roadways to the factory by mobile phone. We were met in the office by Graham Simmons, the Grand Old Man of the British pork-scratchings industry, and by his son Sean, pork scratchings' greatest enthusiast and ambassador.

'I'll show you around in a bit,' said Sean. 'It's Thursday, so we am just shutting off the fryers, so that we can start cleaning. We cook for four days, twenty-four hours round the clock, and clean on Fridays.'

It was clear that Sean was going to do all the talking; that Graham was something of a figurehead.

'I wanted to come and see you, because all pork scratchings seem to come from round here. And I wondered why.'

'There's a tradition of it, isn't there, Dad? It's a Midlands thing, like you get jellied eels in London. But they don't all come from us. There's a place in Rugeley, and one of the big snack companies make them in Warrington.'

'But the bags all say they come from Dudley, or Tipton.'

'That's what it says on the bags, ar. But there's only three places that make 'em. We bag 'em up for people, in their bags, like.'

'So, you don't just do your own brand?'

'Ooh, no. We am making 'em for five or six snack companies, who sell 'em in their own packets. But ours are the best, they have to be, because they've got our name on the packet.'

So there it was. Lots of small companies sell and distribute them into pubs, but there are only three manufacturers, and only one in Walsall. It felt a bit anti-climactic.

'How did you get started?'

'Well, we used to 'ave a butcher's shop in Willenhall, didn't we, Dad? Like all butchers round 'ere, we made our own scratchings in the shop. Not like you get in the pubs, but the real West Midland leaf scratchings.'

'There are different kinds?'

'Ar. I'll show you in a bit. Anyway, the newsagent's down the road asked us if we could let them sell a few bags of scratchings, so we said, yes, like, didn't we, Dad? And we sold 'em about twenty bags a week. But then Trading Standards came into the shop, and said you can't sell those. There's no label on the bags, no list of ingredients, no weights. So we thought, well, we'd better get some labels done, to put on the bags. Dad was against it, weren't you, Dad?

'I was against it,' said Graham. 'Too much bother.' I was coming to suspect that, despite his way with pork, Graham was not the driving force behind Simmons' success.

'But I said, oh coom on, Dad, so we made the labels, and it just slowly grew from there. We gave up the shop to go full-time on the scratchings about ten year ago. Coom and 'ave a look round.'

Sean took us from the office and outside to the main entrance.

'Now, this is where the rinds are delivered. It all comes frozen from Denmark.'

'Why not Britain?'

'The rind isn't so good. I don't know why. Making scratchings is a bit like cooking steak. You can be the best steak chef in the world, but if the steaks is tough, there's nothing you can do, is there?'

'Do you use the same rind for every kind of scratching?'

'No. The scratchings we make for other people coom from a big meat-processing place called Crown. Very good rind, but not the best. No, I found another place out in Denmark, a much smaller place, that does the best-quality pork rind in the world. They don't do as much as Crown, and you can't always get as much as you like, so we can't use it for all our products. That rind just goes for the Simmons' own brand. The quality of the rind is the most important factor in making good scratchings. Coom in.'

We went through the door into the factory. Although we were still not in the main frying room, it was already very hot, like walking from an air-conditioned hotel room into a sweltering Mediterranean noon. Fat hung suspended in the air. As it cooled, it condensed, and formed an emulsion which covered every surface in a slick of fat.

'Mind 'ow you go,' said Sean. 'It's a bit like walking on an ice rink. You do get a bit fatty when you're frying. Last week, I was standing in a newsagent's next to a lady, and she said to the bloke behind the counter, you am frying chips somewhere, so I said, "No, that'll be me. I work in a pork scratchings factory."'

Sean continued, 'Now, originally, pork scratchings were a by-product of lard manufacture. They were what was left over at the bottom of the tub after you'd made your lard. This is the real old-fashioned scratchings, what we call leaf, and you can only get it locally. We still do it for butcher's shops; 150 pound of rind gives about 20 pound of scratchings. The lard goes to a pork-pie factory up the road.'

'Is it right that we're in the middle of a European lard shortage?' I asked.

'Ar. The demand for lard is much higher in the new EU countries than it is over here. Poland has been soaking up a lot.'

Sean showed us the lard press, still in the antechamber of the frying room, and let us try some of the precious leaf scratchings. They were more like crackling than the stuff you get in pubs. Perry was unsure, but I thought it rather wonderful.

'The main part of the business is the ordinary pork scratchings. First you put the rind through these cutters, so that it's diced and sliced, and then it comes through into here . . .' He pulled back a curtain of plastic flaps, and admitted us to the inner temple. The heat intensified, like a blistering wind from the south. Three vast fryers, each at least nine feet high, dominated the room. Two guys were bustling about with brooms and buckets of water, whilst a third was unloading a batch of scratchings from the fryer at the far end of the room, and ladling them into a chute.

'We've just shut the fryers down. We start on Sunday night and cook round the clock for three shifts, turn them off on Thursday afternoons, and spend Friday cleaning. The scratchings go through into the next room for seasoning.'

'How long do they cook for?'

'They am deep-fried for an hour and a half, at 160 degrees. And that's it, really. That's all there is to it. Coom on, let's get out of these lads' way. I'll show you where the ladies work.'

Sean took us into the last room, where the temperature was something approaching merely very hot. Two middle-aged ladies in blue overalls smiled at us as we came in. They were covering the last few scratchings from the fryer in seasoning.

'What's in that?'

'Secret, that is.'

The process could not be more simple. You shred pork rind, fry it up, season it, and Bob's your mum's live-in lover. Lovely gorgeous pork scratchings.

'Try some,' said Sean. So we dipped our hands into the stainless-steel container, and pulled out a handful each of the freshest pork scratchings imaginable, still warm from the fryer. Perry's lips glistened with lard. You could taste Sean's obsession with quality, taste the love that goes into their manufacture.

'I'll get the ladies to bag you up a few. Coom back into the office, and we'll have a coop of tea.'

Over tea and biscuits, Sean told us how they'd built the business up, and how they had been approached by Asda to supply them with Simmons' own-brand pork scratchings.

'We've never done any marketing,' said Sean. 'Have we, Dad?'

'Never needed to,' said Graham.

'Asda approached us. It's all been word of mouth. The Atkins Diet has made pork scratchings more popular than ever,' said Sean.

'Really?'

'Ar. You can eat as many as you like, can't you? No carbohydrates.'

My previous scepticism about the Atkins Diet was badly shaken. I could lose weight by eating lots of these wonderful things? I needed to think about this. One of the ladies from the packing room knocked on the office door, and came through with four vast bags of scratchings, enough to feed an army.

'We got a lovely letter from a lance-corporal came from

Brownhills, serving in Iraq. Said his mam had sent him a bag of pork scratchings from 'ome in a food parcel, and it made him cry because of 'ow much he missed it. So we sent over a load of boxes to the lads over there, so they can have scratchings with a pint in the mess.'

Even though I find a God who disapproves of eating pork scratchings a bit unfeasible, I couldn't help thinking that the Iraqi population, already having to come to terms with an illegal occupying force, would just have their worst fears confirmed by this, by the beery breath of crusaders with pork fat dripping down their chins.

'Anyway, lads, these are for you.' Sean gave us the four bags of scratchings, each bag about a kilogram in weight. Enough pork scratchings to keep our friends and families in pork-based snacks for a year; a magnificent gift.

'Thank you, Sean,' I said, as he showed us back to the car. Perry put three of the bags in the boot with our luggage, to take home, while one of them came into the car with us, to sustain us through the weeks ahead.

'My pleasure. I love talking about pork scratchings.'

Sean Simmons has worked in the family business his whole life, and it is his enthusiasm that has driven G. Simmons & Sons to produce the best pork scratchings in the world. They are the antithesis of processed food; just high-quality ingredients beautifully cooked. I would feed them to a new-born baby, except for one thing. The packets come with a health warning: 'Recommended for people with healthy strong teeth.'

We were staying that night at the Roman Road Hotel, a few miles from Walsall town centre up on Watling Street, so that we go out for the night in leafy downtown Bloxwich. 'Blocco' is right at the edge of the West Midlands conurbation. Two miles up the road, and you are on the edge of Cannock Chase. If you can't do a Brummie accent, but you feel you'd like to give it a go, try starting by saying 'Bloxwich'. It's almost impossible to say it in anything other than a West Midlands accent. It reminded me a bit of Coulsdon or Barnet; one of those small towns right on the edge of a vast metropolis which barely cling to their identity. Birmingham and the Black Country has been a manufacturing centre since at least the fourteenth century. Really, what people think of as 'Birmingham' is a series of towns which have grown into one another, but which at one time would each have specialised in a particular product. In Bloxwich's case, it was equestrian ironmongery.

We had two reasons for wanting to go into Bloxwich for the night. Firstly, Blocco has one of the 'Thirteen Unaltered Pubs of Britain', the Turf Tavern. This would be the second one we'd visited on the trip, after the Monkey House in Defford. But I also wanted to go to Bloxwich to drink in the Queen's Head, tucked away behind the High Street on the edge of a large council estate. Built in the sixties, like the estate it serves, it's run by Val and Ken Horobin, whose son Richard Jarman is a writer and political lobbyist and a pal of mine. I wanted to go to Richard's mum's pub. We arranged to meet Richard there at six.

Since it is one street back from the centre of Bloxwich, the Queen's Head gets a good lunchtime crowd, attracted by Val's home cooking. In the evenings, it's mostly people from the adjacent estate. There are two cavernous bars; we parked the car, walked into the Public, which had two pool tables, a widescreen TV, and young people wearing tracksuit bottoms and baseball caps. I asked the ravishing blonde barmaid for Richard.

'Ow, you most be 'is friends. I'm Kim. Richard's in the other bar with 'is mam. Just through there.'

Perry had the smirk he wears when he likes a barmaid. I think I had it, too. We went through into the Saloon, equally big, with no pool tables and no TV but, instead, a small PA set up in the corner, and a pub singer sitting at the bar, eating braising steak. Richard came from behind the bar, wearing slippers. I introduced Perry; Richard introduced Val, Ken, and Sharon, Kim's equally lovely oppo, who made us smirk again.

They bought us pints, and a smashing braising-steak dinner; braising steak, potatoes, cabbage and runner beans. If we had not been guests, this would have cost £3.25; highly recommended. Richard sat with us, not eating, as he'd already had his tea. He was whispering to me about the book he was working on. It's called

*The A–Z of White Trash*. He was feeling guilty about it. I thought it was a great idea; I was feeling guilty, too.

Our side of the pub was beginning to lively up. Some elderly folk, in their seventies; a few younger couples too, in their late twenties maybe. But mostly the pub was filling with mums and dads in their forties and fifties, dressed up to the nines, come out for a drink and a bit of a sing-song. As the pub slowly filled, the singer fiddled with his PA. He was singing along to backing tapes, and he had a radio microphone; he checked his gear was working, and began his spiel.

'Good evening, ladies and gentleman. My name's Chris Aaron, and if you've never seen me before,' and he looked towards me and Perry, 'I'll just explain a bit about the two halves of the show. In the first half I'll take it easy, and just sing a few songs, and then we'll take a break, and then I'll come back for the second half, and we'll make it a bit rowdier. And as you know, if you've seen the Chris Aaron Show before, I always start with . . .' He clicked a pedal with his foot, and the tape started to play . . . "Let's Face the Music and Dance"!'

I've done gigs like this, in pubs like this, except that I have C.C. Ambler, keyboard player, instead of a tape machine. I do have a radio mike, though. The act is called 'Your Dad'. It's supposed to be an ironic take on the pub entertainer's art. Sometimes we get booked into the wrong place, the irony doesn't come off, people threaten us with violent death, and we revert hastily to being straight pub singers. Singing cover versions of standards in pubs is not cool. In fact, it's cheesy as Wensleydale. But it is fun. It's not rock 'n' roll, no, but it's a crack, and if you can get people singing and having a laugh and then drive home with a couple of hundred quid each, well, I call that a good night. Only once has it gone horribly wrong, in a hellhole in the West End of Morecambe, where the squint-eyed myrmidons of hell gather to sell guns and sup lager. They were not happy with the irony at all, and they said as much.

'But can't you see,' I pleaded, 'we're subverting the genre?'

'Why don't you fuck off?' said one philistine.

'Yeah, and fucking learn to talk English,' said another.

I drew myself up to my full height. 'I am speaking English . . . it is you, sir, who cannot speak his own language.'

The second time he hit me, I said, 'It doesn't matter how much you hit me, I'll still be cleverer than you.'

The landlord stepped in at this point, with the happy result that I am alive today to relate the tale.

Some places like two sets, such as Chris Aaron was doing tonight. The first set always starts as the pub is starting to fill, and nobody listens to you. They order drinks, and chat to their pals while you hack through 'Desperado' in the corner, unloved and unwanted. Chris did really well warming them up, I thought. He goes round the pub with his radio mic, and sings love songs to fat bald men, and sits on their laps and rubs their heads. This causes great hilarity, as I know. Once they laugh, they'll start joining in with the songs, which is the whole point really. A good pub singer isn't singing at people, he's singing with them.

'You do that in your act,' said Perry.

'Not after tonight,' I said.

He came and sat on my lap and rubbed my big bald head, just as I (used) to do to fat bald men in our audience. He sang Take That's valedictory hit 'Back for Good' to me. I sing this in pubs myself, so I was able to join in on the backing vocals. With a belly full of scratchings and braising steak, a singer on my knee, and a song in my heart, I was beginning to enjoy myself. For the last number of his first set, Chris did 'Fools Rush In'. One of the big old girls in the audience joined in with a note-perfect harmony line. He got her up on the mike. I was now convinced this was my gig. So I leapt up uninvited and did some more BVs. Couldn't help myself. Perry didn't know where to look.

After his set, I got talking to Chris Aaron.

'It's me stage name. It's 'cos it's Elvis' middle name.'

Perry got talking to Sharon behind the bar. Turns out she's a pet beautician by day. Perry's barmaid smirk was becoming intolerable. Richard, I felt, could do with a less intense atmosphere. So we skipped Chris Aaron's second set, and walked out into the Bloxwich night, to find the Turf Tavern.

'Thank God for that,' said Richard, as we hit the street.

'No, he's a good singer.'

'Ian, in his second set, he does things like "I am the music man, I come from down your way . . ."'

'But he can only be twenty-five. Where on earth do you learn to sing stuff like that?'

'I dunno. And he's a lot younger than he looks.'

'People like it though,' I said.

'I know. It's difficult for me to understand. Sometimes it feels like I lived in a Martin Parr photograph.'

'What, growing up in a pub?'

'No, that was all right. It was fun.'

Nancy Banks-Smith, the *Guardian* TV critic grew up in a pub in the 1930s and 40s. She wrote about the experience: 'Extrovert humanity boiled around me but I was too much alone. The pub was asleep when I went to school because publicans who work till early morning, clearing up and cashing up, don't get up at eight. In the evening walking through the roaring warmth, sober and shy, was a most solitary sensation.'

I put this to Richard.

'Yeah, it was a bit like that, I suppose. Christmas was always weird, because Mam and Ken were working. No, what I mean is, because of all the things that I've done, I can't just sit in the pub and listen to Chris sing "I am the Music Man" any more, without thinking about Martin Parr photographs. And that's wrong.'

'I feel like that, too,' I said. 'In Newhaven, people find it odd that I wanted to go to university, and exotic beyond belief that I write books. They say I'm middle class, which I suppose I am, in a way, because of the education and t'ing. But when middle-class people hear me speak, they know at once that I'm not one of them. Not that I want to be.'

'But, as you say, you are,' said Perry.

'You end up not quite fitting in anywhere,' said Richard. 'I went to fucking Oxford to study law. Nobody else in Oxford spoke with a Bloxwich accent, so everyone thinks you're common. And then you'd come 'ome, with your carefully modulated vowels, and everyone thinks you're posh. My mam and Ken are really lovely, but they were puzzled about why anyone would want to go to Oxford. I think I worry them.'

'Yeah. I feel awkward in almost any conceivable social situation. What do they think about you being a political lobbyist?'

'They haven't really got a clue what I do, or why.'

'They're going to love you when *The A–Z of White Trash* comes out.'

'God, I know. Do you think it's terrible of me to do it?'

'Yes. But I think it's funny. I would have done it when I was starting out to write. It would be shit if it was done by some middle-class wanker.'

'But that's what you two are,' said Perry. 'It doesn't matter what school you went to, or what your parents did, or what your school friends do now. Fact of the matter is, your ideal night out is dinner at St John's, or going to see a new production of *Hedda Gabler* at the Almeida. You read the *Guardian* and the *Spectator*, and watch Channel Four news. You know who Martin Parr is.'

'Yeah, but this is where we're from,' said Richard, 'and it's become puzzling and strange. Most people don't feel strange at home, do they?'

'There's a line in an old Brinsley Schwarz song, "He gets nervous on the road, but he can't stay at home". That's me,' I said.

'Who is Brinsley Schwarz?' said Richard.

'A pub-rock band from the seventies, he likes,' said Perry.

'Pub rock, you note, not pub singers,' I said, 'though I like them too.'

We had arrived at the Turf Tavern. Richard had never been in there before. There was a bar with Anaglypta on the walls and Oregon pine benches worn smooth by a hundred and more years of beer drinkers' arses. It is a well preserved example of a Victorian urban pub, I would say, rather than a startling survival like the Cider House. The landlady politely explained that she would rather that Perry did not take photographs, as she felt her customers would not like it. Her customers were all men, seven of them, three twos talking quietly amongst themselves, and a fat man with a beard, supping ale on his own. We got chatting. He was a real-ale enthusiast, and a banjo player in a trad-jazz band.

'What's the difference between a banjo and a trampoline?' he asked us.

We said we didn't know.

'You take your shoes off to jump on a trampoline,' he said.

Richard went for a piss.

'It's a bit quiet in here,' I said to the banjo player.

'That's how people like it,' he said. 'People don't come here for a crack. They come here to get away from the wife and kids and to have a good pint.'

'I think that's important,' said Perry.

'Ooh, come and see the urinals,' said Richard, returning. So we did. It was a cathedral devoted to piss. The unaltered nature of the pub revealed itself in its white-tiled glory. People ask me what was the best pub in England, and I still say the Duke of York's in Iddesleigh. But best bog goes to the Turf Tavern, Bloxwich, West Midlands.

We finished our pints and walked back to the Queen's Head. People most certainly go there for a crack. And they take their wives with them. Chris Aaron was just coming to the end of his set. We'd missed 'I Am the Music Man'. Chris finishes with 'Delilah'. So do I. So do all pub singers. It's a good song. Everyone was singing along with red happy faces.

It looked like a Martin Parr photograph. It looked like the people I went to school with, grown up, grandparents now, some of them, out for a good time. It looked like a long forgotten home.

# Friday 16th April

In the morning, heading east, we sampled the new M6 Extension, Britain's first toll motorway. It depressed me. I ate a handful of pork scratchings to cheer myself up. I used to drive once a month from Lancaster to Brighton and back, and I liked to come off the motorway near Cannock, get on to the A5 as far as Tamworth, and then go south to join the M40. It made a change from the monotony of the motorway. There were proper transport caffs, instead of the hateful service stations, so I would stop for a fry-up and a read of the *Sport* and the *Star*, which were left lying about for the edification of travellers. The old A5 skims the far north of Birmingham, but actually it goes through very few towns. When you got on to a switchback section, swooping up and down small hills, you could see how straight the road is, see its Roman origins. Although Watling Street is still there, it is over-shadowed by the new motorway. The Romans worked out the best way through this countryside 2,000 years ago, so the motorway follows its course. But where the A5 is a linear adventure which starts at Marble Arch and finishes at the ferry terminal in Holyhead, a highway into history, the motorway is just a motorway. We came off after one junction, paid our three-pound toll, and went into Lichfield for morning coffee and a wander round the cathedral.

People argue to this day about where the North/South divide has its fault line. Some people say it's the River Trent, others that it's the Mersey. Lichfield is only seven or eight miles as the crow flies from Bloxwich, but it feels much further. The Brummie accent fades away, to be replaced by the Staffordshire voice, a voice which tells you the North cannot be far off. Watling Street was the old border between the Danelaw and Wessex; go a couple of miles either side of the road, and you can hear the difference. Beer is a good measure of cultural difference, too. After Lichfield, we were going on to Burton-on-Trent, for what would prove to be our last flat pints. Somewhere round here would be as good a place as any to say that we had crossed a line.

Before we leave Johnson's Lichfield, incidentally, a quick word from the Doctor: 'A man who exposes himself when he is intoxicated, has not the art of getting drunk.' And you can't argue with that.

The valley of the Trent is unspectacular. Burton sits in flat unappealing countryside, and according to Benjamin Capper's *Topographical Dictionary* of 1808 it was 'reckoned to be unhealthy' because of its low-lying situation. You can see it coming for miles around, as the towers of breweries peep over the horizon. The largest of the towers, a silver-grey grain silo, has 'Coors' written in red letters on its side. So before you get into Burton, you can make no mistake; this is a corporation town, owned and controlled by two of the biggest brewery companies in the world, Coors and Interbrew. Coors took over the brewing in Burton of Bass from Interbrew, who own the brand, and there is some talk of moving it to a different site, which would be a disaster. Burton is not the centre of British brewing by accident. It is where it is for a very good reason, which is its water. There is no better water for brewing pale ales. As we had discovered in Bishop's Castle, most brewers 'burtonise' their water; they add mineral salts to make their water as much like that which occurs naturally in Burton as possible. Like Bath and Malvern, Burton is a town whose fortune has been made by having the right kind of water. Burton sits on top of dozens of springs, the water from which is rich in gypsum. At the mashing stage, before the yeast is introduced, enzymes turn starches in the malted barley into sugars for the yeast to feast upon. Gypsum encourages this process.

The earliest record of brewing in Burton goes back to 1295, when the monks of Burton Abbey were already well known for the excellence of their ale. When Mary Queen of Scots was imprisoned in nearby Tutbury Castle in 1584, her daily tipple was Burton ale. This was not being made by big breweries, but in the ale-houses of the town. Burton ale was famous, but you had to go to Burton to get it; before the addition of hops, which both bitter and preserve and thus turn ale into beer, it would not have travelled at all. Larger beer breweries started to appear during the seventeenth century, and when the River Trent was made navigable in 1712, greater amounts of beer were leaving the town. By 1720, 1,000 barrels a year were being exported to London up the Trent and round the coast, via Hull. Nor was London Burton's most important market; a navigable river to the east-coast ports opened up the Baltic trade, and Burton beer was crossing the North Sea to Denmark and Germany. An influx of capital in the 1740s meant that, by 1780, there were five major breweries on Burton High Street. Yet it would still only have been available in London in small amounts, and probably only in the smarter taverns and inns. Burton beer would have been a luxury, its clear bitterness in contrast to the dark porter that London specialised in.

It was the Prime Ministership of the Duke of Wellington which really put Burton on the map. Firstly, he had agreed that the government should provide some capital to the insanely expensive Liverpool & Manchester Railway, the world's first modern railway. The project could not have been completed without money from the State. The Duke's personal endorsement of the project, by riding on the first train from Liverpool to Manchester, was a potent symbol of the dawn of the Railway Age. Burton's production expanded by a factor of fifty in the years between the arrival of the railway in 1840 and the death of Victoria some sixty years later. St Pancras Station is a monument to the trade; it was designed, at least in part, to handle beer from Burton.

Wellington's other great contribution to Burton was the Beerhouse Act of 1834, an early attempt at liberalisation, which meant that pretty much any house could sell beer if it had a licence. The point was that lots of houses sold their beer without a licence anyway. Rather than to try and stop this trade, the idea of the 1834 Act was merely to regulate it, but it led to the largest period of expansion in the licensed trade in British history. By 1900, the average Briton was drinking thirty gallons of beer per annum. And a gallon of spirits and half a gallon of wine, incidentally, which shows how times have changed. I reckon I drink half a gallon of wine a week. Still, the Duke did all right by Burton, and must deserve a pub in his name, at least.

The writer L.T.C. Rolt arrived in Burton by canal boat. He wrote:

> Walking through Burton's dirty streets, it is impossible for a moment to forget the town's major industry. Brewers' drays or lorries rattle past over the uneven sets, and the air is filled with the pungent aroma of the tall brewhouses and maltings which meet the eye on every hand. These streets are intersected by innumerable level crossings. Every now and again, at the strident clang of a bell, the gates swing to, compelling the traffic of Burton to wait in patient deference while a squat, shunting locomotive, glittering with polished brasswork and bright paint, puffs fussily across with a lumbering trainload of great pot-bellied casks bearing the familiar names of Bass, Worthington, Allsopp or Ind Coope.

Rolt's visit was in 1939. Burton is not like that now. The level crossings have gone, as have the railways, to be replaced by a fierce one-way system. Allsopps and Ind Coope have gone too. Coors and Interbrew own Bass and Worthington between them. The setts have been uprooted and the streets laid to tarmac. Even the aroma has gone, or it had on the day of our visit; it was not like Southwold, which smells of brewing and the sea, or even Devizes, where the Wadworth's brewery scents the air. This may be because most of the processes of brewing have been industrialised to such an extent that smell has been eliminated. The move to closed fermenting vessels was necessary because $CO_2$ is produced during the production of beer, and the brewing industry is doing its bit to cut greenhouse-gas emissions; this may account for the lack of smell. Or we might just have come on the wrong day, as usual, and Burton still smells like Ovaltine for much of the time.

Driving around Burton, looking for Marston's (the Bass Museum, as you may have guessed, was closed), we passed a huge Coors site, and several abandoned tower breweries. We also passed the Marmite factory. Like it or loathe it, it is made in Burton. If, after all, you are going to make yeast extract, what better place than Burton to set up your operation? Marmite was invented here in 1902.

I had arranged for us to visit the Marston's Brewery. I was motivated partly by taste; I like Marston's Pedigree. But mostly I wanted to come there because Marston's is the last of the breweries to use 'The Burton Union', a system of fermentation that uses a vast array of interlinked wooden barrels rather than tanks. Beer takes care and love to brew, as Bill Bainbridge had attempted to demonstrate at the Three Tuns. Wine, by comparison, is fairly easy. On my website (www.ianmarchant.com) I've put up a recipe for making beer, reproduced from Dorothy Hartley's *Food in England*. Have a go. If you read between the lines, it should just be possible to work out from our visit to the Three Tuns how beer is made. The process is broadly the same for most beers; mix hot water and malt, boil it up with hops, let it cool down, add yeast, wait seven days. I knew how beer is made. What I wanted to think about were the living organisms which for the best part of a hundred and fifty years had inhabited the Union.

The visitor centre is got up like a pub, one which also acts as the Marston's Museum. I had arranged this trip especially, and we were the only people being shown round. We were introduced to our guide, whose name was Tracy, a bonny lass in her late thirties, with bottle-blonde hair and the kind of English pear-shaped figure that Perry always goes for. At once, his little smirk came unbidden to his lips. He took her photo. Horribly, she smirked back, pleased that somebody wanted a snap of her.

'Ooh, I don't know that I look me best today,' she said.

'You look lovely, Tracy. Look, you can see.'

Perry showed her the picture on his poncy digital camera, leaning over her shoulder.

'Ooh, you're very good, aren't you?'

It was suddenly clear that I was going to be playing gooseberry for this trip. Off we set on our personal tour of Marston's Brewery, with Tracy in the lead, Perry strategically placed just behind her, and me trailing along in the rear. If she had fancied me, there is no doubt that I would have hung on her every statistic. I admit that. But since she so clearly had the glad eye for Perry, I found it difficult to get interested. Perry, however, was gripped.

She took us to the top of the building, which operates on the same principle as the Three Tuns; the process of brewing starts at the top of the building, and uses gravity as far as possible. She showed Perry the malt, and insisted that he chew a little. She reluctantly let me try some, too. She showed Perry the old mash tuns, and described their construction. She showed Perry some sparging tubes. She explained to Perry how the grist that is left as the wort heads off to the coppers is sold as cattle feed. She told Perry about gypsum in the water, and about the seven wells that Marston's own. She told Perry the capacity of the coppers, the temperature of the rolling boil, and about how Marston's use dried hops, not pellets. She explained to Perry that they use Goldings and Fuggles hop varieties. She showed Perry the whirlpool, where the wort is separated from the last of the grist and the hops. She showed Perry the paraflows, where the hot wort is cooled to the correct temperature for fermentation. She barely paused for breath, and whenever I asked any questions, she directed her answers at Perry.

'And every step of the way, the brewer teks samples to check that the wort is clear and bright,' she said.

'They don't tell you at school, in chemistry lessons or in careers, that if you do well at chemistry, you could work as a brewer, do they?'

'No, they don't, Perry. It's all very scientific really. I applied for a job in the labs here, 'cos it were part-time. That suited me, Perry, because I'm on me own wi' me little boy, you know, but it were above me head, really. You needed the chemistry.'

'I'd like to see your labs,' said Perry.

'Are you full-time here, then, Tracy?' I asked.

'Yeah, and I can't do it really. I'm a part-time fitness instructor as well, Perry, and it's 'ard when you're on yer own.'

'I thought you looked fit,' said Perry.

'Ooh, that's nice of you to say. Well, I'll need to be. This is me last tour. Next week I start work as a postman.'

Up until this point, I'd been quite happy to let Tracy and Perry flirt. It was natural. They were both attractive people, I could see that. Tracy was looking forward to her new life as a postie, and it was hardly surprising that she wanted to lighten up her last tour. But now Tracy took us outside the main building, and into the fermenting room, and this is what I had come to see. I needed her to concentrate on fermentation, rather than Perry's cute buns. We climbed a steel staircase on to a walkway around the room, so that we could look down on the Union.

'Now,' said Tracy, 'this is the last remaining Burton Union set. At one time, lots of brewers used a union for fermenting here in Burton; but Marston's is the last brewery still to use this system.'

The Burton Union is an environment designed to make yeast happy. It is an interconnected labyrinth of oak barrels, ninety or so, linked together with plastic pipes. Along the top of the barrels there runs a long open trough, which foamed with yeast. The trough connects to the labyrinth, and as the beer 'works', it runs from the trough, through the complex arrangement of casks, back up into the trough, and back down into the barrels. This method of fermentation is what makes Marston's Pedigree unique; as the textbooks insist, not really a bitter at all, but the last of the true Burton Pale Ales.

'Each of the casks costs about two thousand pounds to mek,' Tracy told us, launching into one of her breathless perorations. 'You need right sort of oak. They found a forest in Germany, where the trees grow very close together, so that the trunks grow tall, and don't put out many side branches, so there's no knots. These casks are made by our cooper on site. There's only fifteen or so coopers left in England, though there's more in Scotland, because they use casks for making whisky. Each cask lasts between ten to forty years, depending on the quality of oak. Each cask is serviced every two years, and between three and five millimetres are filed away at each servicing. The casks are held together by metal rings, and the heads are sealed using bulrushes . . .'

'What, really?' I said.

'Yeh. They reckon it's the best thing to use as a sealant. It's a shame it's Friday, Perry, and the cooper's shop is closed, or I could have shown yer. But even when one cask is taken out for servicing, the Union keeps working. Its been working now for a hundred and fifty years. So the yeast we use is the same family of yeast that we've used for all that time.'

No wonder this particular strain of yeast has thrived. For a hundred and fifty years, it has been fed an endless diet of sugar, which is to yeast what eucalyptus leaves are to koala bears. It is warm in the Union, and wet, and nobody thinks it rude that the yeast pisses ethanol and farts out carbon dioxide. In fact, it seems positively encouraged. So privileged is the life of brewer's yeast, that it gleefully reproduces itself, by a factor of about four during the process. The Burton Union is a breeding kennel for yeast. Because no other yeast has been allowed in, this yeast is purebred; literally Pedigree.

Every so often, if you are having a session, stoners will speculate that our entire universe could just be an atom in a whole other universe, and the amazing thing is, there's no way of telling. Well, for Mr and Mrs Marston's Pedigree yeast, the Union is an entire universe, a world unto itself. And what, an intelligent yeast might speculate, is the afterlife? They might develop a complex theology. One third of the yeast left at the end of the fermentation process lives on to eat sugar and piss alcohol again while the other two thirds is taken across town to the Marmite factory. Yeast clergymen might threaten poorly behaved yeast with eternal damnation . . . 'Yea, and you shall be drowned in salt, and thy B-complex vitamins shall be extracted, and ye shall be spread thinly on toast . . .'

Yeast are unicellular fungi, and thus not given to theological speculation of any kind. They are all over the shop; on plant leaves and flowers, in soil and salt water. Yeasts are also found on the skin surfaces and in the intestinal tracts of warm-blooded animals. Unpleasant things like athlete's foot, nappy rash and thrush are yeast infections, usually caused by *Candida albicans*, and not by the yeast used in brewing and baking. The friendly yeasts are the related species and strains of *Saccharomyces cerevisiae*. These are the fellers who humans utilise to produce booze and in baking to raise dough.

Fermentation gives off carbon dioxide and ethanol as the yeasts scoff up sugar. The carbon dioxide is trapped within tiny bubbles and results in the dough expanding, or rising, and the beer or wine sparkling. The ethanol results in you singing 'Angels' at a karaoke night down the pub, with your frock unzipped and tucked in your knickers.

Biologists have studied yeast for decades. Biologists love *S. cerevisiae* because it offers valuable clues to understanding the workings of more advanced organisms. Humans and yeast share a number of similarities in their genetic make-up; about one third of our genes are closely related. These similarities show that the genes play a critical role in cell function in both species, or they would have been lost during the billion years of evolution that separate yeast and humans, Marmite from Man.

In 1996 an international consortium of scientists announced that it had finished spelling out the entire genetic map of *S. cerevisiae*. At that time it was the largest genome to be completely mapped, and it opened the door to mapping the human genome.

'The yeast genome is closer to the human genome than anything completely sequenced so far,' said Dr Francis Collins, director of the National Center for Human Genome Research. 'The complete sequence will allow us to move into a whole new area of biology, looking at how all the genetic instructions work together to make a whole cell function.'

In cancer research, *S. cerevisiae* has emerged as an important model for studying control of the eukaryotic cell cycle (yeasts, like humans, are eukaryotes). You've got to hand it to our friend the humble yeast. It may cause personal itching, but it turns out that it gives us not just cakes and ale, but also the key to understanding how we function at the genetic level. All yeast should get to live somewhere as congenial as the Burton Union Set.

'Now,' said Tracy. 'Would you like to see the bottling plant?'

'Ooh, yes please,' I said.

'Come on, then, Perry.'

She took us across the yard, and into a building that was brittle with the sound of jostling glass. Tracy started shouting at us.

'This is one of the largest bottling plants in the UK. As you can see, we don't just bottle Marston's Beer, we bottle for other brewers too. The plant can process twenty thousand bottles an hour. If you want, you can go up on the gantry and have a look. I'll wait for you outside.'

Most mornings, outside a pub, you can hear the sound of a member of staff dumping bottles into a skip, with a great shattering crash. The bottling plant called that to mind; glass is noisy stuff. We climbed on to the gantry. Thousands and thousands of bottles politely queued up, like debutantes waiting to be presented to the Queen. I was reminded of watching *Play School* with my eldest daughter in the early eighties. Through the Round Window, or whichever, they would show films of canning factories, or biscuit production lines, with no voiceover to explain what was happening, just some nice library music. Highlight of a primary carer's morning, that was. It was a Futurist ballet, every morning at eleven. I'd only ever seen it on TV before, but now I was in Sadler's Wells; bottles press forwards, nozzles spurt, bottles twizzle, labels adhere, the bottles pirouette, caps are punched on. It was beautiful.

I found watching the bottling hypnotic, like sitting by a river, except a lot noisier. Sadly, the bottles were waiting to be filled with some noxious bright blue stuff for young people, who like brightly coloured things. The whole plant was choreographed by two white-coated boffins wearing ear protectors, who pointed at things on a computer screen whilst their charges danced past to their own music. Perry took some photos of the operators from the gantry. After all, as the Water Rat says to the Mole, one of the pleasures of being on holiday is watching the other fellow work.

Tracy was waiting for Perry outside the bottling plant, and she took him off for a complementary pint of Pedigree in the visitors' centre. I went, too. Tracy and her fellow guides look after the beer, and because this is Marston's Brewery Tap, they feel they have to look after it better than anyone else.

'The beer isn't ready to drink when it leaves the Union. It's still working,' said Tracy, as she pulled us each a pint. 'You add the finings at the cask stage, ooh, and I hate the smell of that, Perry.'

'It's the swim bladder of freshwater fish,' I said.

'I like the smell of dried fish,' said Perry.

'It needs seventy-two hours' racking. You put what's called a soft peg in it so that it can work. Then you put in a hard peg when it's ready to serve.'

'We got a barrel of Pedigree once for a party we were throwing, when we lived in Llanddewi,' said Perry. And so we did. We provided our guests with a nine-gallon cask of Pedigree, a catering-size jar of pickled onions, and two ounces of home-grown, ready-rolled. The party was adjudged a great success.

'Well, nine gallons is seventy-two pints,' said Tracy. 'Once the beer stops working, it's good for three to five days. If a landlord can't sell seventy-two pints in that time, then he can't really keep cask-conditioned ale. Here we are.' She gave us each a pint of Pedigree.

'I think ours lasted about three to five minutes,' I said. 'Cheers!'

'It should stick to the side of the glass,' she said, and it did. This is the one beer that straddles the North/South divide, and I would therefore choose it as the beer I would give to my Anglophile aliens, if they only had time for one pint. Tracy came and sat with us as we drank our pints, but she wouldn't have one herself.

'No, I'm still working. But I'm going into Burton tonight for a few drinks with the lasses, to say goodbye, like. We're going to Wetherspoon's, Perry.'

'Will you miss the brewery, Tracy?'

'I will, but the hours didn't work out, not now I'm on me own wi' me little boy.'

'Are the breweries still the main employer in Burton?' I asked.

'Oh yeah. I mean, four hundred people work 'ere. But only fifty of them actually make beer. The rest of 'em are in sales and that.'

'I loved your tour, Tracy,' said Perry. 'You're a very good guide, and I bet you'll be a good postman too.'

Tracy laughed.

'We're going out for a drink tonight ourselves, aren't we, Ian?' pleaded Perry.

I agreed.

'I might see you later, then,' said Tracy.

'What are you like?' I said to Perry as I drove around Burton looking for our B & B.

'No, but we are going out for a drink, aren't we?'

'Of course. We'll go for a curry and a few pints. The Burton Bridge Inn sounds good.'

But Perry persuaded me of the merits of Wetherspoon's. Nagged me into it.

We smartened ourselves up at the B & B. We'd each packed a suit for just such an occasion.

'Ough!' I said. 'I think I may have put on a few pounds.'

'Oww. Me too.'

'And is it me, or do we smell of pork scratchings?'

Perry sniffed his jacket. 'Poufffffffffff.'

Then we walked out into the town.

Already at half-seven, great big lasses with haunches like hams were clattering through the pedestrianised streets on their way to the bars. Great big things of girls, with their pierced torsos hanging between New Look tops and micro-skirts from Matalan. Lasses with hair-dos, big old barnets, doused in dye, adventures in hair gone horribly wrong, trailing Charlie in their wake.

Already they were shouting at us, when all they'd had was a half a bottle of vodka between them in Coleen's room while they waited for her to do her face, which Christ knows needed doing:

'Fuckin' look at 'im!'

'You all right, mate?'

'Fuckin' what a state.'

Already at half past seven, stocky men with shaven heads and Nazi necks in leather jackets and aviator shades with walkie-talkies in their inside pockets stood guard at the entrance to Yates, Wetherspoon's, the Lounge. The girls were hanging round the door, joking with the doormen. A night of Europop and alcopops lay before them, with the promise of a laugh, a fight, a shag. The trick is to get pished quick, and then who gives a fuck what happens. Here's a poem, by Catherine Smith:

## Hen Night

By her fifth Bacardi Breezer, she's sweating cobs,
her L-plates have come askew and her make-up's
gothic. The stripper's a big disappointment;

puts his back out giving her a fireman's lift
and ignores her mate asking to squeeze his hose.
By midnight her guts are growling

And, crouched by the bog in The King's Head,
Wave after wave of rice and peas
Leaping like salmon into the bowl, her head pounds,

it hurts to breathe, and she knows
when the ring slides over her knuckle, there'll be
this sour taste, still, this bruising on her knees.

We went for dinner in a smart-looking Indian place on the High
Street, where I had the worst curry I've ever had in a lifetime of bad
curries. It was full of over-cooked tinned pineapple, God knows why.
I couldn't finish it. The old trousers were gripping a bit, which didn't
encourage my appetite. We looked through the window as the night-
time economy of Burton took shape. Lads with comb-forwards, little
strands of hair gelled meticulously to their low brows, Ben Sherman
shirts worn outside slacks. Lads in baseball caps on BMX bikes doing
tricks for the fat lasses, too young or too stupid even to get into Yates.

Now it was our turn. Town centres have become no-go areas,
they say, for anyone who is over thirty, or who doesn't want to get
pished. I didn't want to get pished, not particularly, neither did
Perry, and thirty is a distant memory of hair and not having to get
up for a slash every night, yet here we were in a mythical forbidden zone, outside the law, somehow. If you believe conservative
commentators, this loss of access to the town centre for the
respectable citizenry is a huge social problem. But I can't really
remember anyone very much in the town centre at night. These

bars used to be banks and greengrocer's shops. Did the respectable citizenry used to attend vegetable evenings in the greengrocer's shops? I can't remember that they did. Thatcher personally destroyed the High Street with her bare hands. So what are towns to do? If you've got an entertainment licence, you can stay open till one. Stick in a DJ playing identikit dance music, offer for sale cheap lager and bottles of bright blue stuff with high-alcohol content,* and you got yourself a party. The night-time economy currently accounts for 4 per cent of GDP. Better that the town centre is full of barfing chavs and weeping students, perhaps, than allowing the town centres to die, and abandoning all life to out-of-town shopping centres, out-of-town gin palaces, and out-of-town new-build housing. Actually, that might be a good idea. Bring shops back to the city centre, and send your drinkers out to the malls. No, I stand up utterly for the right of these hideous places to exist, and for the right of people to get lashed in them until their livers dissolve. The only thing I ask is that I am not myself forced to join their company.

At least Wetherspoon's doesn't have music, just the merry scream of binge drinkers, the caustic brring of the mobile telephone, and the insistent bleat of the tills. They did have muscle on the door, and as a general rule, if you are looking for somewhere to have a drink, you should not even consider places with bouncers. But Perry had made his mind up.

I hoped they might refuse us entry, 'Sorry mate, no armchair anthropologists,' but no such luck.

We fought our way through an appreciative crowd to the bar.

'Look at 'im!'

'Where'd you get those specs mate?'

'Should 'ave gone to fuckin' Specsavers!'

The air was thick with the stink of Lynx. Atmosphere, Russ Abbot calls it.

There was no sign of Tracy.

We looked like men in the midst of their midlife crisis, trying against all hope to pull some totty. We ordered two pints of Pedigree.

---

* RTDs, the industry calls them. Ready to Drinks.

This marked us out as old gets. All the lads were drinking lager. All the lasses were drinking Reef or Ice. The crowd was a little older than the girls in the street, but we still beat them all by fifteen years. There was nowhere to sit. Places like this are designed to be stood in. We were surrounded by Burtonians with sharp elbows. We clutched our beer to our chests, while the lotus eaters of Burton-on-Trent did their best to spill it over our one good set of clothes.

'This is no fun,' I said. 'Sorry.'

'Come on! Where's you spirit of adventure? . . . Sorry.'

'I have no spirit of adventure. You know I have no spirit of adventure.'

'Excuse me,' said one of the fat lasses. 'But me and my friend were wondering if you two are queer.'

'As a nine-bob note, my dear,' I said.

'Why don't you fuck off then?'

'Perry, why don't we fuck off, really? This isn't our place. I don't want to stand around while you flirt with Tracy, even if she does turn up. You'll be a great postman. Desperate stuff.'

'She can handle my sacks anytime.'

'Well, she's not here.'

'It's a bit anti-climatic, though, after all the build-up.'

'Life is anti-climactic. Not with a bang, you'll remember, but with a whimper.'

So we went to the Burton Bridge Inn after all. It was nice. A brew pub. We had our last identifiably southern pint, with hardly a head on it. We sat next to a couple discussing whether or not to get a new shed, loosened our belts and supped our ale.

'Thing is,' said Perry, 'this place is good because just round the corner there are shit places. Only people who like good places come here. If there were no shit places to go, then the people who like shit places would come here too.'

'Diversity, that's the thing. Choice. President-for-Life Blairbrown says so.'

'And you can't argue with that,' said Perry.

'We've got to stop saying that.'

'I know.'

# Saturday 17th April

East of Burton, we slipped through the small belt of countryside that barely separates Loughborough from Nottingham, and drove into Melton Mowbray. As we pulled into the town, we finished our first kilogram of pork scratchings, a kilogram which was meant to last the whole trip. Never mind. Lots more where they came from.

Melton Mowbray means hunting. This is the home of the Quorn, the first of the modern fox-hunts. Hugo Meynell was the founder in 1753; they call him 'The Father of Foxhunting'. The owner of Quorndon Hall, just outside the town, he was the first man to breed foxhounds fast enough to keep up with the horses, which gave rise to the modern idea of a fox-hunt; hounds racing ahead of the galloping horses, who jump hedges and ditches in order to keep up. The Quorn were the first to wear the hunting pink, too. The Quorn is still a fast hunt; the country is flat, and the pack has been bred for speed for 250 years. They recommend keeping two or three thoroughbred or three-quarter-bred horses for a day's hunt, where lesser hunts, in slower country, will let you get away with one. Supporters of the hunt will tell you that the sport is democratic; that anyone can take part. I'm sure that's true; anyone, regardless of social origin, who can afford to buy and stable a couple of thoroughbred hunters is free to join in the fun. Mr Jorrocks, the grocer hero of R.S. Surtees' comic novels of hunting life *Jorrocks' Jaunts and Jollities* (1838) and *Handley Cross* (1843) was common as muck, after all. Very rich, but common as muck.

On balance, it must be admitted that since 1066, hunting on horseback with hounds has largely been a pastime, if not exclusively of the aristocracy, then certainly of the idle rich; 'the unspeakable in pursuit of the uneatable' as Doctor Johnson put it. Keeping a hunting box around Melton for the season was *de rigueur* for the aristocrats of the nineteenth century, when there was stabling for 500 horses in the town. Melton became a byword for alcoholic excess. The drunken hunters called it 'larking' and 'ragging'; just the sort of behaviour that Anthony Blanche hoped to avoid by taking Charles Ryder to dine at 'the Spread Eagle' in Thame. To be a 'Meltonian', or a 'Melton Man' meant that you could hold your drink, and join in with a practical joke or two.

According to locals, Melton was the site of one of the most legendary piss-ups in recorded history. In 1837, the Marquis of Waterford and his pals, somewhat the worse for wear, decided that it would be a 'lark' to cheer up Melton, so they got some tins of red paint, and redecorated several houses, the tollgate on the turnpike, and the tollgate keeper. They actually painted the town red; hence the expression. Whatever your feelings about hunting, or the bumptiousness of the landowning classes, you have to hand it to those lads; how many nights have you had which will stay in the popular consciousness for over a hundred and fifty years? Next time you paint the town red, raise a glass in memory of the old-style Meltonians.

There is another sense in which modern pub-goers still live with the heyday of hunting in Melton Mowbray. The landscape of the hunting field is intimately associated with pubs, because it is all but impossible to find a country pub that doesn't have framed hunting scenes on the wall. The most famous artist of the post-Meynell hunt was John Ferneley, a Melton man, whose paintings of the Quorn and their neighbours the Belvoir could fetch up to £400 each. No aristocratic hunting box was complete without one; any self-respecting Melton inn would have to have a print on the walls. A fashion was born which continues to this day, though it will be interesting to see if the prints stay on the walls now hunting with dogs has been made illegal. What will they replace them with? What is characteristic of the countryside now? Prints of West Londoners packing the 4x4 for a weekend in the cottage? Ramblers setting boldly off across Wainwright Country? Low-flying jets? Other hunting artists, such as 'Snaffles', illustrated hunting scenes set around Melton; next time you are in a country pub, take the time to examine the hunting scenes; odds are, they show one of the Leicestershire hunts in full pursuit of poor old Reynard.

Melton Mowbray also means pork pies, you might think, and you'd be right. It's one of those products like Parma ham or Parmesan cheese which are geographically protected under European copyright law. If you think the EU is bunk, remember next time you are doing the shopping, and you get yourself a couple of Melton Mowbray pork pies as a little reward, that they really have been made in Melton Mowbray to a traditional recipe. Stilton is protected in the same way, and is Melton's third great claim to greatness. All Stilton cheese comes from the area centred on the town, so Perry and I thought it would make the ideal place to stop for a ploughman's lunch.

You could get a ploughman's lunch in pretty much any English pub, fifty, a hundred, a thousand years ago, only it wasn't called that. It was called 'bread and cheese'. If the season was right you could get an onion and an apple as well. If the landlady cooked, you might get some pickled vegetables too. The point is, if all else failed, any pub worth its salt could knock you up a bit of bread and cheese. Most of them still can; all that has changed is that the marketing boys added a bit of salad and came up with a spaccy name back in the sixties.

Walking through Melton's busy Saturday market, it certainly seemed that we had come to the right place for a spot of ploughman's. Stalls groaned with Stilton cheese and hand-raised pork pies. We saw WI stalls selling home-made pickles, and stalls with fruit and veg from the fields of neighbouring Lincolnshire. I was struck by the people; by the fact that these faces, and these voices, would have been quite at home buying pork pies in Melton's Saturday market two or three hundred years ago. Here, close to the centre of England, English people are doing what English people have done since time immemorial. Only they are better-looking now, because there has been an injection of new blood, new life, into the Leicestershire countryside. The market abounded in what Saleel calls FBIs; fit British Indians. They speak with the same East Midlands accents as the Anglo-Saxon stallholders, but they are much much more beautiful. Yet another advantage of mass immigration, I would say. We visited Ye Olde Porke Pie Shoppe, which was hugely impressive, if, like me, you are a fat bloke with an insatiable appetite for pork products, and then settled on the Half Moon for our ploughman's lunch.

A couple of pints of Pedigree, half a hand-raised pork pie each, a chunk of pungent Stilton, wet from the press, some sharp pickles and a crunchy local salad were just the thing that Perry and I had been hoping for. While we ate our lunch, everyone else in the dark pub sat hunched over their copies of *Racing Post*, marking their cards for that afternoon's racing. Marking up your card in the pub still seems to me to be the traditional pastime of Saturday lunchtime. I liked Melton Mowbray.

We went back to the car, rescued one of the sacks of pork scratchings from the boot, and kept heading east. Perry was driving, I was navigating. He kept doing that annoying stuttering thing, while I picked out an annoying route. The idea was that we should drive into Lincolnshire by back roads, and head for Skegness on the North Sea coast. When we got there, we would make up our minds what we wanted to do.

South of Grantham, we crossed the A1, at the point where the modern road parts company with the old Roman road that the Saxons called Ermine Street, and then followed the Roman road north towards the RAF College at Cranwell. This part of Lincolnshire is full of airfields, the most militarised landscape we had seen since Salisbury Plain. We jinked across the flat country, where roads are dictated to by the shape of the fields. This is Britain's most fertile area. There are no hedges, or even verges, as the land is too good to waste. The fields come right up to the edge of the road, the sky to the edge of the fields. The roads often follow the course of drainage ditches, and then take ninety-degree turns as the ditch follows its field. Here and there we passed through small villages; Digby, Timberland, Ashby-de-la-Launde, lost under the sky. At Martin Dales, we came to the River Witham, and we stopped for a pint at the King's Head, where the landlord was much tickled by the idea of the Longest Crawl.

'And you've told yer wives yer writing a book? Oh, that's brilliant, that is.'

'No, I am writing a book. I've got a contract, and everything.'

'No, you're killing me. Best excuse I've ever heard . . . Irene!' He called his wife, who popped her head from the kitchen.

'What yer want?'

'Irene, keep an eye on the pub, will yer, luv? I'm just off to write a book about the bars of Ibiza.'

Across the Witham bridge, and we came into one of the oddest towns in England, Woodhall Spa. It is set amongst pines, and the soil is mostly sand. Blink, and you could be on the Surrey heaths. There were at least four large hotels; and there was the headquarters of the English Golf Union; there was no building earlier than 1900. Woodhall Spa cast a spell over me as we drove through the little town.

'Weird place,' said Perry, as we drove on towards the coast.

We drove through Horncastle, which calls itself 'the Town of Antiques'; it is trying to do a Hay, and attempting to attract tourist shoppers. So far as we could tell, they were doing all right, as the pretty little town seemed alive with visitors.

And so to Skeggy, and the sea. We had crossed the country, from Perry's house on the Welsh coast, to the coast at Skegness, and had taken almost three days to do it. If you go slowly enough and take enough back roads, even driving from Aberystwyth to Skegness can feel like an epic voyage.

'I feel like Cortez, looking for the first time out on to the Pacific Ocean,' I said, as we stood on the prom.

'Except there were no donkey rides or miniature golf courses for him to enjoy,' said Perry.

Even in the middle of April, the seafront was already raucous with families from Nottingham and Sheffield come for a weekend. The early echo of summer laughter ran through the waiting amusement arcades, which were starting to fill. The sea was brown, and the wind bitter, but a few hardy children with trousers rolled above their knees were already paddling. Some children sat mounted on mournful donkeys plodding along the beach with the weight of the world on their shoulders.

A man walked past us and said to his girlfriend, who had been complaining about the temperature, 'It's not cold, though, is it? It's bracing.'

The world-famous symbol of Skegness is the Jolly Fisherman, skipping and prancing along the beach in his thigh-length rubber boots and sou'wester, with the slogan 'Skegness . . . It's So Bracing'. There is a statue of the old gentleman on the prom. He was first drawn in 1908 by the poster artist John Hassall for the Great Northern Railway. A hundred years before, in 1808, Skegness had twenty-three houses and a population of 156. It was the arrival of the railway in 1873 that led to Skegness's popularity as a holiday resort. The Duke of Scarborough, who owned Skegness at the time, must have been a wily old bird, because from 1870 onwards he had started to develop the village into the modern town, laying out the wide streets which still give Skegness an attractive and open feel. Billy Butlin opened his first camp in 1936 in Skegness, and I could see why. It's a nice English seaside town, much more fun than, for example, Eastbourne or Morecambe. We got unlucky with the pub, that's all.

It was called Wolfies Bar, a dark blue cavern of a place on the seafront. At half past four in the afternoon, it was only a quarter full, mostly with young men in baseball caps waiting for the football results on the many television screens around the bar. There were also some families sitting by the door, two fat couples in matching velour leisurewear who were drinking lager and smoking tabs and talking about prize bingo whilst studiously ignoring their bored offspring, a couple of kids per couple, who sat eating plates of chips. One of the mothers spoke to her child.

'Fuckin' shut it, will yer, Dason?' she said.

The young men standing around watching the telly nudged one another as Perry and I approached the bar. They thought we were very funny, and they told us so: 'Fuckin' 'ell. Faggots.'

This seemed a bit rich; why Skeggy has not become another Blackpool or Brighton is beyond me, given the state of the Jolly Fisherman as he minces along the beach. Thigh-length rubber boots? He wouldn't look out of place in Old Compton Street. Oddly, no one in Old Compton Street, or Canal Street in Manchester, or in my home town of Brighton has ever shown any sign of interest in getting their hands on me. It only seems to be drunk young chavs who think I fit the bill of what a gay man should look like.

At the bar, all the beer came from taps; chemicals mixed with water, pumped full of $CO_2$, and sold cheap to suit the underdeveloped taste buds of the recently post-adolescent. Cheap lager is shit. My favourite quote about lager comes from a mid-seventies edition of *Coronation Street*, which has stayed with me for thirty-odd years. Ken Barlow goes into the Rover's.

'Good evening, Ken,' says Mrs Walker. 'Will you have a drink?'

'No thanks, Mrs Walker,' says Ken. 'I'm driving. I'll just have a pint of lager.'

Odd that something weak as piss water manages to be the fuel that fills A&E departments every Friday and Saturday night, but there, a certain kind of young man loves a scrap, and not often the kind of young man who has anything other than poor taste or a weak head. Real-ale drinkers might be beardy old gets, but it's not them terrorising the night-time High Streets. You don't hear about real-ale louts. There was no real ale in Wolfies, so we both had a Guinness, for the first time on the trip.

We could have had a cocktail; there was a menu with a hilarious selection of delicious drinks for children: the Blow Job, which is Banana Bols, Baileys and cream; the Slippery Nipple (Sambuca, Baileys and Grenadine); or a Wolfies Wrecker, which is vodka, Pernod and cider, with a blackcurrant top, served in a half-pint glass. Lovely. In tiny letters at the bottom of the cocktails menu it says 'Please enjoy our products responsibly'. While the boys wind themselves up on cheap lager for a fight, the girls drink this vile stuff, which they will regurgitate into the gutters on the way home.

Here was a place I could really give vent to middle-aged grumpiness. Although I know from experience that young stupid men in baseball caps and tracksuit bottoms who drink lager usually just fight amongst themselves, there was an air of unwelcome about the place which shaded into menace. Over by the door, young Dason had finished his chips, and was keen to get outside.

'Dason! Fuckin' get 'ere!' bellowed Mama. Give it ten years or so, and Dason too will be standing in his baseball cap at Wolfies Bar, swallowing lager and menacing strangers. There is no class more conservative than the underclass, no better way of ensuring continuing membership than calling your child 'Dason'.

We waited for the football results (Brighton 1, Peterborough 0), finished our drinks, and got back into the bracing Skeggy air.

'Shit-hole,' said Perry.

'Can't argue with that,' I said.

We walked along the prom to where we had parked the car.

'I suppose we'd better look for somewhere to stay?' said Perry.

'Let's visit the model village first.'

I like model villages. Life is easier at 1/16 scale. This is one of the things my kids hate me for. Visiting the seaside when they were tinies, they wanted me to go with them on horrifying fairground rides, but I forced them instead to stroll around model villages, while I explained the difference between 0- and G-gauge model-railway layouts. The Skegness village is a classic, dating from 1962, set behind a high hedge. There was an ancient lady in a fetching jet-black wig, collecting money in a kiosk by the gate, and a lugubrious old gentleman pulling weeds from a flower bed. We were the only paying customers. A G-gauge model train rattled around the site. The church played scratchy hymns through hidden speakers. Model bathers in old-fashioned bathing drawers played happily in the lido. A hunt, frozen in time, chased a fox across the lawn. The hounds were just taller than the grass. The officer in charge of the fire station was called P. Uppitt. There were oast-houses, and an abbey, both of which in their way hold out the promise of intoxication to the clay inhabitants of the village. Best of all there were two pubs, each representing a different level of pub hierarchy; the George Inn was posh, standing on its own, half-timbered, and three storeys high, while the Nag's Head was a disreputable old boozer, leaning drunkenly against another of the model houses; according to the sign, the licensee was Frank Lee Merry.

'If this isn't England,' said Perry, 'I don't know what is.'

'Amazing that places like this survive.'

I have been unable to find out for sure how many model villages there are in the UK. The International Association of Miniature Parks has fifteen members, from MiniTurk in Turkey to MiniWorld in Canada, but only one UK member, the mighty Bekonscot, the world's oldest model village, near Beaconsfield in Buckinghamshire. Incredibly, there don't seem to be any model-village fan sites on the interweb. Since there are fan sites for everything, this cannot bode well for the future of the UK model-village industry. There is a vacancy waiting to be filled, and I like to think that one of my readers might be geek enough to take it on.

I asked the lugubrious gentleman if they ever had problems with vandals.

'No, the hedge has always kept them out.'

'Did you make the models?' I asked him.

'No! I've not the skill for that! I wish I had! No, I just look after them, paint 'em up in t'winter, keep the garden and the like.'

'Do you get many visitors?' I asked.

'Aye, in the season. It's a bit early yet.'

As we left the village, I said to Perry, 'You know what? I don't really want to stay in Skegness.'

'Why?'

'It looks OK, but I hated that pub, and the model village made me sad.'

'Where do you want to go, then?'

'Woodhall Spa. Let's go back there. We haven't stayed at a really posh hotel yet. Whaddya think?'

'So long as you drive, I'm up for it.'

So we retraced our steps, back inland twenty-five miles or so, to the strange little spa town in the woods, where it is rumoured that Tarby and Brucie have holiday homes, so that they can be near to the excellent golf courses.

Of the four hotels in Woodhall Spa, we fancied the Petwood, a faux-Jacobean sprawl of a place with a car-park crammed full of Beamers and Mercs, and a bouncing bomb outside the entrance, which was odd. We tried to spruce ourselves up a bit in the car, admiring our reflections in the driving mirror. If you were running a four-star hotel, and two old hippies turned up, smelling of Guinness and spliff, with ash spilled down their front, and pork scratchings stuck between their teeth, you might think twice before admitting that you had a room available for the night. But at the Petwood, they are above such superficial considerations. They are class. They did have one (twin) room left at HOW FUCKING MUCH!???

I managed to keep my face under control.

'Thank you,' I said. 'We'll take it.'

'You must be mad,' said Perry, as we struggled into our suits up in the room. There could be no doubt. They smelled of pork scratchings, the pork scratchings which we kept in the boot with all our clothes. All our clothes smelled of pork scratchings.

'No, it's worth it. It'll be a crack. Let's live like kings, just for one night.'

We wandered down into the Squadron Bar, rich in oak panelling and red velvet plush, and with model aeroplanes in cases on the wall. It was rammed with the owners of the Beamers and Mercs, young, good-looking, dressed in their Sunday best, some of them wearing kilts.

'What's going on?' I asked the barman.

'It's a wedding.'

In an adjoining room, we could hear the cheery thump of a wedding disco. Reasoning that, although we smelled a bit, in our suits we could pass for guests, we took our pints through into the reception. There was a sign outside the door. It said 'Celebrating the Wedding of Donald and Marie'.

'Do you think they call him Donny?' said Perry.

The bride and groom, with their mums and dads, uncles and aunties, grans and grandads still sat the top table, behind an ornate cake. Tinies slid about on the floor, in sweet costumes that will prove a source of endless hilarity to their own children when they unearth the photos in thirty years' time. The portion of the guests who had managed to get the most drink down them had started bopping to 'Wake Me Up Before You Go Go'. There was a fine display of young womanly flesh, lightly clothed in gossamer party frocks. Lots of them had Beckhamesque tatts; squirling inscriptions in Sanskrit traced over their naked backs and shoulders.

'That room was worth every penny, I reckon,' said Perry.

'Told you.'

Less attractive were the hairy legs of that section of the male guests who had chosen to wear kilts. Donald's side, we presumed. I went to a corking wedding in Scotland once, where old Perry was best man, and he had to wear a kilt for that, even though he is about as Scottish as a green salad. He has good legs, I must admit, and might have carried it off with a measure of *savoir-faire*. Sadly, he had got bladdered the night before with the bride's father on single-malt whiskies, so his skin was the colour of porcelain, with the same translucency, and instead of joining in a nice foursome reel at the reception with the bridesmaids, Perry spent the whole time in the gents, boaking up his ring.

I too have disgraced myself when called upon to perform the duties of best man. When we were students at Lampeter, Perry and I shared a house with four other guys. One of the lads was going out with a nice lass from the town; they got engaged, and he asked me to be best man. I agreed. Then they split up. Six or seven years later, he met another lass at work, and had gotten engaged to her, and insisted on holding me to my promise to be his best man. Snag was, in the intervening years, he had become a member of the Metropolitan Police force, as was his bride-to-be. All our old pals refused to go to the wedding except me. Emboldened by drink, in my speech I told the story of how the copper had tried to grow a cannabis plant in his room over the course of a Welsh winter by putting a two-bar electric fire next to the plant pots, and keeping it on for three months, and how he had failed to do anything except fill the upstairs of the house with the fetid stink of his socks. This went down quite badly, so I took another swig of champagne, and embarked on the one about how he felt it was dirty to masturbate in bed, and chose instead to crack one off over our bathroom sink, neglecting always to wipe up his man-milk, a most unpleasant experience when you went up there to clean your teeth. I had been certain that the assembled families and cops would love this one, but I was wrong. In fact, the groom's mother started crying.

To be a proper best man, you must stay as close to sober as you can manage. It is a tough gig. There is only one gig tougher, of course, and that is being groom. I can't honestly say I enjoyed either of my weddings over-much. At the first one, I was twenty-one, and fucking stupid. My speech was brief.

'Thank you all for coming here today,' I said, 'to see us take the first step towards getting a divorce.'

How funny I thought I was. How my chums roared. How angry was my new wife; how disgusted were our families. In my defence, I was very drunk. Luckily, the prophecy never came true, as we were spared the divorce court by her death. My second wedding was quiet. There was me and Lily, the two kids, and Perry and Gilly, who acted as witnesses. We split up a year later, the day after getting back from Perry and Shinaid's own wedding. Happy days.

And now it can't be too long before my eldest daughter Charley ties the knot. By tradition, it will be me who picks up the tab. I've been arguing for some years that she should go for a low-key affair, where a carefully selected band of guests, perhaps a dozen strong, would go after the ceremony to the Yorkshire House for a few pints and some pickled eggs. Charley has yet to see the wisdom of this plan. One compensation is that it will be my turn to get the best man pissed the night before the wedding.

By far the best job at a wedding is to be hired as the entertainment. This is a truly great gig. Although you have to lay off the booze until you've finished your set, all the pressure is off. You start quiet while the wedding breakfast is on, play a few oldies for the grans, do something cheesy for the bride and groom's first dance, and finish up with a few rockers so everyone is ready for the DJ and 'Hi Ho Silver Lining'. Then you can get pished yourself, and have a bop. For this, Chas and I charge five hundred quid. (If you are currently planning your wedding, and are looking for a top-class act, why not contact me via ian@ianmarchant.com?)

We left the reception, and went back into the Squadron Bar. A piano player tinkled gamely at a Steinway in the corner while the bright young things of the wedding chattered with rising volume over their drinks. The pianist was a young blonde woman of dazzling beauty, in a dress of multi-coloured sequined splendour.

'She's very good,' I said to Perry.

'I can see why you think so,' he replied.

We went off for a spot of fillet steak washed down with a first-class bottle of Rioja in the restaurant. We could still hear the beautiful piano player from the next room. After our meal, we went to sit in the lounge. The waiter brought us coffee and cigars. We sat back in leather armchairs, and surveyed the world with well fed complacency. The piano player was at the next table, drinking a white-wine spritzer; I invited her to join us, to which she agreed with a professional smile. Musos at a wedding are a kind of superior servant, like an old-fashioned governess. She told us her name was Helen Clarke. I told her that I had enjoyed her set, that I had often played at weddings myself. She told us that she got a lot of bookings at the Petwood, sometimes with her identical-twin sister Sonia, who was a flautist. I tried to hide my disappointment that Sonia had not been there as well tonight.

'We always play for the Dambusters Reunion,' said Helen.

'I'm sorry?' I said.

'RAF Woodhall was where the Dambusters raids took off.'

'So that's why there's a bouncing bomb outside,' said Perry.

'Oh yes. This was the officer's mess for 617 Squadron,' she said. 'The hotel was requisitioned for the duration. The Dambusters came in 1943, and stayed till the end of the war. Every year, they have a reunion here. And we play for them. Last year, there were only four of the gentlemen still alive.'

'Bloody hell,' said Perry.

So this was where first Guy Gibson and then Leonard Cheshire and their officers had spent the war, drinking and playing tennis and shooting at one another between raids over night-time Nazi Germany. It made us like the place even more. Helen would have made a superb forces sweetheart, and I told her so.

She blushed.

'Thank you very much. It is a huge honour to play for them.'

All at once, I decided that when I am old and rich, I will book into the Petwood Hotel in Woodhall Spa, and stay there. I will be a resident guest, like the Major in *Fawlty Towers*. I will have two yappy pugs, called Margaret and Antonia. I will wear an Inverness cape, and walk the dogs in the grounds of the hotel. On Wednesdays, I will play golf; on Sundays, I will go to evensong. I will have an inappropriate relationship with a fifty-something widow who has taken early retirement to live in a bungalow bordering the golf course. In the evenings, I will eat fillet steak and drink Rioja, and after dinner, I will fill my pipe, and smoke it in the lounge, while Helen plays 'We'll Meet Again' on the Steinway Grand. The ghosts of the Dambusters will gather around the piano, and I will raise my glass of after-dinner port, and toast their memory.

At weekends, the ghosts and I will lech at wedding guests in flimsy frocks. I can hardly wait.

## Sunday 18th April

'Where we off to next, then?' said Perry, as we waited for our lattes to cool so that we could swallow our aspirins.

'Well, I've got nothing planned till tomorrow. Tomorrow night we're going to Leeds for a pub crawl with Ziggy.'

'Oh God, we're going to be so ill when we finish this trip.'

'I know.'

We were nursing our hangovers in a seafront café in Cleethorpes. We had driven up through the gloriously pretty Lincolnshire Wolds from Woodhall, after a classy breakfast at the Petwood, which neither of us could quite finish. It was pouring with rain. Thinking about going drinking with Ziggy the next night was hardly conducive to settling our stomachs. I was at Lancaster University with Zig. I met him at a Freshers' Week party on my first night there, in 1989. I was thirty-one, he was eighteen. We quickly discovered that we shared mutual interests. Over the next eight years, we formed a close, even intimate relationship, made more intimate still by the fact that we always seemed to be chasing the same girls. As well as smoking a vast amount of mutual interest, Zig was the most legendary drinking man in my year; in anybody's year. In the Ring o' Bells in Lancaster, they still talk about the night Zig drank thirty-two pints, and how, as the last pint went down, so did he. He liked to take off his clothes when he was pissed, and would dance on stage with my band when we had a gig, waggling his eye-watering cock at our fans, many of whom were female mature students, several of whom were blinded to the fact that Zig has a face like a bucket of frogs by the sight of his porn-star todger. Zig would be expecting us to drink a great deal tomorrow night.

'Let's just take it easy today,' I said, already quailing at what Ziggy might have in store for us. 'Let's get across the Humber

Bridge, and find somewhere to stay around Hull. I could do with a quiet night. In fact, I could do with doing nothing, for most of the rest of the day.'

'Me too,' said Perry.

We drove north from Cleethorpes, and crossed the Humber by the beautiful bridge. There was little to see, as the grey drizzling rain blocked any chance we may have had of seeing the view. Somehow, on a wet and miserable Sunday, Hull didn't appeal. We looked at our maps, and decided that we would try Spurn Head, away to the east, a great sandbank that curls out into the mouth of the Humber like a pirate's hook. The last village in the flat bleak countryside before Spurn is called Kilnsea, and here we stopped for a bite at the Crown and Anchor, hard up against the estuary, with views across the mud flats, to judge from the cars in the car-park, clearly a popular spot. A good old-fashioned Sunday lunch, friendly staff, and the water of the Humber estuary, bubbling and brown like fermenting beer, made us decide that we should get a room here, have a nap, then go for a walk along Spurn Head. A quiet night in the pub would prepare us for the drive to Leeds in the morning. A quiet night would help us face up to the rigours of a night on the town with Zig. We had come a long way, after all, and neither of us had been to this sea-haunted place before.

'Sorry, fellers,' said the landlady. 'Can't help yer. I've only got four rooms, and they're all tekken by lads working at gas plant.'

We looked at our *Good Beer Guide*, and found the Bell, in Great Driffield, a market town some fifteen miles to the west and north. The book said it had over a hundred whiskies behind the bar. That sounded OK. We wouldn't hammer them, but one or two would help us sleep. I phoned ahead, and booked a room, which was too expensive, but neither of us cared; we just wanted to get our heads down for the afternoon. Before we left for Driffield, however, we drove the car along the narrow spit of Spurn Head, and went for a walk, to let the wind hoover up our hangovers.

Spurn Head is really a series of sandbanks, slowly growing on one side with silt from the Humber; and being eroded on the other by the fierce North Sea. On the river side of the Head, the water is calm; fifty yards away, the North Sea rages against the beach, which is strewn with rubbish puked up by the waves. Out to sea, we could see at least a dozen ships waiting for the pilot boats which buzzed to and fro, waiting to be guided through the sandbanks of the Humber to Immingham or Hull. On the calm side of the Head, there is a long pier out into the mouth of the river, from where the pilot boats plied their trade, and where Britain's only full-time lifeboat sits waiting for a call to action. A fog horn brayed. The wind howled. I phoned my eldest daughter Charley, to arrange our visit to Lancaster in a couple of days. I hadn't seen her since Christmas, and I felt sad that it had been so long. Spurn Head is a good place for feeling sad. But at least the fresh air had blown away the last of our sick headaches; we got back into the car, turned our backs on the sea, and drove on through the flat lands towards Great Driffield. As in Lincolnshire, the roads turn at ninety-degree angles as they follow the course of fields and drainage ditches. The rain was relentless; Perry and I were silent, looking forward to our quiet evening.

Great Driffield advertises itself as 'The Capital of the Wolds', and was once an important market town. The glory days of the nineteenth century, when Driffield was the fastest-growing town in the East Riding of Yorkshire have long gone, but the Bell is still a smart old coaching inn, with comfortable rooms. We unloaded our pork-scented luggage, and hit the hay.

When I woke, it was half past six in the evening. I ran myself a bath. When I emerged, Perry was just coming to, and I said I'd see him down in the bar. He said he'd be down in a bit, after his bath. In the entrance hall, I read a sign advertising the Bell's 'Fragrant Retreat', an alternative-healthcare clinic housed in the back of the hotel. They offered Aura Balancing Facials, Hopi Ear Candles, Reiki natural healing and Crystal balancing for your chakras. It was like being back in Glastonbury, though no town on earth could be less like Glasto than Driffield. I got chatting to Sean, the barman, who had only started working at the Bell a few days before. In fact, he had only just moved to Driffield from Didcot, the town next to Harwell, where my father had lived, and where I had first visited a pub. There really were more than a hundred whiskies; I settled for an Islay single malt. Perry came down from the room, clearly refreshed, but still smelling of pork scratchings. We ordered a bar meal, which was brought to us by Karen, receptionist, waitress, and good egg. She was lovely, but the meal was horrible. The hotel manager, whose uncanny resemblance to Basil Fawlty almost scared us, sat at the back of the bar, reading the Sunday papers. Clearly, he was going for a quiet night too.

So now it was eight, and we had eaten, and bathed, and were feeling much better. We agreed that it would be a good thing to go round the town, and get a feel for the pub landscape of Driffield. We asked Karen what the pubs in Driffield were like, and she recommended three: the Tiger, the Full Measure, and the Star. We agreed that we would have a half in each, and then pack it in. So we put on our jackets, and set off round the mostly deserted town centre. We tried the Tiger first, a run-down town boozer, with the kind of ancient interior that, whilst undoubtedly authentic, could hardly be said to be worth preserving. It was only me and Perry in; the landlord, having worked out that we were southerners, assured us that we would like his Sam Smith's.

'After all,' he said, 'the beer down south is as flat as a fart.'

Still, at least it was quiet, and that was the main thing.

We each had a half of foamy northern beer, before moving on to the Full Measure, which was up a side street a few hundred yards away from the Bell. It was full of schoolboys, actual schoolboys in their uniforms. Even my dad, trying to lure the underage drinkers of Wheeler End into his evil web, drew the line at schoolchildren in uniform. Perry and I were at a loss to explain this phenomenon. It was clearly not some kind of 'school disco' night, where adults dress up as school kids and dance to Kajagoogoo records. No, these were kids, some of them no older than fourteen. But why were they in school uniform on Sunday night? They were drinking tequila shots, and screaming at the solitary barmaid, who could have been little more than eighteen herself. She had no control over the boys, and it was the first pub we'd been into which I seriously felt should lose its licence. It was exactly the kind of place you would not go to spend a quiet night, so we downed our halves, and made for the last pub on Karen's list, the Star, in a street which ran along the side of the Bell. It was just gone nine; one more half, then bed, we agreed.

We passed the Bell, and turned the corner. The lights of the Star were glowing about fifty yards down the dark street, on the right-hand side. We crossed over the empty street towards the pub. Another fifty yards on, but on the opposite side of the road, was a large pair of double doors which led into the Bell car-park, poorly lit by the yellow glare of a streetlight. A lad in a baseball cap with the brim turned up was holding a girl against the doors by her neck. She was screaming blue murder. An unwelcome realisation lurched inside my guts. There was no one else about. This was down to us.

Perry said, 'I suppose we'd better do something.'

'Yeah. I suppose so.'

As we walked towards them, still on the opposite side of the road, we could see the couple begin to take shape. She was a plump, short pretty girl with bottle-blonde hair pulled back so tight she looked like a Hollywood actress of advancing years, victim of a dozen facelifts. She could not have been more than fifteen or sixteen, and she was screaming, crying, wailing at the top of her voice. A yoof, eighteen or so, in regulation chav gear – tracksuit bottoms, hoody, baseball cap, low brow, bad teeth – pinned her against the doors of the garage, and was screaming in his turn into her face. We could see now that he had her gripped by the front of her top, his face an inch away from hers.

'DO YOU FUCKIN' 'EAR ME, YOU FUCKIN' SLAG!!! YOU FUCKIN' ORE!!! DO YOU FUCKIN' 'EAR ME!!! I'LL FUCKIN' TWAT YER, YER FUCKIN' SLAG!!!'

We were level with them now, still on the other side of the street. I didn't want to do this, this wasn't my job, why was there no one else to do this but us? It seemed unfair. But I knew it had to be done, and the closer we came, the calmer, the more in control of the situation I felt.

As I crossed over the street towards the couple, I called out to the girl, 'Are you all right, love?'

'No,' she sobbed.

'Fuck OFF!' said the yoof. It was clear that he was very drunk.

Perry was right behind me, I knew.

'Would you like us to walk you up the road to the phone box, so you can phone your mum?' I said, all the time talking to the girl, ignoring the boy.

'Yes please,' she said, her sobs subsiding a little.

'I told you faggots to FUCK OFF!!' said the yoof. Now I turned my attention to him, armed only with my one small nugget of self-defence know-how, which I had been taught by an old board-marker called Tony. My first day of working for William Hill's in 1979, it was Tony who trained me how to write up the results of horse-races, how to make proper tea, and how to look after myself if ever I got in trouble in the sometimes alarming atmosphere of the bookmaker's shop. He called me Educated Evans, Educated for short.

'Educated,' he said, 'there's three kinds of people you NEVER have a go at. They are ———s, ———s, and blokes over forty.'

'Why not blokes over forty?'

'Look at you, Educated. You are strong and fast' (I was twenty-one). 'Now look at me. I'm forty-eight and fat and slow. If you come at me, I know that I've only got one chance, and that I've got to hurt you. If the fight goes on, you'll win every time. An old guy *has* to hurt you. He's got no choice.'

So here I was, twenty-five years later, and the yoof was young and strong and fast and I was forty-six and fat and slow. So I knew that if he did come at me, I would have to hurt him. Also since he was pissed, although his emotions might be running at something of a high, his reactions would be slower than mine. One more thing in my favour: there were two of us, and we were both twice his size. Only if he was very stupid would he actually have a go.

'Come on, son,' I said. 'Calm down. It's OK. Leave her alone. You go that way, we'll walk her up the phone box, and you can call her tomorrow and say you're sorry.' I touched him on his forearm. I'm not sure which was worse from his point of view, that I

272

had touched him, or that I had implied that he might have done something for which to be sorry.

'We're fuckin' engaged,' he said, which I'm sure was all the justification he needed for his behaviour.

'Not now, we're not,' sobbed the lass.

'Come on, love,' I said. 'Come on. We'll find the phone box, and your mum can come and pick you up.'

'I TOLD YOU FAGGOTS TO FUCK OFF!'

And he came at me. It was very strange. It seemed to happen very slowly. In retrospect, I seem to have had time to explain to him why he shouldn't attack me . . .

'Don't have a go, son, because we're bigger and older than you, and there's two of us, and you're pissed, and we're sober . . .' but of course, it happened much too quickly for explanations. I felt as calm as I had ever felt, as though I was watching Devon versus Cornwall in a Minor Counties cricket match on a drowsy afternoon in June. As he swung his first clumsy punch at my head, I stepped to one side, and grabbed the little fuckwit in a headlock.

I don't think I've ever felt less worried about anything in my whole life. The yoof was struggling as I held him round the neck, but I said to his ex-fiancée, 'Off you go, love. You go up on to the High Street and phone your mum. We'll keep him here.'

The girl ran up the street, towards the phone boxes. And I had a prize, held under my arm, trapped in my power, a struggling yoof, a witless chav, a little cunt in a baseball cap. It was too good a chance to miss. Suddenly, at once, my calm melted away to be replaced by livid anger, and I twatted him, twatted him hard in the face, like this, TWAT TWAT TWAT, three times in quick succession. I felt my fist in his face, and I loved it. I still love it now. I loved each punch. TWAT . . . for your girlfriend, for all the times you've hit her and threatened her and terrorised her, for all the women you've terrorised and will terrorise, for my mother and grandmother, living in fear of Cruiser . . . TWAT . . . because of what you are, what you wear, what you represent, the sneaking crimes you commit, the petty sneaking thefts, the pointless aimless vandalism, the joyless stupidity of your empty mind, for what you are doing to England, fucking useless

dregs of the Earth, you and all the people like you . . . TWAT . . .
for me, for the pleasure of it, for the sensual delight, because I can,
because I love the feel of my knuckles against your flabby mouth,
your flat nose, your vacant eyes.

But now the point of Tony's argument about age difference and
violence began to make itself felt. I had got in first, and stopped
him and, I hoped, hurt him. But he was stronger and faster than
me, more agile and much much nastier. He was struggling free, like
a slimy eel. Perry stepped in to help me restrain him, and he managed
to get his nails into Perry's cheek. He wriggled and shook us off,
and he was gone, running up the street, shouting after the girl,

'GEMMA!! GET 'ERE, YOU FUCKIN' SLAG!!! GEMMA!!!!!'

So I pulled out my last weapon. My mobile phone.

'Leave her alone,' I called after him. 'I'm phoning the police if
you don't leave her alone.'

We chased up the road after him, rounded the corner. He had caught
up with her, had manoeuvred her into a shop doorway, and was screaming in her face again, while she sobbed in fear. There seemed little
point in taking him on again. It was beautiful, punching his face, but
it hadn't worked. I dialled 999, and asked for the police. I explained
that we had been witness to violent and threatening behaviour, that
the yoof was still screaming at her, and threatening her, and that she
wanted help, and that we'd done about as much as we could do. I
gave our address as the Bell, Great Driffield.

I offered the yoof one last chance; held out one last diplomatic
solution.

'I've phoned the police. Walk away. Go away. Leave her alone.
We'll look after her, the police will take her home. Piss off.'

But he ignored me. We stood a few feet away, knowing that there
was no point in temporary restraint, followed by her escape, followed
by him chasing after her again. This needed ending. We watched
in case he hit her, and waited for the polis. Within a minute, two
at the most, a squad car came round the corner, blue light flash-
ing. The yoof jumped back from the girl.

'Did you see that?' he said to the first copper who got out from
the squad car. 'She pushed me.'

'All right, son,' said the copper. 'Get away from the girl. Just calm down.'

'You can fuck off an' all, yer cunts. We're fuckin' ENGAGED!'

The driver of the squad car got out, and came across to the couple. 'There's no need for swearing, son.'

'I know my fucking rights, you fucking cunts. Didn't you see her push me? What are you fucking going to do about that?'

'Son, if you don't stop swearing, I'm going to arrest you for disorderly conduct.'

'Just you fuckin' try, you fuckin' wankers.'

'All right, if that's what you want; I'm arresting you on a charge of disorderly conduct. You have the right to remain silent . . .'

'YOU'RE NOT PUTTING THEM FUCKING CUFFS ON ME.' He started to struggle against the two coppers, who were trying to pin him down, to get the cuffs on, while he wriggled and fought. I was quite gratified to see that two policemen couldn't restrain him either. One of the policemen managed to get a hand to his radio, and called for assistance, while they tried to control the little moron. Within another minute, a police van pulled up, and two more coppers got out. One helped his two colleagues get the yoof to the pavement, face down, and pin his hands behind his back and snap on the cuffs, while the fourth went across to comfort the girl. The yoof was screaming now.

'Why don't you arrest them?' he said, looking at us. 'They're faggots, but you don't fuckin' care about that, do you?'

'It's not illegal,' I said, but I'm afraid my feeble attempt at wit was wasted on him. The three coppers manhandled the squirming yoof towards the van, when, O horror of horrors, his baseball cap came off. This was too much for him. The proud badge of his stupidity fell on to the pavement.

'Me cap!' he wailed. 'Me cap's fallen off!' That's when me and Perry started laughing. And as they got him into the van, and just before they closed the doors on his evil little face, he let fall one last priceless gem: 'This is a nice way to spend yer birthday, int it?'

And the doors slammed, and the van drove away.

I went across to where the policeman was talking to the girl. He had given her a handkerchief.

'I hope we did the right thing, calling the police,' I said to her.

And she looked at me, and gave me the most beautiful smile, and said, 'Yes. You did. Thank you so much for helping me.'

And I felt like Lancelot.

'Can I take a statement from you lads?' said one of the two original polis who had turned up. We told him what had happened, though, I must admit, I neglected to mention hitting the yoof in the face. He asked if we would be happy to appear in court; we said yes, of course. They put the girl into the squad car, and drove off, presumably taking her home. It was just gone nine-thirty.

Back in the hotel, Karen the receptionist, Sean the barman, and Basil Fawlty the manager were waiting for us. One of the polis, not realising at first that we were standing by the whole time, had gone into the Bell to look for us. Basil was anxious lest we had caused trouble; Karen was anxious lest we had been hurt. We told them what had happened; Basil relaxed, and Karen glowed at us. I felt like Lancelot squared. Sean poured us each a whisky, and I started to shake. What if he had a knife? What would fat old, sad old Lancelot have done then?

And then came the post-match analysis. Part of me wanted to say, 'Poor little lad. What chance does he have in life? There are no jobs for stupid people any more. He's got no future. He must have been brutalised at home. And the drink companies exploit kids like that, and fill them with cheap booze, and it's not his fault he can't handle it, poor wee baby.' But that's not really what I think.

Really, I can't buy into relativistic accounts of behaviour at all, despite a lifetime of *Guardian* reading. Plenty of people live in poverty, bad housing, are the victims of an education system which serves only to prepare people for life in a call centre. Plenty of people get pissed. My mother was brutalised at home, in conditions of unthinkable squalor, and she didn't take it out on anybody else. What I really think is this: there is evil at work in the world. Some people are evil. That kid was evil. Not naughty, not misguided, or led astray. Evil.

Evil; not what you expect, when all you want is a quiet night.

## Monday 19th April

In the morning, on our way from Driffield to Pocklington by back roads through the Yorkshire Wolds, we were waved down by a middle-aged woman standing in the middle of a lonely crossroad.

'You can't go this way. There's been an accident; the road is blocked a little further on. You'll have to go down there,' she said, pointing to the left. We followed her advice, and a few miles on, we were stopped again, this time by two policemen.

'You can't go this way, lads. There's been an accident.'

'But we were sent this way because of the accident,' I said.

'Different accident. You'll have to go back to Warter; they should have diversion signs up by now.'

'Do you think we're trapped in a Hammer film?' said Perry. 'Nobody escapes alive.'

But we did escape from Great Driffield. By following a lengthy series of diversions round the back lanes, we came to the attractive town of Pocklington; crossed the River Derwent, thundering with flood, bypassed York, and stopped for lunch in Tadcaster, the Burton of the North.

'I'm not that hungry, actually,' I said.

'Neither am I.'

Our second empty kilo bag of pork scratchings lay in the passenger's foot well.

'Ian, we've got to do something about the scratchings.'

'I know.'

'In three days, we've each eaten a kilo. All our clothes smell of pork scratchings. The boot of my car will clearly always smell of pork scratchings.'

'A pleasant reminder of our excursion, I'd have thought.'

'We've got two bags left,' said Perry, 'and they've got to go.'

Tadcaster is rather genteel, in the way that some Yorkshire towns are, except for all the breweries. You cross the River Wharfe into the town centre. There are antique shops, teashops, ladies' dress shops ranged along the wide High Street. On one side of the street is the Old Brewery, a fine eighteenth-century brick building which masks the Samuel Smith brewery from the casual passer-by. At the top of the town, impossible to disguise, is the John Smith's brewery, a nineteenth-century tower, where they make horrible foamy beer, but first-class TV adverts. On the way into town, we had passed another big brewery, a Coors place. The breweries are here for the same reason they are in Burton: the water is very good. The town smelled of yeasty malt. We smelled of stale pork.

With plenty of time to spare before we were due to meet up with Ziggy in Leeds, we visited the offices of Sam Smith's to see if there was anyone available to show us round. There was not, not right then; but if we came back later, there would be a tour going round. No good; Ziggy was expecting us. So we settled for a pint. We chose the Howden Arms, a friendly Sam Smith's pub opposite the John Smith's brewery.

'No one in Tadcaster drinks owt but Sam's,' said the landlord, and I can see why. If I was forced to take northern beer to a desert island, I'd take Sam Smith's.

'Why do you think it's better than John Smith's?' I asked.

'Sam's is still a family concern. They tek care about what they do. Just recently, they 'ad to re-do the mash tun, and they did it in real gunmetal. Had to go all the way t' India to get it.'

We told the landlord and his small group of lunchtime regulars about the trip, and about how we'd been to a pork-scratchings factory. No, THE pork-scratchings factory.

'Do you like pork scratchings?' Perry asked the assembled company. They agreed they did, and I was dispatched back to the car for one of our two remaining bags.

'The pork scratchings are on us!' I announced on my return.

The kindly landlord bought us each an excellent pint of his beautifully kept foaming ale, which no other landlord who we encountered in the course of our travels had the good sense to do, even when informed of the nature of the project. Perhaps we should have made it plainer to our hosts that we were open to crude bribery, though it is difficult to see how we could have done, short of having 'Your Name Here' tattooed on our foreheads.

Just think, it could have been your pub. Instead, it's the Howden Arms, Tadcaster, which wins the Longest Crawl Yorkshire Pub-of-the-Decade Award.

Mind you, we brought rare pork gifts from the South. The scratchings smoothed our passage. The regulars huddled round the sack. Luckily, they all seemed to have their own teeth. When we left, they raised their hands in farewell, crunching and chewing behind their smiles, their lips dusted red with faintest trace of MSG.

We arrived in Leeds, parked the car in the university district, and were still too early to meet Ziggy, so we went for a drink in the student union. We found the Terrace Bar, a bright modern and very large space designed for vertical drinking, and bought coffee. To start drinking *before* Ziggy would be a huge mistake. In order to smoke, we had to sit out on the terrace, which was full at three-thirty; it was the first day of summer term. It was a cold and blowy afternoon under a bright sun with no warmth in it. Everyone was trying to soak up a little sun and stay warm at the same time. The tables were crammed with students wearing inappropriate overcoats. The wind picked up plastic glasses, empty packets of crisps, flyers advertising happy hours in town-centre bars: 'Two shots for one', 'Ladies drink Free', 'All you can drink for a tenner'.

We found two places to perch with our coffees on a bench at the end of one of the wooden tables. The rest of the spaces were taken by half a dozen hearties in rugby shirts, drinking lager, trying to read the *Sun* in the wind, and discussing the fastest route to intoxication. They had been to a bar the night before where flavoured vodka had been on offer. They didn't much like the chilli-flavoured vodka, feeling that it was 'too kebabby'. Management-science students.

On the table next to us slouched a student band with their guitar cases propped against their knees, the drummer tapping away with his sticks on the table. Girls in short skirts and shades sat silently by as their menfolk charted their route to the top. Little could they expect that their future sat beside them on the next table, twenty-five years on, turned from wannabe rock gods into two old geezers who used to play a bit and were now trying to look up their girl-friends' skirts.

So five rolled round, and we made our way to the Parkinson Building, completed in 1950, a neo-classical barn of a place whose white tower is the university's best-known landmark. We entered through the portico into a cavernous entrance hall; two porters sitting at a reception desk were dwarfed by the scale of the place. They showed us the philosophy corridor, leading off from the hall; Leeds is an old-fashioned modern university, to still have its philosophy department at its centre. In the medieval universities, theology, the queen of sciences, rooted in the authority of the past, lay at the heart of the university's life. Study was an act of worship, which would help to reveal the will of God.

After about 1800, modern universities started to evolve across Europe; the first was the University of Berlin; University College London is the oldest British example. These new universities wanted to place philosophy (especially German Enlightenment philosophy) at the centre of their enterprise. Philosophy held the promise of a rational understanding of the world; logic and epistemology were deemed essential keys to unlocking the secrets of a knowable universe. With philosophy at their heart, the new universities led the way in science and engineering. Above all, the new universities were engaged in the Newtonian task of understanding the mind of God.

Now there is another new kind of university, which dates from the late 1980s. The philosophy department has been shipped out from its central place to a couple of Portakabins on the edge of campus, and their offices have been given over to the business school. Study is now a test of fitness for the workplace; Her Majesty's Secretary of State for Education decrees that there is too much medieval history taught in universities. Focus groups assess the cash value of God.

It was good, therefore, to see how central the philosophy department still is to Leeds University. It has the largest department outside Oxford, and their offices are ranged along the corridor, and overflow into one of the wings that have been built on to the back of the Parkinson Building. All the staff have beautiful wooden nameplates on their doors. One of the nameplates said 'Dr Seiriol Morgan. Director of First Year Studies'.

We knocked on the door, and a voice from within boomed, 'WAIT!'

The door opened, and out shuffled a weedy youth in a baseball cap and with an evident flea in his ear. He was followed by Ziggy, who laughed and said, 'Mr Marchant! Mr Venus!'

'Dr Morgan,' I said in reply, and gave him a hug.

'Come in,' he said. 'I've just told off my last slacker of the day.'

Inside, the office was lined floor to ceiling with philosophy books, except for a cooler fridge full of beers, with a few bottles of spirits on top.

'Now, as I've finished for the day, I can offer you a drink,' said Zig. 'What's it to be?'

We each had a tinnie, while Zig outlined what he had in store for us.

'First of all, you can give me a lift back to my house. I only moved in on Friday, so it's a bit spartan. Then I thought we could go and have a curry, before we go out. But I am lecturing tomorrow, so I can only have eight pints.'

'Does this count as one of the eight?' I asked, holding up my tinnie.

'Good God, no! This is just a little something to help you unwind. Drink up. And we'll get going.'

We found the car, and drove Ziggy home, a mile from the campus.

'It was an old student house,' said Zig, 'so it came with all the furniture.'

It was the kind of three-storey four-bedroom house that Zig had lived in ever since I had known him, with the same kind of shagged-out sixties three-piece suite and cowboy-wired electric cooker and ratty carpets stiff with dust; except this time he owned it. Extraordinary. Zig owns a house. I don't own a fecking house.

'It's cool,' I said. 'It really is.'

'I haven't got any food, but I've got some milk, teabags and sugar, in honour of your arrival.'

'Milk and one, please, Zig,' I said. 'Shall I pop one together?'

'You can, Mr Marchant, but I have given it up. Alcohol is my exclusive drug of choice these days. I like that alcohol buzz, but I need five pints to make it happen.'

Extraordinary. Zig owns a house, and has nixed the puff. He made us some tea, and took us on a guided tour of his property.

'I'll need to get lodgers in, but I'm only having fabulous women,' he said. At last. The unadorned Zig I knew and loved.

We set off to find a curry, which is easy and fun in the big northern cities, and then we were off to our first pub, which was called the Pack Horse, opposite the Parkinson Building. It was brown, the true colour of pubs, and was three-quarters full of people who could only be junior lecturers and doctoral candidates. In an upstairs room, a band was rehearsing; we heard the thump of an inexpert kick drum through the floor. I bought Zig the first of the eight.

'So, Zig,' I said, 'Drinking. Is getting pissed compatible with the good life?'

'Ah. Now . . . it all depends . . .'

Getting professional philosophers to talk can be difficult. Some are worse than others. My pal Big Doctor Dave can hardly bear to tell you the time, for what, after all, is time? Zig is better than some, and can be persuaded to offer an opinion, but like all philosophers he is trying to be precise. In one of his lectures, if you take your notes carefully, you will be able to follow his thought processes with accuracy. In the pub, in a series of pubs, it was going to be difficult to keep up. So, this is what I think Ziggy said, with grateful thanks to my tape recorder, and if I misrepresent his thought, well, then, he'll kill me.

'You could argue,' he said, 'that there are two broad accounts of the good life; what you might call eudaemonism and Cyrenaicism.'

'I hear you,' I said.

'But he doesn't understand you,' said Perry.

'Well, again, very broadly, eudaemonism is the view that

practical philosophy aims to tell us how to achieve the "good life". Eudaemonists disagree with one another about what the good life is – virtue, knowledge, the maximisation of pleasure, virtue and knowledge. But they all agree that we should be focusing on life as a whole and asking how we can achieve eudaemonia by taking into account the long-term consequences of our actions.'

'Sorry, what's eudaemonia?' I said.

'Well, happiness. Eudaemonists say that real happiness takes into account long-term consequences. So you can get pissed, but not too often, if it affects your course-of-a-lifetime happiness.'

'And what about Cyrenaicism?'

'Ah, now, the problem with the Cyrenaics is that the only writings that we have left about them were written by people who violently disagreed with them. Cyrenaicism wasn't a particularly popular or long-lived movement, so far as we can tell. The top dogs were Aristippus, Aristippus the younger and Aristippus' daughter Arete, and that's pretty much it.'

'And what did they think?'

'Cyrenaics, at least allegedly, argued that there is no happiness distinct from particular ephemeral pleasures, so the goal of all our actions should be short-term pleasure without any concern for the long-term consequences. So they would advocate getting loaded at the expense of long-term health.'

'I'd say they were doing quite well, as it goes,' I said, 'especially among students.'

'Right,' said Zig. 'Next pub.'

This turned out to be the Palace, spangly with mirrors and the new Leeds middle class.

'Now,' said Zig, as we settled down with our pints, 'the best-known advocate of eudaemonism is, of course, Aristotle.'

'Of course,' said Perry.

'Yes, of course,' said Zig. 'If you're thinking about drinking, you have to think about Aristotle. He's got an intellectualist account of agency which presents human action as basically governed by our perceptions of what is good.'

'Zig, I beg you . . .'

'It means he says that human actions are under the sway of reason, our highest faculty, and that which separates us from the beasts. The way to live a good life is to cultivate the powers of reason and through them to come to see what is genuinely good, which will motivate us to pursue it.'

'But reason tells me that I shouldn't smoke, that it is bad for me, but I still do it.'

Zig smiled at me, as he would at a bright first-year. I had managed to raise a philosophy 101 question.

'Exactly, Mr Marchant. It's the same problem facing the widely ridiculed claim attributed to Socrates in Plato's *Protagoras*, that "virtue is knowledge".'

'Widely ridiculed?' said Perry.

'By philosophers, Mr Venus. By philosophers.'

'Oh.'

'So what's the problem again?' I said, two thirds of the way down pint two.

'Well, surely lots of people in lots of situations act in ways that they know not to be good, like you and smoking, or by getting repeatedly bladdered at the expense of your long-term health. So it doesn't look as if good action comes from our knowledge, but from some other non-cognitive faculty of the mind – the will, as Augustine would later call it.'

'The one who evangelised the English?' said Perry.

'No, Mr Venus. The other one. *City of God, Confessions*, that one.'

'Oh,' said Perry.

'Aristotle's response is to distinguish real knowledge from the kind of inferior "knowledge" we have when we are able to give a verbal account of something without fully grasping the meaning of what we are saying. Aristotle says that when you say "Smoking is bad for you", but you keep on smoking, then you are like the drunk mouthing the words of Empedocles.'

'How dare he say that about me?'

'You have the latter kind of knowledge but not the former, which requires practical wisdom, like you'll have when you get cancer. You understand the ostensible meaning of the particular words, but not the message that they convey. If you really, truly grasped the import of your actions, you wouldn't do them. Right, next pub.'

Zig strode through the streets of Leeds at a rate of knots which Perry and I, with twelve years more of non-Aristotelian behaviour than him, struggled to keep up with. Our next pub was the Dog and Duck, and here I really started struggling to keep up with the philosophy too, because I had my third pint, which doesn't help, and because there was a band getting ready to play. Just looking at them filled me with loathing.

They were called Hi/Way 49, and they were all older than Perry and I, if such a thing is possible. They had New Wave of British Heavy Metal haircuts, which are indistinguishable from a mullet. NWBHM was big in the late seventies, a period for which these guys had an evident fondness. Twenty-five years ago, when Hi/Way 49 were a NWBHM band proper, these haircuts already looked shite. Now they are calamitous. They had Zapata moustaches, and wore 'Classic Rock' T-shirts. The keyboard player, I swear to God, was wearing a Uriah Heep T-shirt.

'Will you look at these fuckers?' I said.

'What's up with you? Stop fuckin' moaning,' said Zig. 'I'm trying to tell Perry about Augustine.'

'No, because, look at them. Jesus. I had a Uriah Heep album. When I was fourteen, and it was 1972 . . . oh dear, and the bass player's got a radio pick-up . . . what a wanker.'

'Shut up,' said Perry.

'Why do you need a radio pick-up? What, are they going to play stadiums? The tosser is standing next to his amp. Just fucking plug it in. Old-boy hobby bands; they can't play, but they go and buy all the latest gear.'

There were about twenty-five people in, but as soon as the singer stepped up to the mike and said, 'Good Evening, we're Hi/Way 49, and we'd like to start with a song by Free called "Wishing Well",' twelve of them drank up and walked out. The singer and lead guitarist couldn't sing and play at the same time, though he could do Kossoff-by-numbers on the solos. The drummer was devoid of all rhythmic sense. Only one of their wives/girlfriends could be bothered to turn up and sit through it. Monday nights, if you are playing in a pub, is the graveyard shift, the grimmest, most dead-end gig there is. You must love it a lot to still be playing Monday gigs in your fifties.

'Do you like Gary Moore?' asked the singer/guitarist of the remaining dozen people in the room.

'No, I fucking don't. Please can we go?' I said.

'I'm half-way through my pint. Surely you can put up with one more?' said Zig.

'Oh my God . . . they're doing a bass solo . . .' I said, my hand held to my mouth.

And they did. All bass solos are wrong, except the one on Glen Campbell's version of 'Wichita Lineman'. I tugged at Ziggy's sleeve, until he'd finished his pint, and we stood outside on the pavement.

'What is your problem?' said Ziggy.

'It can't be conducive to the good life to be stuck in your youth,' I said, 'especially one where you can only listen to "Classic Rock".'

'Don't you think we all are?' said Perry. 'We still listen to the Clash.'

'I still go to raves,' said Zig.

'Yes, but the Clash were good. Unlike Gary Moore. Unlike NWBHM. And when I go and play in pubs, I don't pretend that I belong to the Clash; I sing Nat King Cole songs, in a suit, because I'm middle-aged. And when we started losing our hair, we didn't think to grow it into mullets. We shaved our heads.'

'Right,' said Ziggy, 'next pub.'

The next pub was called the Regent, right in the heart of the city.

'I like this one,' said Zig, cracking into pint four. 'This is a proper pissheads' pub.' Three toothless old ladies sat around a table, supping gin; an ancient tramp was asleep in the corner, with his plastic bags around him.

'So, Zig, what were you trying to say about Augustine?' said Perry.

'It's Augustine who brings "the will" into it. If we still know-ingly do things that might prevent us from enjoying the good life, then it can't be knowledge that brings us virtue. According to Augustine, of course, virtue has its source in God, but our will is divided into "the two loves": man's love of God, and thus virtue, and our love for ourselves, which leads away from virtue, owing to our sinful nature. Our love for ourselves causes love for various objects, and those loves exert an influence on us whatever happens. So basically we act on whatever is the most powerful love or combinations of loves at any particular time. But unfortunately the evil love is naturally the stronger, since we will have been in the habit of gratifying bodily pleasure, pursuing money, getting pissed and so on, and habit increases the power of desire. Evil love will outweigh our desire to do what we know to be good. Hence the agent can be quite literally incapable of resisting temptation in a situation when his urge for some gratification has swelled to such a degree that it outweighs the loves opposing it, such as the love of God. So the agent can find himself resolving many times to be good, but forever carrying on doing evil.'

'Like lots of people who come and see me,' said Perry. 'They keep resolving to give up the drink, but they keep on drinking.'

'That's right. The love of drink is a more powerful love than the love for God. It is for me, anyway,' said Zig. 'Right . . . next pub.'

This was Whitelock's, the oldest pub in Leeds. It was full, and noisy, and we stood at the bar as Ziggy bellowed philosophy at us, and drank pint six. I'd given up trying to keep pace with him after hearing Hi/Way 49's bass solo. It took the heart out of me. I tried to pay attention to Zig's shouted exposition of Augustinian philosophy.

'But there is some room in Augustine's account for agency! This is because our loves are not static, but fluctuate in strength over time! In the presence of the beloved object the love will be stimulated and strong! Away from the object, though the pleasure will be lodged in memory and hence the love ever-present, it will likely be in weaker form, especially if not indulged in for some time! Then it would be countered by a coalition of other desires which would not be effective if it were properly active . . .'

'What?' I bellowed.

'What do you mean, "What"?'

'I didn't hear you! Could you repeat it?'

'Which bit?'

'All of it!'

'No . . . come on. One last pub.' We were outside, and walking towards Zig's final selection of the evening.

'So, could Augustine help me help people control their drinking, do you reckon?' asked Perry.

'Perry is trying to teach people how to manage their drinking, without having to resort to abstinence,' I said.

'Abstinence?' said Zig. 'Abstinence, boy? That will never do. Augustine thinks we are too weak for abstinence, but that we might be capable of moderation.'

'So what do you think? Can we conquer the love of drinking a bottle of whisky a day, and replace it with a love of drinking a glass of dry sherry after dinner?' I asked.

'Why not? Augustine is about strengthening the will. If you stimulated a coalition of other desires, such as wanting not to piss the bed or not to lose your job, and damped down the love of drink, then you could strengthen your will not to get fuckin' totalled. Augustine's point is that we should learn to accept our limitations. Wisdom lies in anticipating and avoiding situations in which you might lose control. Here we are. The Horse and Trumpet. I'd better have two pints.'

It was nearly closing time. I bought Zig his two pints, which made up the eight, and so he was happy.

Ziggy felt perfectly capable of walking the mile or so back to his house, but me and Perry were having none of it. We caught a taxi. Our taxi driver had a beard and wore a shalwar kameez.

'Excuse me for asking, friend, but are you a follower of Islam?' I asked.

'Yes, sir, I am.'

'How do you find it having to pick up drunks on their way home from pubs and clubs?'

'Well, I don't like it, but it is my job.'

'Does it seem strange to you, that that's what people want to do with their spare time?'

'I asked a passenger last week. Why do you drink, I asked him. He told me that it was because he feels pressure in his head. When I feel pressure in my head, I pray. Or read the Holy Qur'an.' Of which I'm sure Augustine would approve, since it is exactly the love of God, and hence virtue, that stops Muslims from drinking.

Back at Zig's, he dug out a bottle of Scotch, while we complained that there wasn't anything to eat.

'Hang on,' said Perry. 'We've got the last bag of pork scratchings in the car. I'll go and fetch them.'

Alas, our love of fried pork skin was stronger than our love of not being fat bastards. Much stronger. But at least we'd solved the problem of what to do with the scratchings.

## Tuesday 20th April

In the morning I felt, in the immortal words of Withnail, as though a pig had shat in my head. I can't speak for Perry, though he looked bloody dreadful, but Zig was as bright as a perky Welsh button, all booted and suited and off for another day explaining the difference between necessary and sufficient causes. A mere eight pints were hardly going to give him a thick head.

'Always a pleasure, Dr Morgan,' I said.

'Good to see you, Mr Marchant. Where are you off to next?'

'Lancaster tonight. But first we're going to a pub with no beer.'

A little of the colour drained from his cheeks. 'No, that can't be right.'

'I'm afraid it is.'

Leaving Leeds we took the M62 and crossed from Yorkshire into Lancashire, England's funniest county. The people are funny (Peter Kay, Victoria Wood, Les Dawson, Eric Morecambe); the weather is funny (or at least, if you didn't laugh, you'd have to cry); and the place names are funny: Ramsbottom, Bacup, Clitheroe. We turned up the M66 towards Rawtenstall to find Fitzpatrick's Herbal Health Bar, the last temperance bar in Britain.

Temperance is one of the Four Virtues, the much less popular counterparts of the Seven Deadly Sins. It is the quality of restraint and moderation. As W.T. Marchant points out in his book from 1887, *In Praise of Ale*, 'Every moderate drinker knows that, all things being equal, the moderate drinker is, take him all round, a better average man, with not only a higher power of work, but a greater pleasure in executing it, than the total abstainer.'

And you might think that you can't argue with that. Temperate, which is to say moderate, and thus Augustinian, drinking is a thing of joy to behold forever. In the early nineteenth century temperance was taken to mean just that, and the early Temperance movement was founded to promote moderate drinking, after the excesses of the Georgian age.

The first half of the eighteenth century was moderate only in its religious beliefs. After two and a half centuries of religious wars across Europe, toleration became the order of the day (except for left-footers, obviously). People went along to a mild church service on Sunday mornings, and that was about it. Ranting was off the menu, and was replaced by scientific and philosophical enquiry. But in their appetites, the English, unleashed from the yoke of Puritanism, went a bit mad. This was the Age of Gin, just as much as it was the Age of Enlightenment. Although politicians, magistrates and churchmen were concerned at the levels of alcohol abuse, there was no real question that anyone would be expected to give up drinking. Alcohol, after all, was good for you, a tonic.

The religious revivals of the mid eighteenth century brought religious fervour back into English life, at around about the time that the social implications of drinking to excess were becoming clear. In 1804, two doctors, Dr Rush in Pittsburgh and Dr Trotter in Scotland, both published books on the dangers of alcohol. It had never occurred to anyone that there might be health implications in taking one over the eight, with spirits in particular singled out as a cause of ill health. The first society set up to dissuade people from taking spirits was started in Saratoga, NY, in 1808. It was always linked with the Evangelical movement, but it was never intended to stop people drinking beer or wine. It took an Augustinian approach; it was a temperate movement.

Temperance came to life this side of the Atlantic in Ireland. The first British society was the Ulster Temperance Society, founded in 1829, and it soon became a popular cause; by 1830 there were twenty-five societies in Ireland and two in Scotland, from where it spread south into Lancashire and Yorkshire. The British and Foreign Temperance Society was the first national organisation, set up in 1831. The great evangeliser of temperance was 'Father Matthew', an Irish priest, who preached throughout Ireland, England and the US, and who was reckoned to have 5 million adherents by 1845.

And in Leeds, in 1847, the Revd Jabez Tunnicliff and Mrs Ann Jane Carlile set up 'The Band of Hope', which quickly grew into the most important youth movement of the nineteenth century. Kids would 'Sign the Pledge', swearing never to touch a drop, and they would have a weekly meeting, where they would learn about clean living, and sing Temperance hymns, like this one by the evangelist Ira Sankey:

Hark! The Temperance Bells are ringing; joyous music fills the air,
Strength and hope their tones are bringing to the homes where
   dwelt despair.
Long the tyrant foe hath taken cherished loved ones for his own;
Now his cruel power is shaken, soon will fall his tottering throne;
Brothers come! The hosts are forming! Let us join without delay;
Bright the hills with tints of morning; dawning of a better day . . .
Hear the bells! Joyous Bells! Chime the anthem of the free! Hear the
   Bells! Merry Bells!
Sound the temperance jubilee!

By 1900, there were 10,000 Bands of Hope in the UK holding weekly meetings, and they reckoned to be in regular contact with 10 per cent of the total population, the majority of them children. In 1909, there were 480,000 members. Itinerant lecturers were made available to schools to warn children of the perils of drink, lectures which were always welcome, as they used magic lanterns to illustrate the talks. The Bands of Hope Union was one of the first organisations to see the power of moving pictures in getting their message across. It is not surprising that such a large organisation still survives; now they are called Hope UK, and they are still working with young people in drink and drugs education, still from a Christian perspective.

By 1850, with the exception of the Bands of Hope, the Temperance movement was in decline. Their mistake was to move from calling for people not to drink spirits, to demanding total abstinence from all alcohol, and to putting political pressure on politicians to move towards Prohibition. This was decided at a meeting in 1836 in New York, and although their greatest political moment was the passing of the Volstead Act, in 1919, which led to Prohibition in the States, socially they had lost the argument. The children who were signing the Pledge at seven and eight years of age, were not growing up into non-drinkers. The movement had become intemperate, and being a teetotaller was not something that most people wanted to try. (The tee, incidentally, has nothing to do with tea. It's an intensifier, like 'M for Murder'.)

During its heyday, however, the Temperance movement had been powerful and popular, and a string of businesses had sprung up to service the demand for alternatives to alcohol. In the North-West of England in particular, Temperance hotels and pubs could be found in most towns. Now, there is just one left.

We parked up the car, and walked through Rawtenstall. No one loves East Lancashire, except the people who come from there, and all my friends who come from Ramsbottom, Burnley and Accrington moved away years ago, though they still get defensive if you take the piss. Rawtenstall is run down; most of the shops in the sixties arcade were boarded up and empty. Fitzpatrick's was tiny; it stands on a corner, and looks from the outside like a cross between an old-fashioned health-food shop, an old-fashioned chemist's, and an eccentric museum. Most of the business comes from selling herbal remedies. But, as the owner explained as he pulled our pints (Perry had Sarsaparilla, I went for the Dandelion and Burdock), he still sells enough of the old-fashioned tonic drinks to make it worth while. There is a bar at one end of the shop, and two tables with chairs, so that you can sit and enjoy your pint.

'This was a pub, once, many years ago,' the owner told us, 'called "The One Too Many". It's still haunted by the last landlord.'

'I'm not surprised. You can't expect pub landlords to approve of Temperance bars. Do you drink yourself?'

'Too bloody right I do,' he said.

The drinks are available as cordials, as well as on tap, and while we were drinking, an old lady came in and bought a bottle of Dandelion and Burdock.

'The old folk still drink it as a tonic,' explained the owner. 'It's like a traditional Lancashire food, now. That Hugh Fearnley-Whatsisname came here, and now you can buy it on Bury market, where they sell black puddings.'

The owner was keen on his wares, and Fitzpatrick's is a beautiful little shop, and it was well worth stopping by to try a non-alcoholic pint, but I must say, I could barely get my Dandelion and Burdock down. It was horrible. If this is what Temperance drinks were like, its unsurprising that there is only one bar left that sells them. But then, I don't like fizzy soft drinks at all, so perhaps I'm not best placed to judge.

'Mine was nice,' said Perry.

'Really? I can still taste mine.'

'We'd better go and have a pint, so you can get rid of the taste,' he said.

We drove north, to Clitheroe, where we stopped for a lunchtime sharpener at the New Inn so that I could clear my palate, before heading north and west through the Forest of Bowland, a vast stretch of moorland, mountain and river valley rumoured by the locals to be the Queen's favourite part of her realm. There is a road through the Forest which leads from the tiny village of Dunsop Bridge over the high fells to Lancaster, by way of the mountain pass known as the Trough of Bowland. Dunsop Bridge claims to be the geographical centre of the British Isles, which seems counter-intuitive, until you remember that 'The British Isles' include Ireland. The road up through the Trough clings to the side of the stream which tumbles down from the watershed. From the top of the pass, you look out on a new world; unarguably, this is the best view in England. To the north lie Morecambe Bay and the Cumbrian Mountains. To the west you look over the fertile flatlands of the Fylde to Blackpool Tower and, on a very clear day, across the Irish Sea to the Isle of Man. And then a slow descent into Lancaster, past the Ashton Memorial in Williamson's Park, 'The Taj Mahal of the North', which makes the city so memorable from the motorway.

The area immediately below Williamson's Park is known as Little Scotland, because the streets are all named after Scottish towns . . . Perth Street, Ayr Street, Dundee Street, etc. I lived in this part of town for eight years. My daughter Charley still lives there. So do my good friends Saleel and Madeleine, with whom we were staying. This was no social visit. We were staying for a purpose. We had come to Lancaster to play some hardball quiz.

People have always played games in pubs. That's why the Chequerboard is one of the oldest pub signs still in existence. There are many regional pub games, like Aunt Sally, as I had played in Oxfordshire, or the strange medieval game of Bat and Trap, still played in parts of Kent. Even in the case of something as relatively simple as skittles, there are many regional versions; in the South-West, for example, skittles is something akin to ten-pin bowling, played in a long alley, where the idea is to knock over the skittles with your bowls. In Northamptonshire, however, skittles is entirely different: wooden 'cheeses' are thrown at pegs on a table, which are caught by a wide net. In the North, skittles is uncommon, but plenty of pubs still have their own bowling green. Most pubs can find you a pack of cards and a cribbage board, or some dominoes, and both games are played seriously in pubs, at league level. Americans expect to find shove ha'penny and table skittles (the one with the ball on a pole); but I wish to contend that three games now dominate games-playing in pubs. These are pool, darts, and quiz.

Pool tables started to appear in pubs only as recently as the 1970s, but life is now unimaginable without them. Now and again, you still find their precursor, a bar-billiards table, the bar referring to the gate which stops the balls coming back to the bottom of the table after twenty minutes or so, rather than the fact that you find them in bars. People argue that bar billiards is a traditional English game, which the brash American upstart has swept aside. But bar billiards is based on a game called Russian billiards, which seems to have originated in Belgium, and which was imported into this country only about a hundred years ago. Landlords liked it because it doesn't take up much room, since players only strike from one end, not because it was authentically English. Pool is a much more exciting game.

Except when I play.

Don't get me wrong; I'm not so bad. I've held my own in pub

teams. I fancy myself a bit, though admittedly, so does everyone who plays pool regularly. But I like pool for its contemplative nature, rather than for its excitement. I model myself on that old Zen master of the green baize, Terry Griffiths. I prefer the quiet charm of the safety to the pizzazz of the chancy pot. I prefer seeing my shots teeter on the edge of a pocket to merely slamming them home. I like closing down opportunities for my opponents. I walk around the table, taking a bead on various shots, chalking my cue, having another look, having a swig of beer and a suck on a fag, taking a decision, looking up at the shot, then putting my head down, which means I'm looking over the top of my specs, not being Dennis Taylor, so I have to look up again, just to make sure that I've got it right, and TAP, the cue ball glides towards one of my balls, kisses it, and rolls behind the black ball, right up against the cushion. Your shot, *amigo*.

It drives people mad, which panics them into making mistakes. I know no other way.

Of darts, I can say little. I don't have the hand/eye co-ordination. I'm scared of sharp pointy things. Although I am a camp follower of the mathematical arts, arithmetic is not my strong point, and you need to be good at sums if you're going to amount to anything as a darts player. And yet darts is a subject which inflames the hearts of millions of men and women world-wide. One of these men is the poet Peter Sansom. His long-held ambition was to make it as a professional darts player. In his youth, he spent hours in front of the practice board in his room. But slowly, sadly, he came to realise that he wasn't quite cutting it, so turned his hand to poetry instead. I asked him if he would write something for me about darts, and he was kind enough to send me this. I don't know much about darts, but I know what I like.

### Finest (Half) Hour

Coming to nothing
from 501 a dozen times a match,
not to mention wall-to-wall practice, over a season
you clock up a fair few miles of seven foot nine and three quarters,

and yet you seldom see a physique from it. Or you do.
Still, you take it on to live the dream, with the Crucible
next door, spectactular when *for those of you watching in black and white
the pink's behind the blue.* And, sponsored by the same fags,
it flourished for a while in snooker's shadow, an unlikely
spectator sport, three in a bed or needing
fiveinbits.

I had
Keith Deller's spring-loaded nickel tungstens,
and I shook on the oche, lighting one off another.
Play the board not the man, that's the mantra
till in the end the arrows throw themselves,
a kind of meditation. I'd love to live by it,
but when your middle game's a ton, sixty, forty-five
and he's steady one-forties, it comes home.
And it came home, and it was time
to move on.

It's hard to let go
of hope, though, and there are times even now
I relive that night, that night of nights
the pints paused halfway, when two sets down from nowhere
the one-eighty went in and he went shy at tops
and shy at tops again, and if you can't finish
you're buried, and the whole match turned round.

Leg after leg, if I dropped a dart it went in the sixty,
right to the wire, till in the spotlight
of the team the room the pub holding its breath
I was looking at treble twenty,
treble eighteen,
bull.

I may not know my arrers, but I too have lived my moments of
joyous sporting achievement. I am, at heart, a betting-shop

intellectual, Educated Evans, a saloon-bar know-it-all. My game is quiz, and I am the bomb, brothers and sisters.

A quiz night in the pub is my idea of the perfect evening. Landlords like them too, as they tend to guarantee a crowd on an otherwise quiet night; Wednesdays are quite common. I started playing back in the eighties, the decade which marked the start of the modern quiz era. You know the kind of thing. Teams of four or five friends sit round a table, with a piece of paper and a pencil. The team is encouraged to come up with a funny name. A question master with a microphone stands at one end of the pub, and asks questions in rounds. Sometimes the quizzes are dedicated to pop music, film, or sport, but more usually the questions are general. Players whisper answers at that member of the team who is writing down; after each round, you hand your answers to the team on the next table, who mark your sheet. At the end, the team with the highest score picks up twenty quid or so.

This kind of quiz is called 'Table Quiz', and it is a lads' game. I was in a team called 'Benny the Cat' with Ziggy and a couple of other mates in the early nineties, and we usually came in the first three when we turned up somewhere to quiz. We were pretty good. We thought we were hard-line quizzers. But we weren't. We were lads. Oh, I still enjoy it; still enjoy the smug satisfaction of going up to collect your winnings, the hostility from the teams who came second and third, who are still bickering with the quiz master about whether or not Northampton is a city (it isn't, you stupid twats). Yes, and I've seen tempers lost and friendships broken over table quiz. I've seen grown men throw beer mats at sobbing women. But I say again, it's a lads' game. The real thing is the terrifying battle of nerves and bluff that is the Lancaster City Quiz League. Before I tell you anything else about Quiz League, bear in mind this astounding fact: the results are printed in the sports page of the *Lancaster Guardian* every Friday, occasionally with match reports.

In spring 1995, I had a crack-up. I became a nutter for a few years. Nutters are no fun. All my pals despised me, except Saleel, who kept me alive, thus revealing himself to be not a pal but a friend. Going out, unless to the doctor's to cry, was impossible. I discovered the joys of televised golf. One night, six months or so into my life of horror, the phone rang, and I must have been in a good mood, because I answered it.

It was a muso guy I'd met a few times at the Lancaster Musicians' Co-op, called Tom Crippen.

'Marchant,' he said. 'You miserable bastard. Do you want to be on the Yorkshire House Quiz Team tonight?' It was half-five on Monday evening.

'Yeah. I do.'

'Be here by eight.'

I hadn't got dressed for about a fortnight, my child had been living off a diet of Crosse & Blackwell Full English Breakfast in a tin, and the fecking cat had just had another load of kittens under the settee. The place was damp with kitten piss, and stank of fermenting cat shit. No amount of visits from community psychiatric nurses could lure me from my little home-made hell to take an interest in anything other than watching the telly. Tom Crippen it was that got me out the door.

I walked into the pub at eight, expecting to find the tables thronged, but instead the place was empty except for Tom.

'Where's the quiz?'

'Here.'

'Where are all the other teams?'

'What do you mean? This is Quiz League. There is only one other team: Heysham Cricket Club C. And they're not here yet.'

He explained how it worked. Right across the whole Bay area, from Galgate up to Hest Bank, all the pubs and clubs had a Monday-night Quiz League team. There were so many teams that the league was split into six divisions. Tom's magistrate father was in one of the top Division One sides. The Yorkshire House had entered a team in the league for the first time, and so we were starting in Division Four A. This was our first match.

'Each week, one of the Division One or Two sides take turns to sit it out,' said Tom, 'and they set the quiz. Happens to each of the top-flight sides once a year. You get the questions to the League Secretary by Friday. The secretary photocopies the questions, which the team captain of the home side picks up before eight-thirty on Monday night. Each team has four players, each assigned a number which signifies where they sit, and thus where the questions fall. The home team provide a question master and a scorer/timekeeper. At eight-thirty everyone all across the Bay City opens their envelope, and the questions are asked in rounds. Eight rounds of eight questions; each of the eight players answers one question per round. In turn; no conferring. You've got one minute. If you get it right, you get three points. If you don't know the answer, you can pass it to another member of your team, within the minute, for one point. Also no conferring. If they get it wrong, it goes to the other side. They've got five seconds; one point if they get it right. Team with the highest score at the end is the winner, and gets two league points. Next week, we play away, then home, until we've played all the teams in the league twice. The team with the most points at the end of the season gets promoted. Have you got 35p?'

'Why?'

'It costs 35p per player.'

'Do we get anything if we win the league?' I asked.

'Yeah, I think we get a book token.'

'Cool.'

And so I met the small band of brothers and sisters of the Yorkshire House Quiz Team, seasons 1995–6, 96–7 and 97–8. At Number Four, Bold Tom Crippen, flame-haired son of Orkney, rock 'n' roll guitarist, sports fanatic, grammar-school drop-out. At Three, Mighty Mike Edwards, mine host, landlord of the Yorkshire House, stout descendant of Chesterton's anarchist landlord Humphrey Pump. At One, Naughty Neil Lent, our saucy captain, military historian, sociologist, and ladies' man. I felt honoured to be offered the Number Two shirt, right in the engine room of the team's midfield. And here comes our utterly impartial question master Raving Ronnie Baker, and his glamorous timepiece-toting sig-other Miss Sarah Fiske! Little then did we small band of six know that we were about to embark on one of the great achievements in recent Quiz League history.

That first night, I did all right. I answered five of my eight questions correctly, and picked up three passes. We won. After the game, I went home, and stayed in bed for the next six days while kittens took over our house. But the next Monday, I made it to Quiz again, and the following week, and on through the winter and into the spring, and we just kept on winning.

I started looking forward to something: Monday nights. I began to use Monday as a day when I could do things, like bits of shopping and housework. By Christmas, I had managed to get myself into therapy, also on a Monday, before I went to quiz. Monday became my good day, and it got me liking good days, and wanting more. My therapist persuaded me to try medication. By spring, we were division champions, with two games still to play. With the title in our pockets, the *Lancaster Guardian*, noting news from the lower divisions in their Quiz round-up, singled out the Yorkshire House as 'the team of the future'. We were QPR, and I was Rodney Marsh.

Over a season, we had tested one another's mettle. The ideal score is the so-called 'full house', where you get all eight of your questions right, scoring 24 points. I was getting high teens, low twenties most weeks, and a full house a couple of times a season. Tom Crippen in the tricky Number Four seat (which meant you often had to answer the last question), was also picking up points into the high teens, with an occasional 20. Mighty Mike, solid by my side at Number Three, would always give you a steady knock of 12, 15, every week. Naughty Neil, our captain, was less predictable, sometimes scoring 5, sometimes scoring 22. But Number One is a nasty seat; you get the first questions, you soak up pressure. When you are captain, your first duty is to win the toss to decide which side goes first. All the other teams, if they won the toss, would go first; Neil always put us in to bat second. It was our secret weapon.

Over the course of our championship season, we had learned the elaborate system of hand signals which indicated who on your side was willing to try for a pass; five fingers for utter certainty, four for almost sure, three for an educated guess, two for a rough guess, and one finger meaning, 'If nobody else is willing, I'll have a wild stab in the dark.' Neil, as captain, had to learn the difference between four fingers from Tom, or two from me; Mike's threes were always better than my threes, because he's a modest man, and I'm a know-it-all.

Highlight of that first season was Prize Night, when all the teams from Lancaster City Quiz League come together in the Phoenix Club to reward quiz excellence. Starting with the Division One winners and runners-up, then Division Two, and so on and so on, right down to Four A and Four B, the players go up to collect their trophies; one big one to be kept in the pub for the year, and five small ones for the players and the QM, to keep for ever. Mine has pride of place beside my desk; in slate, four inches high, bearing the proud crest of the league and a small brass plaque: Division Four A Winners, 1995–1996. All the players also got an envelope, containing a £20 book token. Superb. And after the prize-giving, a buffet made by the ladies, followed by five fiercely contended rounds of table quiz, just to help the players relax into the summer break.

When we gathered again the next autumn, we found ourselves in Division Three A. The teams were better. Competition became stiffer. The gamesmanship became more evident. When we played at home, Quiz took place in an alcove off the bar. On one side of the alcove was a high bench where we always sat. Our opponents sat opposite; we had provided them with low barstools so that we were always taller than they were. Increasingly, me and Neil were doing a little double act to discomfort our opponents. I know this isn't a terribly grown-up or funny thing to do, but we would pretend to be gay, do our Kenneth Williams and Hugh Paddock bit. We'd whisper sweet nothings in one another's ears, as the other team tried to think. This throws your more macho opponents right off, though it should be used sparingly if you're playing in one of Morecambe's rougher pubs.

Open hostility finally broke out in a match with the Golden Lion B. They really wanted to win. We did, too, but we kept it hidden. Their Number Two was a fucker called Sean, who would stand up and shout his answers, and give his teammates high-fives if they got an answer right. Tom and Mike were imperturbable, while Neil and I camped it up, which enraged Sean even further. We won, of course. Sean was spitting bricks. At the end, it is traditional that the teams shake hands with one another; Sean refused to shake, stalking off to the bar for a pint of Theakston's. His team apologised for him, but the die was cast. All season we vied for second and third in the league with Golden Lion B. Only two teams could go up. In the end it was us who finished runners-up, and Sean and his pals were left behind as we were promoted again. This year, our plaques were smaller, wooden, saying Division Three A Runners-up, 1996–1997, and the book token was only worth a tenner. We didn't care. Promoted in successive seasons.

And so we come to 1997–8. The competition was sharp in Division Two, but hostilities were kept in check. And yet, we kept grinding out results. As the season went on, it became clear that we could be promoted yet again. And I had my night, my night of nights, in a match with Gregson B. Three of the players for Gregson B were indifferent quizzers, hardly Division Two material. But one of them was a guy called Steve Allan, who had won *Mastermind*, in 1992. It was an honour and a pleasure to play against one of the all-time quiz greats; his elegant full house that night was as near perfect as a game of quiz could be. But it was not enough to ensure victory. We were three points ahead going into the final round. Their Number One fucked his question, but Steve took it, and Neil fucked his, but I held on to the point. Still three up to us. Steve, sitting opposite me at Two clipped his question effortlessly into the long grass. We were level, but if I could get my question right, we'd be three ahead again, with Mike and Tom still to go for us, and their Three and Four mere makeweights.

'Question four,' said the QM. 'For Number Two. Who was the last Chancellor of the Exchequer to die in office?'

There was a sharp intake of breath all around the table. Nasty question, no doubt.

'Iain MacLeod,' I said.

And Steve Allan, winner of *Mastermind* 1992 smiled at me, and said, 'Nice one.' It doesn't get better than that.

At season's end, it went right up to the last game, but we won, taking runners-up spot again. We had been promoted from Division

Four A to Division One in three seasons. It was some kind of record. On Prize Night, Tom and Mike told us they wouldn't be playing next season. They both felt that had gone as far as they could, and would be hanging up their boots. They were hardly to be blamed. After three seasons of glory, Division One could only be anti-climactic. But, still, Neil and I thought we were honour-bound to give it a try. We recruited two new players, my friend Saleel, and Neil's friend Nik.

Well, Sir Alex Ferguson did win stuff with kids, but we stood no chance. Saleel's encyclopaedic knowledge of films and cricket and Nik's sturdy courage at Four would need a few seasons to mature, to make them into the fine quizzers they are now. In that first humiliating season, they were less certain of their ground, and needed coaxing to produce a guess. Guessing lies at the heart of the quizzer's art. If your question is 'Which Dickens novel centres around the court case of Jarndyce vs. Jarndyce', you don't say, 'I don't know.' You say *David Copperfield*. So you're wrong. But since you didn't know the answer, you also don't know that it's not *David Copperfield*. It might have been; one time in three a good guess will pick you up points. It can also help your team-mates waiting for a pass. If they are thinking 'Well, it's either *David Copperfield* or *Bleak House*', and you say 'Don't know', you have done nothing to help your team. An incorrect guess has often opened up a scoring opportunity. And there are things that all quizzers must know, and they didn't, not at first. If you don't know the name of the astronaut who was left in orbit around the moon on the Apollo Eleven mission, or the identity of the first person killed in a railway accident, then you are not ready to play quiz at any level.

It was December before we won our first game, and we stayed glued to the foot of the table. No longer were we playing the B and C sides, but the big boys in the A teams. Quiz League is a monument to the glories of working-class autodidacticism. These guys really knew their onions. All the way up through the divisions, we'd been playing against people who spent their spare time reading encyclopaedias. We had all been forced to memorise the state capitals of the US, the longest rivers in the world, and the winners of the five Classics since the war. These guys took it much further.

'How do you do your research?' I was asked by a member of Britannia A, the Manchester United of Quiz League, before a particularly severe tonking.

'Er . . . read the paper?'

This was not the right answer. The right answer is that you live and breathe trivia. You memorise everything, any list you can lay your hands on. You lay off the porn, and spend your evenings surfing quiz websites. You never miss *Fifteen to One*. You *are* quiz. And we weren't. Native wit had only taken us so far; we were still QPR; and QPR reserves, at that.

Tom Crippen had given up the game, but his father most definitely had not. He played for one of the Division One teams, and they beat us both home and away, to his evident delight. I'd met Tom Crippen's dad on Prize Nights, but I'd never played him before. He sat opposite me, at Number Two, and is one hey of a quizzer; I could see where Tom got it from.

Towards the end of the season, I had to endure a court appearance, for non-payment of council tax. I sat in the waiting room of Lancaster Magistrates Court, dressed in my suit, surrounded by chavs in tracksuit bottoms, who knew that no matter what they wore, they were going down. My name was called, and the usher showed me through into the courtroom, built in the seventies, in a style which managed to capture the exact atmosphere of my old headmaster's office. I stood in the dock; I didn't have a solicitor. Ranged against me was a team of three lawyers from the city council, all younger than I. In came the magistrates; Tom Crippen's dad was chairman. He gave me a stern look, and addressed himself to the case. Lancaster City Council's argument was simple. I hadn't paid any council tax for years. My defence was shaky, since they were quite right. I hadn't. Tom Crippen's dad turned to me and asked if I had anything to say. I explained about the struggles of being a single parent; about how my depression had taken away my already limited administrative abilities, so that all I had managed to do for the best part of three years was to throw away any envelopes that I thought might come from officialdom. I explained that I had been writing a book, which had taken up a lot of time. The city's team of solicitors smiled and leaned back in their chairs.

Tom Crippen's dad turned right and left to confer with his fellow magistrates. One was an elderly gentleman with horn-rimmed spectacles and a tweed jacket, who looked at me as one might at dog shit that talked; the other was a middle-aged lady who might as well have been wearing a badge saying 'I hate fat bald hippies'. They whispered together, and nodded in agreement. Tom Crippen's dad turned to address the court.

'All payments revoked,' he said. 'Costs against the city council. If the city council wish to continue to bring cases of this kind against vulnerable yet hard-working people, let this stand as a reminder of what is likely to happen. Case dismissed.'

I tried not to smirk at the solicitors as we filed from the courtroom. After all, I had only been spared £750, which I did, in all fairness, owe them; whereas they had sustained a serious blow to their professional prestige. I should feel compassion in victory. But I just couldn't help it; I came out of that room a happy man, and the chavs in the waiting room saw my joy, and said, 'Nice one mate.'

Next time I saw Tom Crippen's dad was in the Phoenix Club on Quiz League Prize Night. I thanked him very much. He smiled.

'You should have seen their faces from where I was sitting, Ian,' he said of the solicitors. 'Oh, they didn't like that at all, did they?'

We were not at Prize Night to collect a prize; we were there for the buffet prepared by the ladies, and a bit of table quiz. We had been relegated after our first and only season in Division One; the beginning of a six-year slide back to Division Four A. We struggled the following season, back in Division Two, my last season with the team. Sometimes Raving Ronnie Baker would sit in, and Sarah, our old timekeeper, would QM. He was a good man to have at Three while we brought the new blood on. But it was my favourite season of them all, in many ways; well again, book published, fines revoked, walking down the hill to the pub with my friend Saleel at eight o'clock on a Monday, through rain and snow and spring sunsets over the city by the bay.

All very well and good. But today is Tuesday. Quiz was last night. I could write about Quiz League for ever, but I wanted Perry to get some photos. What to do? I spoke to Saleel on the phone when I was planning the trip, and he said that I should leave it to him, that he would fix up a friendly with the Brit D, a team whose captain is our pal George Green. Saleel and George would set the questions. (You can find all the questions and answers on my website, www.ianmarchant.com.) So we arrived at Saleel's house, and his beautiful smile at the door reminded me again of all the help and support he had given me during my missing years. He fed us, as he'd fed me so often when I had nowt; and, as we had done hundreds of times before, we walked from his house at eight towards a dodgy old pub to do battle with people who still believe in the virtues of self-improvement.

We were playing in the Britannia, actually the nearest pub to Saleel's house. It's a bit of a shit-hole by anybody's standards, but is the spiritual home of Lancaster City Quiz League, its Wembley. This is the home of the mighty Brit A and Brit B teams, locked together in eternal combat at the top of Division One. Brit C aren't half bad either. Brit D, however, are a wee bit dodgy, and we had to fancy our chances. Friendly or not, we had attracted a couple of supporters; Professor Sue and her husband Tony, who we'd met in the airport waiting room on Scilly. And I'd spoken to my eldest daughter Charley from Spurn Head, and I had told her what time we were going to be at the Brit, and arranged to meet her and her partner Greg there, so that she could see her old dad wield his quiz racket.

'If by some chance we miss the quiz, Daddy,' she'd said, 'then we'll see you in the Yorkshire House after the game.'

I felt sure that she wouldn't want to miss sitting silently at the bar, while eight middle-aged people answered questions about gardening in the corner, but to my surprise, she wasn't there when we arrived.

'Charley will be here in a minute,' I said to Perry.

'Good.'

Our team assembled. Miss Sarah Fiske was QM, and Nik was timing. At One, Naughty Neil. At Two, me. At Three, Raving Ronnie Baker. And at Four, Whitbread Prize-winning poet Paul Farley, which you have to admit is quite cool. The Whitbread/Costa Prize has come to rival the Booker over the last few years. It has separate categories for novel, first novel, biography, children's book and poetry; Mr Farley picked up the poetry gong in 2003 for his collection *The Ice Age*. No one can question Whitbread's commitment to modern literature. It's only a shame they don't brew any more. They own Brewers Fayre, Travel Inns, Costa Coffee, and suchlike, rather than making honest ale. Old Samuel Whitbread, the most innovative brewer of the eighteenth century, would be spinning in his grave. It would be good if they combined the two major literary prizes. Imagine the prize-giving ceremony; held in a Brewers Fayre pub, with jars of pickled eggs and packets of peanuts from the cash-'n'-carry.

Not many quiz teams have a Whitbread Prize winner on board. Admittedly, Farley might not be your first choice. D.J. Taylor is a Whitbread winner with a fine quiz brain; Mark Haddon would be useful in a tight corner, too, I reckon. Paul Farley, though, is a pub man and a great poet, perhaps the greatest of his generation, and God only knows plenty of great poets have enjoyed a drink. Since he looks like a cross between Paul Scholes and Alan Ball, and sounds like Emlyn Hughes, it's reassuring to have him on your side.

Our opponents, the Britannia D, were made up of several old quiz lags, all of whom we'd played against at one stage or another. Their Number One was quite handy, I knew of old. After four rounds, the score was Brit D 28, Yorkshire House A 33. Neil was playing a stormer; with three questions right, and four passes, he had scored 13 points. I had already missed my full house by getting the year of Balaclava wrong by one; I was on 10 points. Ron was on 6, and Farley was on 4. The Brit's Number One was also on 13, and my opposite number had 9. But they were falling apart in the lower orders; their Three and Four were on 3 points each.

At half-time, I looked around, anxiously awaiting the arrival of my daughter.

'Where is she?' I asked Perry, who had spent the first half of the match whispering with Professor Sue and Tony.

'Well, if I'd known what it was going to be like, I'd have made sure I met up with you later, too.'

'Whaddya mean?'

'It's the dullest thing I've ever witnessed.'

'How can you say that? Have you got photos of the hand signals?'

'Well, yes. But as a spectator sport, it's up there with gin rummy.'

'We'll be going now, Ian,' said Professor Sue, stifling a yawn. I gave her a kiss.

'You're lucky,' said Perry to Sue and Tony, and they left laughing. Bunch of heathens; perhaps my ambition to take Quiz League to the Olympics is a little premature. I bought Farley a pint of Guinness.

'The important thing in a pub is connecting with the myth,' he said. 'All pubs have their own guiding myth, and if you can tune into that, you'll have a good night. Where did you start?'

'Turk's Head, on St Agnes in the Scillies.'

'I've had a few pints in the Turk's Head.'

'What was the myth, do you think?'

'Real nice tidal vibe you get into down there. Bought a lobster off a fisherman at the bar, but I made a bollocks of jointing it. Overrated, if you ask me. Crab is where it's at.'

The second half of the game was called. Neil's form continued, with two correct answers, and a hat trick of passes on a round about cricket, which I certainly didn't know he had in him. A total of 22; a very good captain's score. I stepped up for a proper Number Two second-half innings. Three correct answers (failing to identify the actor who does the voiceover for Lisa Simpson), and a swingeing seven passes; Charley would have been proud of her old dad, if she'd been there to see it. Twenty-six; what you need from your striker. Ravin' Ron managed one correct answer, and saved a pass, for a match total of 10 points, whilst Farley kept up the tail end with two correct answers and a pass, for a total of 11. Yorkshire House A, 69 points. The opposition fell apart; their Number One only managed 7 points, their Number Two scored a 6, whilst their backfield crumbled, scoring only 1 point between them in the second half. Britannia D, 42 points. Lovely. We stood at the end of the game, each to shake hands with the other, and then we each put our 35p's into the centre of the table. Without paying 35p, it doesn't feel right, somehow.

With Quiz over, and no sign of Charley, it was time to be moving on to the Yorkshire House, our home ground in every conceivable way. It is ten minutes' walk down the hill from the Brit. My specs misted over as we opened the door. The Lancaster Bus Club stood at the bar, and the same jar of pickled eggs stood on the end of the counter. C.C. Ambler and Gary Holland and Tom Crippen sat around the fire, and there, there, my daughter, my darling girl, sat at a table with a vodka and coke and Greg and four of her pals; and like the end of a corny old black-and-white movie, the door closes behind us, and you are left on the pavement, secure in the knowledge that for tonight, at least, we have reached some kind of resolution.

# Wednesday 21st April

If Dunsop Bridge is at the geographical centre of the British Isles, and Lancaster is the nearest city to Dunsop Bridge, then it stands to reason that Lancaster is the most central city in the British Isles. Londoners may gasp, but it's true. It's easy to get to anywhere from Lancaster. It's a little under half-way between Land's End and John o'Groat's. Manchester is about an hour away; Leeds, about an hour and a half. A couple of hours will see you in North Wales, two and a half in Newcastle or Dumfries. The M6 slips right past the town, but manages to be discreet enough about it so that you don't notice it's there until you need it; three and a half/four hours to London, and about the same to Glasgow. The main London-to-Glasgow rail line comes right into the town centre; Lancaster is about half-way between the two by rail as well. There are trains for Manchester, and Leeds, and even Barrow, if that's your bag. You can catch a boat at Heysham for the Isle of Man, and Belfast in season. And it is on the doorstep of the wildest landscapes of England. Across Morecambe Bay to the north, the Cumbrian Mountains, honey-combed with lakes and traffic jams, tower away from the mud flats. To the south, the Fylde starts to open out, the empty flatlands, like a little Lincolnshire, flat as you like all the way to Blackpool. South-east, and you are back in the Forest of Bowland, climbing towards England's best view. And to the north-east, apparent from the moment you pass under the motorway a mile from the town centre, you can see the Pennine mountains, Pen-y-Ghent, Whernside, and Ingleborough, still with a lick or two of tired snow in the frost pockets, even now in late April. And up in them thar hills is the highest pub in Britain.

Everyone knows where the oldest pub is, or the smallest; it's in the next village, or a few towns over, or just into the next county;

there are dozens of claimants. Sticking my neck out a mile, I'm going with the Ferryboat Inn, Holywell, near St Ives in Cambridgeshire, as oldest, and the Old Smith's Arms, at Godmanstone in Dorset, for smallest. I await your views with interest.

But as to highest, there can be no argument. At 1,763 feet above sea level, the Tan Hill Inn is a clear winner. It is between nowhere and nowhere, on Arkengarthdale Moor, deep in the deepest deepness of the deep Pennines. It is the Slaughtered Lamb, the Crow and Crown, the ultimate pub in the back of the back of beyond.

Tan Hill is a two- or three-hour drive from Lancaster, mostly along narrow mountain roads. We drove through Ingleton, and on to Hawes, stopping half-way between the two so that Perry could take some pictures of the Ribblehead Viaduct, one of the Seven Wonders of the Industrial Age, a testament to the Victorian impulse for the conquest of nature dumped in the middle of desolate moorland.

Then into Hawes, and through the Buttertubs Pass, and up into the high country beyond Keld. It was raining in Hawes; as we climbed, the rain turned to sleet. There were no other cars up there to see our dipped headlights coming towards them on the single-track road. We passed through the occasional 'village', each a small settlement of five or six houses, hunched under the shoulder of a mountain. The sleet started to firm up as we climbed higher still. We passed the last of the 'villages'. Bogs came right up to the verge of the road. Tall wooden poles marked where the verge lay, so that travellers in heavy snow could keep to the roadway. Our snow was too late in the year to stand any chance of lying, but it was enough that we needed the windscreen wipers to flap away the soft wet flakes. The peak of Mirk Fell was lost in snow clouds as we arrived in the middle of the middle of nowhere; it was late afternoon, but you could see the lights of the pub from miles away, like a pub on Mars. There were no other buildings in sight in the wet grey moorland uplands. So here, at last, we got our quiet night. Mrs Baines the landlady showed us to our room. She said that we were lucky to get it, as there were not too many walkers about because of the weather. She is very busy in clear weather, she told us.

'Nice spring weather we've been having, too,' she said.

'It's been snowing,' I pointed out.

'Nice spring weather for Tan Hill. We got snowed in for six weeks a couple of years back.'

Tan Hill survives because it is on the Pennine Way, and 90 per cent of business comes from ramblers. If the Pennine Way didn't come past the door, there would be no walkers; Alfred Wainwright, in his guide to the Pennine Way, points out the bleak unloveliness of Arkengarthdale Moor, and says that walking across it is like walking through porridge. The inn was built because it stands at the meeting place of three important drove roads over the Pennines. What looks like wilderness in the British Isles never is. Even this barren moorland has been altered, shaped, farmed. As my pal Big Doctor Dave argues, Britain is a garden, not an untamed wilderness in a state of nature; this bit of it is a boggy alpine garden, tended by generations of sheep farmers and gamekeepers.

After dinner, Perry stayed for a while in the firelit bar, talking to the handful of walkers who were out in this weather, while I went back to our room to write up my notes. There is a sense in which the Tan Hill Inn, as well as being the highest pub we had come to, was also our last. Tomorrow we would cross into Scotland, and Scottish pubs are very different; less like houses – less public, in a way. Sitting in my room at Tan Hill seemed an ideal opportunity to look back on where we had come from.

Time and again, I reflected, on our journey through England and Wales we had met lots of welcoming friendly people who were out for a few drinks with their pals. This is the default state of affairs in pubs. The fight could have been avoided, if we had turned the corner five minutes earlier, or if we hadn't chosen to take a hand. Other than that, we hadn't seen any trouble at all, and, as time passed, the more we enjoyed the fight anyway. We hadn't seen much of the vertical and subsequently horizontal binge-drinking, 'the scourge of the city centres', which generates so much political heat. We had avoided the areas where it happens, except perhaps in Burton, where girls had taken the piss out for me for being a bit funny-looking. I *am* a bit funny-looking, and if you are a bit funny-looking too, then I can see you might find town centres uncomfortable on Friday and Saturday nights. But if you don't want to go to a shit party with loads of students and chavs, then you don't have to go. If you don't fancy it, there are still plenty of good, interesting cool places where you can get a half-decent pint, and you will find intelligent students and articulate chavs there too. All the cunts are up the High Street; so what? At least they're not in your local.

And what will you do with the town centres? The Tories drove businesses from the town centres in the eighties, drove them into retail parks on the arterial road. Councils had little choice but to allow more pubs and clubs and bars to open in the abandoned shops and banks, or let the town centre die. The night-time economy is currently 4 per cent of GDP, and set to rise.

It is largely a myth that respectable middle-aged people have been excluded from town centres at night, because they were never there in the first place. Why would they be? As I have argued, there never was anything to do at night. People talk about the difficulties of going to the cinema or the theatre, but lots of cinemas are out in the malls anyway, and theatres kick out well before the pubs. There is noise, and heat, and vomit, but actually, you are only really under threat if you have been looking at Jason's bird, or if you spilled his pint.

My brother Trapper was in a pub once, when someone knocked against him, and spilled a drop, the merest drop of his pint, as he tells the story. Trapper turned round, and emptied what was left of his pint over the guy's head.

'Now you can buy me another pint,' said Trapper.

The guy twatted Trapper, who fell to the ground.

'All right then,' said Traps, as he got up from the beer-soaked floor, 'just make it a half.'

Moral is, don't tip beer over people's heads and you'll probably be all right. Or you could follow the advice that one of Wellington's officers gave to the Iron Duke. Wellington came across the officer, a colonel, in a state of advanced inebriation.

'Look here, sir,' said Wellington, 'what would you do if you met one of your men in the condition I find you?'

The colonel drew himself up, saluted the Duke and replied, 'I should not condescend to speak to the brute, sir.'

If 'binge-drinking' is to be controlled politically, somebody is going to have to do something about the nature of the English people. Our culture has Saxon roots. The Saxons got off the boats, 1,500 years ago, pissed out of their heads and itching for a scrap. Their idea of heaven was a place where cows gave beer rather than milk.

It is one of our deepest cultural engrams, the idea of drunken leery Englishmen. Englishness has at its root a bunch of North European economic migrants on the make, sat around a log fire in Jutland or Schleswig-Holstein, arguing about the best way to get things done, who, after a few beers, got themselves all wound up because Eodwyn had been looking at Erminilda's tits. Folks called them the Saxons, and lots of them were, though some of them were Jutes and some were Angles. Why did they drink beer? Because the water was unclean, and they fermented it. It would never have crossed their minds that you could purify water by boiling.

They'd been coming over for a bit, perhaps from the middle of the third century, and one of the last acts of the Empire in Britain was the establishment of a series of forts along what was called 'The Saxon Shore' to try and keep the buggers off. As the Empire completed its slow withdrawal from Britain, the Saxons offered 'military advice' to the British king Vortigern, which is always a mistake on the behalf of those who are being advised. They found in Britain a confident affluent society of people who still felt themselves to be citizens of the Roman Empire, even though the legions had gone twenty or more years before. The Saxons were hungry, and the British weren't. The Saxons operated in independent bands; the British expected central control. By the time the British threw up leaders like Ambrosius and Arthur, the Saxon tribes were at the gates of Glastonbury, and thousands of Britons were escaping to the partly abandoned Roman province of Armorica in Gaul. Britain was strong enough to take back much of the island, in the period roughly between

490 and 520. After that, the game was up, and Johnny Saxon started to come over in numbers; recent evidence would suggest, relatively peacefully, to farm rather than to burn. The English had arrived. Mine's a pint.

The British already had wine, roads, organised farming, functioning towns, at least one city in Londinium, and a vibrant Christian culture. The Saxons brought over democracy, beer, and mindless violence under the influence; sadly, they trashed the city, which stood abandoned for 200 years. The Vikings brought indifference to adversity, pagan zest for life and more beer. The Normans brought the class system, and more wine. The Jews, the Hanseatics, the Huguenots, the Dutch, brought wealth and knowledge, Protestantism and gin. The Afro-Caribbeans brought Rastafari and radical politics and rum; the Indians brought food and tea and grandmotherly kindness, and now the Russians and Poles are sending us the fruits of the finest education system in the world, along with a measure of vodka. That's what Englishness is . . . and if you read down the list you'll find mindless violence under the influence of alcohol right at the root. Ain't no use in saying it ain't there.

Swift said, almost 300 years ago that 'There is no nation yet known in either hemisphere where the people of all conditions are more in want of some cordial to keep up their spirits than in this of ours'. And you can't argue with Swift.

Fact of the matter is, if you put cheap booze in front of the English, lots of them will enjoy getting falling-down drunk. Our masters decreed that we should live and die by the market, and the market quite clearly calls for another bottle of something. According to the Government's Alcohol Harm Reduction Strategy (AHRS; someone wasn't thinking, were they?), alcohol causes 1.2m. violent incidents, including some 350K cases of domestic abuse a year. Approximately 17m. working days per annum are lost due to alcohol-related absence. Half of all street fights, and over half of admissions to Accident & Emergency departments occur in just two hours of the week – the last hour before closing time on Friday and the hour around closing time on Saturday. I repeat, if restriction hasn't worked, then liberalisation deserves a go.

As an example of good practice, AHRS cites the case of Stroud, where the incidence of disorder in the town centre has dropped due to a new approach by the local council. They've improved the street lighting, started renovating town-centre buildings, offered incentives to people to live over shops, committed themselves to improving civic design, and have initiated an innovative programme of public art in the town. They've also started encouraging events back into the city centres, like farmers' markets and music. It works. People have started taking pride in their town centre. Unsurprising; that's how all town centres should be. But that's still not enough.

City councils, if they want the night-time economy to continue its growth, at the same time as cutting back on public disorder, have to commit to proper street-cleaning, up to a European standard. This would include washing the streets, and there is nothing like a big machine squirting water to make people go home quietly. Above all, the one thing government could do to improve all our lives is to provide cheap subsidised public transport which runs both night and day. The benefits would be practically limitless; cutting back on fights at taxi ranks would be the least of it. And how do you fund it? By scrapping our nuclear weapons.

What you'd do about the kebab shops, I don't know.

It still seems to me that the big worry is not that young people go out and drink more than the State says is good for them on Friday and Saturday nights. What worries me is the virtual disappearance of any kind of underground, of alternative ways of living. At Lampeter, the biggest drinkers were the rugby team and the ordinands, that is, the young men who had been accepted to train as vicars in the Church of Wales. The rugby team all expected to go on and join large firms as management trainees, whilst the ordinands knew that if they didn't get pished and shag around while they were students, they were never going to get another chance, as their parishioners were hardly likely to approve later in their careers. What these groups shared in common was a realisation that their futures were mapped out for them. In the past, it was medical students who used to drink too much. The student years were their years of freedom, and flaming youth was expected of them. Those of us who had no intention of becoming vicars, doctors, or management trainees, and who expected a life chock full of freedom, could take it a bit easier.

Now, no one has years of freedom. Turning on, tuning in and dropping out are historical phenomena. From cradle to grave, we are tested and measured, and prepared by the education system to take our allotted place in 'the world's fourth-largest economy'. As Toni Morrison says, we are not citizens, we are consumers. That is our job. President-for-Life Blairbrown says that he wants a society based on merit and ability, rather than class. Thing is, you could escape from your class; I did. From the iron grip of a meritocracy, there is no escape. If you have no ability, if you have no 'merit', what are you supposed to do then? Might as well get pished. An underclass is the inevitable result of meritocratic society; read the book, Mr Blairbrown. It has been around since the fifties. It's called *The Rise of the Meritocracy*, and is by Michael Young.

And if all the psychometric tests show that you are suited to working in the human-resources department in a large branch of Tesco, why, that's what you'll do. And you'll work like a dog for no reason you ever really know until you are sixty-five or seventy, paying off your student debt, paying off the mortgage on your new-build mock-Georgian house on the outskirts of Kettering, consuming like a good consumer should, buying and buying and buying on credit, watching the telly, reading about the 'love lives' of 'celebrities' in life-style magazines, and end up putting your children through the same system that has imprisoned you. If that was your future, wouldn't you go and get blathered at weekends? They are drinking to forget.

So, young people, your drinking habits are a problem. Politicians are worried about your productivity. Politicians want you to stay well and work hard because they will need you to pay their pensions in twenty years' time. They are trying to turn this country into Eisenhower's America; respectable, clean, hard-working, buttoned down. Imagine the future; it is not a boot stamping on a face, for ever. Too crude. It is Stepford. Much nicer.

I am worried that you are so dull, that all you can think of to do on a weekend is go get legless in a city-centre bar and shout at people. The more you allow yourselves to be herded together, the less chance you will have of freedom in your lives. Don't let people turn the world into America 1954. Politics should not be the higher management. Have a look at Paris 1968, and see if that doesn't seem like more fun. There is a beach under the call centre.

Enough ranting into a notebook for one night. I went next door to the bar, to join Perry and the walkers for a last one. As my illustrious ancestor W.T. Marchant says in *In Praise of Ale*, 'Beer is one of those daily expected and daily enjoyed simple pleasures which give man's life its local colouring.' In what is undoubtedly the highest, but also one of the most isolated pubs in England, we took our simple pleasure, like millions of other people, sitting in pubs, talking to friends and welcoming strangers.

'Scotland tomorrow,' I said.

'Aye,' said Perry

'Verra different.'

'Aye. The noo.'

# Thursday 22nd April

In the morning, it was spitting sleet as we set out from Tan Hill on the road down from the moors, to pick up the A66 at Brough. The A66 is a relatively fast road, and we'd spent three weeks trying to avoid them. But the crack now was to get on to the M6 at Penrith, and head up to Glasgow as quick as we could.

'I've got a mate who's just moved to Glasgow from Bath,' I said to Perry as he drove. 'I think you'd like him; shall I give him a bell?'

'Why not?'

I wasn't sure if my pal would be free, since he'd moved up for a new job, but I tried his mobile. 'Mr Brook?'

'Is that Mr Marchant?'

'It is. How are you, Chris?'

'Indifferent. I've just packed my job.'

'But you've only just got it.'

'I know. It's a fucker.'

'Do you fancy coming out for a drink tonight?'

'Yeah, but I'm in Glasgow.'

'So are . . . hang on . . . Perry! Can we come off at the next turn?'

'What, this one?'

'Yes!'

'Why?'

'I want to go to Longtown . . . sorry, Chris. We're on our way up to Glasgow now.'

'No.'

'Yeah. You free tonight?'

'I certainly am. Where shall we meet?'

'Don't know, mate. It's your town.'

'OK. How about the Pot Still, on Hope Street. What time will you be there?'

'Six-ish.'

'See you later.'

'That's fixed,' I said to Perry. 'Nifty junction work back there.'

'I'm following the signs to Longtown, is that right?'

'Yeah, cheers.'

'Why are we going to Longtown?'

'To see a munitions factory. Almost forgot it was here.'

A little way out of Longtown, out in the flat country that Cumbria isn't famous for, almost up against the Scottish border, is M.o.D. Longtown, now proudly advertising itself as part of the 'Research and Defence Logistics Organisation'. What it is, is a bomb factory. This is one of the places where the State develops its new weapons. We drove alongside the perimeter for a time. There isn't really much to see from the road. There are hedges and a chain-link fence. The few buildings you can see from the road are low-lying.

'Why this?' asked Perry, as we drove over the road that runs alongside the site.

'This place is the reason we have opening times,' I said. 'In the First World War, this was the country's largest munitions plant. It employed 25,000 people, and most of them lived in Carlisle. They kept on turning up for work pissed, so in the 1915 Defence of the Realm Act, all pub opening times were restricted. Pubs could only open between eleven and three, and then between six and ten-thirty. The government hoped to control drunkenness. Before the Act there were 250 convictions for drunk-and-disorderly conduct in Carlisle per annum. After the introduction of the Act, the conviction rate went up to a thousand.'

'People saw the shorter opening times as an inducement to drink,' said Perry.

'Exactly so. The government reacted by bringing all the pubs in a 320-mile-square area around Carlisle under State control.'

'Was that successful?'

'From the State's point of view, yes. You couldn't buy rounds, you couldn't buy chasers with your pint, all advertising of alcohol was banned; all sorts of measures were brought in to control drinking. And the only beer they sold was brewed by the government brewery in Carlisle, which, by all accounts, was as weak as piss water. We should have gone to Carlisle, really.'

'Why? It's not State-owned now.'

'No, but it was up until 1971. It was one of the Tories' first privatisations. After the war, the Carlisle pubs were put in the hands of the State Management System, the SMS, and it was pretty popular. They dropped some of the crazier restrictions and upped the quality of the beer. And they employed Harry Redfern.'

'Who he?'

'He the architect who built the best pubs of the twentieth century. Characterful, family-friendly, lots of comfortable places to sit, easy to supervise. He had complete control over the building and renovation of all the pubs under SMS control. Redfern's pub designs became the model for good pub architecture for years to come.'

'Shall we have a drink and a bite of lunch in Carlisle?' said Perry.

'No. I'm through with English pubs. Last night I was writing that the Tan Hill was our last one. If you drive another three miles, we'll be in Gretna. Let's go there.'

So we did. Hello, Scotland.

Funny old place, Gretna. I drove up there one night from Lancaster with a girlfriend on a romantic whim. We got there about ten past closing time. We parked in the car-park next to the Old Smithy, where they used to do the weddings for which Gretna was famous. We looked in the Old Smithy Gift Shop window at some kilted dolls in plastic tubes and tins of shortbread with pictures of Highland cattle on them. Then we turned around and saw two men tumble out of the pub and start punching one another.

'I've been five minutes in Scotland,' said my friend, 'and I feel I've seen it all.'

She was being unfair, of course. She hadn't had a deep-fried Mars Bar.

So me and Perry bowled up for lunch in what I suppose must be the first pub in Scotland, the Crossways Inn. We looked gloomily at the McEwans beer taps and our first Scottish menu, and ordered Guinness with steak and chips. If you are expecting me to go on about the second-worst cuisine in Europe, you can wait a bit.

'It's weird,' said Perry. 'One moment you're in the North, and you cross some arbitrary line, and all of a sudden you're back in the South.'

'Yes, it is weird, but it's not arbitrary. We have entered a new cultural universe.'

Most places on borders are unlovely; think Dover, or Hounslow. And Gretna is, I'm sure its most loyal residents would agree, unlovely. But in the windows of the gift shop at the Old Smithy, you are offered your first real clue to the character of Scotland. Scotland is kitsch.

A couple of hours' drive, and we were in Glasgow. We'd booked a hotel in the centre of Glasgow, in a street parallel to Sauchiehall Street, which is Glasgow's Oxford Street and Soho rolled into one. After a shower, we set out to find the Pot Still. Lost again in a city centre, we stopped to ask the way to Hope Street of a couple who were selling newspapers and rattling tins on behalf of the Scottish Socialist Party. They were friendly and funny. We introduced ourselves. His name was Andrew, and hers was Senga.

I explained to them why I was here. Which was to see if people really do drink Buckfast Tonic Wine in Scotland.

'Och, Christ yes,' said Andrew. 'I remember going to a Miners' Social Club in the seventies where they sold it on tap.'

'I used to work in an off-licence in Airdrie, and we sold thirty cases on a Saturday night,' said Senga.

'Bloody hell. Is that mostly to street drinkers?'

'Street drinking is illegal in Glasgow, which is mad, because it's a social problem, not a criminal one,' said Senga.

'That's right,' said Andrew. 'The polis aren't interested in sorting it out. They don't think it's their problem, either. There needs to be places people can go, youth clubs and the like.'

'We used to get pished at our youth club,' I said.

'Aye, so did we,' said Senga. 'Many's the half bottle of Bucky I've shared on the swings.'

'Aye, we drunk Bucky too. Alkies and teenagers. No one else is going to touch it, are they? It's like cough medicine,' said Andrew.

'Did you know,' said Senga, 'that the most common weapon of

attack on a Glasgow Saturday night is a broken Bucky bottle?'

'I didn't. You can't really get it in England.'

'A couple of socialist MSPs wrote to Buckfast Abbey last year, to ask if the monks felt OK about selling the stuff, but they got no reply,' said Andrew.

'If it is a social problem, rather than a criminal one, you'd think the church would be interested, wouldn't you?' I asked.

'You would, aye,' said Senga.

Andrew and Senga pointed us in the direction of the Pot Still. I could see why Chris had chosen it. It had a Victorian interior, in brown wood and mirrored glass. It had a few business types enjoying a quick one after work, several couples having a drink before dinner, and three elderly gentlemen, clucking over that morning's *Racing Post* and turning over a small pile of dud betting slips. All well and good. What set it apart from a London pub were the hundreds of bottles of whisky behind the bar. The selection was vast. This is why the beer is rubbish in Scotland, I reckon, because the whisky is so very excellent.

Perry can't drink too much of the stuff since he got arse-holed with the father of the bride at that Scottish wedding, but I was looking forward to a few days and nights of taking a dram at every available opportunity. I asked Dave the barman for his whisky menu. There was whisky from all over Scotland; from Islay, from Speyside, from Campbeltown, from the Highlands, and from the Islands. I asked Dave what he'd recommend. He said to try the cask-aged Highland Park 1977, from Orkney. It had just won a big competition, where distillery managers from all over Scotland had picked their favourite. It was £8.60 a nip. That's two and a half bottles of Bucky. But this much I have learned in life; that except in the case of home goals, quality is always better than quantity.

I looked at the price again. £8.60 for a drop of whisky. Makes you think.

'Dave, can you give me a receipt for this?' I asked. (I'm STILL waiting to hear from HM Treasury whether vintage whisky, drunk in the name of research, is tax-allowable!)

'Yes sir, I can.'

'Then let's do it, Dave!' I said.

'Yessir!'

Dave poured the golden old spirit into a whisky glass, and I started to raise it towards my lips.

'Not without a drop of water, sir,' said Dave, shocked. He handed me a small jug, and I added a few drops of water to my whisky.

'You must always add a drop of water, sir. It releases the oils.'

As the whisky touched my tongue I understood, really for the first time, why getting rich might be worth all the bother.

Chris Brook arrived at this point, looking like a cross between John Cooper Clarke and W.H. Auden, as tall as me and three times as thin.

'Ere y'are, Brooky. Try this,' I said. He sipped my whisky.

'That's good. That's very good. What's that?' You can still hear Bradford buried under Bath in his voice.

'It's a 1977 cask-aged Highland Park, sir,' said Dave.

'I'll have one of them,' said Chris.

'Eight pounds sixty,' I said.

'Are you mad? Pint of Guinness, please.'

'I'll get that, mate . . . can you stick it on the receipt, Dave?'

'No problem, sir.'

I introduced Chris and Perry, and I started to outline the nature of the project to Chris.

'Where are you going after Glasgow?'

'Islay and Jura,' I said.

'Really? Fuck. Jura. Jura is amazing. Have you ever been before?'

'No. You?'

'Well, yeah. I went over when Bill and Jimi showed the film, didn't I?'

'Did you?'

'Yeah. I did the book of the film. Didn't you know?

'Chris, I didn't. God.'

'What film?' asked Perry.

'*The KLF Burn a Million Quid.*'

'You were there? When the KLF burned a million quid?' said Perry.

'No. That was just Bill, Jimmy and Gimpo. Gimpo owns the film, and the ashes of the money. When they showed the film in the village hall on Jura, I went over with them, and then turned the film and the debate in the village hall into a book. Jura. Man, I love Jura.'

I love the KLF. If you are unfamiliar with their work, then you need to know that they were a pop and art-terrorism group who had a couple of big hits in the 1990s, and who took all the money they ever earned from the music biz, in cash, and burned it in an abandoned boathouse on the Isle of Jura. It was one of the reasons I wanted to go over to Jura, to pay homage to one of a tiny handful of conceptual art works that put their money where their mouth is.

Chris is a performance artist. One of his best-known shows is a Beefheart tribute act, performed in collaboration with that great and good man Sir Gideon Vein. They recreate *Trout Mask Replica*, using an old analogue synth and some kazoos. It has not proved an easy route to success for them. Chris has little or no interest in pleasing a crowd.

'Since I packed the job I've just been sitting in my flat for two weeks, trying to write. Jura. Fuck. I could really do with getting away.'

'Come with us,' said Perry, whose modest share of our advance was ring-fenced from any expenses which might accrue during the course of the trip.

'Booof!' I coughed.

'Really?' said Chris.

'Of course,' said Perry. 'We've got a room booked. Ian pays for all the booze and grub on expenses . . .'

'Not quite expenses as such,' I started to explain.

'I'd love to. Wow. Thanks. I'd love to see Jura again.'

So that was that. Brooky was coming with us.

'We're leaving at eight in the morning,' I said.

'Eight? In the morning?'

'Yes.'

'Well . . . I'll see. I'd love to go to Jura again. But, eight you say?'

'Yeah. It's a long drive to the Islay ferry.'

Chris pulled a face.

'Well . . . I'll see how I feel.'

So Brooky wasn't coming with us after all.

'Do you know anywhere we could eat, then?' I asked.

'Yeah. How about the 13th Note? That's pretty cool.'

We walked across town. Chris and Perry were talking about the disappearance of the underground press. I was looking out for off-licences.

'I guess it's too soon for you to get to know anyone much,' I said to Chris.

'There's only one guy I know in the whole of Glasgow, and I keep trying to avoid him.'

We arrived at the 13th Note, which gave the impression of being largely painted in eau-de-Nil. The bar was one large room, but downstairs was a small venue. Posters advertised forthcoming gigs. Always a great place to see bands, is Glasgow. Always got something interesting up its sleeve. A chalkboard behind the bar advertised a menu of both drink and food. If all pubs are either an inn, an ale-house or a tavern, this was a tavern. Perry and I walked up to the bar, ordered some drinks, and started thinking abut what we might like to eat. Chris hadn't made it to the bar. He'd been engaged in conversation with a rascally-looking man, aged in his late twenties, with hooded eyes and a permanent smirk, who, to gauge from the lack of clear focus in his eyes, was very pished indeed. Or something. Perry and I found a table, and Chris joined us.

'Would you fucking believe it?

'What?'

'You know I said I only knew one person in Glasgow?'

'Yeah?'

'And that I was trying to avoid him?'

'That's him, isn't it?' I said.

'Yes,' said Chris.

One of the difficulties of writing non-fiction is that coincidences happen. If you are writing fiction, you are free of this kind of thing. Nobody believes coincidence in fiction, so it is easily avoided. But in non-fiction, you are called upon to deal with it. Professor Sue and her husband Tony sitting in the departure lounge at St Mary's Airport. Turning a corner at just the wrong moment in Driffield. Chris Brook meeting the one person in the whole of Glasgow he wanted to avoid, minutes after telling me about him. But what are you going to do? In real life, things happen which make our narratives seem fictional. In fiction, events of this kind can never be allowed.

'He's coming over when we've had our food,' said Chris. 'His name's Kenny. He's an artist. I met him on a British Council junket to Moscow a few years back.'

'What's up with him?'

'Well, he's all right. But he can be a bit mad when he's pissed. He likes blowing things up.'

'For fun? Or politics?' said Perry.

'No. For art.'

'Chris, I can't help noticing that everything on the menu is vegetarian,' I said.

'You'll have to be brave,' said Chris. 'The vegetarian haggis is all right.'

So that's what I had. It was all right.

When we had finished eating, Kenny staggered across, and I told him what we were doing.

'I'll take yer to sum fucken great pubs,' slurred Kenny.

'What I'd really like to see is an off-licence,' I said.

'Get sum carry-oots, like? Good idea. Youse can all come back to mine. I've got some horse.'

'No, not really. What I want is to meet some Bucky drinkers.'

'You're talking to one, mate. I love my fucken Bucky, me.'

'I'd like to see them in action.'

'All right. Let's just have another drink, and I'll take youse to an offy.'

We ordered drinks, while Kenny reminisced with Chris about blowing things up in Moscow.

'Do y'mind that explosion I did in the undergroond bunker?' asked Kenny.

A look of pain crossed Chris's face. 'Yes, I do Ken. I was deaf for weeks afterwards.'

'Aye. That was fucken daft, actually.'

We finished our drinks, and Kenny led us, somewhat uncertain on his pins, through the broken streets of Glasgow's East End. Ken is no fool. He was pissed, but he knew what I was after. In a cosmopolitan city like Glasgow, there will be wine merchants selling fine wines, and quiet respectable off-licences. I'm sorry if I'm perpetuating old ideas about Glasgow; but I wanted to see Bucky drinkers in their natural habitat, and we weren't going to find them in the suburbs.

'That's Glasgow Green,' said Kenny. 'In the old days, everyone would come doon here on holidays, and sit by the river. Not so much now.'

His smirk widened, and we turned into a wide street still lined with tenements. There were a few shops; a Bangladeshi supermarket, a tailor's, and an off-licence. I felt a shock, both of indignation and fear. We had left one economic zone, where bohemian vegetarian bars flourished, and entered another, where people still lived in semi-derelict tenements. The street was badly lit; the predominant impression was that it was brown, brown with decay. Net curtains flapped at lightless windows. There was no one about, so far as I could see. No cars. Perhaps I've led a sheltered life, but I'd never seen such glaring poverty so close to a city centre. Kenny knew his stuff; he told me that, back in the seventies, the East End of Glasgow was officially the most deprived inner-city area in Europe. Population dropped from 150K at the 1951 Census to 80,000 by 1971 and to 45,000 by 1976. 35,000 people left in five years.

'Bloody hell, Ken.'

'I live roond here. It's cheap to live roond here.'

'Can't say I'd fancy it.'

'Would you not? It's nice to visit, but you wouldn't want to live here, is that what you're saying? Lots of journalists feel like that.'

'I'm not a journalist.'

'Are you not? What are you, then? One side of this street is Catholic, and one is Protestant. Which are you?'

'Protestant.'

Kenny narrowed his hooded eyes.

'Ah'm Catholic,' he said.

We arrived outside the offy.

'Was this the kind of thing you had in mind?' asked Ken.

When I am rich and elderly, I shall paint. I'll paint in the school of Jeff Koons and Damien Hirst. I won't actually touch the brushes or anything. My subject will be light. I'll hire art-school graduates who can paint in the style of Joseph Wright of Derby, and get them to paint scenes like this; a dark brown street of tenements, uncertain dim lights behind dirty windows, like the moon on a foggy night, and the open offy door a warm yellow beacon over the wet pavement.

'This is just the thing, Ken.'

'Ah may not be a cynic myself, but I understand the workings of the cynical mind.'

Inside, the shop was divided into two. On one side, an array of colourful bottles ranged over well stocked shelves, looked after by a white guy, the kind of whiteness that you only really see in Scotland, bleached whiter still by harsh strip lighting. He was younger than me, I reckoned, but the absence of teeth and hair made it difficult to estimate his age. On the other side was the area where the customers stood to place their order. The two parts of the shop were divided by a bandit screen in blurred Perspex, no longer as see-through as once it was, harrowed by scratches and starbursts of stress marks. There was no question here of self-service, of a leisurely consideration between bottles of merlot and cab sav. You came up to the bandit screen, and asked for what you wanted, which the offy guy dug out for you from the shelves.

'Yes, mate?' he said.

'A bottle of Buckfast, please,' I said.

'Do you want it cold?'

'You keep it cold?'

'Aye!' He pointed to a chiller cabinet, where rows of Buckfast Tonic Wine lay in wait for those bon viveurs who enjoy a chilled glass of Buckie after dinner.

'No, just as it comes.'

I handed him his £3.49 and he gave me my bottle through the

gap at the bottom of the bandit screen, wrapped in a brown paper bag. I told him that I'd been to Buckfast Abbey a few weeks ago, and asked him if he ever drank it himself.

'I used to, aye. Buckie was my poison. But I've not touched a drop for fifteen years. I'm a recovering alcoholic.'

'Isn't that difficult, working here?'

I remembered Fleur, the retail manager at Plymouth Gin, another recovering alcoholic who sold booze for a living.

'No. Not when you see the people we get in here . . . yes, mate?'

An ancient street drinker in a filthy overcoat had come into the shop, clearly very drunk, but working very hard to appear sober.

'Pulse,' he said.

The shop worker bent down, and pulled out a litre plastic bottle of white cider.

'One-fifty.'

The old guy pushed a pile of coppers under the bandit screen, which the shop guy counted into his till. It was right to the penny. The Pulse was put into a paper bag, and slid under the screen. The old guy grabbed it, and limped out of the shop, to drink his prize, and to start collecting more coppers for the next bottle.

'How much Buckie do you sell in a night?' I asked.

'Och, usually fifty bottles or so. Yes, mate?'

A couple had come into the shop, drunk as skunks, their ages impossible to estimate. Their faces were caved in by their lack of teeth. She was wearing a filthy Kappa tracksuit in turquoise, a raw and livid scar running down one side of her face. He was on crutches; he leaned on these to hand over his money.

'Pulse,' he said, handing over three 50p coins.

Once more, the plastic bottle in the paper bag was slid under the bandit screen. Now another guy came into the shop, perhaps slightly less drunk than the others; with a few more teeth; slightly better dressed.

'Yes, mate?'

'Buckie, chilled,' he said.

'I've just been to Buckfast Abbey,' I announced to the assembled company.

'Where's that?' said the Buckie buyer.

'It's in Devon. It's where they make the stuff.'

'We call it Fuckfast,' said the guy on crutches.

'You can't really get it in England,' I said.

'Can you not?' said the Buckie buyer.

'Ah come frae Coatbridge,' said the guy on crutches. 'You can get as much as you like there.'

'Rutherglen is the Buckie capital of the world. In Rutherglen, the streets run wi' Fuckfast,' said the Buckie buyer.

'Why do you drink it chilled?'

''Cos then it disnae taste so fucken shite,' said the Buckie buyer, making his way back into the ruined street.

'Ah've seen you before,' the woman with the scar on her face said to me. 'Are you no' one of they American wrestlers?'

I had to admit I was not. I said goodbye to the guy in the shop, and went back out on to the pavement, where my friends were waiting. The guy on crutches and the woman with the scar made their way uncertainly up the dark street.

'Have you seen enough deprivation for now?' said Kenny.

'Yes thanks, Ken.'

'Come on, then. I'll show you some of the new Glasgow.'

Ken led us through streets of warehouses. As we moved away from the East End, it became clear that more and more of the warehouses were marked for development, or were in the process of being converted into loft spaces for the increasingly affluent urban middle class. Three or four blocks away from the night-marish off-licence, Kenny took us into the bar of a brand-new designer hotel, the Brunswick. It wasn't busy; apart from us, there were a few well-dressed young couples chatting at tables. Everyone looked like they could be members of Franz Ferdinand or Belle and Sebastian. The lighting was discreet, the décor art-school; expensive branded lagers were available on tap. We all had Guinness.

'This is the world's first post-industrial city,' Kenny asserted. 'And post-mercantile. The population is starting to climb. All these warehouses are being converted into apartments and bars and shops.

It won't be too long before the development reaches the East End, and then all those people will be driven out too.'

'Where will they go?'

'Further and further oot, I guess. They won't fucken care, so long as they can still get a drink.'

Me and Perry and Brooky drank up, but Kenny said that he was going to stay for another.

'Would you like the Buckie?' I asked him. It was difficult for Ken to understand that we didn't want it, that I had bought it so that the off-licence guy would talk with me. He looked at me suspiciously from under his hooded eye-lids.

'Do you no' want it?' he said.

'No Ken, we don't. You can have it and welcome.'

'Well, if you're sure . . .'

I handed him the paper bag with the bottle of Fuckfast, and left him at the bar, now barely able to stay upright on his stool. We walked with Chris back towards our hotel, and turned into Sauchiehall Street. The countless bars were chucking out, and a river of pissed-up people were spilling on to the streets. Getting wellied, they call it in Scotland. Vomit slicked the gutters. Girls were screaming with laughter, tripping over on the pavement. It might not be to everyone's taste, but at least they gave off an air of having enjoyed themselves. Here at least, Glasgow seemed like a place where the link between drinking and fun had not been broken. Half a mile away, drinking was not something that was done for fun, but out of necessity. You don't drink Pulse, or Buckfast Tonic Wine for fun.

We came to our hotel.

'So, Chris, will we see you in the morning?' I asked.

'Eight o'clock?'

'Yes, sorry. We can't wait around. Like I say, it's a long drive out to the Islay ferry.'

'Hmmm. I'd love to come, but eight o'clock . . .'

'See how you feel in the morning.'

Chris wandered off into the night. Shame he was such an idle bastard. It would have been good to have him along for the next part of the trip.

# Friday 23rd April

But, bless his heart, there he was, at eight o'clock on a cold wet Glasgow morning, with a grin and a little back pack and raring to go. So I rescued the car, and off we set on the four-hour drive to Kennacraig, where the ferry to Islay was due to depart at one.

If you don't carry a map of Scotland in your head, you might imagine that all the islands are well to the north of Glasgow, but this is not the case at all. Kennacraig is on the same latitude as Glasgow, about fifty miles due west in a hovercraft, but over a hundred by road, as you have to skirt round the north end of Loch Fyne. It doesn't really take four hours, more like two and a half, but I drive slow, and like to stop for breakfast, elevenses, lunch, tea, dinner and supper. We were at the Caledonian MacBrayne ferry terminal at Kennacraig with an hour to spare, and that was with a couple of stops. We were first in the queue to get on to the boat by at least twenty minutes.

I love Scottish ferry terminals. They are in the most remote places imaginable. Kennacraig sits half-way down West Loch Tarbert, which bites into the western coast of the Mull of Kintyre. There isn't a Kennacraig village as such, just a gaggle of low buildings and some parking spaces, clinging to the side of a wild sea loch. And Kennacraig is one of the more developed ferry terminals, because boats go from here to Islay, Jura and Colonsay. It actually has an office and a coffee machine. We watched the Islay boat come up to the loading ramp, and disgorge the mostly local traffic. There are few tourists on the islands at this time of the year, so the vehicles were two whisky tankers, a butcher's van, an empty builders' merchant's truck and a handful of cars. And then it was time to load us up, and as soon as we were parked up on the car deck, we hurried off to do the thing that all experienced Caledonian

MacBrayne passengers do at the start of a Hebridean voyage. We went to the cafeteria, and had Calmac lasagne and chips.

Calmac lasagne is just the thing to line the stomach if you think you might be in for a bumpy crossing, but it can make you feel a bit blue. Sea travel, I maintain, is melancholy by its nature, a feeling which is hard to shake when you are bloaty with carbohydrates. After lunch, I felt I wanted to be alone, and walked on deck in grey drizzle, thinking about the empty pointlessness of existence, watching as the shores of West Loch Tarbert slid by like my life. But then, as the lasagne started to wear off, we came to the mouth of the loch, and passed the north of the island of Gigha on the port bow. The sun had broken through the clouds, and Gigha was golden. I chewed some Rennies, and life seemed like it might be worth living after all.

The crossing from Kennacraig to Port Askaig on Islay takes about two and a half hours. Brooky joined me up on deck, and we watched as the mainland fell away, and the Paps of Jura came closer. As we came to the entrance of the narrow strait that separates Islay and Jura, it became obvious that the boat was working harder to make progress against the flooding tide. We saw the ferry between Islay and Jura, little more than a landing craft, swept along on the flood as it fought its way between the two islands. I was reminded that tides are fast in this part of the world. Between Jura and the island of Scarba to its north is the Gulf of Corryvreckan. The Corryvreckan is a fearsome tidal whirlpool, where Orwell was nearly drowned with his son. Orwell was the reason I wanted to go to Jura. Famously, he wrote 1984 there, in a house called Barnhill, seven miles from the nearest road, an inconvenient spot at the best of times, but especially so if you are dying of tuberculosis. But it wasn't Orwell the satirical novelist that I wanted to think about, but rather Orwell as creator of the most important pub in the intoxicated landscape, the Moon Under Water.

But whisky was the reason for coming to Islay. There are nine functioning distilleries on the island, and it vies with Speyside as the most important whisky-producing area in Scotland. A moment's thought shows this is unfair. Islay vies with nothing, and nowhere, because Islay whisky is almost as distinct from Scotch as Scotch is from Irish, or from bourbon. There is no whisky like Islay whisky; and you love it, or hate it. If you love it, the fact that it smells like TCP is what makes it so wonderful. If you hate it, you hate it for the same reason. Perry and Brooky and I are all gaga for the stuff.

We climbed from Port Askaig on to a plateau of peat, dotted here and there with small villages, and drove as fast as we could the twenty miles across the island to Port Ellen, and then up the coast to the Ardbeg Distillery, where we hoped to catch the last guided tour of the day. I knew that it would be touch and go whether we made it or not. All nine of the distilleries run tours, but Ardbeg was Perry's favourite, and theirs was the latest tour to set off, at four. If we drove like lunatics, we could just make it across the island in time. Since Brooky doesn't drive, and I turn into an elderly Buddhist monk behind the wheel, much too interested in the process of the journey to concern myself with anything so trivial as destination, driving like a lunatic fell to Perry, navigating fell to me, and skinning up to Brooky.

The first turning to the right as you come out of Port Askaig on the road to Port Ellen has a brown heritage sign with a picture of what looks like a pagoda pointing the way to the Caol Ila and Bunnahabhain distilleries. To do all nine would take at least a week, and we had two nights, so we passed them by. There are mountains on Islay, which rose on the horizon to our left, but they are all dwarfed by the Paps of Jura, which filled the rear-view mirror. Mostly, the interior of Islay is flat, the road straight across the dark peat. As we passed occasional cars on the road, we noticed that all the drivers waved at us, and as we came into Port Ellen, past the maltings, we noticed that all the pedestrians waved at us too. We waved back.

Brooky extinguished our second joint, and said, 'I could do with some sweeties.'

'So could I,' said Perry. 'And I want to send Shinaid a postcard.'

'I could do with a piss,' I said.

So we stopped in Port Ellen to conduct a little business. Three stoned middle-aged men in a sweetshop and looking for lavatories are not to be hurried. It was clear that we were not going to make the tour after all.

'Pouffffffffffff,' said Perry, when I told him this as we got back into the car.

As you leave Port Ellen, you pass three of Scotland's most famous distilleries in the space of three miles, Laphroaig, Lagavulin and Ardbeg. The still buildings looked a bit like Chinese pagodas, which explained those brown heritage signs with the symbol of the pagoda, directing you to distilleries which welcome visitors, which we were to see all across the whisky-producing areas of Scotland.

The Ardbeg Distillery is hard by the sea. Waves wash against the rocks underneath the back wall of the warehouse. All the buildings are painted a brilliant white, but on the wall that looks out to sea, Ardbeg is written in huge black letters, lest anybody coming from the sea should mistake that they have arrived in Islay. For anyone who likes factories of any kind, it is especially thrilling to find such beautiful industry in such lonely surroundings. On the landward side of the distillery, mountainous hills stand out from the sea. At this time of the year, in drizzling rain, they looked bleak and unwelcoming. This place is the essence of Romance; you can imagine Heathcliff and Cathy bounding towards one another on the hills, with a glass of Ardbeg in their hands.

Despite the frantic drive from the ferry, we had missed the tour by about twenty minutes, but the lass in the visitor centre told us that we could try a wee nip of something, which was some compensation. We had a go at the several Ardbeg malts ready and waiting for the tourists; the stench of antiseptic rose invitingly from the tasting glasses. As we wandered around the shop, the tour arrived to try a dram for themselves. There were six of them, all young men, all carrying expensive camera equipment and all Japanese. The tour guide, dressed in a fetching tartan outfit, chattered gaily about the different kinds of whisky they could try and subsequently buy, but I got the impression that their English was fairly limited. It didn't seem to matter, as they all tried the whiskies with an air of enraptured awe. Whisky enthusiasm is big in Japan, and by enthusiasm I don't mean merely liking a drop after dinner. There are real enthusiasts, fanoraks, nutters, who collect rare bottles, and who clearly save up for years to come on distillery tours.

We drove south from Ardbeg, back towards Port Ellen, watching seals playing in the water beside the road. This was the last tour we could have attached ourselves to that day on the whole island, and we had blown it. We stopped to look at Lagavulin and Laphroaig, both built on the same model as Ardbeg; hard against the sea, white painted buildings, still rooms topped with the distinctive pagodas.

Next to the Laphroaig Distillery there was a field full of tiny flags; lots of American and Japanese ones, but also British, French, German and Dutch.

'What's that about, I wonder?' I said to my chums.

'Er . . . I think they've split this field up into plots a foot square, which they then sell to the Friends of Laphroaig,' said Brooky.

'How do you know that?' said Perry.

'Erm, because I am a Friend of Laphroaig, and I own one of those plots,' said Brooky, somewhat shame-faced.

'No! You twat!' I said.

'Yeah, I know. I don't know what came over me.'

'How much was it?' said Perry.

'Can't remember. It was years ago. It's the only land I've ever owned.'

We leaned on the fence, and stared out over the desolate field at the Brook Estate; more a bit of fenced-off peat bog than a field in the conventional sense.

'I've never been to see it before,' said Brooky. 'Just think, one of those flags is mine.'

'Yeah,' said Perry. 'You could go and stand on it, if you knew which one it was.'

'Yes. You could put up one of those tall loo tents that you see on campsites.' I said. 'Or a sentry box.'

'Yes,' said Perry. 'Or a mobile-phone mast.'

'Why fuckin' not?' said Brooky. 'It is mine.'

Having missed the tour, we set off back towards Ballygrant, a village not far from Port Askaig, where I had booked a (twin) room in the local pub. I hadn't told them about Brooky, so I hoped there would be room at the inn. On the way back across the island, we stopped in Bowmore, the island's administrative capital, which was so happening there was a curry restaurant and a nightclub. I suspected that Ballygrant might not be so lively.

The Ballygrant Inn is set back from the main Port Askaig/Port Ellen road, and stands in well manicured grounds. I explained to the landlady, who introduced herself as Ruby, that our party had increased by one, and was this going to be a problem?

'Och, not at all. That's fine. We've a family room you can have.'

She took us upstairs to a good-sized room, where there was a big double, and two bunk beds. I'm afraid I pulled rank, on the basis that I was paying for the room, and I nabbed the double, leaving Perry and Chris to argue about who should go in the top bunk. We freshened up, and went down to the bar.

Ruby was there to greet us, and she introduced us to her husband Dave. I told them why we had come to Islay, and they told us that we were lucky, that tomorrow night was curry night, but, in the mean time, what would we like to eat? As is well known, Scotland is not at the forefront of world cuisine, so I always try to order something plain, hoping against hope that they can't cock it up. I opted for the lamb chops. I felt encouraged that it might be pass-able, since there was actually Draught Bass behind the bar, a fabulous rarity in Scotland.

The Ballygrant Inn serves as a community centre for this part of the island. There is an internet café, and four lads sat at computer terminals, playing on-line games. There was a full-sized pool table, which the three of us were looking forward to trying later. There was a piano, and Dave told me they had some great sing-songs in there sometimes. I was already beginning to like the Ballygrant very much, when they brought out the lamb chops, fat, perfectly cooked, with crisp green vegetables and fluffy mash. I've had worse at Simpsons-in-the-Strand. We fell to.

While we were eating, six lads dressed up to the nines came in, ordered beer, and started playing what looked like a fairly serious pool tournament. Ruby told me that they were painters and deco-rators working locally.

'They're not locals though, Ian. They're over from the Uists.'

I've never been one to find painters and decorators romantic, but the mention of the Uists did it for me. Even on Islay, the Outer Hebrides seemed exotic, a world away, where people lead a life of unimaginable wildness.

After dinner, the conversation turned to whisky. Although they are not all labour-intensive, the distilleries are by far the largest employers on the island, as well as being the main source of tourism. Dave turned me on to Bruichladdich.[*]

'It's rare, isn't it?' he said.

'Certainly is, Dave.'

'The Bruichladdich Distillery had been mothballed for years, but they've just recently reopened. They do tours on a Saturday morning.'

'Really?'

'Aye. I'll find their brochure.'

So it looked as though we were going to get to see an Islay whisky distillery after all.

I asked Dave about illicit production on Islay.

'Well, you can never be 100 per cent, but I'd say that almost certainly there are no illegal stills on Islay.'

'Why not, do you think?'

'Well, in the old days, all the distillery workers would get two or three drams of the clear stuff every day.'

'What's the clear stuff?'

'Well, that's the pure alcohol before it goes into the casks for ageing. It gives you a quick buzz rather than the slow whisky burn. The head brewer had a special jug that he brought round the drams in, all carefully measured oot by the excise man. Did ye know that in the old days an excise man actually lived at the distilleries?'

'No.'

'Aye. But even with the excise man there, there was enough of the clear stuff aboot that nobody needed to make their own. My mother worked at Lagavulin, and if any of us had colds, she'd always bring home a bottle of clear spirit.'

---

[*]Brook Laddy.

'Did it work? Did it clear up your colds?' asked Perry.

'It did, aye.'

So there you are, mums; a nice traditional Islay cure for the baby's cold; a wee dram of pure alcohol.

The painters and decorators from the Uists had finished their tournament, and were heading off for the nightclub in Bowmore, so the three of us got on the table. First I played Perry, in a frame which he was lucky to win, in my view. Then I watched as Brooky crucified Perry. Brooky's game was all about potting. The Terry Griffiths in me stirred, and when it was my turn to play Chris, I offered him a cash wager.

'How much?' said Brooky.

'A tenner,' I said.

'You're on.'

It was not often during the course of our trip that I'd wished for television cameras to film our doings, but that frame of pool deserved recording for prosperity. Brooky played like a short-sighted Ronnie O'Sullivan, madly biffing away at long pots, while I played like Griffiths on downers and beer, taking as long as I could over my crafty safety shots. Chris was going bonkers with impatience, and although some of his flashy pots were going home, I had carefully constructed a finish. Brooky had one ball left to sink before the black, whilst I had three, but his ball was stuck under the cushion as I came up for what I knew was the last time, and biff biff biff biff I cleared the table.

Beautiful. It's great to be present at the birth of your kids. Who can ever forget passing their driving test? But nothing can compare to a crisp tenner changing hands after a game of pool. Even if it is a Scottish one.

## Saturday 24th April

After our first night in the family room, Perry and I awoke as fresh as Cliff Richard's sheets, but old Brooky was looking a bit rough, and even an oak-smoked Loch Fyne kipper for breakfast did nothing to lift his spirits.

'What's the matter, Chris?' I asked.

'I'm fucking knackered.'

'Did you not sleep?' asked Perry.

'Sleep? How could I sleep? Sharing a room with you two is like sharing with a horse and a bear.'

'I'll lend you some earplugs tonight, Chris,' said Perry.

'Come on,' I said. 'A nice trip round a distillery will be just the thing to lift our spirits.'

Dave had been true to his word, and had found out that the only distillery visit available on a Saturday was to Bruichladdich. A fairly short drive towards Bowmore, and then turning right for Port Charlotte brought us to the site, overlooking Loch Indall to the mountains on the east of the island. The buildings did not look so smart as those of the distilleries on the southern coast, but our guide Mary was cheerful and full of enthusiasm for her subject, and as the tour progressed, it became clear that this shabby air contributed to the charm of the whisky.

'Noo, how about a wee dram to start the tour?'

Mary poured us all a glass, and asked us to say where we were from.

There were ten on the trip. Apart from the three of us, there was a mother and daughter from 'Darwin Australia', come to visit Islay for the first time since their ancestors were cleared a hundred and fifty years before; a lone Japanese whisky enthusiast from Osaka, lugging a sturdy camera tripod, who was reminded by Mary that flash photography was not allowed in the still room or warehouses; two excellent guys from Haywards Heath, brothers, country-music enthusiasts, and Brighton and Hove Albion fans; and a fantastic girl with a pointy nose with her baldy fiancé. Mary knew this girl already. She was nanny to the managing director of Bruichladdich. This was her fiancé's first trip to Islay, and me and Perry and Chris all admitted afterwards that we had felt instinctively that she would be much better off with one of us.

All of us, it later transpired, had a thing about girls with pointy noses.

A dram taken against the cold, we set off around the site. In the early stages of the manufacturing process, it is really no different from Ash's moonshine. The first step is to make a weak beer from malted barley (the distillers call this the 'wash'), which is then run three times through a huge copper still. What is different is what happens next. Ash's hooch, like gin, is ready to drink as soon as it has been through the still, but whisky must be aged for at least eight years before it is ready to drink, preferably in a wooden barrel.

'Why does Islay whisky taste like . . . well, like God's bog cleaner?' asked Brooky. 'Is it from the water?'

'No. We burn peat during the process of drying the malt, which produces phenol.'

Phenol is another name for carbolic acid, which makes an excellent disinfectant. That's why Islay whisky tastes like the stuff they use to clean the cludgies in Paradise. And it smells of iodine, too. Laphroaig was still available in America during Prohibition, because of the smell. It couldn't possibly be something you'd drink for fun, the officials thought. It was bottled as 'Medicinal Spirit'.

'Islay whiskies are graded according to their phenol content,' said Mary. 'This is a measure of the influence of the peat at the time of malting. Bruichladdich has a phenol content of about four parts per million. But we also make a malt called Octomore, which is the peatiest whisky ever distilled. And that's got a phenol content of sixty parts per million.'

'That's butch,' I said.

The distillery was mothballed in the 1980s, and reopened in

2001. Bruichladdich had stuck to the old labour-intensive methods of distilling, while the other bigger distilleries modernised in tune with a Thatcherite ethos. Bruichladdich couldn't compete, and distilling stopped on the site. All the whisky that was ageing in oak sherry casks was left to age, but the warehouse doors were locked and sealed. The 2001 saviours were Murray McDavid, bespoke bottlers of fine single-malt whisky, who understood that times had changed, and that traditional methods of distilling had become in themselves a USP. What was necessary was good marketing; so it is that Bruichladdich is both the most traditional and the first post-modern distillery. They use the lowest-possible tech in the process of manufacture and employ seventeen people; it has remained the most labour-intensive distillery in Scotland. Mary took great pride in the antediluvian mash tun, and in the wooden tally sticks which are used to measure quantity throughout the process of distillation. Yet the whole place is alive with webcams, of which there are dozens. George Orwell would probably not have been surprised, but I was.

Customers can buy their own casks, and then look at them on webcams for eight years. This might seem excessive, not to say somewhat dull viewing, but it gives buyers who live off Islay a chance to talk to their casks. Yes, that's right. Talk to them. People do; it's a tradition to say good-morning to your whisky.

'I've got a cask in my name,' said Mary, 'and I always remember to say good-morning when I'm in the warehouse.'

We were trying to concentrate on the tour, but all three of us were thrown by the nanny with the pointy nose. Perry and I had an excuse, in that we'd been largely free of female company for three weeks, but Chris Brook is just mucky. We all had different methods to try and get a smile out of her. Perry was perhaps the most successful, as he buzzed around with the camera, and few pretty girls can resist a snapper. Brooky's approach was dictated by the state of his health; he was being pale and interesting, and clearly hoping that his shades made him seem mysterious. He got at least one smile. He has a natural advantage with the ladies, since his face looks like a road map of the area around Lou Reed's house, and lasses go for a bit of craggy. I was least successful, since I kept asking spoddy questions about whisky production, and spoddy never wins fair lady. In fact, I think I was pissing off the whole group, though not as much as the Japanese enthusiast, who kept stopping and setting up his tripod to take pictures of spirit safes and pot stills. At least old Perry has steady enough hands not to need a tripod; he took photos of the Japanese photographer and the pointy-nosed nanny.

'Do you sparge the wash?' I asked Mary, as we examined the mash tun.

'Och, I don't know,' she said. 'It's full of funny words. We'll ask the Operations Manager when we get back to the shop.'

The only thing which really made the pointy-nosed nanny laugh was Mary's impersonation of their mutual boss, the managing director, which created the impression that the Bruichladdich Distillery is a good place to work.

Mary took us into the warehouse to visit the casks. There is a sense in which the warehouse is what sets whisky distilleries apart from other producers of spirituous liquor. Without cask ageing, it's not malt whisky. The casks are all pre-loved. Some of them have previously held bourbon, and others sherry. These days, they use rum and port barrels too. Experts can tell the difference between whisky which has been aged in a sherry cask used for the first time, and a sherry cask which is being used for a second or third time. They can also tell whether or not the whisky has been kept in a warehouse which is inland, or by the sea.

Non-smokers.

In the warehouse, dimly lit, the walls were black, and ranks of casks marched away into the gloom.

'Noo,' said Mary, 'the walls are black with a particular fungus that feeds off the angels' share, which is what they call the evaporating spirit in the air. You can see why we don't allow flash photography.'

This is why so many distillery warehouses look so shabby from the outside. No matter how often you paint it white, the fungus still creeps through.

'Where's your cask?' asked Brooky.

'Och, shall we all go and say good-morning?' said Mary.

And we all did.

'I've got a cask, too,' said pointy-nosed nanny.

'Can we see yours?' said Perry.

'I don't know where it is.'

Our resentment of her fiancé reached boiling point. To think that in eight or so years, just as the magic was starting to wear off, your bride would be coming into a good amount of cask-aged whisky . . . it was beyond our wildest dreams.

We finished, as all good tours must, in the gift shop. Mary introduced me to Pete, the Operations Manager, who assured me that because they used an open mash tun, there was no need to sparge anything.

'It's a crack working here,' he said. 'I used to work for Bowmore, but this is much better. We all chip in at whatever's necessary. Steve the financial controller was working on the bottling plant last week. The people are great, and they all take pride in what they do.'

The pointy-nosed nanny and that lucky bastard her fiancé headed off. The rest of us all tried a nip of 'the clear stuff', except for Brooky, who said he didn't feel up to it after the night he'd had. Perry, rock 'n' roll to the last, washed down a couple of codeine with his share; for his back, he said.

Now it was midday, and we wanted to get over to Jura for lunch. Back down at Port Askaig we watched as the Jura ferry swept towards us on the tide. On the other side of the strait, we could see that the ferry landing was no more than a concrete ramp and a hut. The Paps were crowned in cloud. We drove on to the ferry, which struggled against the tide as it made the short crossing.

'Fucking hell,' said Brooky. 'Jura.'

Which says it all.

Though I suppose I'm going to have to try and do better.

My old pal Big Doctor Dave, a professional philosopher to rival Zig, insists that there is no such thing as wilderness in the British Isles, and that this is a problem if you are thinking about British ecology, since most ecological models presuppose a state of prelapsarian authenticity, which is nowhere to be found. Britain, says Big

346

Doctor Dave, needs a different ideal; instead of yearning for a return to wilderness, we need to understand that Britain, and most of Western Europe, is a garden. Even on the moors up to the Tan Hill Inn, you could see that this is the case. But Jura is outside the garden model; it is wilderness, and I am English, and I struggle still to understand it. Ruby, the landlady of the Ballygrant Inn had told me the night before that there are supposed to be places on Jura where nobody has ever set foot, though how you could tell this, I have no idea. But even now, looking through my notes, and looking at pictures that Perry took on Jura, I feel overwhelmed, and all I do is start staring out of my window, and dreaming about the scale of the thing, the clouds around the Paps, the desolation and emptiness, with which no other landscape I've ever encountered can compare.

Jura. Fucking hell. What to say? It's big, for one thing, thirty-five miles long by ten miles wide. About a hundred people live on Jura, almost all of them in the village of Craighouse, although there are a few farms and hunting lodges scattered up the east coast. The west coast is empty, inaccessible except by foot; it is here that you might find Ruby's untouched plot. If you imagine the southern end of Jura as a clock face, then the ferry landing is at half-seven, Jura House is at six, and Craighouse at four. We drove from the ferry towards Craighouse along the island's only road, which runs from Feolin Ferry, through Craighouse, to the hunting lodge of Ardlussa. After that, if you want to see where Orwell completed 1984, you have to walk seven miles.

Before you reach Craighouse, you pass the celebrated gardens of Jura House, at the tip of the island, but set a little way back from the sea.

'Down there,' said Brooky, 'is the boathouse where they burned the million quid.'

Ok, so, now, I'm going to say it, though I probably shouldn't. The two greatest works of British art in the twentieth century were carried out on Jura, in the wilderness. The first was the completion of 1984. The second, and here I feel an entry in Pseud's Corner coming on, was the burning of one million pounds in cash by the KLF.

In a nutshell, what they did was very simple. Firstly, they showed how wit and intelligence can still find a place in the Hit Parade with three or four singles of bare-faced cynicism and Situationist playfulness (it's odd that the Situationists found their most fertile ground in the not always terribly bright world of popular music). Then they announced their retirement from music, and set up the K Foundation, whose aim was to take all the money that the KLF had made in the music biz, and do away with it. They offered the K Foundation Prize for the Worst Work of British Art, to be awarded on the night of the Turner Prize-giving ceremony; the unfortunate Rachel Whiteread won her twenty grand from Turner, and was immediately awarded forty grand by the K Foundation. Whiteread must have had a sense of humour by-pass, because she needed a great deal of persuasion to take the money, which she gave to charity. Visual art is a closed little world; in order to have your piece accepted as 'a work of art', you need to have it authenticated as such by 'the art world'; and so it becomes a self-perpetuating freemasonry. Publishing, music, the theatre, are all much more open. The British art establishment still think that Tracey Emin's unmade bed is art, whereas the KLF is not. I would wish to argue that even before they came out to the boathouse on Jura, they had done more to make people think about art and its value than poor old Trace will ever achieve.

So then the KLF, Bill Drummond and Jimi Cauty, drew out all the money they had left, in cash, a million pounds, and came to the abandoned boathouse on Jura, and torched it. If that isn't conceptual art of the very highest order, I don't know what is. For a full account of what happened, you could get your hands on Brooky's book, *The KLF Burn a Million Quid*, or you could read Bill Drummond's excellent *45*, the best book about rock music ever written. After the burning, they gave the ashes to Gimpo, their roadie and amanuensis, himself an accomplished conceptual artist, who had filmed the burning. Apart from his film, and Chris's book, there is nothing left; a pilgrimage to the boathouse where it happened would be a fine thing. But time was against us.

'Perhaps we can go and look on the way back if we have time. I want to try and get to Barnhill.'

'We'll never get there, man,' said Brooky. 'It's miles from the end of the road.'

'Have you been there?' I asked.

'Yeah. Me and a mate camped here after the showing of the film, and we drove as far as we could, and then walked. It took us nearly three hours. And there's nothing there except the house, so you turn round and come back.'

'Let's see how far we get, anyway,' I said.

We came into the village of Craighouse, where the two most obvious buildings are the Isle of Jura Distillery, and the Isle of Jura Hotel. The distillery was closed, but we looked into the small gift-shop window at miniature pot stills full of malt whisky, and a bottle of the distillery's most famous vintage, which is, of course, the 1984.

The Isle of Jura Hotel is not pretty, but it doesn't need to be, since Jura isn't either. The building is blocky and pebble-dashed, and its job is to stand against the elements, to offer a warm haven in the wilderness. We went into the bar. The first thing that Perry and I noticed were the murals, painted somewhat after the style of Lenkiewicz, in that they showed what were obviously local characters in fantastic situations; a mermaid sat at the hotel bar, a regular trying to stroke her bum.

There was only one guy in; a drunk guy in his late thirties, whose eyes reminded me of Kenny in Glasgow. He introduced himself as Paddy. Behind the bar was a ginger-headed guy, the spitting image of Gordon Strachan after a night on the tiles. He was very very pished indeed. Triumphantly so. We were going to have to place an order with him for lunch.

All three of us went for the venison casserole; as they say, on Jura there are 5,000 deer and one whisky. Deer-stalking is Jura's only real industry, and it seemed churlish not to eat some of the fruits while we were here. Also, three of the same should just fall within the compass of what the barman could understand.

Chris was telling us about the showing of the film. We asked Paddy how the islanders felt about the burning. (People often say that it was a waste of money; that they should have given it to fecking charity. In pubs, they tell you that they could have built a hospital with the money.)

'It was their money, like,' he said. 'Besides, I did all right oot of it.'

'How come?'

'Well, it's no easy to burn money in an open fireplace. It's light. Lots of it went up the chimney without burning at all. Me and my sister collected a couple of hundred poonds each, just by walking along the beach.'

'And did you spend it? Or frame it?' asked Perry.

Paddy looked puzzled.

'I spent it,' he said.

'Philistine,' said Brooky.

The hotel manager brought out our excellent venison casserole.

The very drunk barman said, 'Mind you don't drop it, yer fat cunt.'

He was drinking Irn-Bru and vodka. He held his glass up to the vodka optic, and pressed the rim of the glass against it, but his grip was clearly not what it once was, and the force of the optic pressed the glass from his hand. The glass fell to the ground and shattered. And did he clear it up? No, he got another glass, drew himself a nip of vodka, and topped it up with Irn-Bru.

Call me old-fashioned, but if I was the hotel manager, I would be sacking this guy on the spot, and I doubt that there is an industrial tribunal in the land which would fail to back me up. Being pished behind the bar and smashing glasses would be enough in itself. But calling your boss a fat cunt, in hearing of the customers? Rather than showing this oaf the door, the hotel manager got a dustpan and brush, and cleared up the glass that the barman had broken. Blackmail was the only explanation I could come up with. The pished barman must have caught his boss in rubber nappies or something, and filmed it.

A two-seater helicopter clattered in from the direction of the Mull of Kintyre, and landed on the hotel lawn.

'Some cunt frae Glasgow bringing his shag for lunch,' said the barman.

'He's incredible,' I said to Perry.

'The most pissed person we've seen on the trip,' said Perry.

Chris told us that the south of Jura was owned by the Riley-Smith family, who made their money from brewing.

'Sam Smith's, in Tadcaster. That was theirs,' he said.

'We went to Tadcaster, and drank Sam Smith's,' I said.

'Well, Jura is what they did with the money,' said Chris.

So this wilderness was in a way the product of brewing and selling beer. A landscape pickled in alcohol. We finished our lunch, and got back in the car, heading north. The road clings to the coast, and we watched seals basking on the rocks and swimming out to the Small Isles in Craighouse bay through the clear water. Then the road climbs through a forest, before emerging on to a high watershed. In front of us lay Loch Tarbert, which almost bisects Jura. On high hills beyond the loch, the red deer were moving across the brown heather. We got out for a stretch. I didn't want to go too far away from the car, or Perry. Chris walked a few hundred metres off into the emptiness, and seemed almost to disappear, like a figure in a landscape by Caspar David Friedrich, insignificant and powerless. This place is too romantic; I like England, fields and woods and walled gardens. I could live on Islay, but not here. It is much too much.

We drove on for another ten miles, through this seemingly untouched landscape. Big Doctor Dave would argue that even this is not the state of nature, but a pastoral version of it; that the deer are farmed, the heather is burned. You can keep Rousseau, I thought. Give me Alan Titchmarsh anytime.

We came to the locked gate that represented the end of the road. Beyond this, there is just the roughest track, and you are going to need a Land Rover or a tractor. The road has been widened slightly, to provide parking for three or four cars, so that visitors can walk the seven or so miles to Barnhill. It has been left unchanged since Orwell lived there, from 1946 to 1949. It is available for hire, but even without seeing it, I knew that it must be haunted, haunted by Winston and Julia, a house of profound horror. There is no mains water, and no electricity. It was seven miles away, on foot, and we had just over an hour to catch the last ferry back to Islay.

'You were right, Brooky. We're nowhere close, are we?'

'Well, it's about seven miles down the track.'

'We haven't got time, anyway, have we?' said Perry.

'Or the inclination,' I said. 'This is close enough, maybe.' Standing at the gate of this empty road, I was dumbstruck by Orwell's pigheadedness. To come here, on your own with a child, with severe tuberculosis seemed like madness. But Orwell knew what was necessary for him to be able to finish the book, so come here and finish it he did, at the ultimate cost of his health.

To be here for an afternoon was almost too much. But I'd wanted to see how close we could get to Orwell, because you can't think about pubs any more without taking on the Moon Under Water.

On the 9th of February 1946, the *Evening Standard* published Orwell's essay, 'The Moon Under Water, and, as Stephen Earnshaw says in *The Pub in Literature*, 'the sentiments in this description have lasted until the end of the 20th Century as the dominant ideal of what the English pub is'. I buy into these sentiments, as Chesterton would have also. I'm prepared to bet that most readers would too. Orwell's ideal pub has 'draught stout, open fires, cheap meals, a garden, motherly barmaids and no radio'.

It is down a side street, so casual drunks never come across it; it has a large clientele, a great many of them regulars, and 'atmosphere' is paramount to beer. Orwell even stipulates that the beer should be served in china mugs, such as we had seen the cider drinkers using at the Monkey House. He admits that such a place doesn't exist. But Earnshaw is right to say that this vision of what a pub should be still carries a great deal of potency. CAMRA has an inventory of pubs whose interiors are largely preserved; in practice this almost always means the Victorian interior preferred by Orwell. Music in a pub, unless it is specifically a rock 'n' roll pub, or a place where people like a sing-song, or a vertical drinking establishment for young clubbers, is seldom appropriate. There is a company that builds pubs like the Moon Under Water, called the Traditional Pub Company.

One of Orwell's abiding concerns is with the food. The dining room, he insists, should be separate from the main body of the pub, and should serve plain food at lunchtime only. (Orwell could eat the most disgusting food, using it almost as an instrument of self-torture.) But when the dining room is closed, you should always be able to get liver-sausage sandwiches, cheese and pickles (what, no 'Ploughman's'?), and mussels. The pub garden is full of mums and kids; there are swings and a slide. And although the kids are officially banned from the pub, they keep spilling into the back bar, often to order drinks for their parents: 'This, I believe, is against the law, but it is a law that deserves to be broken, for it is the puritanical nonsense of excluding children and therefore to some extent, women from pubs that has turned these places into mere boozing-shops instead of the family gathering-places that they ought to be.' And you can't argue with that.

At the time he was writing, so far as Orwell was aware, there were no pubs called the Moon Under Water, but now there are several, inspired by his ideal. In calling your pub the Moon Under Water, you are making yourself hostage to fortune, and, of course, none of the ones that I have visited have come remotely close. The best known is on Leicester Square in London, and is a Wetherspoon's pub. If they had called it the Shite Hole, no one would have been quite so disappointed. As it is, however, it cannot fail to let you down. Don't go there. Don't have anything to do with anyone who wants Orwell's ideas to live. Don't watch *Big Brother* or *Room 101*. Don't let yourself be caught on CCTV. Don't do the lottery.

We turned the car around and drove back down the island. We didn't pass any cars, but as we came through Craighouse, three children waved at us. We arrived back at Feolin just in time to catch the last boat to Islay.

It was curry night back at the Ballygrant. Every month, Dave and Ruby do their curry nights, which are very popular. People come from all over Islay for a night out. There is draught stout, an open fire and a garden. There are children in the bar, playing pool, and connecting to the internet. Motherly Ruby knew our names, and what we were drinking. I'm not saying it was 'The Moon . . .' but it came as close as anywhere. The Ballygrant, like Islay, is too warm to be like the moon, too human. Ruby and Dave were by far the friendliest people we stayed with. Jura is like the moon; beautiful, terrible, cold.

After our curry, it was back to the bar. Brooky clearly had something on his mind.

'Fancy a rematch?' he said.

'Double or quits?' I said.

'You're on.'

Poor old Brooky. I was worried that he could not afford to lose another tenner. I had enjoyed the pleasure of having his tenner in my pocket all day. Why shouldn't I share my pleasure? Nothing could take that away. So I let him win, and handed back the tenner cheerfully.

One of the ten-year-olds who had been playing pool earlier put 50p on the table, and challenged Brooky. Old Brooky hardly had a chance to make one of his flashy pots before the kid was tucking the black away. I thought I'd show the lad a thing or two, so I challenged him in turn. The impatience of youth meant that he had cleared the table before he had time to learn anything about the Zen game.

'Youse two are shite,' he said.

'And you can't argue with that,' said Perry.

'Stop fucking saying that,' said Brooky.

# Sunday 25th April

'Did you sleep a bit better, Chris?' I asked over the breakfast kippers.

'No, not really. Is that right you both have girlfriends?'

'It is odd, isn't it?' said Perry.

This was to be a day of goodbyes and driving, and very few pubs.

First we said goodbye to Ruby and Dave, who had made us so welcome on Islay, and we then we drove across the island to Port Ellen, to catch the morning ferry back to Kennacraig. Next to us in the queue for the ferry were the Brighton-supporting country fans that we'd met yesterday at Bruichladdich. They'd been on Islay for four days, visiting all the distilleries. The natural intelligence and genial good nature of the Brighton and Hove Albion supporter shone from their honest faces.

Then we said goodbye to Islay. As we came out from Port Ellen, we passed the three south-coast distilleries, Laphroaig, Lagavulin and Ardbeg, their names painted large and proud on the sides of their warehouses for the benefit of seafarers like us. Behind Islay: the empty slopes of the Paps of Jura, clear from cloud.

Then we said goodbye to the spring sunlight, as we burrowed into a fog bank. We came down from the deck to sit and drink coffee in the cafeteria. Other passengers, who had not just eaten Ruby's excellent kippers were tucking into Calmac lasagne and chips, for which it is never too early.

A two-hour drive of stunning loveliness north from Kennacraig brought us to Oban, where we were going to say goodbye to Chris Brook. Oban is a good-looking town, the kind of place you see illustrated on the cover of the *People's Friend* in pastel colours. Our first stop was the train station. Although we'd always planned to drop Brooky off here, none of us had actually gone so far as to check the train times to Glasgow. Brooky had a five-hour wait, and we were all hungry, so we went to the Oban Inn for lunch, where we had creamy haddock in crisp batter with thick home-made chips. I was beginning to doubt the 'second worst cuisine in Europe' thing. I proposed a toast, which came from the pages of Dean Ramsay's *Reminiscences of Scottish Life and Character*, published in 1857: 'May the hinges of friendship never rust, or the wings of love lose a feather.'

'Hear hear,' said the guys. We clinked our glasses of Guinness together.

Reluctant to say goodbye to our friend, we went for a wander around the town, which in my case always means checking out the bookshops. Oban has a branch of Ottaker's, and I got chatting to the manager about the project.

'Every morning, at about half past eight, I walk down through Oban to open the shop,' she said, 'and every morning, at about that time, the distillery lets off a great cloud of whisky-scented steam, which I have to walk through. I always smell of whisky at work. Come to think of it, most days Oban smells of whisky, too.'

Now it was three o'clock, and Perry and I had a long way to drive. Chris still had three hours to wait for his train, but the spring sunshine was back, and he said that he was going to go for a walk. We shook hands, and were back on the road.

'Bet you anything he misses the train,' I said.

One of the problems with socialism is that equality will always be bounded by what Sartre called 'facticity'. Some people are cleverer than others. Some are better-looking. And some people will get to live in Crawley, whilst others find themselves on the West Coast of Scotland. It doesn't seem fair that so much beauty has been allocated to one place. We drove mostly in silence, unable to take it all in. Jura was fearsomely beautiful, but the drive up from Oban to Fort William was beautiful in a more human way. Some of the best-preserved prehistoric sites in mainland Scotland are on the coast road north of Lochgilphead; best of all, the Kilmartin Stones. The Gaelic for Scotland is Alba; another memory of Albion, the White Isle, Land of the God Over the Seas, home to a race of giants, who were expelled by Brutus, leaving only their stone circles. The Old People held this coast sacred, and so should we.

We stopped in Fort William, which is not a pretty town as such, no more pretty than Crawley. But Ben Nevis topped with snow towers over the town, and we walked up beside the Caledonian Canal to Neptune's Staircase, the flight of locks which lifts boats up from the sea on the start of a journey towards Loch Ness and the Great Glen. Mind you, Crawley is handier for IKEA.

One last long drive took us from Fort Bill to Mallaig, where we were to spend the night. If the drive from Kennacraig to Oban had been lovely, and from Oban to Fort William lovely again, this last leg topped them all. It is quite a fast road, and largely free from traffic, a political road, one which signifies how keen the politicians have been not to abandon the isolated West Coast towns, and to keep open the links out to the islands. As we topped the brow of a hill, a seascape full of islands.opened up in front of us; Muck and Eigg, Rhum and Skye.

We were staying in Mallaig with Mr Bruce and Mrs Jeanette Watt in their B 'n' B.

'Look, Ian,' said Perry. 'The Broad and Narrow Way.'

In the entrance hall of their house hung a nineteenth-century print, showing travellers choosing between the broad, easy route of pleasure and drink to Hell, and the hard narrow way of sobriety, which leads to Salvation. Each step on the several paths was illustrated by a biblical incident. God was represented at the end of both paths by the symbol of the all-seeing eye in the pyramid.

'Do you know this?' I said.

'Yeah,' said Perry. 'I used to see it at farm sales in West Wales all the time. It's a really well known illustrated Temperance tract.'

Presbyterianism has been synonymous with Lowland Scottish life since the sixteenth century, but it was less popular in the Highlands, where Catholicism managed to cling to the rocks. A series of Evangelical revivals, starting in the 1820s, killed off the last of the old religion, which gave way to the somewhat dour spirituality that can now be found throughout the Highlands and Islands. The Temperance movement arrived in an area that had been renowned for singing and dancing and drinking, and put a stop to them all.

Dean Ramsay, a liberal Edinburgh churchman, did not approve: 'I have known persons who held that a man who could not drink must have a degree of feebleness and imbecility of character . . . Some of the old school would have looked with ineffable contempt on the degeneracy of the present generation in this respect, and that the temperance movement would be little short of insanity in their eyes.'

I told Mrs Watt why we were in Mallaig, and I'm not sure she approved. We were here to catch her husband's boat in the morning, so that we could visit Britain's Most Isolated Pub.

Perhaps because we were a little early in the season, none of the three or four small restaurants in Mallaig seemed to be open, so we walked up to the West Highland Hotel at the top of the town, and watched the sun sink behind Rhum. Another excellent meal served almost to depress us; when were we going to get proper bad Scottish food? We both agreed that this was such a romantic spot it was wasted on the two of us; that we needed to come back with our wives and girlfriends to get the full effect.

I have one abiding legacy from the West Highland Hotel; I started drinking 'half and half' there, one of the national drinks of Scotland, and have not looked back to this day. A half and half is a half of beer and a dram of whisky (not in the same glass, incidentally), and it goes down very nicely.

The manager at the hotel told us that Mallaig was a cosmopolitan place.

'There are people here from Eyemouth, from the East Coast, even from Ireland,' he said. I'm not in a position to argue with this, but it is a very very beautiful place, a good place to spend an evening with a friend, or a fortnight with a lover. We needed an early night, after driving the best part of 150 miles to get here.

At least, without old Brooky to put us off our strokes, we could snore with impunity.

# Monday 26th April

It was never the idea, when I set out on this trip, to tick too many boxes, like oldest pub or smallest pub or even really the highest, even though we had ended up there. Rather I wanted to follow the drunken road and see what kinds of pubs we ended up in. I wasn't sure that visiting the most remote pub on the British mainland would add much to the mix, especially since it isn't on a road, and would therefore seem to exclude itself from my notion of Chesterton Country, a place where weary travellers and beery cheery locals could sit by the fire and swap yarns about the Common Market, and what a bad thing it is, except for the farm subsidies, obviously.

Britain's Most Remote Mainland Pub is called The Old Forge, and it is in the village of Inverie, on the Knoydart Peninsula, between Mallaig and Kyle of Lochalsh. Its remoteness is due to the fact that there are no roads which connect to Knoydart, so there are only two ways to get there; you can walk in across the mountains from the nearest road, which is twenty miles away, or you can take Bruce Watt's boat the *Western Isles* out from Mallaig. It had taken the best part of a day to get to Mallaig, and tomorrow we would have to cross Scotland to get to the whisky-producing area of Speyside. And I doubted that it would be a great pub. I pictured it as being a bit like a camping barn, dismal, dull, relying on a handful of damp smelly walkers to eke out a precarious living.

But it had been Perry's idea, and I didn't want to diss his ideas, after dragging him round and forcing him to take pictures of barmaids for a month. And then there is Knoydart itself, which recommended me further. After years of ownership by absentee landlords, some benevolent, others not so, in 1999 the Knoydart Trust raised enough money to buy the estate, 18,000 acres of mountain and coastline. Knoydart is owned and controlled by the eighty or so people who live there. It is remote both from the world, and, as we were to discover, from the State, to some extent.

The *Western Isles* leaves Mallaig for Inverie at 10.15 sharp, five days a week in summer, and three in winter. Mrs Watt cooked us a proper Scottish breakfast, with pudden. Pudden is a bit like Christmas pudding, but you fry slices and serve it with eggs, bacon, sausage, black pudding and flat bread. Breakfast done, we said goodbye to Mrs Watt, and drove the car down to the ferry terminal. The plan was to go across to Knoydart with Mr Watt, and then to come back on the return boat, which would give us ten minutes to pick up the car and then drive on to the last ferry of the day to Armadale, on Skye.

'It'll be tight,' said Mr Watt, 'but we might just make it. The return trip is longer, because we have to go up to Tarbert.'

Almost everywhere on the West Coast of Scotland is called Tarbert. It can be confusing.

The *Western Isles* can take up to eighty passengers; today there were perhaps thirty. About a third of the passengers, clearly locals who have become indifferent to the scenery, were sitting in the below-deck cabin, out of the fresh wind. The rest of us were sitting on deck, catching a little sun. A couple of guys going over to do some painting sat in their overalls, reading the *Star* and the *Sport*. The rest of the passengers were walkers with waterproof trousers tucked into thick woollen socks. Some had binoculars round their neck, hoping to catch a glimpse of birds, nature, etc. There was also a quantity of freight; boxes and parcels and crates, some bottles of wine.

The sea was the colour of a Gordon's Gin bottle, as we watched Mallaig drop behind us. From Mallaig to Inverie across Loch Nevis is about ten miles, and takes just over an hour. The walkers were scanning the sea for life, while the painters swapped newspapers.

'Look!' said a walker. 'A dolphin!' And she was right; off to port, maybe a hundred metres off, the unmistakable fin and humpback, rocking through the calm water.

Inverie looks how I imagine Grytviken must look on South Georgia. It is a row of houses at the base of high mountains, a precarious stain of human settlement caught between the sea and the hills. As the pier came closer, we could get a look at the tiny village, and at the pub that we had come so far to drink in; painted white, single-storey, with a new extension built on to its side. The walkers were collecting their stuff together, looking forward to a pint before setting off, I guessed. The locals were emerging from the cabin, and the painters folded away their newspapers. The Old Forge didn't look dank; maybe if the walkers went for a drink *before* setting off, the place might not smell too bad. The *Western Isles* docked at Inverie, and the walkers surprised me by setting off up the road away from the pub, like those hardy souls who go round a National Trust property before visiting the tearoom. I like to go to the tearoom both before and after the trip. Perry and I were off the boat and straight into the bar. I was also surprised to see three or four cars and a van parked by the pier head; I thought the point of Knoydart was that there no roads.

All my illusions were shattered as soon as we stepped through the door of the Old Forge. The low-lying frontage disguised the fact that it is quite a big place, with an attractive modern bar, and a dining and dancing area in the newly built extension done out in stripped pine and nauticalia, looking out through wide windows at the splendours of Loch Nevis. There was a modern menu chalked up behind the bar, and a cheerful young barman, who told us he was here for the season. Most miraculous of all, there was Adnams on draught, which we'd last seen to the south of Walsall. This is a sign that the pub is busy; if you can't get through a firkin a week, it's not worth keeping. There were four or five people in there already, drinking latte from the Gaggia machine and unfurling newspapers which had just come in on the boat. There was nothing there which you wouldn't see in a bar in Crouch End, except for the views across Loch Nevis. In fact, you could pick the place up, drop it anywhere in a smart part of London, and you'd go there, which is not something you could say of many Scottish pubs.

We ordered coffee, and got talking to one of the locals, a slight foxy man with a permanent smile, aged in his comfortable fifties, a decade when men can go mad, jack it all in, and come to live on desert islands, or, at least, desert peninsulas. I told him that the Old Forge was not what I had expected. Was, in fact, about ten times better than I had thought.

'We're very lucky,' he said. 'Heart of the community, this is.'

His name was John Sellars, and he only moved to Knoydart a few months ago, from Buckinghamshire. He ran a computer business, and said that he could do it just as well here as anywhere. He'd just put his wife on the boat, because she had a doctor's appointment in Mallaig.

'We just wanted to live in a place where you had some say in what goes on in the community.'

'And is it friendly? Welcoming of incomers?'

'Really, it couldn't be more so. Like lots of these isolated communities, they really want people to come and live here, and to get involved. I've got half an hour or so before I need to get home. I'll run you up the road, and show you round a bit.'

We drank up our lattes, and followed John outside. He beckoned us into his Land Rover.

'I didn't think there were roads on Knoydart?'

'Oh yes, ten miles or so. The point is that they don't connect to anywhere.'

He drove us up the road away from the pub, in the wake of the walkers.

'How do you get the cars over?'

'There's a boat like a landing craft based in Mallaig, called the *Spanish John*, that brings cars and vans out here, and to the Small Isles. They had to bring three vanloads of furniture round for us when we moved in, which was almost too exciting. Quite a rough day. But we made it.'

I remembered seeing the *Spanish John* in the harbour that morning, loading a Fiesta.

'Some people keep a car at Mallaig, and a runabout for over here. Look at the cars. They've got no tax, no MOT, and most of them haven't got insurance.'

'Don't the DVLC mind?'

'Well, what are they going to do? I think it counts as private land.'

We drove a little way along the peninsula, past the small church and the Big House, up to the end of the road, where it turned into a track. The walkers were striding away up the mountain.

'Munroists, lots of them,' said John. 'There are three or four Munros on Knoydart.'* 'Not all of them, though. Some of them will walk round to Tarbert and pick up the afternoon boat there. Some of them just go for a walk round, come back to the pub for lunch, and catch the afternoon boat back from Inverie. I'll show you the other way.' He turned the Land Rover round, and we went back to the village and beyond the pub, a mile or so up the single-track road.

'Up in the hills, we've got our own hydro-electric plant, which provides all our power,' said John.

'Do you all own that, too?'

'Yes. Knoydart is part of the community-power movement, which aims to help small communities meet their own power needs.'

We drove away from Inverie, and up into the hills besides the loch.

'I carry on for a couple of miles,' said John, 'but if I drop you off here, you can walk back to the pub. How's that?' We thanked John as he dropped us off.

We started walking back into Inverie. The road was lined with gorse bushes, which smelled of Malibu.

'Would you fancy living here?' asked Perry.

Rain was starting to work in from the west; we turned up our collars. We walked back towards the village, and passed the community school, where four or five kids were rorting about on the lawn, oblivious to the weather. We looked across Loch Nevis to the high ground which hid Mallaig from view, and out to the Small Isles, which the rain had blurred into the background of the sea.

'I'd love to give something like this a try. I really would.'

This is a place where day-to-day living would be an adventure, co-operation with neighbours the only possible way to survive. But

---

*A Munro is a Scottish mountain over 3,000 feet. A Munroist is someone who is trying to climb them all.

it would be made easier by the fact that it has a bloody good pub.

On our return visit to the Old Forge, we plumped for the Adnams, after more than a week without proper beer. From the menu, neither of us could resist the venison burgers. There were half a dozen or so couples in taking lunch; a couple of local ladies in thick sweaters, some of the less hardy of the walkers, and a pair of cheerful-looking guys in suits, with their trousers tucked into their wellies. They were vets, on Knoydart for a couple of nights to inspect the local cattle. It might be free of MOTs and the DVLA, but DEFRA gets everywhere.

'This is very good,' I said, munching my way through my venison burger.

'Yes,' said Perry, 'but it was a bit dear.'

We told the barman that we had come to Knoydart for no other reason than to have a drink in this pub, and he went to fetch the landlord.

His name was Ian Robertson. He and his wife Jackie have been running the place for about three years, and they have transformed it into one of the best pubs we had seen in Scotland. Atmosphere, beer, food, everything was just right.

'Well, we make use of the remote thing. It makes us a place that people want to come to. We've got a good website. We get lots of walkers in the season, we've got berthing for ten boats, so we get quite a few sailors in. We run a folk festival; that brings in loads of people, too. It was last week; you should have been here then. Great crack. Look, here's a CD that was recorded at last year's festival . . . please, take one. And then you've got all the locals. A pub has to be somewhere that the locals want to come. We're open every day, all day, and we can always cook up some food. We do a dawn breakfast for the Munroists. And now, look . . .'

He looked around at the bar, at the dining area that converts to a venue, or a meeting hall, at the draught Adnams and the Gaggia machine, at the chalked-up menu of contemporary Scottish cuisine, and through the windows to Loch Nevis.

You can't argue with that.

We walked back along the row of single-storey cottages that

comprise Inverie, and went to the tiny shop and post office. The young guy behind the counter told us that he had just been appointed Knoydart's postman, and that he worked ten hours a week. A red post-office van sat outside the post office, the only really legal vehicle we had seen. I suppose, what with it being the Royal Mail and all, you can't really get away with not taxing it, even if you are confined to the ten miles of Knoydart roads.

When the boat came in, all the members of the community who happened to be about unloaded the slightly larger amount of boxes than had been brought over on the morning boat. John Sellars was there, helping to unload crates of wine for the pub, and to meet his wife, back from her appointment at the doctor's. The postman came down and handed the mate of the *Western Isles* what looked like an empty mail sack. Then we were back on the boat, heading further down Loch Nevis to the settlement of Tarbert.

'That was a good idea,' I said to Perry.

We were the only two left on deck. The rain had taken hold, and was blowing in from the sea behind us. We were cold, and wet, but how often do you get to cruise up the Scottish equivalent of a fjord? I didn't care how bad it got, I wanted to see everything. In front of us, far up the loch, I could see what looked like a miniature castle, with a central round tower, and a long hall behind. It sat low down by the water.

I asked the mate what it was.

'That's Sir Cameron Mackintosh's place. He's had it built for him.'

'The impresario?'

'Aye.'

'Is there a road?'

'No. That's Tarbert.'

'How often do you come up here?'

'Three times a week.'

Tarbert consists of Sir Cameron's mini-castle, an old chapel, and a house of familiar shape.

'That used to be a pub, many years ago,' said Mr Watt.

'Really?'

'Aye. The herring boats all used this place, when there was herring fishing still going on. Before they built the railway into Mallaig, Tarbert was much more important.'

'How does Cameron Mackintosh get out here?'

'Well, he charters a boat, doesn't he? He has lots of MPs out here to stay. Peter Mandelson, Chris Smith, they've all been.'

As we came into Tarbert Bay, a white-haired lady came out of the old pub with a mail bag in her hand, and stood on the slipway that led down from the front of her house into the clear water. The mate of the *Western Isles* pulled the tender alongside, and stepped down into it with the mail bag he had been given by the youthful post-man at Inverie. Up until this moment, Knoydart had seemed incred-ibly remote, but seeing this old lady who lived on the side of a sea loch, with no neighbours but occasional visits from Cameron Mackintosh and MPs with an interest in musical theatre, I realised that I hadn't really known what isolated meant. The tender of the *Western Isles* buzzed across to the old lady, tiny in the shadow of moun-tains which climbed away to get lost in the rain. The mate handed over his mail bag, and she dropped hers into his hand. Are they avid letter writers in Tarbert? Or would she, after her thrice-weekly deliv-ery, be opening an envelope from the Reader's Digest telling her that she had already won £10,000? Does this little old lady live here on her own? I like the quiet life myself, but this was ridiculous.

So was standing in the pouring rain. The clouds had closed off much of the view. I asked Bruce Watt if we were going to make the Armadale ferry.

'Mibbee. Mibbee no,' he said. Perry and I went down into the cabin to join the walkers. The windows were streaked with condensation. We beat up the loch, and rounded the corner into Mallaig bay.

'Will ye let these London lads off first?' Bruce Watt asked the other passengers as we came into berth. 'They're in an awfa' hurry.'

We landed at Mallaig at ten to five, and we actually jogged. I jogged to the car, while Perry jogged to the ramp of the Skye ferry to tell them we were coming. Neither of us had jogged in a long while, but we made it on to the ferry, last car on. A month in the pub hadn't made us any fitter; luckily for us, the crossing over to Skye from Mallaig is only about twenty-five minutes so there isn't time to eat Caledonian MacBrayne lasagne and chips. And then we were on Skye.

I'd done no more than set foot on the island, when I walked across the Skye Bridge from Kyle of Lochalsh, a few years before, but Perry knew it fairly well, having spent a week hill-walking here in the company of Wee Boab, our ex-guitarist.

'I don't know, mate,' I said as we drove across the island. 'I'm beginning to lose it.'

'Beginning?'

'Yeah. It's just . . . all this is so beautiful, and so empty, and so alien. Too much. Where did you go with Wee Boab?'

'We walked up one of the Cuillins. We were above the clouds. It was . . . like the black steeples of churches sticking up through the snow. Like in the old Baron Munchausen story? Where he's travelling through thick snow, and ties his horse to a spike coming out of the ground, and in the morning the snow is melted and the horse is tied to a church spire?'

'It's so different from England, isn't it?' I said. 'England is framed by woods and fields and villages and towns, home, familiarity. The frame helps you understand the picture. This is like a trip, unframed; sea and sky and rock coming at you all the time, in your face. Too much. I think you must start shutting down before you begin to open up. What does a few day trips say about the West Coast? I'd love to live up here, and write romantic novels and listen to the Beach Boys.'

'Good luck.'

We came into Portree, another of the Scottish fishing harbours I'd seen illustrated on the cover of one of my mum's copies of the *People's Friend*. We parked in the main square, and went into the Isles pub to ask if they had any rooms, which they did.

It was all right, the Isles, even though it is a Highland theme bar. I don't think I'd ever seen one before. There was a fake turf roof over the bar, held in place by fibreglass stones. There was scumbling on the window frames, a limewash on the walls, there were hand ploughs suspended from the ceiling, and there was a picture of that particularly horrible man 'Bonnie Prince Charlie' hanging over a gas fire designed to look as though it were really burning peats. But the half and halves went down a treat, and I had an excellent steak.

It was clear that there were no locals in the Isles; that although the place was three-quarters full, we were all tourists. I felt something like pity for the French family who sat talking in horrified tones as they tried to eat their food. They had made the mistake of ordering wine with their dinner, and they looked really sad and unhappy as they tried to drink it. The father's face as he nosed the bouquet was a picture. He trawled the depths of human misery. This is probably why Scottish explorers like Mungo Park and David Livingstone opened up new areas of the globe, while the French stayed at home reasoning. The Scots could eat anything the world threw at them, but Johnny Frenchman only knows how to dine well. It must make travel an unpleasant business.

I hope the Highland theme-bar craze doesn't spread from Skye to the rest of the UK, but if it does, can I make one request? In the Isles in Portree, they were playing Dido; fairly quietly, but loud enough that you could still hear the poor love bleating away. I honestly think I'd prefer bagpipe music. No Dido, ever.

# Tuesday 27th April

We were taking it in turns to drive through the Highlands, so that at least one of us would be able to gawp out the window. I drove across Skye at a comfortably sedate pace, one which I felt matched the mood of the West Highlands; Perry got impatient after we'd come across the Skye Bridge, and had taken over, and now we were high in the Highlands, snowfields on the mountains, and we were listening . . . to . . . Radio . . . Two . . . and . . . his . . . fecking . . . foot . . . was . . . pumping . . . up . . . and . . . down . . . on . . . the . . . fecking . . . pedal . . . and . . . we . . . stuttered along for mile . . . after . . . fecking . . . mile.

A pub appeared, as if from nowhere, which was about right, as that's where we were.

'Lets stop for coffee,' I begged.

This was the Cluanie Inn, just below the snowline on the Five Sisters, at the west end of Loch Cluanie, very high, and very cold, even in late April, even in weak sunlight. The Cluanie Inn·is one of those peculiarly Scottish places, not quite a hotel, not quite a pub, not really an inn, with a grandparentish air, as though remembering better, or at least different, times.

I took over the driving; slower, but a nice smooth ride. As I drove, we dropped. As I'd said to Perry yesterday, being in the midst of the mountains, especially when they were reflected in a sea loch, felt like a trip, and leaving them behind was exactly like coming down, even though the comedown was driving along the shores of Loch Ness past Urquhart Castle, and thus not half bad. And yes, of course you watch the water on Loch Ness, just in case.

We arrived in Inverness, 'the Capital of the Highlands'. Everywhere is the capital of something these days. We were here to buy underpants. All ours were horrible; the last wash we had managed was in Lancaster, and we don't have the knack of washing our knickers in hotel sinks, like women do. We tried TK Maxx, but it won't do, not really, not at our time of life. We found an M&S, and assured our comfort for the last few days of the trip. As it was twelve-thirty, our bodies had began to crave their first drink of the day. There is no doubt that we had built up resistance over the course of a month; we liked to take drink earlier every day, and we liked a few more of an evening now than we had at the beginning of the trip.

We were both suffering physically, there is no doubt about that. Perry's back wasn't getting any better, and his sinuses had begun to play up. I'd had a migraine in Walsall, and I felt like I was getting one now, when my normal pattern would be about two a year. Only my foot remained steadfastly well, after its dunking in holy water. The rest of me was rubbish. Only a month ago, it had been the other way round.

'I could just about kill a drink, my friend,' I said.

'Me too . . .'

We went to Hootenanny's because it is owned and run by Kit Fraser, raconteur, friend and patron of poetry, scion of aristocratic families, ex-coal miner and all-round good egg. Kit is currently running the Publican's Party, and claims that he can deliver the Scottish Parliament to the SNP if they are prepared to have the political courage necessary to fight the smoking ban, which Kit feels will be disastrous for Scottish pub life.

'Everbody will drink at home. It's the end for pubs. But we can stop them, if we can sign up half the pubs in Scotland.'

But Kit wasn't there, so we had a half and half and some Thai crackers; authentic Scottish cuisine if ever there was. We examined our new pants, like girls do, and looked forward to our last night on the mainland.

For tonight we would drink malt whisky, because we were going to the 'Malt Whisky Capital of the World'. Which sounds grand, until you discover that the Malt Whisky Capital of the World is really a small run-down Morayshire town called, unfortunately, Dufftown.

Bad enough that your town is designated Duff, but the fact that the town is nothing without the alcohol industry could lead the unsuspecting visitor to assume that one of the world's most famous beers is made there. This, of course, is Duff Beer, drug of choice for Homer Simpson and his best friend Barney Gumble. It comes in many varieties: Duff Lite, Duff Dry, Duff Dark, Lady Duff, Tartar Control Duff and Henry K. Duff's Private Reserve. In the neighbouring county of Shelbyville, they drink Fudd, which is quite different from Duff, even though it comes from the same vat. Duff Beer is promoted by Duff Man, and the Duff Brewery operates a popular theme park just outside Springfield, called Duff Gardens, where you can see the Duff mascots, the Seven Duffs: Sleazy, Queazy, Edgy, Surly, Tipsy, Remorseful, and Dizzy. Duff is an American slang term, essentially meaning 'fat arse'.

Sadly, you can't buy Duff Beer in Dufftown, unless you are very rich, and prepared to trade on eBay. In 1996 a resourceful South Australian brewer, seeing an obvious promotional opportunity, started brewing a beer which he marketed as Duff. Twentieth Century Fox took out an injunction, and he was prevented from making it. A few people hung on to some crates of Duff; they currently sell on eBay for about $10,000 each, the ultimate Simpsons collectible.

If Duff beer is not to be had in Dufftown, malt whisky most certainly is. This is the home of Glenfiddich and Mortlach, a personal favourite. There is a well known Whisky Shop, and a Whisky Museum, and no distillery tour of Scotland is complete without a visit to the town. We drove out from Inverness towards Speyside, looking forward to a whisky feast.

The signs were good, the closer we got to Dufftown. The Spey is a beautiful river, fed by the high mountains, flanked by woods, crossed by superb bridges and lined along its length by distilleries. As you enter Morayshire, the sign says 'Moray, Malt Whisky Country'. And the more you follow the river, the more distilleries you see, their pagodas letting off steam which rises from behind the trees. The road signs point to Glenlivet, Tomintoul, Knockandhu; and there are brown heritage signs, too, showing the way to Glenfarclas, Strathisla, Glen Grant, Cragganmore, each of the signs bearing the proud mark of the pagoda. Every ten minutes or so, we were passed by whisky tankers, heading off for the bottling plant. Whisky country is about right.

We passed the Tormore Distillery, a strange kitsch Italianate building behind an ornamental pool, and, in the manicured gardens, a collection of topiary pot stills which somebody had taken a great deal of time to clip. Tormore advertised itself as 'The Home of Long John'. Perry wanted to stop and take some photos. I wanted to get to the Whisky Shop and the Whisky Museum, but the Tormore Distillery is so odd-looking, it seemed rude not to stop. As well as the distillery itself, there was a curve of ten houses ranged around a green, clearly at one time homes for distillery workers, but now empty, all bar one. A carillon hidden in the distillery's bell tower chimed the hour, and I was just thinking that this must be a good place to work when a jobsworth came and hassled us off the site, saying that it was closed for maintenance, and was unsafe for visitors.

So we were back in the car, and we passed through Charlestown of Aberlour, a smart comfortable place, with a good-looking wide High Street. The Aberlour distillery is here, as is the Walkers Pure Butter Shortbread factory. This was as Scottish a town as could be; this is where whisky comes from, and also tins of shortbread with pictures of Highland cattle on the lid.

'Do you want to stop?' said Perry.

'No. I want to go to the Whisky Shop, and the Whisky Museum.'

The closer we got to Dufftown, the more the whisky sights piled up. There was the Speyside Cooperage, with vast piles of whisky barrels in the yards, Munros of them. They had a visitor centre, which was just closing, but we determined to come back the next day. Closer and closer to Dufftown, and there is Dewar's, its bonded warehouses blackened with the fungus we'd seen at Bruichladdich. And on the outskirts of the town, Glenfiddich, probably the most famous of the malt whiskies, with workmen laying asphalt on a large new visitors' car-park. The sign told us we had arrived: Dufftown. Malt Whisky Capital of the World.

Well, of course, both the Whisky Shop and the Whisky Museum

were closed. The shop had screens up on the window, and was deserted, but there was life in the museum. We spoke to a nice man, who refused to let us in, even though we'd driven nearly 200 miles to get there.

So, here we were in the Malt Whisky Capital of the World, and the attractions were thin on the ground. But we had arranged to stay, and had taken all day to drive the wild width of Scotland to get here. Besides, tomorrow we could go visit the Speyside Cooperage and then head up through Glenlivet on old smugglers' roads. It was fine.

'You are a twat,' said Perry.

'What makes you say that, friend?'

'Because everywhere we've been has been closed.'

'It's a symbol.'

'Of what?'

'Blairbrown's Britain?'

'Why?'

'Well . . . anyway, it doesn't matter. I'm sure we'll find lots of things to see tomorrow.'

'Pouffffffffffffff!'

There was one restaurant open. It was called the World Famous Glenfiddich Restaurant and Lounge Bar and it was a temple to kitsch, painted in green and gold. Inside there were pictures of Elvis done in silk tapestry, and 45s nailed to the wall. There were electric water statues, and glitter balls, and tins of shortbread. We thought it was too good to miss; we checked the opening times, as I think Perry would have killed me if we'd found one more closed thing.

We had booked into the Fife Arms Hotel, run by a couple of such staggering antiquity that I felt sure they were both about to drop down dead, especially in view of the fact that strong drink had clearly been taken.

'This,' the landlord announced in the remains of a Yorkshire accent, 'is the home of the quarter gill. Thirty-five mills. It's a perfectly legal measure, but most landlords are too mean to use it. Here, when you ask for a drink, you get one.'

The landlady, though it would be ungentlemanly of me to call her mutton dressed as lamb, did seem to be wearing lots of lacy frills and ruffs, which I can't say suited her entirely. She took us out back to where we would be staying, in a small mews of motel rooms.

'Ooh,' she said, 'I'm in a room with two young men. I must mind my reputation, or people will talk.'

Perry's back was very bad after a day sitting in the car, and I still felt the buzz of a migraine starting behind my eyes. It was five o'clock in the afternoon, and we both fell asleep on the (twin) beds.

There was a knock at the door which woke us up. Perry answered it in his new boxers.

'Och, looks like it's my lucky day,' said the landlady. 'And me a respectable married woman.'

'Can we help you?' said Perry.

'Och well, I was just wondering if you young men would be wanting dinner?'

'No, thank you.'

'Well, if there's nothing else.'

We each had a shower and felt a bit livelier, so we thought that we could probably face the bar. The landlord was a little redder in the face than earlier in the afternoon. I ordered a half and half.

'This,' said the landlord again, 'is the home of the quarter gill. Thirty-five mills. It's a perfectly legal measure, but most landlords are too mean to use it. Here, when you ask for a drink, you get one.'

'Yes indeed,' I said.

We finished our drinks, and went off to the World Famous Glenfiddich Restaurant and Lounge Bar. It was only us in. We sat in the middle of a store of Scots gimcrackery. The World Famous Glenfiddich Restaurant and Lounge Bar, according to the sign in the window, sold whisky, antiques, and tablet, as well as food. Tablet is one of Scotland's lesser-known delicacies, seldom exported beyond its borders. It's a bit like fudge, but only a bit. Given that I was trying to shake off a migraine, this was probably the last place we should have come, with the sparkle of glitter balls, and the tinkling drone of electric water fountains. And then, at last, the authentic Scottish food, for which we had waited, but had not previously materialised: tough steak, anaemic oven chips, and insanely over-cooked vegetables.

Although the World Famous Glenfiddich Restaurant and Lounge Bar was a train crash both in terms of its décor, and the food, the owner was a really nice guy, and was keen for us to try some of his more obscure whiskies, including a 'manager's dram' from Glenrothes and a sherry-cask-bottled Aberlour, which we did.

Getting pished on malt whisky seemed like the perfect solution to our health problems.

We popped our heads round the door of the bar of the Fife Arms, to say goodnight.

'Och, it's my young men,' said the landlady.

'This is the home of the quarter gill,' the landlord assured us. 'Thirty-five mills. It's a perfectly legal measure, but most landlords are too mean to use it. Here, when you ask for a drink, you get one.'

'I feel like shit,' said Perry, as he got into his (twin) bed.

'At least we got some new underpants,' I said.

# Wednesday 28th April

Jerome K. Jerome was quite right. There are few pleasures in life that can compare with watching people work. I could quite happily sit in a call centre all afternoon, just watching people quoting others happy, saving them up to a hundred pounds by welcoming them back to BT and helping them switch the balance on their credit cards. Oddly, there are few opportunities for watching office workers, and most trips to visit workplaces happen because manufacturing industry is becoming so rare. Tourists are thrilled that a tiny handful of people still know how to make things.

Perry and I like to go on canal trips. Once, we took our wives for a wet week's spree on the canals around Stoke-on-Trent, so that we could visit factories where they make lavatory bowls, and watermills where they grind flints for the manufacture of glazes. Lily still cries when I remind her of the trip. I remember, on a long-ago voyage with friends, a place south of Birmingham where the canal actually went through a factory; actually went into the building. On either side of us, men were hard at work on grinding wheels while we drifted through their factory at three miles an hour with a bottle of wine open on the cabin roof, and a spliff in the steerer's hand. Happy days.

It is one of the great regrets of my life that I have never really been able to hold down a job, unless you count afternoons writing up the results of horse-races, which my wife never did. Work always looks such fun to the outsider, but I suffer from a genetic disinclination, and have been forced to scrape a living by singing in pubs and the like. I imagine that the money is the best bit, but I always found it hard to make the link between what I had to do, and the cash people gave me for doing it. Piecework I especially didn't get. I once valeted cars in a car wash for a summer. You got paid per car cleaned. Everyone else could do one an hour, but I did two a day, and not very well, at that. So everyone else got a hundred quid a week, and I got twenty-five. But who had enjoyed themselves the more, I ask you.

Perry is more of a worker than I, but only a bit. We were both delighted to be standing in the visitors' gallery at the Speyside Cooperage, watching skilled men working with intensity and love, pulling old barrels apart, checking them for leaks, replacing the hoops, tightening them up, shucking reeds into the barrelheads, and rolling newly refurbished barrels out to the storage area.

'They're all on piecework,' said our tour guide.

The guys were working at a feverish pace; none of them would be going home with twenty-five quid at the end of the week

'They serve a five-year apprenticeship before they become journeymen. The journeymen all own their own tools.'

The concentration, the single-mindedness of these guys was astounding, and all under the eyes of visitors. There are machines for helping to shape replacement staves, but 90 per cent of what these men do is exactly what coopers would have done 500 years ago. Take the heads. The heads of wooden barrels are still sealed with rushes, just as Tracy had told us at Marston's. The reed beds are on the River Great Ouse; out there on the river, there is still someone whose job it is to cut and collect bulrushes for coopers to seal barrels with, and so the reed beds are another feature of the intoxicated landscape.

Before our guide let us in to see the coopers at work, she'd made us sit through a PowerPoint presentation, the start of which I managed to stay awake for. It explained that there are three kinds of barrel, size apart: these are dry, for grain; white, for domestic use; and wet, which is the kind most coopers still make and repair. I learned that drunkards were made to wear a cask in punishment for their sins, and that this was known as a 'drunkard's cloak'. I was reminded that Nelson's body was brought back from Trafalgar in a barrel, pickled in brandy. After that the PowerPoint presentation moved on to talk about how new barrels are made, and I nodded off. There was steam and fire in my dream, I remember. New barrels, however, are not really what's wanted, not in Britain. Mostly, at the Speyside Cooperage, at least, they are repairing old ones, since the industry derives flavour and colour from old barrels.

Wooden barrels, I had come to realise, are hugely important to the production of fine alcoholic drinks. Wood has memory; it sucks up flavour in one place, and releases it in another. I remembered the cider-tasting in Churchingford, where the sweetness or otherwise of the cider was dictated by what kind of barrel it was kept in. After only four or five months in either a bourbon or a sherry cask, the strength, colour and flavour of the cider was dramatically affected. Then at Marston's, we'd seen the great Union sets, the labyrinth of wooden barrels which that fine old firm of brewers still insists makes their beer taste unique. And malt whisky is simply not malt whisky if it isn't kept in a wooden cask for at least eight years.

The Speyside Cooperage has made something of its visitor centre, realising that there are lots of tourists who are coming to Speyside on whisky tours. Most importantly, there was a tearoom, where the visitors could sit and talk about the quality of the work they'd just seen. On the wall of the tearoom was a map, a map showing how the brewing industry was spread about Britain; where the barley-growing areas could be found, where the breweries and distilleries clustered, where there were hop-yards and cider orchards. It even showed famous brew pubs: the Blue Anchor in Helston, the Three Tuns in Bishop's Castle. It was a map of the places where we had been, and the biggest cluster of distilleries on the map showed us where we were. Which was just outside Dufftown.

In the grounds of the cooperage are barrels which are so big that there are tables and benches inside. These are made in Germany, and they are called picnic casks because you can sit in them, and, er, have a picnic. And there is a miniature train of barrels for the kids to sit in. In fact, it's Dufftown's answer to Duff Gardens.

From Speyside Cooperage, we drove back down to Charlestown of Aberlour, and back past the Tormore Distillery, until we came to the sign for Glenlivet, and followed the road up into the glen, famous in Scottish history. This was the centre of the illicit whisky trade between 1790 and 1830, producing whisky which was regarded as the best in the world. The Glenlivet Distillery was actually open, and we hadn't missed the tour. The buildings are pebble-dashed and nothing to see from the outside, except for the stains, the blackened stain of the fungus that feeds on the angels' share, which is everywhere in this part of the world. You have one fungus that helps produce alcohol, and another one that feeds on it.

'Do you want to go on the tour?' Perry asked.

'No, fuck it. One more tour and I'll set light to my eyebrows.'

The visitor centre at Glenlivet is a cracker, and if you don't fancy the tour, there is a very good museum. It shows, in photographs and dioramas, the history of the illicit whisky trade, and the slow process of legitimisation brought about by the 1823 Excise Act.

There is no recorded start date for the distillation of whisky. If distilling in Europe and subsequently England had been a consequence of alchemical technique, this was not the case in Scotland. They just seem to have been at it for ever. One of the opponents of the gin trade in eighteenth-century England pointed out how much healthier were the water drinkers of the Scottish Highlands than the gin drinkers of London. A weary Scottish excise collector wrote in reply that 'The ruddy complexions, nimbleness and strength of these people is not owing to water-drinking, but to the aqua vitae, a malt spirit which is commonly used in that country, what serves for both victual and drink'.

'Uisge beathe' is what the Highlanders called it in their own language, and it was made all over Scotland in small domestic stills. The Highlanders were not regarded as drunkards, because whisky was so ordinary; people would take a dram for breakfast, not to get falling-down drunk, evidence would suggest, but to warm them for the day. An analogy might be coca leaves, which South American peasants chew to get them through a hard day without much food.

States need money for wars, and taxing alcohol has always been a good way of raising revenue. The first attempt to tax whisky was made by the Scottish Parliament, who passed the Act of Excyse in 1643, to help pay for the Scots war with Charles I, an Act which was confirmed after the Restoration in 1660. After the Act of Union between England and Scotland in 1707, the English excise laws were made to operate in Scotland too. But all these attempts to raise revenue from whisky were worthless, because of the impossibility of tracking down who made it. Everyone made it, pretty much everywhere. The best that could be managed was to tax counties, according to a rough estimate of how much was being made in any one year. As with the Gin Acts in England, attempts at tightening control led to an increase in illegal production. The Wash Act of 1783 increased the complexity of an already unworkable tax-collection system. It operated in favour of large producers of lower-grade Lowland whisky, made from a mixture of malted and unmalted grains. This is grain whisky, made in vast industrial stills, good for funerals, but little else. These days, it's blended with selected malt whiskies to produce your Johnnie Walkers and your Famous Grouses. Everyone knew that the Highland stills, especially those in Glenlivet, were producing whiskies of far higher quality, so demand was high, but production was on the scale of the home still, each producing maybe fifty gallons a week.

In the Excise Act of 1814, stills with a capacity of less than 500 gallons were made illegal. This suited the big Lowland producers, but meant that almost all of the Highland distillers were made into criminals, which led to the final boom in illegal production. It was the Highland stuff that people in Edinburgh and London wanted, but it had just been effectively outlawed. In the decade between 1814 and 1824, the 'smugglers' who made the whisky were involved in a small-scale war with the gaugers, as they called the hated excise men. Given the nature of the terrain, the gaugers waged a hopeless war in the face of tradition and a demanding market place. Hundreds of gallons were coming out of the glens every week, carried over the high Cairngorms on smugglers' roads to the ports of Aberdeen and Peterhead. In 1824, there were reckoned to be 400 illegal stills operating in Glenlivet.[*]

---

[*] This does not mean that there were 400 smugglers in Glenlivet, as most operations would have had four or five stills, while several were known to have had up to twenty.

The Duke of Gordon, a major Scottish proprietor, proposed a compromise. He said that excise should be cut to a level which would be affordable to the people who were making the good stuff, and that the limit on still sizes should be reduced to forty gallons, on payment of a £10 annual licence. George IV, was recruited to the cause by Walter Scott, who advised the King on his visit to Edinburgh in 1822 to ask for the 'real Glenlivet'. Highlanders were pleased that their highly illegal product received such a generous endorsement from His Majesty. It was like the Queen going on a visit to Kabul and asking for a wrap of the real Afghan Brown. The Treasury and Parliament saw sense, and the Duke's proposals were passed into law as the 1823 Excise Act.

The smugglers were much less keen. In fact, they threatened to destroy the stills of anyone who went legit. But in 1824, one of the Duke of Gordon's tenants, called George Smith, with the help and encouragement of the Duke and the laird of Aberlour, who gave him a pair of pistols, decided that the game might be worth the risk. In his own words, 'in 1824, I, George Smith, who was a robust young fellow and not given to be easily "fleggit" determined to chance it.'

Smith, a carpenter and a farmer, who was distilling about a hogshead a week was ridiculed and attacked by his neighbours, who felt that he had betrayed the cause of the smugglers. But George kept his pistols tucked in his belt and 'watched his kiln by night for years'. People in the South wanted Glenlivet whisky, and now they could have it openly and legally, and because the excise was set at a reasonable level, it could compete with the illegal stuff. Liberalisation is inclusive; it brings people within the law. Restriction is exclusive, as it puts them outside it. By 1850 George Smith was the largest and best known of the Highland distillers. As others of the smugglers realised that legitimisation could bring prosperity as well as peace from the gaugers, they too wanted to lay claim to the famous glen; but in a court case at the end of the nineteenth century, the Smith family won the right to the name. Other whiskies can say they are made in Glen-Livet, (which has to be hyphenated) but there is only one daddy. THE Glenlivet.

As we went into lunch, the tour finished, and a by-now-familiar mix of Americans, Dutch and Japanese came into the gift shop for the tasting. We managed to mingle with them, that we might take a wee dram ourselves. Suitably fortified, we drove up from Glenlivet to Tomintoul, which claimed to be the highest village in the British Isles. There we picked up the A939, which was built by General Wade in the 1720s. The Wade roads were planned so that troops could be moved about quickly in order to assert control over the Highlands following the 1715 uprising. The Wade roads proved invaluable to the smugglers, and this road, 'The Lecht Road', which led from Speyside across the high Cairngorms to Ballater and on to Aberdeen, was the main, unpoliceable artery of the trade.

There were still patches of snow that high, blobs hidden from the spring in folds on the hillsides. And there must have been a great deal of snow up here in the recent past, because at the top of a high mountain pass, we passed through the Lecht Ski and Activity Centre, though there were no skiers and no activity of any kind that we could detect. Chair lifts ran up the hillsides, stilled now until the next winter.

The Cairngorms are higher, on the whole, than the mountains on the West Coast, but they lack the sea, and the human community, and after a bit, you can't help but go, 'Yeah, mountains, cool, but what else you got?' We came down from the hills to Balmoral, but the Queen wasn't in, so there was nothing to do but head for Aberdeen, and the Northlink ferry to Shetland.

I was driving as we came into the outskirts of Aberdeen, when the migraine that I had been brewing for a day or so struck. There is a strange moment at the beginning of a classical migraine when you suddenly notice something missing from the field of your vision, and you wonder why. With me, it was the speedo. It had gone, and I felt a momentary panic, before I remembered that it must be a migraine. Then the blind spots spread, and what you are left with is like looking at a TV whose vertical control has gone.

'Perry,' I said. 'I'm sorry to be a bore, but I've got a migraine, and I can't see properly. You'll need to drive.'

'Don't worry, mate. There's a street coming up on the left; can you see it?'

'Got it . . .'

I pulled off the main road, drank two litres of water (far and away the best cure, if you can keep it down), and tried to sleep in the passenger's seat while good old Perry drove through Aberdeen to find the ferry terminal.

If you've never had a migraine, you're probably thinking, 'Oh, he's just got a bad headache. Hung-over, probably.' Migraine sufferers will tell you that a headache is just the most common of the symptoms, and not the worst. As it happens, I no longer get a headache at all, not really. Migraine, in the classical model, is a sickness of childhood, and it should get better with age. I can control mine, postpone them, anyway. I knew that if I could drink lots of water, sleep, and then have a cup of tea, I'd be all right. No headache, then, but a feeling of disgust that is always with you; just writing about migraine makes my skin crawl.

So to get to the ferry, I had to rely on my buddy, as I had now for almost a month. My girlfriend, all of my girlfriends, probably all girlfriends, have been unimpressed by the quality of male friendship.

'You never call one another,' they say, 'except to fix things up.'

'No, but we email.'

'Yes, lists of your twenty best reggae albums, or "Ten AOR tracks that I shouldn't like but I do". And so on, but you never really talk, do you? Except in jokes.'

'Don't be ridiculous. We talk all the time.'

'Yes, about politics and football and how much you hate young people in baseball caps. But never about your feelings.'

'But I've got you, my angel.'

In the words of the late Alice Thomas Ellis, men love women, women love children and children love hamsters.

That male friendship is different from female is beyond doubt, but that doesn't make it less valuable. Jokes are a good way to communicate feelings, I'd say. Standing next to someone at the match while you both scream at the halfwits on the pitch is cathartic. Male friendship can be more casual, but also more flexible; no one knew that Brooky was coming to Islay until I phoned him on spec. This quality of companionship is one reason, perhaps, why the pub remains a largely male space.

Women, by and large, don't go to the pub on their own. Some of them do but, on balance, they don't. Sociologists have been off round the pubs, and find that women who use pubs and who they classify as broadly working-class go about once a week, often to see friends they have known since school; middle-class pub women go less often, often to meet a group of friends before 'going on' somewhere. Women feel, on the whole, excluded from pubs, because they don't like drunk men, who they think are likely to make advances, or at least comments. When asked to categorise pubs, women were coming up with the ale-house/tavern/inn model, expressed as rough, respectable and posh; but when pressed, the women surveyed said they wouldn't go in any of them on their own. Both the rough pubs and the posh inns are especially exclusive, with the cosmopolitan taverns being most attractive to women.

The fact that children were until very recently excluded from pubs doesn't make them more attractive to women, of course. Perry argues that it is fine for men to have a space of their own, free from domestic pressure, but then he wasn't married to old Lily, who will kill me if I agree. Much as I'd like to. On the other hand, if I disagree, I'm going to look like a wuss, scared of his ex-wife's extraordinary grasp of feminist theory, and her vast storehouse of examples from my life which illustrate the shitness of men. What I reckon is that one of the factors that has led to pubs becoming male is this idea of the difference in degrees of friendship. I don't think pubs are about keeping company with your friends, which is the primary female mode of social interaction. The pub is about spending time with your mates. And women don't have mates.

They don't. My girlfriend has nobody in her life who is the equivalent of, say, Tom Crippen in mine; we used to be on the quiz team together, so we went out every Monday night; and sometimes I'd go round his house and play him at golf on his Nintendo. Women don't go around playing golf on their friend's Nintendos. They talk to one another, about stuff that is important to them. About their relationships, their children, their feelings. After twelve years or so of being mates with Tom Crippen, I have no idea how he feels about anything, outside of West Ham United and thrash metal. Nor do I wish to know. It's his business how his relationship is going. Pubs are ideal for these kind of pally, matey relationships. Men have lots of mates, but few friends. I reckon I've got five, and one of them was looking after me while I fought the migraine.

Men are kind to other men when they are unwell, because only men really know what it is to be ill. My friend Perry Venus found the ferry terminal and parked the car before nudging me gently into the world.

'How are you feeling, mate?' he asked.

I opened and closed my eyes. We were leaving Perry's car behind at Aberdeen. I looked at the odometer. We had travelled 3,050 miles since leaving the heliport in Penzance four weeks ago. You could add about 500 to that, I reckoned, if you added together all the sea journeys and the trip over to Scilly, and the driving we had to do tomorrow in the hire car that was waiting for us in Lerwick. Three and a half thousand miles; it's a long way to go for a drink.

'I feel like death warmed over. But I can see again.' We checked in with Northlink, but were told that it was an hour before we could get on to the boat and into our cabin so that I could get some proper sleep. We walked across to the Quarter Deck pub opposite the ferry terminal; a modern building tacked on to the side of a multi-storey car-park. Didn't look very promising; the last thing we expected to find was 'the craic'. But there it was, like we'd seen nowhere else.

The pub was full of fiddlers and accordionists and banjo players, sitting around having a session at four in the afternoon. Packed with them. Instrument cases lay all over the floor; pretty girls in hippy dresses sat on bags, tuning soulful guitars.

Perry found me a table. I closed my eyes against the light, and tried to enjoy the sound of seventeen folk bands separately running through a few numbers.

'What do you want, mate?'

'Tea, water, and an explanation.'

Perry brought back all three.

'It's the Shetland Folk Festival starting tomorrow,' he said. 'They're all waiting for the boat. How you feeling?'

'So long as I can sleep for a bit, I'll be fine.'

I closed my eyes; migraine makes you photophobic. After an hour, we were allowed on to the boat, and they gave us the keys to our clean and comfortable cabin, and I got my head down for a couple of hours.

I felt wobbly and disorientated when I woke up, but then I always do. There were the doings for tea in the cabin, and I made myself a cup, washed down a couple of aspirin, just out of habit really, and walked up on deck to try and find Perry and what the night might bring.

We were still in the harbour, surrounded by strange-looking boats, which I guessed must be support vessels for the oil rigs. It was ten to seven, ten minutes before we were due to sail, and I looked over the rails with some lads who played in a band called the Real Macaws, all of us driven on deck both by the freemasonry of smoking and a romantic urge to watch the coastline drop away. Perry came up as the lines were cast off; and we were under way for our last pub. *The* last pub.

We went for a walk round the boat, both too keyed up to settle down to lasagne and chips. In every nook and cranny below deck, behind every bulkhead, there were people playing. Round and round we walked, through groups of Cypriot bouzouki players and Croatian bagpipers; through duos and trios and groups. The boat was alive with music, as we watched the coast slip past.

'Is it time for the lasagne and chips?' said Perry.

'I'll come with you, but I might stick to thin captain's biscuits.'

After dinner, more walking on deck, watching as the coast darkened, and the flares of oil rigs appeared on the horizon. The Real Macaws were up there too, smoking some odd-smelling stuff, which they were kind enough to share. Now my head felt strangely light, and I became convinced that the thing I needed to clear it was a nice half and half. We went down to the bar, and settled down with our drinks.

'Your Dad,' said a voice from behind my head.

I turned to see a couple of guys in their late twenties who seemed vaguely familiar, a great big one and a little slim one.

'Yes?' I admitted.

'It is. It's Your Dad. We appeared on the same bill as you at Bath Fringe a couple of years ago. You were fucking funny, mate. Mind if we join you?'

I remembered their act, which included a clever and funny re-invention of the Wilson, Keppel and Betty sand dance. Their names were Matt and Gareth, aka the Barnard and Jones Variety Spectacular, and they told us they were off to Shetland to compere some of the events at the folk festival. They asked if we were going over to play at the festival and I admitted that, no, we were going for a pint in the last pub in Britain, so that I could write a book about it. Matt and Gareth told us they were both running outside stages at Pilton Festival in a couple of months' time. I play on a little stage in the Green Fields, while Perry works for the safety crew, and we all arranged to meet in the Tiny Tea Tent. We chatted about Glastos past, and Glastos to come, and I managed to blag a gig on Matt's stage. We had become mates, like men do.

'Is book-writing your main job then, Dad?' asked Matt.

'I suppose it is, really, these days,' I admitted.

'Is it humorous? Like *Round Ireland with a Fridge?*'

'That's a funny book,' said Perry.

'Isn't it?' said Gareth.

'What will you do next? After you've written this?' said Matt.

'I don't know.'

'You could go round meeting all the other humorous travel writers, and kill them, and write a book about it,' said Gareth.

'Now that,' I said, 'is a really good idea. I'll put you in the acknowledgements.'

# Thursday 29th April

I should have been getting an early night, God knows, but here we were, in a bar on the Shetland ferry in the middle of the North Sea, and we were having one of the best nights out we'd had all month. The bar stayed open all night, and all night the Croatian pipers and Cypriot bouzouki players jammed, while the comics tried to top one another's jokes. Out on deck the Real Macaws were smoking tea and watching gas flares blaze across the water. I think any lingering mystery about what makes a great pub was lifted; a great pub is simply one that is full of people you like who are enjoying themselves.

But it all got to be too much. I was dog-tired after my migraine, and I knew that I couldn't really have more than a couple of drinks, if I wanted to be able to face the morning. Once again, I had proved myself little more than a fellow traveller in the company of real pissheads. Even so, it was almost two before we got back to the cabin and sleep. A reeling sleep, with jigs still sounding in my ears; a rolling sleep as the shallow-draughted ferry lolloped across the waves. And I knew Perry was being brave, because he doesn't like the sea.

I dozed for about four hours, and woke at six, much too excited to sleep. Gabby Chris Garrand and Rachel Hazell had both told me that I had to get up in time to see Sumburgh Head appear off the port bow. And there it was when I went up on deck, the colour of an olive floating in a cocktail sea. There was cold in the air, a real bite of it. There was only one other guy up there, and we got to talking.

'Do you know how far we've come?' I said, a shivering morning fag in my hand.

'It's 260 miles from Aberdeen to Lerwick,' he said.

He told me about the ferries; how the boat we were on, the MV

*Hrossay*, had been purpose-built for this run; the shallow draught allowed for speed, but it could make for a rough ride.

'Eleven million a year, that's how much subsidy Northlink get from the government. Shetland couldn't survive without it.'

Passengers started to appear on deck as the café opened for breakfast. Perry came up with the camera to record our arrival. The sun was trying to fight off the cold, and the sky was a brilliant Scandinavian blue as we slid between Bressay and the mainland of Shetland, and into the berth in Lerwick. Northlink Ferries, being decent sorts, don't make you get up at seven-thirty to disembark. You don't have to be off the boat till ten, and the café stays open, so you can have a bit of a lie-in. That's exactly what Perry and I planned to do on the return leg, but now we were raring to go, and we joined those few passengers who wanted to be up and at 'em. Our friends from the night before were all taking advantage of a nice long lie-in. They would need it; they'd told me that Shetland's folk festival is regarded as more than averagely hectic, a 72-hour bender for all concerned.

The first thing I noticed about the ferry port in Lerwick is that it is bilingual; all the signs are written in English and Norwegian. So difficult is it to find a map of the British Isles which shows Shetland in its true position, it is hard to picture that it is actually further north than Bergen, and closer to the Norwegian port than to Aberdeen.

Then I noticed some of the signs pointed out, both in English and Norwegian, the hopelessness of bringing drugs on to Shetland; and then I noticed the polis, with a cheery-looking sniffer dog. He must have had a bit of a cold, is all I can say, if he wasn't picking up on all the musos who came staggering into the terminal building. He sat cheerfully wagging his tail at people who might as well have been bathing in eau-de-skunque. Good dog!

At the hire-car desk, we were second in line. The guy in front of us was an American, and he was very nervous about what he should do on single-track roads. The hire-car lady explained that there were passing places, and all he had to do if there was anybody coming was to pull over.

'And you'll find that lots of them will pull over for you anyway,' I said.

'Whoever is nearest the passing place should back up,' said the lady.

'Yes. But you should give priority to buses and trucks,' I said

'Jeez, I've been worrying for days. I've never driven in Scotland before.'

The hire-car lady said, 'This isn't Scotland, sir. This is Shetland.' I listened to her voice, and it wasn't really Scottish at all. Much more Scandinavian than anything else.

Orkney and Shetland were the last members of the archipelago to count as British; before 1468 they were Norwegian, when they were mortgaged by King Christian of Norway and Denmark to the Scottish Crown as part of the marriage settlement of Margaret of Norway to James III of Scotland. It just goes to show what happens if you don't keep up the repayments – Scotland kept the islands in perpetuity.

We drove up Mainland. Within minutes of leaving Lerwick, the road was climbing up hills and crossing peat bogs. Mainland had the bleakest landscape of any we had visited; there are no trees on the islands, except the occasional pampered freak in a garden, because of the high winds. The road divides in two: one sign pointed to the Sullom Voe oil terminal, from where we could see gas flares behind the shelter of hills; the other, to the ferry for Yell. We sat waiting for the ferry, and watched it come sashaying across the sound. This first crossing took twenty-five minutes. Built after the landing-craft model of the ferry between Islay and Jura, but with room for twelve cars, the ferries are run by Shetland Council. Sadly, there is no caff, no lasagne and chips. Chris Garrand had told me that people drive like lunatics between the ferries, so as not to have to queue, but we were happy to wait. There was something in the air. All the migraine fog had lifted from my head. Perry was smiling, which almost worried me. He even seemed to enjoy the boat trip over to Yell.

The lunatics raced off across the island, but we decided to go the long way round, and we hacked up the east coast of the island. It seemed more pastoral than the Inner Hebridean islands, prettier, but also sadder, more lonely, lost. This was, by far, the best weather we'd had on the whole trip. I felt enchanted; we got out and walked over the machair to an old ship's figurehead that looked out over the sea to Fetlar. And in the sun, it was like having early spring back. Slow to arrive this far north, the daffodils were coming into bloom, and new-born lambs skittered in the small fields.

And if that wasn't enough, at the end of Yell, by the place where the ferries cross to the out islands, there is a small miracle of a café, called the Wind Dog. Rachel Hazell had told me it was good, but now I could see why she thought so. It is really not much more than a prefabricated hut, but it does internet access, it has a library, there are some carefully selected local crafts for sale, there is proper coffee, and superb cakes, and an astounding view over to Unst and Fetlar.

It's run by a guy called Andy, a New Zealander in his early thirties. He's an opera singer by vocation, and he and his partner had bought the house that stands a quarter of a mile away from the café, in order to open up a centre for singers.

'It was cheap. And we figured that the clean air would be good for the voice.'

But funding is always difficult at the early stage of any project like this, and having bought the house, they needed an income, so when the run-down old café by the ferry landing came up for sale, they took it on, and have turned it into one of the best caffs in Britain, an object lesson in how to run a rural business.

'We're very lively here,' said Andy. 'We run a book club, and creative-writing classes. It's always busy.'

Lively is a relative term, I guess. There was no one else in that morning, waiting for the ferries to Fetlar and Unst. There was a Spanish lady helping Andy, so presumably there must be a rush sometimes. There are 900 or so people who live on Yell, and there's no real pub, so the Wind Dog must be important to the locals. I mentioned to Andy that I'd heard about the Wind Dog a thousand miles away, in North Devon, when I had been told about it by my friend Rachel Hazell.

'Oh, is that you? Rachel was through here yesterday, heading over to Fetlar. She left you a message. Hang on.'

He dug around, and found a note from Rach: 'Hello, Ian and Perry! Welcome to the Wind Dog. Give me a ring when you can.'

I tried her mobile, but failed to get through. Given where we were, waiting for a boat to Ultima Thule, it would have been surprising if the reception was great.

'I like Rachel,' said Andy. 'She was running a bookbinding workshop in here three days ago.'

I liked the Wind Dog. I loved it, in fact, and would have to choose it as my favourite café in the UK; not just because of the friendliness of the service and the excellence of the coffee, but because of its mad location, here on the very edge of things. In fact, I bought the T-shirt.

Now there was just one short hop to make, from Yell to Unst, and we watched the ferry swing up to the ferry landing, and drove on with two other cars and a fishmonger's van. The ticket collector asked us why we were going to Unst, and I told him that we were going for a drink in the last pub in the British Isles.

'Mm, you should come up to the bridge and meet the captain,' he said. 'He'd be thrilled to hear about that.' So I followed the ticket guy up the metal stairs to the small bridge, where I spoke to the captain and mate, and watched as Unst swished closer.

The crew of the MV *Fivla* were full of smiles, but, like lots of Shetlanders, they didn't talk much, though they were interested to hear what the Scillies are like. Shetlanders, we were discovering, are friendly and shy.

But the captain did remind me of one salient point. 'The Baltasound is the last pub. But there's a bar at RAF Saxa Vord that is further north. The Baa Bar it's called.'

'But we'll never get in there, will we? In the current climate?'

'Oh, yule have no problem at all.'

So we drove from the MV *Fivla*, and on to the last inhabited island, the counterbalance of St Agnes in the Scillies, and started to cross Unst. It is treeless, like all of Shetland, but the beaches glittered in the sun. We drove past a stone at the side of the road that had a woman's face painted on it in white, which we both admitted we really didn't like the look of. The west and centre of Unst are mostly uninhabited; its 500 inhabitants cling to the south and east coasts. As across lots of the islands of Scotland, there are not actually villages as such on Unst, but townships, scattered agglomerations of crofts and houses, the largest of which is Baltasound, which spreads itself around the eponymous bay.

And here at last, was the last pub, the most northerly pub in the British Isles, the Baltasound Hotel. Set perhaps a quarter of a mile back from the pier, it is a square blocky building in grey granite, with a wooden extension built on to its side, and a mini-campus of chalets ranged around a green. On the side of the building, in fading paint, it said 'The Baltasound Hotel. Britain's Most Northerly Pub'. We parked the car, and walked around to reception. There was a friendly lass in a baseball cap waiting to greet us.

'Hello,' she said. 'You must be Mr Marchant and Mr Venus! You've come from the Scilly Isles to have a drink here!'

We admitted as much.

'Your friend phoned. Hang on, I've got a message for you.'

It was from our friend Gilly, who had come on the piss-up in two breweries in Bishop's Castle.

'Congratulations,' it said, 'on completing the Longest Crawl.'

'Now,' said the receptionist, if you'll come with me . . .'

She led us out from the reception, and round the side of the building. We saw a sign painted on the wall, saying 'Bar'.

'Here we are,' she said, opening the door. 'The public bar of the Baltasound Hotel. Britain's most northerly pub! Come back to reception when you've had your drink, and I'll show you your chalet.'

It was dark brown with nicotine and unlove. One ancient customer sat at the bar, a silent smiling Shetlander. A taciturn barman in a brown home-knitted cardigan asked us what we wanted, which was a pint, even thought it was 80 Shilling; I'd begun to develop a taste. The barman was in his late fifties, as shabby as the bar. And I sat in the window, looking thoughtfully north, while Perry ponced around taking photos of me.

We asked the barman if we could get anything to eat. He pointed wordlessly to the menu chalked up behind the bar.

'Sausage Egg and Chips', it said.

'Well, that suits me just fine,' I said.

'Me too,' said Perry.

The smiling Shetlander sat looking at us, while the taciturn barman ignored us all. They didn't speak to one another, and certainly not to us. I found it unnerving. Silence makes me want to chatter. I told the guys why we were there.

'We've been travelling for a month to get here,' I said. 'We've been travelling between the two most distant pubs in the UK. We started at the Turk's Head, on St Agnes, in the Scillies, and, now, we're here.'

The Shetlander smiled and nodded, and kept staring at us. The barman raised his eyebrows. He brought us our sausage, egg and chips, which we ate in silence, looking out through the window to Baltasound harbour. There was talc on the landing pier.

'Well,' I said when we'd finished. 'Fair words butter no parsnips. Can we put this on our bill?'

'No,' said the barman. 'You have to pay now.'

'OK,' I said.

Lunch over, the last pub ticked off, and the Baa Bar at RAF Saxa Vord not open till the evening, Perry and I girded our loins to do something we hadn't done for a good while. We were going for a walk.

We got back into our hire car, and drove north. RAF Saxa Vord dominates the north end of the island, with its golf-ball dome, but we took the road that led towards the Herma Ness bird sanctuary, which is the end of it all. We drove as far as we could, and then started to walk. The glorious weather of the morning had given way to drizzling rain. Peat bogs only really look their best in bright sunshine, and we started to walk through a landscape of brown peat, dull, windswept, but exhilarating. There was a footpath from the car-park, with a sign telling us that it was closed for refurbishment, a sign which we happily ignored. When it is finished, the walking will be easier, but we had to pick our way across the empty bog. The skuas that we had been warned about long ago in a London pub by Chris Garrand wheeled aggressively above our heads, but although they made warning swoops, it was probably too early in the season for them to have their chicks yet, and although they threatened, they didn't attack. So we walked and we walked through the peat, our boots sticky with it, towards the horizon and the sea. Each horizon turned out to be false, and new hills opened up before us as we breasted each one. My specs were blurred with rain. But then, one last false horizon, and we could see that we were approaching the cliffs' edge. In the sea, we could see the rocks of Muckle Flugga and the last lighthouse. Try and compute this; it is further from Muckle Flugga to the border between England and Scotland, than it is from the border to Land's End. And so we walked until we came to the last hill of all, and we stood twenty yards or so from the cliff edge, and we could go no further, because we had come to the end of Her Majesty's domain.

'We are the last men standing,' said Perry, and he was right. It was coming up to five. Behind us, south of us, people were leaving work, kids were home from school, people were starting to cook dinner, perhaps going to the pub for a quick one after work. All of them. We were the most northerly men in Britain. Everybody else in the British Isles, all 60 million of them, were south of us. We were the first and last men, alone at the end of everything.

It felt strange; lonely, as who wouldn't in this lonely place, with high cliffs and chippy skuas and wind and rain, dressed in frankly inappropriate outdoor wear, which is just about the naughtiest thing you can do. We began the long walk back across the peat, due south.

There is something in the mineral composition of Unst which causes it to glitter. There is iron pyrites on the island; and they've just found platinum and gold up there, too. On our return to the car, we both found that where we had been walking, our jeans were covered in a glittering powder. We looked like members of the Glitter Band; fat, middle-aged, dumb, but with sequins sewn on our loons.

On the way back to the Baltasound, we passed the most famous structure on Unst, which is, of course, the legendary bus stop. This is the only bus stop which has its own website; you can find a link to it through my site. Somebody looks after the stop. There is an easy chair, an old microwave cooker with a stuffed cat sitting on it, and a computer, not working. No visit to the island is complete without calling in and, er, well, sitting there. We did.

Then it was back to the Baltasound for dinner, which is served in the hotel side. It was quite the most extraordinary menu I'd seen in years. There were three things on it: chicken tikka masala, poached salmon, and steak. It was like being taken back to the seventies in a time machine, which was appropriate in view of our glittering trousers. I had the salmon, because it's hard to get wrong, but they did. There is nowhere else to eat on Unst. And where was the folk festival? Matt and Gareth told us that it happened in small venues in all the islands; on Out Skerries, on Fetlar, and even, for the first time this year, on Foula, that extraordinary island, the most isolated of all the inhabited islands of Britain, where they keep the Julian rather than the Gregorian calendar, so that they are always nine days adrift of the rest of us. But not on Unst. Not in the Baltasound, which would have been the most obvious venue. I sensed that whoever was running this place did not grasp the first principles of hospitality. Apart from me and Perry, there were exactly eleven people in the dining room of the Baltasound, and nine of them were ancient ladies winding themselves up for an exciting game of bingo.

The other two were a couple of men, one in his late fifties, the other a lad of twenty or so. They had both made some effort to tidy themselves up, perhaps feeling the social pressure of having 'dinner' in a 'hotel'. The lad had carefully combed his hair forward over his brow, and had plastered it down with hair gel, while the older guy had combed his back, and stuck it down with brilliantine. Two stupid haircuts, separated by thirty-five years of bad hairdressing. They sat silently at the bar, waiting for their chicken/salmon/steak. We tried to engage them in conversation, but they had clearly decided to act like Shetlanders. They were in fact, from Essex, and were up to do some painting on the radar dome at the RAF base.

The lad might have liked to talk, but the older guy was such a miserable old get, and was so clearly uninterested by anything that wasn't him, that we gave up the struggle of trying to talk. We ate our meal in silence, and looked out the windows again. The bingo got going.

Now there was just one thing left to do, which was to get into the mess at RAF Saxa Vord, which is, beyond all dispute, the most northerly bar in the British Isles. The receptionist at the Baltasound said that we'd get in, no trouble.

'I've had some great nights up there,' she said, which was just as well, because nobody was going to have a great night in the Baltasound, ever. So we got back into our car, and made one last northern excursion. It was still light, noticeably much lighter than anywhere else we'd been, even at nine o'clock at night.

RAF Saxa Vord is a listening post. It is staffed by radar operators; there are no aircraft as such, though there is a place where helicopters can land. Twenty-four hours a day, 365 days a year, highly and expensively trained young men and women sit in darkened bunkers, scouring the skies for incoming ICBMs launched from Soviet Russia.

Hang on, you say. Are we still worried about that?

Well, apparently we are. The operation has been scaled down, and as a consequence the population of Unst has fallen dramatically. We saw a lot of empty service houses on the edge of the base. But there are still people there, guarding us from . . . well, International Terrorism, now I guess. After all, the International Terrorists could launch one of their weapons of mass destruction, and fire it at us, and it would be here in forty-five minutes, raining anthrax down on British cities.

Oh no, hang on, that's not right, either.

Well, anyway, there they sit.

I imagined that such a sensitive base would be all but impregnable, especially in the current climate. Johnny International Terrorist would give his eye teeth to blow it up. Post-9/11 slash 7/7, it seemed hardly credible that two fat chancers like ourselves would be able to penetrate to the heart of Britain's intelligence network. We drove past the guardhouse, loaded down with cameras and recording devices. Nobody stopped us. We parked the car, and decided that we'd better go back to the guardhouse, to tell them we were here, and what we were doing.

Inside sat an aircraftwoman with her feet on the desk, reading a paperback novel.

'Hello,' I said.

'Hello. Can I help you?'

She took her feet off the desk, and looked up from her book.

'Yes, hello. We were told that it would be OK for us to go for a drink in the Baa Bar.'

'Yes, I expect so,' she said. 'Er . . . have you got any ID?

'Well, not really. I've got my credit card, if that would help.'

'Let's have a look.'

I handed her my credit card, which she looked at, and handed back.

'Oh, it'll be fine. Just walk round the corner, past the NAAFI, through the double doors, and down the corridor.'

On the wall outside the Baa Bar is a sign saying 'RAF Saxa Vord. The UK's Most Northerly Mess'. It was a small room, decorated in sky blue with some cartoon pictures of sheep and penguins painted over the bar. We smiled at the barmaid and looked at what she had to offer. There was one draught lager, some tins of lager, some bottles of lager and two optics, one of vodka, and the other of Famous Grouse. There were three bored youths with neat haircuts sitting at the bar, while two others put the covers back on the mess snooker table. The youths ignored us. They were talking about how great it is to get pished. I ordered a Grouse, and Perry had a Budweiser. It really was a very small room, with just three tables, and four barstools, and it felt smaller than it was. We tried to talk with the youths; we told them that we had come a long way, and been to a lot of pubs, to get here. But they didn't know how to talk to people, had no response. I guess it must make you tense, knowing that the safety of the realm lies in your hands. When the ICBMs come, it's these guys who'll be giving us that all-important five-minute warning. We got nothing out of them but a grunt. So we sat in embarrassed silence, looking out the window at the most northerly rain in the British Isles. We finished our drinks, and left. There was no sign of the laconic guard as we left the base and turned the car for home.

# Friday 30th April

One last breakfast for Perry to photograph.

The sky was a rain-washed blue, a lapis-lazuli sea lapped at the shore, and the sun was butter-bright. It was a perfect spring morning on the last island. Who could not be glad to be alive?

'Lovely morning,' we carolled at the radar-dome painters from Essex as they came into the dining room of the Baltasound for their breakfasts.

'Nyeh, so far,' sneered the miserable old get.

'The forecast is very good,' said Perry.

'Nyeh. I know it is. But it changes in five minutes up 'ere. All we know is, we'll 'ave weather all day.'

We checked out of the last pub, both of us feeling that it was wrong. All wrong.

There was one last place that I had arranged to visit on Unst, which was the Valhalla Brewery, run by a guy called Sonny Spence. Everything on Unst is the most northerly something in the British Isles so the Valhalla is the most northerly brewery. Sonny's is a one-man operation, but he sells his beer all over Shetland. Except, of course, in the Baltasound Hotel, where everything was wrong. Sonny told us about Unst. He'd been born on the island, one of nine. Seven of his brothers and sisters still live there.

The beer was excellent; Sonny made us try the Simmer Dim, named after the weeks in midsummer when the sun dips only briefly over the horizon, and night doesn't come to Shetland. He has real marketing savvy; he does about eight bottled beers, each with a distinctive label. 'White Wife', one of his brews is called. He told us about the stone we had noticed yesterday coming across the island with a woman's face painted on it.

'That's where you see the White Wife. They say she drowned

herself from grief in the loch. My brother was driving past the stone one night, felt that something was wrong, turned and saw the Wife sitting next to him in the passenger seat.'

He told us about life on the island.

'It's getting much harder, now the oil is nearly through. We used to have Chevron up here, but now they've gone, and the RAF are winding down, and the airport is closed. Used to be a thousand people lived on Unst. Now it's more like five hundred.'

'What do you think of the pub?' asked Perry. Sonny made a face.

'Oh, it's sad. None of the locals use it. I'd love to take it over, and turn it into a brew pub. It's for sale . . .'

'All pubs are,' I told him, and he laughed.

'Aye, I can see why.'

'How much do they want?'

'Two hundred and fifty K. Too expensive. But if I could raise the cash, I'd take it over tomorrow, and bring it back to life.'

We said goodbye to Sonny, and started a slow drive down through the islands. Our ferry was due to leave Lerwick at seven in the evening, and would arrive in Aberdeen at seven the following morning. From Aberdeen, we would take it in turns to drive to Crewe, where I was going to stay the night in the Railway Hotel, so that I could catch a train back to Devon on Sunday morning. Perry reckoned that he'd be good to drive from Crewe straight back to West Wales. It took us a month to get here, and two days to get home.

We caught the ferry from Unst back over to Yell. The crew of the MV *Fivla* invited me back up on to the bridge, and asked what I'd thought about the Last Pub. I made a face.

'It's run without love,' I said, and the Shetlanders smiled.

Back in the Wind Dog Café, over elevenses, I started to develop a fantasy. Suddenly, from nowhere, I had half a million pounds. I would go into partnership with Sonny, and we'd take over the Baltasound. It looked to the outsider to be in good order, and the sixteen pine chalets that were gathered around the green in front of the hotel were well kept and comfortable, and would be good to go, at least for starters. The main hotel building didn't look like it would need too much structural work, which meant that we could spend money knocking it about inside.

The first thing we'd do is to gut the shabby old public bar. On our visit, it was modelled on an ale-house, but what's needed is a tavern. It needs to be modern and light, in order to attract in the widest possible number of locals, men, women and children. It needs a Gaggia machine, and Sonny's Valhalla Ale straight from the brewhouse. It would have Guinness, of course, and, since you have to have lager on tap, you'd make sure it was Hoegaarden, or Leffe. There should be a selection of thirty or so malt whiskies, nothing mad, just a selection of some of the best from the Highlands and Islands. The default gin would be Plymouth, and cider would come from Herefordshire; Dunkerton's by preference. The walls would be the colour of conversation. No recorded music, but you'd encourage local players to come and have a weekly session. And once a week, you'd do a table quiz. There would be a good-sized TV, which would be turned off at all times, except for big occasions, like football internationals, which people like to watch together. The staff would be selected on the basis of their conviviality, rather than their efficiency, which can be learned.

The food would be cooked with love, by a proper chef, one who is ambitious and looking to make a name. There are fish in the sea at the bottom of the garden, and lamb in the fields behind; you need local ingredients, and your menu needs to have one foot at least in the local cuisine. We'd pay a premium for local ingredients; if someone started a smokehouse on the island, for example, we'd use their kippers, and happily pay top dollar. You should be able to get something half decent for a fiver a head at lunchtime, and a tenner at night. People who just wanted a drink should be made to feel as welcome as those who wanted a meal. In the dining room, you could serve a more upmarket menu, perhaps two or three nights of the week, as well as your breakfasts for the guests. There is room too for a quiet lounge, perhaps with a few computer terminals with interweb access. You could do all this and still leave room for a good-sized hall, with a proper piano and a house PA. The Folk Festival would be invited in straightaway, and you would start to build a reputation as a place that people wanted to come and play. You'd make it a room that people wanted to use for weddings, and for christenings, and good old-fashioned funeral teas. The green in front of the hotel needs to be a sturdily built playground, with places to sit when the weather is good. You'd listen to what people wanted to do, and fit the space to suit local demand.

We'd change the name. It would be called 'The Northern Lights'. You'd have an excellent website, which would make it seem attractive as a place to come. The Old Forge on Knoydart capitalised on being the Most Remote Pub; we'd market ours as the Most Northerly. You need to make people come there because of its uniqueness. At the time of the Simmer Dim, we'd run all-night events. In the darkness of winter, you'd run northern-light weekends, and encourage amateur stargazers to come and stay. You'd run bird-spotting weekends. You would make sure that it was a place that intrepid yachtsmen wanted to come. You'd twin with the Turk's Head on St Agnes.

It was my Moon Under Water, and just as real.

I finished my coffee.

'Well, that's it, then, friend,' I said.

'Yes.'

'Downhill all the way from here.'

'Certainly is.'

'What are you going to do when you get home?' I asked.

'Cut back on the drink, for one thing.'

'That's how the poem ends.'

'What poem?'

'"The Rolling English Road":

My friends, we will not go again or ape an ancient rage,
Or stretch the folly of our youth to be the shame of age,
But walk with clearer eyes and ears this path that wandereth,
And see undrugged in evening light the decent inn of death;
For there is good news yet to hear and fine things to be seen,
Before we go to Paradise by way of Kensal Green.'

'Can't argue with that,' said Perry.

# A NOTE ON THE AUTHOR

Ian Marchant has written two novels, *In Southern Waters* and *The Battle for Dole Acre*, and his first work of non-fiction, *Parallel Lines*, was published by Bloomsbury in 2003. He used to run a second-hand bookshop, and is a comedian, singer, songwriter and cabaret performer.

# THE PUBS

To write *The Longest Crawl*, Ian Marchant did the longest pub crawl possible in the British Isles starting at the Turk's Head on St Agnes in the Scilly Isles and ending at the Baa Bar on Unst in the Shetlands. In between he describes: Nero's in Okehampton; the Eagle in New Radnor; the St Austell Brewery in St Austell, Cornwall; the Rose and Crown (aka Eli's) in Huish Episcopi; the Atlantic Bar on St Mary's; the Coach and Horses in Soho, London; the French House in Soho, London; the Colony Room (aka Muriel's) in Soho, London; the Blue Anchor in Helston; the All Nations Inn in Madeley; the Old Swan in Dudley; the Three Tuns in Bishop's Castle; Plymouth Gin Distillery in Plymouth; the Dolphin in Plymouth; Buckfast Abbey near Buckfastleigh; the Valiant Soldier in Buckfastleigh; the Barrelhouse in Totnes; the Corney & Barrow Wine Bars in London; the Tucker's Maltings in Newton Abbot; the Yorkshire House in Lancaster; the Hunter's Moon in Beaworthy, Devon; the Laurels in Petrockstowe; the Torridge Inn in Black Torrington; the Eagle in Farringdon Road, London; the Dartmoor Inn near Tavistock; the Stagg Inn in Titley; the Duke of York's in Iddesleigh; the Merry Harriers near Taunton; the George and Pilgrims in Glastonbury; the Avalon Vineyard in East Pennard; the Pennard Country Wine Bar at the Avalon Vineyard; the Blackthorn Cider factory near Shepton Mallet; the Bell in Bath; the Hat and Feather in Bath; the Rummer Tavern in Bristol; the Three Tuns in Bath; the Royal Pump Room Hotel in Bath; Wadworth's brewery in Devizes; Young's brewery in Wandsworth, London; the Pelican in Devizes; the Black Swan in Devizes; the Bear in Devizes; the George and Dragon in Potterne; the Stage Post in West Lavington; the Bustard Inn in Salisbury Plain; the Bell in Amesbury; the Prince of Wales in Newhaven; the George in Amesbury; the Dickens Coffee House and sports bar in

Amesbury; the Three Cups Inn in Stockbridge; the Hospital of St Cross and the Almshouses of Noble Poverty in Winchester; Gales Ales Brewery in Horndean; the Star in Petworth; the Bull's Head in Ewhurst; the Parrot Inn in Shalford; the Fox and Anchor at Smithfield Market in London; the Barbican in London; the Hogshead in the City of London; the Bell Brewery in Shoreditch, London; the Meux Brewery in Grey's Inn Lane, London; Wetherspoon's in Hamilton Hall, Liverpool Street, London; the Lamb in Leadenhall Market, London; Blackfriars at Blackfriars Bridge in London; the Old Mitre Inn off Fleet Street in London; the Citie of Yorke on High Holborn in London; Lincoln's Inn and the Inns of Court in London; the Seven Stars near the Royal Courts of Justice in London; the Hope and Anchor in Islington, London; the Paradise Bar in Kensal Green, London; the Windsor Castle in Notting Hill, London; the Cheshire Cheese on Fleet Street, London; the Chequers in Wheeler End; the Kicking Donkey in Harwell; the Leathern Bottle in Harwell; the Three Tuns in Hay-on-Wye; the Spread Eagle in Thame; Fothergill's restaurant in Thame; the Fox and Hounds in Great Wolford; the Redesdale Arms in Moreton-in-Marsh; the Lygon Arms in Chipping Campden; the Lygon Arms Hotel in Broadway, the Cotswalds; the Cider House in Defford, Worcestershire; the Foley Arms Hotel in Great Malvern; the Royal Oak at Bringsty Common; the Talbot Inn in Knightwick; the Six Bells in Bishop's Castle; the White Horse in Clun; the George Borrow Hotel near Devil's Bridge in Wales; the King's Head in Lampeter; the Union Bar in Lampeter; the Cwmann Tavern in Carmarthenshire; the Ivy Bush in Lampeter; the Talbot in Tregaron; the Roman Road Hotel in Walsall; the Turf Tavern in Bloxwich; the Queen's Head in Bloxwich; the Coors brewery in Burton; Marston's Brewery and Bass Museum in Burton; Wetherspoon's in Burton; Yates in Burton; the Lounge in Burton; the Burton Bridge Inn in Burton; the Half Moon in Melton Mowbray; the King's Head in Martin Dales; Wolfies Bar in Skegness; the Squadron Bar in Petwood; the Crown and Anchor in Kilnsea; the Bell in Great Driffield; the Tiger in Driffield; the Full Measure in Driffield; the Star in Driffield; the Old Brewery in Tadcaster; the Howden Arms in Tadcaster; the Terrace Bar in Leeds; the Pack Horse in Leeds; the Palace in Leeds; the Dog and Duck in Leeds; the Regent in Leeds; Whitelock's in Leeds; the Horse and Trumpet in Leeds; Fitzpatrick's Herbal Health Bar in Rawtenstall; the New Inn in Clitheroe; the Britannia in Lancaster; the Ferryboat Inn in Holywell, Cambridgshire; the Old Smith's Arms in Godmanstone, Dorset; the Tan Hill Inn on Arkengarthdale Moor in the Pennines; the Crossways Inn in Gretna Green; the Pot Still in Glasgow; the 13th Note in Glasgow; the Brunswick Hotel in Glasgow; the Ardberg Distillery on Islay; the Laphroaig Distillery on Islay; the Ballygrant Inn in Ballygrant, Islay; the Bruichladdich Distillery on Islay; the Isle of Jura Hotel in Craighouse on Jura; the Moon Under Water pubs including the one at Leicester Square, London; the Oban Inn in Oban; the West Highland Hotel in Mallaig; the Old Forge in Inverie; the Isles in Portree, Skye; the Cluanie Inn in Loch Cluanie; Hootenanny's in Inverness; the Tormore Distillery in Speyside; the World Famous Glenfiddich Restaurant and Lounge Bar in Dufftown; the Fife Arms Hotel in Dufftown; the Speyside Cooperage near Dufftown; the Glenlivet Distillery in Glenlivit; the Quarter Deck at Aberdeen's ferry terminal; the Baltasound Hotel on Unst, Shetland; and the Valhalla Brewery on Unst.

# A NOTE ON THE TYPE

The text of this book is set in Garamond 3. It's one of several versions of Garamond based on the designs of Claude Garamond, It is thought that Garamond based his font on Bembo, cut in 1495 by Francesco Griffo in collaboration with the Italian printer Aldus Manutius. Garamond types were first used in books printed in Paris around 1532. The Linotype version of Garamond from 1936 is based on the American Type Founders design by Morris Fuller Benton and Thomas Maitland Cleland. Many of the present-day versions of this type are based on the Typi Academiae of Jean Jannin cut in Sedan in 1615.

Claude Garamond was born in Paris in 1480. He learned how to cut type from his father and by the age of fifteen he was able to fashion steel punches the size of a pica with great precision. At the age of sixty, he was commissioned by King Francis I to design a Greek alphabet; for this he was given the honourable title of royal type founder. He died in 1561.